Claiming the
American Wilderness

ALSO BY HUNT JANIN
AND FROM MCFARLAND

*The Pursuit of Learning in the
Islamic World, 610–2003* (2005)

*Medieval Justice: Cases and Laws in France,
England and Germany, 500–1500* (2004)

*Four Paths to Jerusalem: Jewish, Christian,
Muslim, and Secular Pilgrimages,
1000 BCE to 2001 CE* (2002; paperback 2006)

*Fort Bridger, Wyoming: Trading Post for Indians,
Mountain Men and Westward Migrants* (2001)

*The India-China Opium Trade
in the Nineteenth Century* (1999)

Claiming the American Wilderness

International Rivalry in the Trans-Mississippi West, 1528–1803

Hunt Janin

McFarland & Company, Inc., Publishers
Jefferson, North Carolina, and London

The illustrations kindly provided by Alecto Historical Editions are by the Swiss artist Karl Bodmer, who traveled extensively in the Trans-Mississippi West during 1832–1834.

LIBRARY OF CONGRESS CATALOGUING-IN-PUBLICATION DATA

Janin, Hunt, 1940–
    Claiming the American wilderness : international rivalry in the Trans-Mississippi West, 1528–1803 / Hunt Janin.
        p.   cm.
    Includes bibliographical references and index.

    ISBN-13: 978-0-7864-2551-8
    (softcover : 50# alkaline paper) ∞

    1. West (U.S.) — History — To 1848.   2. West (U.S.) — International status — History.   3. West (U.S.) — Discovery and exploration.   4. Indians of North America — First contact with Europeans — West (U.S.)   5. United States — Territorial expansion — History.   6. United States — Foreign relations — Europe.   7. Europe — Foreign relations — United States. 8. Explorers — West (U.S.) — History.   9. Pioneers — West (U.S.) — History.   10. Indians of North America — West (U.S.) — History.   I. Title
    F592.J34   2006
    978'.01 — dc22   2006007708

British Library cataloguing data are available

©2006 Hunt Janin. All rights reserved

No part of this book may be reproduced or transmitted in any form or by any means, electronic or mechanical, including photocopying or recording, or by any information storage and retrieval system, without permission in writing from the publisher.

On the cover: *Shooting the Rapids (Quebec)*, Frances Anne Hopkins, oil on canvas 36" × 60", 1879 *(Library and Archives Canada Acc. No. 1989-401-2)*

Manufactured in the United States of America

McFarland & Company, Inc., Publishers
   Box 611, Jefferson, North Carolina 28640
   www.mcfarlandpub.com

Acknowledgments

I COULD NOT HAVE WRITTEN this book without the help of many scholars and friends who have been generous with their time and critical comments. Chief among them is Petronella van Gorkom, a Dutch editor who has done her usual fine job of producing a coherent text from my rough drafts.

Special thanks are also due, in alphabetical order, to Dr. Kathryn Abbott, Dr. John Logan Allen, Dr. Mike Allen, Robert Applegate, Tom Beaman, Adán Benavides, Richard W. Blumenthal, Dr. Paul Brand, Dr. Colin Calloway, Dr. Denys Delâge, Carola DeRooy, Richard Francaviglia, Jerry Green, Diana Hadley, Dr. Thomas Kavanagh, Dr. Richard Kitchen, Dr. Carlos A. Leon y Leon, Olivia Little, Dr. Paul Mapp, Ian McLeod, MariaElena Raymond, David W. Rickman, Jane Sanchez, Lady Tunnicliffe, Dr. Dick Wilson, and Dr. W. Raymond Wood. Whatever errors or misjudgments may remain in this book are my responsibility alone.

The illustrations kindly provided by Alecto HIstorical Editions are by the Swiss artist Karl Bodmer, who traveled extensively in the Trans-Mississippi West during 1832–1834.

Hunt Janin
St. Urcisse, France
Spring 2006

Contents

Acknowledgments v
Introduction 1

1. The Indians: Coping with the Europeans and Americans 9
2. The Spaniards: Children of the Sun 48
3. The French: Lords of Rivers and Lakes 96
4. The British: From Rupert's Land to the Pacific 127
5. The Russians: "Soft Gold" — The Richest Fur in the World 157
6. The Americans: To All Points West 165
7. Epilogue: The Six Rivals: A Summing-Up 182

Selected Chronology, 1492–1804 203
Appendices
   1: The Lewis and Clark Expedition 215
   2: Mirrors of the Trans-Mississippi West: George Catlin and Karl Bodmer 220
   3: The Coming of the Horse 223
   4: Firearms on the Early Frontiers 225
   5: Protecting Northern New Spain from the Apaches 232

  6: A Spanish Requerimiento   233
  7: The Treaty of San Ildefonso   234
  8: Coureurs de Bois and Voyageurs: The Men and Their Boats   236
Chapter Notes   241
Bibliography   255
Index   265

A most terrible Storm at west with thick snow and excessively high Drift. The poor fellows who have made a Hut were nearly suffocated in it — all were obliged to come into the Tent which however small is obliged to contain us all 16 in number. The Dogs are drifted over with Snow that we walk on them without seeing them, such is the effects of the Storm and Drift, that it is almost as dark as Night, and we cannot actually see distinct 10 yards before us, altho' we are in the bottom of Gully full 50 feet beneath the level of the Plain — yet it as much as we can Keep from being buried under the Snow, it is without Doubt the worse day I ever saw in my Life. We have no Meat, fortunately yesterday I picked up a Marrow Bone of a Buffaloe which had been pretty well Knawed by a Wolf — and this is my day's allowance.

> Journal entry for 22 January 1798 by the British-Canadian fur trader David Thompson, who used snowshoes and dog teams to trade with the Indians of North Dakota and Manitoba (quoted in Wood and Thiessen, *Early Fur Trade*, pages 121–122).

Introduction

THIS BOOK FOCUSES ON ONE important aspect of North American exploration that is not well known to most readers today: the opening up, in the sixteenth through the eighteenth centuries, of the diverse lands and coasts of the United States lying west of the Mississippi River. It is a unique book because it uses a *prismatic approach* (defined below) to survey and summarize the international rivalries that took place in the Trans-Mississippi West over a period of nearly 300 years.

This era stretches from 1528, when the shipwrecked Spanish *conquistador* Cabeza de Vaca[1] was washed ashore on San Luis Island (off the west end of Galveston Island on the east Texas coast), to 1803, when France sold to the United States a vast tract of land now known as the Louisiana Purchase. The book you have in your hands is a broadly based general survey that offers a wide-ranging account of remarkable events that occurred because six rivals had parallel histories and conflicting interests in the Trans-Mississippi West. In rough order of their appearance on this stage, these rivals are the Indians; the Spaniards; the French; the British[2]; the Russians; and, finally, the Americans.

The historian John Logan Allen summarized the state of play very well. He wrote that, with the exception of the Indians, these powers "all cast covetous glances at western North America as the key to ultimate control over both the economic and the political destiny of the entire continent."[3] Aside from professional historians and well-read enthusiasts, however, not many readers today know what President Thomas Jefferson knew very well: that the Trans-Mississippi West was not an empty land but had long been the site of differing aspirations and conflicting claims of sovereignty. The historian James P. Ronda makes this point more eloquently:

Thomas Jefferson knew that as his explorers moved over the visible world of rivers, mountains, and plains, they would also pass through a more important world — a sometimes-invisible universe of Indian politics and European rivalries. He grasped what had long escaped others, that the American West was a crowded wilderness.[4]

The Trans-Mississippi West became, in short, an arena of intense military and commercial competition for nearly 300 years. In 1801, a famous British fur trader — Alexander Mackenzie — whom we will discuss in more detail later, published an account of his epic overland journey to the Pacific Ocean. Mackenzie strongly implied that the fur-rich Pacific Northwest should become a British colony. This possibility greatly alarmed Jefferson, who read Mackenzie's book in 1802: Jefferson wanted the fledgling United States to stretch, unbroken, from coast to coast.

He knew that his new country claimed all the lands east of the Mississippi, except for the Spanish possession of La Florida, i.e., the Gulf Coast between the Florida peninsula and the province of Pánuco in Mexico. Most of the Trans-Mississippi West had belonged to Spain — but in 1800 Spain had secretly given the Louisiana Territory back to France. Spain, Britain, and Russia variously claimed the Pacific coast. Canada was British. The historian Carolyn Gilman tells us: "Thus, when Jefferson looked west, he saw a gameboard of European boundaries that seemed like the most important aspect of the land."[5]

To solidify American possession of the newly acquired Louisiana Territory, in 1804 Jefferson sent out from St. Louis, Missouri, an exploratory expedition jointly led by U.S. Army Captain Meriwether Lewis and Lieutenant William Clark. This famous venture successfully reached the Pacific Ocean at the mouth of the Columbia River and returned to St. Louis in 1806 with the loss of only one man (due to a ruptured appendix). The adventures of Lewis and Clark are summarized in Appendix 1.

The history of the Trans-Mississippi West begins long before the Louisiana Purchase and the Lewis and Clark expedition. Most of the books written about this region in recent years, however, have addressed only these or later events. For this reason, a book on the earlier days of the Trans-Mississippi West may be a timely contribution.

Studies of the Trans-Mississippi West have traditionally used a chronological approach, presenting the complicated history of this region in a single continuous narrative. In 1953, for example, the historian Bernard DeVoto won the National Book Award for his masterpiece, *The Course of Empire* (1952). In it, he chronicled the years between the "discovery" of America by Christopher Columbus in 1492, and 1805, when the Lewis and Clark expedition reached the mouth of the Columbia River.[6]

More recent studies of the Trans-Mississippi West have also used a chronological format. Cases to the point are Colin Calloway's *One Vast Winter Count* (2003), Elizabeth John's *Storms Brewed in other Men's Worlds* (2nd ed., 1996), and David Weber's *The Spanish Frontier in North America* (1992). In contrast, we will use a unique *prismatic approach*. Just as a prism breaks down a beam of sunlight into its component parts, this book takes the history of the Trans-Mississippi West between 1528 and 1803 and breaks it down into its component parts. Focusing on one rival at a time (with some brief but necessary overlaps and flashbacks), the book thus has six chapters and an epilogue.

The prismatic approach strives for conciseness, simplicity and clarity. It has one clear advantage and one potential drawback. The advantage is that in introducing the very complex history of the Trans-Mississippi West to the general reader, it does a good job of sorting out a tangled skein of people, places, events and dates. The Selected Chronology in the last pages of this book shows just how complicated and disjointed this history can be when it is presented chronologically.

The drawback with the prismatic approach is that the international rivals in this region sometimes made their decisions sequentially, although often only after a long time lag. In 1741, for example, the Russians, who were harvesting sea otters furs to sell to the Chinese, landed at Sitka, Alaska, and later began to hunt sea otters south along what the Spaniards called the "California" coast. (The geography of the Pacific coast was not well defined at this time, so when the Spaniards referred to California they meant the entire unoccupied Pacific coastline of North America.)

It was not until 1769 that the Spaniards become so worried about Russian intentions in California that they decided to colonize California themselves. They did this by establishing presidios (forts) and missions there to prove that it was Spanish territory, that they were occupying it, and that they were resolved to keep it out of Russian hands.

The prismatic approach can deal with such sequential events simply by looking at them from two points of view, in this case, the event as seen first by the Russians and then by the Spaniards.

One important objective in this book is to recapture the spirit of adventure that was the driving force prompting so many generations of Europeans and Americans to risk their lives and their fortunes exploring unknown lands, waterways and cultures. Thus, rather than merely chronicling daily life in the Trans-Mississippi West, this book focuses instead on heroic (or misguided) expeditions and other noteworthy adventures. A vivid example of the former is the 1798 journal entry by the fur trader David Thompson, which is used as the epigraph for this book.

The first task will be to look at ten groups of Indians who had early contacts with Europeans or Americans. These Indians competed with not only the Europeans and the Americans but, even more frequently and much more violently, with each other. The spotlight will then shift to each of the five other rivals in turn, highlighting their objectives, their hopes and their fears. These are briefly summarized at the end of each chapter.

An epilogue with a scorecard recapitulates their objectives and tries to assess just how well or how poorly these rivals fared in their respective quests in the Trans-Mississippi West. It highlights some of their later experiences in North and Middle America, reaching beyond the time of the Louisiana Purchase (1803) and well into the late nineteenth century and the early twentieth century.

Eight topics, which are relevant and interesting in their own right, have been placed in appendices so that they do not interfere with the flow of the text itself. Locations are usually identified by their modern place-names, even if they did not exist as independent entities at that time. For example, as a legal entity the Dominion of Canada dates only from 1867; moreover, Canada did not exercise full control over all its own affairs until 1931.

A legal historian might therefore argue that no one could properly define himself or herself as "Canadian" until 1867. Technically, it could be held, such a person should be referred to only as a French settler; an English settler; an Indian; or a Métis—a person of mixed French-Indian ancestry. In practice, however, people living in Canada considered themselves Canadians long before that time. In a journal kept by a fur trader in 1754, there is an early reference to "Canadian" traders, e.g., the partners and employees of the Montreal-based North West Company.[7] By the same token, in 1793, a Hudson's Bay Company fur trader recorded in his journal that "Two Canadians from the Misisurrie River arrived [at] the Canadian houses," bearing "a great Quantity of Beaffaloe Robes."[8] For this reason, the term "Canadian" will occasionally be used here, either on its own or in hyphenated form, e.g., British-Canadian or French-Canadian.

One important objective of this book is to reach a wide audience and encourage a new generation of readers to learn more about the Trans-Mississippi West. Thus rather than being a narrowly focused academic work written for the scholar, this book is instead a broad-brush approach for the general reader. Offering insights distilled from a range of primary and secondary sources, it focuses mainly on the highlights, not on the details, of the times being discussed.

Because of their frequency and complexity, the European wars of the era will be mentioned only briefly or not at all, even though they had some effects in the Trans-Mississippi West. These wars, with the names of their American phases shown in parentheses where appropriate, include:

- 1688–1697: War of the League of Augsburg (King William's War).
- 1702–1714: War of the Spanish Succession (Queen Anne's War).
- 1718–1720: War of the Quadruple Alliance.
- 1740–1748: War of the Austrian Succession (King George's War).
- 1756–1763: Seven Years' War (French and Indian War).
- 1796: Spain's declaration of war against Britain.

Endnotes are used not only for attribution but also to elaborate on points mentioned in the text. Four additional matters need our attention now: defining the Trans-Mississippi West; understanding the concept of the Passage and its corollary, the pyramidal height-of-land theory; reasons for the illustrations used here; and recognizing the importance of the quotations used in this book.

As used here, the term "Trans-Mississippi West" requires a special *expanded* definition. Some of the important events discussed here, e.g., the fur trade of the northern Great Plains, took place in western Canada, so it is critically important to include this area, too. As Map 1 shows, we will therefore be dealing with the vast swath of territory lying

- North of the Texas coast and the border between the Mexico and the United States.
- South of an imaginary linking York Factory (the Hudson Bay Company's trading post on the western shore of Hudson Bay) with the region around Sitka, Alaska.
- East of the Pacific coastline between Sitka and San Diego, California.
- West of a line that connects York Factory and New Orleans by following the meandering courses of the Nelson, Red, and Mississippi rivers.

This huge area—roughly about some eight million square miles—is the expanded Trans-Mississippi West discussed in this book. It embraces eight of the ten physiographic provinces of North America: the Coastal Plains, the Interior Lowlands, the Interior Highlands, the Canadian Shield, the Great Plains, the Rocky Mountains, the Intermontain Basins and Plateaus, and the Pacific Mountains and Valleys.[9] Only two physiographic provinces are *not* included—the Piedmont and the Appalachian Highlands.

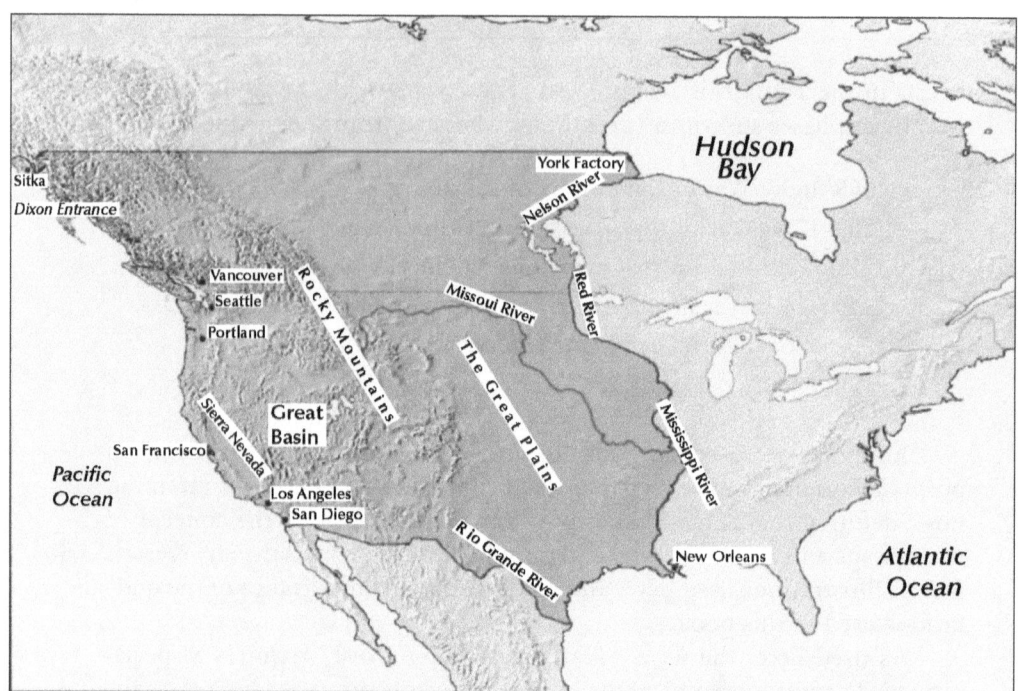

Map 1. The Expanded Trans-Mississippi West. (Map by Jordan Gibb. Data source: U.S. Geological Survey.)

Our expanded Trans-Mississippi West embraces the highest and the lowest points in the United States: Mount Whitney (14,495 feet) in the Sierra Nevada mountains of California, and Death Valley (282 feet below sea level), also in California.[10] It has a range of climates and natural resources to match these extremes. Defined so expansively, this region has had many different appellations, some of which overlapped. These include:

- The Louisiana territory, which extended, very roughly, west from the Mississippi River all the way to the Rocky Mountains.
- The *frontera septentrional* (the frontier provinces of northern New Spain[11]), which was the first of the four viceroyalties created by the Spaniards to govern the lands they had conquered in the New World.
- The Oregon Country, which was only vaguely defined (it included Vancouver Island, Washington, Oregon, Idaho, and the western parts of Montana and Wyoming) and which was variously claimed by the United States, Britain, France, Russia, and Spain.[12]
- The western part of Rupert's Land, a gigantic and poorly defined region that formed the drainage basin of Hudson Bay.

What do we mean by the Passage and the pyramidal height-of-land theory? All the European and American rivals in the Trans-Mississippi West had one thing in common. They risked their lives to find the navigable waterway that they believed cut across North America and flowed into the South Sea, i.e., the Pacific Ocean. Jefferson put it with his usual clarity in his formal instructions to Meriwether Lewis:

> The object of your mission is to explore the Missouri river, & such principal streams of it, as, by it's course & communications with the Pacific Ocean, may offer the most direct & practical water connection across this continent, for the purposes of commerce.[13]

In the interest of simplicity, we shall call this mythical waterway the "Passage." Contemporary students of the subject, however, knew it by many different and overlapping names. The most common of these were:

- The Northwest Passage.
- The Mer de l'Ouest (the Western Sea).
- The Sea of Verrazzano.
- The Ourgan (or Oregan), also called the Great River of the West.
- The Rio San Buenaventura.
- The Strait of Anián, which in 1570 the Flemish cartographer Abraham Ortelius placed, in the first modern atlas of the world (*Theatrum orbis terrarum*, or *Theater of the World*), roughly where Alaska is today.
- The Canal de Floridablanca.
- Lake Thoyago, source of an enormous river flowing into the Pacific.
- The passage to China, Japan, or India.
- The Northern (or Northwestern) Mystery.[14]

Writing in about 1598, Richard Hakluyt, whose *Principal Navigations, Voyages, Traffiques and Discoveries of the English Nation* is the foremost Elizabethan compendium of English adventures, described the Passage to Cathay (a medieval European name for China) as being located

> on the north and northwest part of America: where through our merchants may have course and recourse with their merchandise, from these our northernmost parts of Europe, to those Oriental coasts of Asia, in much shorter time, and with greater benefit than any others, to their no little commodity and profit.[15]

Regardless of its exact name and its supposed configurations, European and American explorers sought the Passage with great eagerness. If only it could be found, they reasoned, it would greatly facilitate European and American trade with China, Japan, Southeast Asia, and India — and it would probably make their own fortunes. In fact, discovering the Passage became such an important objective that in 1745 the British Parliament offered the huge reward of £20,000 to any British subject (other than a member of the Royal Navy) who could achieve this feat.

A closely related geographical myth was the pyramidal height-of-land theory. This held that the headwaters of four major river systems in North America all flowed from a central pyramidal height-of-land somewhere in the West and that one of these rivers would provide easy access to the Pacific.

A few final matters:

The notation *sic*, which shows that a given spelling or punctuation used in a book accurately reflects the original text, does not appear in this book. The reason is that many of the writers cited — Lewis and Clark are perhaps the most famous examples— spelled phonetically and punctuated their work very erratically. The quotations used here retain all their original vigor — and are much easier to read — without the frequent interjection of *sic*.

Between 1528 and 1803, the main period covered in this book, contemporary illustrations depicting the Trans-Mississippi West were of such limited artistic merit that none of them are used here. The first two artists with any lasting claim to fame were George Catlin and Karl Bodmer, who did not set to work in the American West until the 1830s.

Both these men worked conscientiously with their subjects and had the opportunity to experience the culture of the Plains Indians first hand and in some depth. Bodmer's illustrations figure so prominently in this book simply because they are much better than Catlin's. Appendix 2, Mirrors of the Trans-Mississippi West: George Catlin and Karl Bodmer, discusses these two painters and their work.

You will find in this book an unusual number of first hand "I-was-there" quotations. It would have been easy enough to shorten or paraphrase them but they appear in their present form for one very good reason: they convey the flavor of the Trans-Mississippi West much better than any other version possibly can. Because they are in many cases the actual words of those who played memorable roles in the Trans-Mississippi West, they are arguably the most important parts of this book.

1

The Indians: Coping with the Europeans and Americans

THE INDIANS WERE IN THE New World first: indeed, the Canadian government now officially refers to its Indian populations as the First Nations or the first peoples.[1] In 1645, the Jesuit missionary Andrés Pérez de Ribas addressed an intriguing and fundamental question: where did the Indians come from? His answer:

> Much has been studied and written concerning how these people reached the New World, separated as it is from the Old by such enormous seas. I will not pause here to relate the ideas and debates on this subject. These can be reduced to the most likely opinion, which is that these people arrived from Asia overland to the north or crossed some narrow stretch of sea that was easy to cross and remains as yet undiscovered.[2]

This opinion is strikingly close to our present secular understanding. (Some Indians today still retain their traditional religious beliefs, e.g., that their ancestors emerged from the center of the earth.) During an Ice Age, low water levels laid bare a vast area of land at the Bering Strait. People from Asia moved across it, perhaps in phases, and then gradually spread out into the Americas, adopting different life styles attuned to the different environments they encountered.[3]

By world standards, there were not many Indians living in the Trans-Mississippi West during the early nineteenth century: an educated guess is slightly more than 500,000 people.[4] They were fragmented into a large number of tribes. Lee Sultzman, an American writer, identified about 240 tribes in the continental United States alone (excluding Alaska).[5] On a smaller canvas, during their own odyssey from St. Louis to the mouth of the Columbia River, Lewis and Clark met nearly 50 different tribes.

Given their enormous geographic and cultural diversity, it does not make any sense for us to try to generalize about Indians as a whole. Each tribe was in many ways unique and coped with the Europeans and Americans in its own way. It is more sensible for us to look instead at a *representative sample* of Indians, limiting our search only to those who were living west of the Mississippi and who had early contacts with European or Americans. We will discuss ten such groups. They include (early contact dates are in parentheses):

- The Pueblo Indians (1539) of the Southwest, who in the seventeenth century rose up against their Spanish overlords and drove them out of Pueblo territory for twelve years.
- The Apaches (1541), who became in the words of a Western observer "one of the toughest human organisms the world has ever seen" after Comanches pushed them westward into the arid lands of New Mexico and Arizona.[6]
- The Caddo Indians of East Texas and Louisiana (1542), who played a key role as middlemen in intertribal trade and who were courted by Spaniards and Frenchmen alike.
- The Sioux (1660), who were forced out onto the northern Great Plains by other tribes and who would become the biggest single obstacle to American settlement there.
- The Comanches (1706), who blocked European advances across the southern plains, thanks to their mastery of the horse. (See Appendix 3 — The Coming of the Horse.)
- The Mandan Indians of the upper Missouri (1738), whose farming villages were the hub of a trading network where horses and produce of the plains were exchanged for guns and other European or American goods.
- The maritime traders of the Pacific Northwest coast (1741), who bartered the pelts of the sea otter (*Enhydra lutris*) with European and American seamen. Clark, whose spelling and capitalization (or lack of it) is erratic at best, reported that "one of the Indians had on a roab made of 2 Sea Otter Skins the fur of them were more butifull than any fur I had even Seen."[7]
- Mission Indians of California (1769), who were among the most

diverse peoples, culturally and linguistically, of North America but who fared very poorly under mission rule.
- Blackfoot Indians of Alberta and Montana (1790), who became the strongest and most aggressive military power on the northwestern plains.
- The Nez Percé (Pierced Nose) Indians of central Idaho and adjacent areas of Oregon and Washington (1805), for whom the visit of Lewis and Clark spelled the beginning of the end of their prosperous culture.

A number of caveats are in order here. The first is that, technically speaking, there were no such thing as "Indians" in the popular understanding of this term. Instead, there were groups of indigenous peoples *who were called Indians by people other than themselves.*[8] A tribe usually defined itself in very exclusive terms, using phrases, for example, which can be translated as The People; The Real People; or The People, Preeminently. However, because there is no demonstrably better term to use when referring to the native inhabitants of North America, we will refer to them here either by their tribal names (which were usually bestowed on them by outsiders) or simply as Indians.[9]

The second caveat is that the reader should not accept at face value every assertion in the citations used here. None of the ten groups of Indians we will discuss left any written records of a given battle, event or cultural phenomenon. Except for some Indian paintings on buffalo hides,[10] virtually all our accounts come directly from European or American sources. These accounts, which often depict Indians in a negative light, were used to justify repressive policies against them. Examples are not hard to find. The *conquistadors* claimed that the Pueblo Indians were "a people without capacity," "stupid," and "of poor intelligence."[11] A notation on a Spanish map drawn up in 1777 says of the Comanches: "This nation is very warlike and cruel."[12]

The third caveat is that an introductory survey such as this cannot hope to offer an encyclopedic coverage of Indian life. Our goal here is a more modest one: to sketch out the lives of some of these Indians in a few broad strokes. We can then better understand the military and commercial competition that was taking place — Indians against other Indians, or Indians against Europeans and Americans.[13] We will revisit some of these tribes in later chapters when discussing their European and American rivals. What is important to keep in mind at the outset is that as Daniel K. Richter has pointed out in his excellent study, *Facing East from Indian Country: A Native History of Early America* (2001),

> If anything ... emerges from the shadows of the sixteenth century Indian discoveries of Europe, it is a persistent theme of conflict and distrust.... Most striking of all is the way in which the arrival of the newcomers exacerbated conflicts of one Native group with another.... Both within and among Native communities, contact with the new world across the seas inspired bitter conflicts over access to what the aliens had to offer—conflicts that would spiral to unimaginably deadly levels in the decades ahead.[14]

We must always remember, too, that Indian cultures and Indian patterns of behavior were not monolithic but were extremely diverse. Some tribes wanted to live in peace; others relished constant warfare. Some got along reasonably well with the Europeans and Americans newcomers; others preferred to conduct guerrilla warfare against them. All the Indians, however, tried hard to maintain their own independence in the face of what would prove to be, by the last half of the nineteenth century, the unstoppable advance of the Europeans and Americans.

When they could, the tribes tried to play the foreigners off against each other. The Indians had to be ready to change their allegiances on short notice because, politically, the ground could suddenly shift out from under them. After the French and Indian War, for example, a map published in the *London Magazine* in 1765 was—correctly—entitled: *Louisiana as formerly claimed by France, now containing part of British America to the east & Spanish America to the west of the Mississippi*.[15]

Sometimes the Indians tried to order foreigners off their lands permanently. The tribes of the powerful Iroquois Confederacy lived in New York, Pennsylvania, southern Ontario, and Quebec. In one well-documented case on the eve of the French and Indian War, Tanaghrisson, a leader of the Iroquois, told the French in 1753:

> Fathers, Both you and the English are white, we live in a Country between; therefore the Land belongs to neither one nor t'other: But the Great Being above allow'd it to be a Place of Residence for us; so Fathers, I desire you to withdraw, as I have done our Brothers the English; for I will keep you at Arms length: I lay this down as a Trial for both, to see which will have the greatest regard to it, and that Side we will stand by, and make equal Sharers with us. Our Brothers the English have heard this, and now I come to tell it to you, for I am not afraid to discharge you off this Land.[16]

The French commander, Paul Marin de La Malgue, rejected Tanaghrisson's demands; the English traders were equally unresponsive.

The final caveat is that the conventional European and American usage of the words "explore" and "discover" is misleading. These foreigners were, to use an American expression, the new kids on the block. From the Indian point of view, there was very little, if anything, in North America left to discover or explore: the Indians had done so long before.

The Pueblo Indians

The Pueblo Indians lived in compact apartment-like villages made of stone or adobe. These were located on the Colorado Plateau in the arid regions of northwestern New Mexico and northeastern Arizona. Each of these villages, known as pueblos from the Spanish word for village or town, made its own decisions, guided by a council consisting of the leaders of indigenous religious societies.

The Pueblo Indians grew corn, made pottery, wove cotton cloth, and greatly valued their independence — especially the right to practice their own religion. They sought a harmonious relationship between human beings and the cosmos.[17] They believed that unless the proper religious ceremonies were conducted properly, people would fall ill, there would not be enough rain for the corn, and social discord would prevail. Supernatural beings known as kachinas were associated with rain and fertility. Represented in ceremonies by elaborately costumed and masked kachina dancers, they bridged the gap between humans and the gods.

The Pueblo Indians were great traders. Before the coming of the horse, the Plains Indians made long journeys on foot to the eastern and northern pueblos. They brought with them buffalo meat, buffalo robes, animal fat, and Indian slaves to exchange for Pueblo corn, cotton blankets, and ceramics.[18] The Plains Indians moved such heavy loads by using dogs to pull a travois. This consisted of two wooden shafts, with a net or a platform strung between them.

The Pueblo Indians' contacts with the Spaniards began in 1539. That year the Franciscan missionary Marcos de Niza, preceded and guided by the North African slave Estevánico, reached the Zuni pueblo of Háwikuh during a search for the legendary riches of the mythical Seven Cities of Cíbola. This long-running legend sprang from an eighth century Portuguese story.

Allegedly, in the year 714 seven Catholic bishops and their followers, laden with riches, fled from the Muslim conquest of Portugal and made their way across the Atlantic to a mythical land known as Antillia, located in the West Indies. When, however, the Spaniards failed to find appreciable amounts of gold or silver in Antilles, the legend itself migrated westward. The Spaniards gradually become convinced that the treasure-trove they sought was located not in the West Indies but in the North American Southwest — in an El Dorado known as Cíbola.[19]

The Spaniards eventually became so heavy-handed in their quest for wealth and power that in 1680 the Pueblo Indians launched a broadly based, well-coordinated surprise attack against their Spanish oppressors. This is now known as the Pueblo Revolt. The Indians destroyed churches and killed many people. Out of New Mexico's total population of about 2,800 foreigners (which included the Spaniards, their dependents, and their non–Pueblo slaves), the rebels killed over 422 Spaniards, including 21 Franciscan missionaries. This is how Pedro Namboa, an 80-year-old member of the Tewa tribe, explained the uprising to his Spanish interrogators:

> The resentment which all the Indians have in their hearts has been so strong, from the time this kingdom [New Mexico] was discovered, because the religious and the Spaniards took away their idols and forbade their idolatries; they have inherited successively from their old men the things pertaining to their ancient customs, and he has heard this resentment spoken of since he was of an age to understand.[20]

Pedro Naranjo, a Pueblo Indian captured by the Spaniards, gave them this first-hand account of what happened under the direction of the charismatic leader of the rebels, Popé, a Tewa medicine man, who lived in San Juan Pueblo. Popé ordered that his followers

> instantly break up and burn the images of the holy Christ, the Virgin Mary and the other saints, the crosses, and everything pertaining to Christianity, and that they burn the temples, break up the bells, and separate from the wives whom God had given them in marriage and take those whom they desired. In order to take away their baptismal names, the water, and the holy oils, they were to plunge into the rivers and wash themselves ... there would thus be taken from them the character of the holy sacraments.[21]

Yet another Pueblo Indian, Pedro García, told the Spaniards that the leaders of the revolt had promised their followers that

> The Indian who shall kill a Spaniard will get an Indian woman for a wife, and he who kills four will get four women, and he who kills ten or more will have a like number of women; and they have said that they are going to kill all the servants of the Spaniards and those who know how to speak Castilian, and they have also ordered that rosaries be taken away from every one and burned.[22]

Remarkably, the Pueblo Indians succeeded in driving the Spaniards out of their territory for twelve years—a feat that no other North American Indian tribe would ever be able to match. A wide range of opinions has been put forward to explain the reasons for the Pueblo Revolt. This uprising is particularly striking because it occurred so unexpectedly and after such a long period of relatively peaceful coexistence between Indians and Spaniards—after an era, in fact, that was marred by only occasional and localized clashes.[23] It is therefore instructive for us to review some of these opinions here.

The stage was set for the revolt when Pueblo populations began to fall prey to the combined effects of disease, drought, and intertribal warfare. Many died of starvation, as Friar Juan Bernal reported in 1669:

> For three years, no crop has been harvested. Last year, 1668, a great many Indians perished of hunger, lying dead along the roads, in the ravines, and in their hovels. There were pueblos, like Las Humanas, where more than 450 died of hunger. The same calamity still prevails for, because there is no money, there is not a *fanega* [about 1.6 bushels] of maize or wheat in all the kingdom, so that for two years the food of the Spaniards, men and women alike, had been the hides of the cattle which they had in their houses.... And the greatest misfortune of all is that they can no longer find a bit of leather to eat, for their herds are dying.[24]

The situation was so grim that, by 1680, 50 of the 81 pueblos that had been full of people in 1598 had been abandoned.[25]

Contemporary Spaniards offered other explanations for the rebellion. Clearly, they claimed, it was the work of the devil—or even of their own Christian God, who was furious with the Spaniards because of all their sins. On the other hand, after reviewing official reports of the uprising, the seventeenth century scholar Carlos de Sigüenza y Góngora laid the blame squarely on the shoulders of the Indians themselves. "Perhaps it was the idle life of their pagan neighbors which inspired them," he wrote in Mexico City in 1693, "or, more likely, their inborn hatred of the Spaniards."[26]

As time passed, a more balanced view began to emerge. Writing in 1778, the Franciscan friar Silvestre Vélez de Escalante found that the revolt had been based on two factors. The first was "the love which many of the old men retain for their ancient mode of life, for their idolatry." The second was "the vexations and bad treatment which they have suffered from some Spaniards in many pueblos, [as well as] the persecution of those Indians who are taken to be wizards."[27]

Nineteenth century historians moved closer to the explanation that some scholars favor today. In 1883, L. Bradford Prince concluded that "Religious feeling was a very strong element among the causes which led to the revolution and a bitter hatred [of] the Christianity of the Spaniards was evinced in every act during the struggle."[28] A great historian of the West, Hubert Howe Bancroft, concurred: the revolt, he wrote in 1889, was "founded ... largely, on religious grounds."[29]

Scholars still differ on how much weight should be accorded to this "religious" explanation but most historians agree that the competition between the Indians' traditional religion and Spanish Catholicism was an important factor in the Pueblo Revolt. Some carry this analysis one step further. As David J. Weber pointed out in 1999 in *What Caused the Pueblo Revolt of 1680?*,

> Informed by anthropologists, ... historians now know that Pueblos regarded the proper observance of their traditional religious ceremonies as essential to their earthly as well as their spiritual well being ... Spanish attempts to squash Pueblo religious practices, then, did not merely threaten Pueblo religion but threatened the Pueblos' very existence.[30]

Competition between the Pueblo Indians and the Spaniards thus took place not only at the physical level, that is, the Spanish conquest of Pueblo lands and the Pueblo Revolt itself, but on a religious level as well. Conflict was probably inevitable between two different and mutually incomprehensible worldviews. The Indians wanted to defend their traditional religion against Spanish efforts to suppress it by force. The Spaniards wanted to prevent any resurgence of "idolatry," which they saw as a threat to the Christianity they had tried so hard, but with only limited success, to impose on Indian minds. In fact, Friar Francisco de Jesús María Casañas wrote in 1696 that despite more than a century of efforts by Franciscan missionaries, the Pueblo Indians were "still more drawn more by their idolatry and infidelity than by the Christian doctrine."[31]

Moreover, the Pueblo Indians had enjoyed their years of freedom and long remembered them. After the 1680 revolt, there were other localized uprisings, but beginning in 1692 Diego José de Vargas, the new governor of New Mexico, decided to rely on diplomacy rather than on force to persuade the leaders of 23 pueblos to accept Spanish control again. He was successful. Few of the churches reopened, however, and most of the villages continued to practice their ancient religion, perhaps with a slight admixture of Roman Catholicism. Nevertheless, a 36-page *Mercurio volante* (news flash) would gush enthusiastically in 1693:

> Innumerable tribes were brought back to the fold of the Catholic Church, and an entire realm was restored to the Majesty of our lord and king, Charles II, without wasting a single ounce of powder, unsheathing a sword, or (what is most worthy of emphasis and appreciation) without costing the Royal Treasury a single maravedí [a small coin worth about 1/34 of a real]."[32]

The trauma of the revolt did not, however, heal easily. In about 1703, Juan de Villagutierre y Sotomayor, a narrator for the Council of the Indies (*Consejo de Indias*, i.e., the supreme governing body of Spain's colonies in America from 1524 to 1834), would write, movingly, from Madrid:

> Rarely does one see [Pueblo Indians] traveling, one or two by themselves, even though the journey might be a long one, when they were not singing all the way about the happy or sad events of war and peace and other things that had happened to their elders which they enjoyed when they were free, from which it is clear that their desire to return to their former freedom is ever present.[33]

The Apaches

The Apache domain was initially extensive, spreading out over parts of Arizona, Colorado, New Mexico, Texas, and northern Mexico. Scholars have traditionally divided the Apaches into Eastern and Western branches (split into numerous subgroups),[34] depending on whether the group in question lived east or west of the Rio Grande River. Most groups lacked a central tribal organization and relied on the band (a collection of small local groups) as their basic military, economic and cultural unit.

The Apaches survived by a variety of means, depending on the groups in question and on the seasons. They hunted buffalo, antelope, deer and bear. They gathered mescal and other wild plants and grew corn, beans, pumpkins and watermelons. They traded with the Pueblo Indians or with other sedentary peoples. Sometimes they raided neighboring tribes. Beginning in the late 1600s, the Apaches attacked Spanish outposts as well.

The first Western contact with the Apaches came in 1541 when the Coronado expedition, which was looking for the mythical golden city of Quivira, met them on the plains of southwestern Kansas. European geographers were understandably vague about where Quivira was located. In his 1570 atlas, *Theatrum orbs terrarum*, the Flemish cartographer Abraham Ortelius admitted that "These regions further to the North [i.e., north of New Spain] are still unknown."[35] He placed Quivira about where San Francisco is today.

The Spaniards called the Indians they met on the Great Plains the "Querechos." The name "Apache" probably comes from the Zuni word *apachu* (enemy) but may come from *Awa'tehe*, the Ute word for this tribe. The Apaches, however, referred to themselves as *Inde* or *Diné* (the people).[36] They became the most feared adversaries of the Spaniards. The Apaches had acquired horses early in the seventeenth century, first by trading with the Pueblos and later by stealing from the Spaniards. Writing in 1669, Friar Juan Bernal tells us that

> The whole land is at war with the widespread heathen nation of the Apache Indians, who kill all the Christian Indians they can find and encounter. No road is safe; everyone travels at risk of his life, for the heathen traverse them all, being courageous and brave, and they hurl themselves at danger like people who know no God nor that there is any hell.[37]

During the eighteenth century, Apache attacks on the Spaniards increased further for two reasons. First, the powerful Comanches, who had traded for guns while the Apaches were still armed only with lances and bows and arrows, drove them away from their traditional hunting grounds. (For the importance of guns in the Trans-Mississippi West, see Appendix 4—Firearms on the

Early Frontiers.) Second, the Apaches could no longer get corn from the Pueblos by trade because the Spaniards themselves were eating most of the surplus corn of the Pueblos.[38]

Well-mounted and, later, armed with firearms, the Apaches became a formidable force. Since the late 1600s, they had fought against the Spaniards. They stepped up their attacks during the eighteenth century because they were being driven out of their traditional hunting grounds by the more powerful Comanches. Spanish officials estimated that between 1748 and 1772 the Apaches killed more than 4,000 people and stole or destroyed property valued at over 12 million pesos.[39] At one point, a dangerous "Apache corridor," definitely off-limits to the Spaniards, effectively isolated New Mexico from other parts of New Spain.[40] The Apaches became such an intractable problem for New Spain that, in 1777, the Spanish authorities drew up a 16-point questionnaire to determine what was known about them and their plans. (For this questionnaire, see Appendix 5 — Protecting Northern New Spain from the Apaches.)

Women played an unusually important role in Apache life. In 1778, Governor Juan Bautista de Anza of New Mexico warned his colleagues not to underestimate the combat strength of the Apaches. He agreed that while there were about 5,000 Apache warriors, he insisted that

> To these should be added an equal number of women, who, if they do not make war in the same way as the men, aid it in whatever actions the Apaches undertake, as has been observed in fact. Thus they form a reserve corps, round up the horses while the men attack our troops, and, finally, even when they serve no other purpose than to make the parties larger, the enemy succeeds, by increasing the number of individuals, in creating the well-founded idea that they are more formidable.[41]

Finally recognizing that with the very limited resources at their disposal they could never defeat the Apaches militarily, the Spaniards decided to make peace. They therefore signed peace treaties in 1790 and 1793. About 2,000 Apaches then settled in the *establecimientos de paz* (peace establishments), which were precursors of the Indian reservations of a later day.[42] Nevertheless, sporadic raiding still continued in Texas. It increased appreciably when the Mexican struggle for independence began in 1811 and led to a marked decline in law and order.[43]

The Caddo Indians

The Caddos were a scattered confederacy of tribes that spoke a similar language. Their name comes from a French abbreviation of the word *Kado-*

"Herds of Bison on the Upper Missouri"
(©2005 Alecto Historical Editions www.alectoUK.com)

hadacho (real chief).⁴⁴ They lived in villages in a pine-forested world strung out along the lower Red River and its tributaries in eastern Texas, southwestern Arkansas and northwestern Louisiana. This was an ideal location for intertribal trade: here the Indians of the carbohydrate-rich southeastern woodlands, which were perfectly suited for growing corn, beans, and squash, could meet tribes from the protein-rich Great Plains, which were perfectly suited for buffalo hunting.

First-hand reports of Caddo life speak of occasional ritual human sacrifices and cannibalism. The French explorer Jean-Baptiste Bénard de la Harpe tells us that in 1712 a Caddo war party took six Indian prisoners during a foray against a western tribe. The Caddos ate four of these men on the journey home.

When the Caddo warriors reached their village, they wrapped cords around the captives' arms and bound them to a wooden framework, facing the rising sun. After about half an hour, the captives were taken down from the framework and forced to dance. In the evening, having not been fed anything during the day, they were again tied to the framework to face the setting sun. The next morning they were, for a third and last time, suspended for a look at the sun.

Fires were then lighted and earthen pots filled with water were heated. Two old medicine men, each carrying a knife and a bowl, stabbed the victims repeatedly. As their blood gushed out, it was caught in the bowls and poured into a cooking pot until it was clotted. It was eaten by the medicine men. The bodies were cut down and dismembered. Each Caddo family received a portion, which it promptly cooked and ate. The Caddos concluded this ceremony with a dance.[45]

There were about 8,000 Caddos. They were relatively prosperous and treated the early Spanish and French travelers courteously. Rather than being a geographically centralized tribe, the Caddos lived in some 25 communities belonging to three major confederacies.[46] A semi-sedentary people with a hierarchical social structure, they built houses that were rounded frameworks of wooden poles covered with grass thatch. They cultivated corn, beans, squash, sunflower seeds, melons and tobacco. They also hunted black bears (valuable for their fat), deer and, in the western reaches of their territory, buffalo as well.

Father Anastius Douay was a member of the French explorer La Salle's 1687 expedition that was looking for the Mississippi River. He reported that one large Caddo village he visited consisted of hamlets of ten or twelve beehive-shaped dwellings, some sixty feet in diameter, each of which provided shelter for eight or ten families. The village stretched over "at least twenty leagues."[47]

The Spaniards had first learned about the Caddos in 1542 when the expedition of Hernando de Soto and Luis de Moscoso wandered across their lands. At that time, thousands of Caddos lived in mound villages flanked by huge fields of corn. Gradually, however, drought, disease and migration greatly reduced the population. Echoes of this early Caddo prosperity persisted, however, and eventually reached Spanish Franciscan missionaries. They heard legends about the "Kingdom of the Tejas," said to be a rich Caddo confederacy located near Beaumont, Texas. The word Tejas comes from a Caddo term meaning friends or allies. It passed first into Spanish and then into American usage as "Texas."[48]

Important trade routes crossed Caddo territory and the Caddos played an active role in intertribal trade. They could offer both raw materials (corn, salt and *bois d'arc*, a wood used to make bows) and finished products (bows, baskets and pottery). They readily included European goods in their intertribal exchange network. Thanks to other Indian middlemen, long before the Caddos had developed their own commercial relations with the Spaniards they already knew a good deal about Spanish goods. French explorers found that one Caddo village in Texas already had many items of Spanish origin: silver dollars, silver spoons, horses, clothes, and even a papal bull[49] (an official papal letter or document), which exempted Christians in New Spain from fasting during the torrid summer months.[50]

Because of the Caddos' pivotal role in intertribal trade, Spaniards and Frenchmen were soon competing for their allegiance. In this commercial competition, the French were ultimately successful for three reasons:

First, unlike the Spaniards, the French had come to the New World only as traders, not as overlords. They were far more interested in North American furs than in North American souls. In contrast to the Spaniards, the French were thus not seen by the Caddos as posing any long-term threat to Caddo lands or ways of life.

Second, the French were much better at creating and maintaining the bonds of "fictive kinship," i.e., kinship ties which are fictional but which are marked by similar obligations and affections as real kinship ties. Henri Joutel, who kept a journal during La Salle's 1687 expedition, tells us that the Caddos offered them food, lodging, and women in order to establish such ties. The Caddos also went through the important ritual of smoking the calumet (peace pipe) with them.[51]

Finally, French traders were simply better businessmen. They could and did offer a much wider range of goods—and better quality goods— than Spanish officials or missionaries. French traders eagerly accepted Caddo products—bear and deer hides, chamois, tallow and horses—and gave the Caddos European goods in return. Most crucially, unlike the Spaniards, who were forbidden to sell firearms and ammunition to the Indians, French traders were happy to do so.

This process turned out to be a two-edged sword for the French, however. Without realizing the full consequences of what they were doing, French traders sold guns to mutually hostile tribes—e.g., the Pawnees, Wichitas, Apaches, Crows, and Blackfoot—who were also deadly rivals of the Comanches. For good measure, French traders even added their own promises of military protection as well. This trade and these assurances led the Comanches to dislike and distrust the French for arming their enemies.[52]

The French laid out for the Caddos a veritable cornucopia of treasures. These included not only firearms and ammunition but also metal knives, hide scrapers, axes, hoes, and needles; brass kettles; blankets; yards of colorful cloth; glass beads; copper bangles and bells; and, for tribal dances or war parties, vermilion to be painted on the face.[53] These items were in such demand that by 1750 it was being joked that every Caddo town had its own resident French trader.

In contrast, the Spanish outposts were so poor that they could barely meet their own material needs. Both the Caddos of Spanish Texas who lived near the isolated mission at Los Adaes, and the Spaniards themselves, preferred to trade clandestinely with the French at nearby Natchitoches. This was the westernmost French outpost in Louisiana and the oldest permanent settlement there.

The Arroyo Hondo, a little stream between Los Adaes and Natchitoches, thus became the *de facto* boundary line between the rival Spanish and French empires in North America. Contraband trade became a way of life on the borderlands between French Louisiana and Spanish Texas. This was indeed ironic. Los Adaes, which the Spaniards had established to protect their possessions in the Southwest from French encroachment, now found itself dependent on Natchitoches, which from 1720 to 1744 was commanded by a French adventurer, Louis Juchereau de St. Denis. He claimed that his marriage to Manuela Sánchez, the lovely granddaughter of the Spanish commanding officer, proved his desire to become a Spanish subject. The Spaniards, however, continued to view him as a French secret agent.[54]

In Texas, unable to win the allegiance of the Caddos through trade, the Spaniards tried to use Franciscan missionaries to solidify their position, but they singularly failed in this attempt, too, thanks to opposition from the French.[55] Acting on the advice of St. Denis, the Caddos subtly asserted their independence from the Spaniards. For example, they agreed to build churches for Spanish missionaries but they refused to become farmers, to relocate their dwellings around these chapels, or to accept baptism unless on the point of death. Faced such passive resistance, the missionaries decided to resort to force and bend the Indians to their will.

In 1716, Friars Isidro Félix de Espinosa and Antonio Margil de Jesús therefore complained to the viceroy: "We do not have a single gun, while we see the French giving hundreds of arms to the Indians."[56] Shortly thereafter, these two friars petitioned the king of Spain to send them fifty soldiers, who would be deployed to burn the Caddos' places of worship. This would force the Indians to "assemble in their mission and build houses" and would prevent them from running away.[57]

The longed-for Spanish troops were never sent, however, so force could not be used. The upshot was that by 1768 the Spaniards had to admit the failure of their missionary efforts among the Caddos and had to abandon efforts to convert them. Nevertheless, by the end of the eighteenth century, cumulative pressures from European and American settlers became so great that Caddo life was severely disrupted. It was said that the Caddos had become "wanderers on their land." Recurrent epidemics greatly reduced Caddo numbers, so that by 1801 there were only about 1,400 Caddos left.

The Sioux

The single word "Sioux" obscures a very complex reality: the Sioux were many and had many names. The three main branches of the tribe were the Santee (Eastern Sioux), the Yankton, and the Teton (Western Sioux). These Indians called themselves, respectively, the Dakota, the Nakota, and the Lakota. There were numerous tribal subdivisions as well.

There is some scholarly debate today about the meaning of the word "Sioux." Traditionally, it was thought to signify "snake" or "enemy" but this translation now appears to be an error, based on an alternate meaning of a related word.[58] What is clear is that before about 1650, the Sioux dwelt around Lake Superior and lived off wild rice, beans, fish, and deer. The French fur trader and explorer Pierre Esprit Radisson provided the first written account of this group in 1660. Describing them as "a wandering nation, and containeth a vast country" and as "the best huntsmen of all America," he tells us how Sioux ambassadors gave the Frenchmen gifts of food and smoked calumets with them. These calumets, said Radisson, were "pipes of peace and of the wars, that they pull out very seldom — when there is occasion for heaven and earth."[59]

The Sioux asked the French for guns to defend themselves against their enemies. At that time, the Sioux were armed only with bows, arrows tipped with stag horn, and wooden war clubs.[60] Their lack of firearms forced the Sioux to move. Ceaseless fighting with the Ojibwes, who had guns, and with other warlike tribes near the Great Lakes, coupled with a desire for better hunting grounds, eventually drove the Sioux farther west.

Some of them settled in what is now southwestern Minnesota. In 1670–1671, the Jesuit missionary Claude Dablon offered the following comment:

> These regions of North America have their Iroquois [i.e., their dominant tribe]. They are a certain people called the [Sioux], who, as they are naturally warlike, have made themselves feared by all their neighbors.... They live near and on the banks of that great river called Missisipi, of which further mention will be made.[61]

Other branches of the Sioux moved out onto the plains of present North and South Dakota, where they became well-mounted migratory buffalo hunters. European explorers frequently commented on their highly competitive military attitudes, variously describing the Sioux in the mid-eighteenth century as "carrying on war from time immemorial ... continually forming war parties to invade one another's territory"; waging "perpetual war" over contested hunting territory; and carrying on wars "without interruption for more than forty winters."[62] Writing in about 1797, the Scottish-Canadian fur trader John Macdonell described the Sioux as "the most powerful nation in all the interior country," i.e., on the northern Great Plains, and as "the most savage and barbarous of any nation of the plain Indians."[63]

By the time of Lewis and Clark, the Sioux were solidly entrenched on the northern Great Plains and were a force to be reckoned with. Clark quickly recognized their military power and their relatively prosperous way of life. He was quite impressed by what he saw, noting in his journal in 1804:

> The Scioues Camps are handsom of a Conic form Covered with Buffalow Roabs Painted different colours and all compact & handsomly arranged, Covered all round an open part in the Centre for the fire, with Buffalow roabs, each Lodg has a place for Cooking detached, the lodges contain from 10 to 15 persons. a Fat Dog was presented [to the Lewis and Clark expedition] as a mark of their Great respect for the party of which they partook hartily and thought it good and well flavored.[64]
>
> [The Sioux are] a Stout bold looking people (the young men hand Som) & well made. The Warriors are Verry much deckerated with Pain[t] Porcupin quills & feathers, large leagins & mockersons, all with buffalow roabs of Different Colours. The Squars wore Peticoats & a white Buffalow roabs with the black hair turned back over their necks and Sholders.[65]

Clark also took note of a remarkable brotherhood of warriors:

> I will here remark a SOCIETY which I had never before this day heard was in any nation of Indians, four of which is at this time present and all who remain of this Band. Those who become Members of this Society must be brave active young men who take a VOW never to give back [retreat] let the danger be what it may, in War Parties they always go forward without screening themselves behind trees or anything else ... in a battle with the Crow Indians who inhabit the *Cout Noir* [the *Côte Noir*, i.e., the "Black Mountains" of northern Nebraska and both Dakotas] out of 22 of this Society 18 was killed, the remaining four was dragged off by their Party [because they would never retreat if left alone].[66]

Clark added that these men "stay by them Selves, fond of mirth and assume a degree of Superiority — Stout likely fellows."[67]

Lewis, however, considered the Teton Sioux to be the "the vilest miscreants of the savage race and must ever remain the pirates of the Missouri, until such measures are pursued, by our government, as will make them feel a dependence on its will for their supply of merchandise."[68] Cheyenne Indians told the explorers that the Cheyennes were at peace with all other

"Horse Racing of Sioux Indians near Fort Pierre"
(©2005 Alecto Historical Editions www.alectoUK.com)

Indians "except for the Sioux with whome they have ever since their remembrance been on a difencive war."⁶⁹

In 1806, U.S. Army Lieutenant Zebulon Montgomery Pike, was sent out to explore the Arkansas and Red Rivers and to learn more about the adjacent Spanish territory. He ventured as far north as Lake Leech, Minnesota, near the Canadian border. Pike judged that the Sioux were "the most warlike and independent nation of Indians within the boundaries of the United States."⁷⁰

The worldview of the Sioux accurately reflected their own military power. They understood that power on the northern plains reposed chiefly in the hands of the Indians themselves—namely, the Sioux; the village tribes, e.g., Pawnees, Arikaras, Mandans, and Hidatsas; and the nomadic warriors, such as the Cheyenne and the Arapahos. We may well ask: just where did the Europeans and Americans fit into this picture? The answer, in Sioux eyes, was that they were only bit-players on the stage, to be manipulated as the Indians themselves saw fit.⁷¹

The Sioux were not very impressed by the Lewis and Clark expedition. They considered it not as an emissary from a vastly more powerful and therefore potentially dangerous culture but as proof that the Americans now wanted to compete with them for control of intertribal trade in the region.[72] U.S. Army Captain Randolph B. Marcy's authoritative, well-written account, *The Prairie Traveler* (1859), would become the principal manual for westward-bound pioneers in the second half of the nineteenth century. Drawing on his own 25 years of experience of frontier life, Marcy gives us such a vivid first-hand account of the prairie tribes, including the Sioux, that it is worth quoting here at some length:

> The prairie tribes have no permanent abiding places; they never plant a seed, but roam for hundreds of miles in every direction over the Plains. They are perfect horsemen, and seldom go to war on foot. Their attacks are made in the open prairies, and when unhorsed they are powerless....[73]
>
> No people probably on the face of the earth are more ambitious of martial fame, or entertain a higher appreciation for the deeds of a daring and successful warrior.... The attainment of such a reputation is the paramount and absorbing object of their lives; all their aspirations for distinction invariably take this channel of expression. A young man is never considered worthy to occupy a seat in council until he has encountered an enemy in battle; and he who can count the greatest number of scalps is the most highly honored by his tribe. This idea is inculcated from their earliest infancy. It is not surprising, therefore, that, with such weighty inducements before him, the young man who, as yet, has gained no renown as a brave or warrior, should be less discriminate in his attacks than older men who have already acquired a name. The young braves should, therefore, be closely watched when encountered on the Plains.[74]
>
> The prairie tribes are seldom at peace with all their neighbors, and some of the young braves are almost always absent upon a war excursion. These forays sometimes extend into the heart of the northern states of Mexico, where the Indians have carried on successful invasions for many years. They have devastated and depopulated a great portion of Sonora and Chihuahua. The object of these forays is to steal horses and mules, and to take prisoners....[75]

When the American artist and writer George Catlin visited these tribes in 1832, this is what he found:

> I am now in the heart of the country belonging to the numerous tribe of Sioux or Dahcotas, and have Indian faces and Indian customs in abundance around me. This tribe is one of the most numerous in North America, and also one of the most vigorous and warlike tribes to be found, numbering some forty or fifty thousand, and able undoubtedly to muster, if the tribe could be moved simultaneously, at least eight or ten thousand warriors, well mounted armed.[76]

Given the attitudes, abilities and numbers of the Sioux, it is not surprising that, as noted earlier, they would become the biggest single obstacle to American settlement of the northern Great Plains.

The Comanches

The nomadic Comanche buffalo hunters and raiders were not a single "tribe" but were instead organized into 13 or more autonomous bands. Their name is probably a Spanish pronunciation of the Ute word *komántcia* (literally "anyone who wants to fight me all the time").[77] They were originally part of the Shoshonean group but gradually moved out onto the Great Plains. In this process, they displaced the Apaches.

The huge, roughly circular area controlled by the Comanches was known as the *Comanchería*. It covered — very approximately, since it had no formal boundaries — central and northern Texas, the western half of Oklahoma, southwestern Kansas, part of southeastern Colorado, and the eastern third of New Mexico.[78] At its high point in the early nineteenth century, the *Comanchería* encompassed about 240,000 square miles.

One of the first tribes to acquire horses, chiefly by stealing them from the Spaniards, the Comanches became some of the best horsemen in history. The artist and writer George Catlin was astounded by Comanche horsemanship. He proclaimed: "I am ready, without hesitation, to pronounce the Camanchees the most extraordinary horsemen that I have yet seen in all my travels, and I very much doubt whether any people in the world can surpass them."[79]

The Comanches were extremely skilled buffalo hunters as well. It is estimated that about 30 million buffalo roamed the territories west of the Mississippi. They were the main food source of the Plains Indians. Athanase de Mézières, a former French army officer now in the service of Spain, traveled extensively through the southern plains in the 1770s and provided the first definitive descriptions of the cultures, geography, flora, and fauna of northern Texas. The Comanches, he says, were "a people so numerous and so haughty that when asked their number, they make no difficulty in comparing it to that of the stars."[80] They became "skillful in the management of the horse, to the raising of which they devote themselves."[81] This meant they could effectively exploit the buffalo — that apparently inexhaustible protein resource of the Plains.

As Mézières explains,

> The buffalo alone, besides its flesh, which takes first place among healthful and savory meats, supplies [the Indians] liberally with whatever they desire in the way of conveniences. The brains they use so often to soften skins; the horns for spoons and drinking vessels; the shoulder bones to dig and clear off the land; the tendons for thread and for bow-strings; the hoof, as glue for arrows; from the mane they make ropes and girths; from the wool, garters, belts, and various ornaments. The skin furnishes harness, lassos, shields, tents, shirts, leggins, shoes, and blankets for protection against the cold —

truly valuable treasures, easily acquired, quietly possessed, and lightly missed, which would liberally supply an infinite number of people, whom we consider poverty-stricken, with an excess of those necessities which perpetuate our struggles, anxieties, and discords.[82]

The first documentary reference to the Comanches is only a passing one. It dates from 1706, when Sergeant Major Juan de Ulibarrí, then en route from New Mexico to recapture apostate Pueblo Indians who were living with the Apaches on the plains, was told by Indian leaders at Taos pueblo that Comanches and Utes were about to raid the pueblo.[83] The earliest substantive ethnographic comments about the Comanches appeared twenty years later, when in about 1726 Brigadier Pedro de Rivera, posted in El Paso, wrote a brief description of life in New Mexico. This is what he tells us:

> Each year at a certain time, there comes to this province a nation of Indians very barbarous, and warlike. Their name is Comanche. They never number less than 1,500. Their origin is unknown, because they are always wandering in battle formation, for they make war on all the Nations. They halt at whatever stopping place and set up their campaign tents, which are of buffalo hide and carried by large dogs, which they raise for this purpose. The clothing of the men does not pass the navel, and that of the woman passes the knee. And after they finish the commerce which brought them there, which consists of tanned skins, buffalo hides, and those young Indians they capture (because they kill the older ones), they retire to their wandering until another time.[84]

The Spaniards in New Mexico understood very well the power of the Comanches and the difficulty of coping with them. In 1750, the governor of New Mexico, Thomás Vélez Cachupín, reported that

> Although the Comanche nation carries on a ... trade with us, coming to the pueblo of Taos, where they hold their fairs and trade in furs and in Indian slaves whom they take from various nations in their wars, and in horses, mules, knifes, belduques [Bowie knives], and other trifles, as always, when the occasion offers for stealing horses or attacking the pueblos of Pecos [southeast of Santa Fe] or Galisteo [south of Santa Fe], they do not fail to take advantage of it. During the five-year term of my predecessor, Don Joaquín Codallos, as many as 150 of the Pecos perished at their hands.... On the occasions when the Comanches have entered Taos ... I have reproached them for their malice and lack of good faith toward us. They excuse themselves by blaming others of their nation, saying that among them are warlike captains who commit outrages and those who are well disposed are unable to prevent them.[85]

Writing to his successor in 1754, Cachupín warned him that Spain did not have the military strength to protect its outposts from Comanche attacks. French-Comanche trade, he reported, was already well established. The French were trying hard to win the allegiance of this fierce tribe. "If this

1. The Indians

"Indians Hunting the Bison"
(©2005 Alecto Historical Editions www.alectoUK.com)

tribe should change its idea and declare war," he concluded, "your grace may fear the complete ruin of this [colonial] government."[86]

The first major Indian attack on the Spaniards in Texas was the 1758 sack of the mission-fort at Santa Cruz de San Sabá, located near Menard, Texas, about 125 miles northwest of San Antonio. Comanches were blamed for this assault, but many other Indians also formed part of the 2,000-man force that destroyed San Sabá. The well-armed Indians burned San Sabá to the ground and killed eight of its residents, including two priests. Eyewitnesses reported that the attackers had been equipped by French traders: they carried "French arms, bullet pouches, and very large powderhorns."[87] Father Miguel Molina, one of the survivors, recounted that he was "filled with amazement and fear" when he looked into the courtyard:

> I saw nothing but Indians on every hand, armed with guns and arrayed in the most horrible attire. Besides the paint on their faces, red and black, they were adorned with the pelts and tails of wild beasts, wrapped around them or hanging down from their heads, as well as deer horns. Some were disguised as various types of animals, and some wore feather headdresses. All were armed with muskets, swords, and lances, and I noticed also that they had brought with them some youths armed with bows and arrows, doubtless to train and encourage them in their cruel and bloody way of life.[88]

"Comanche Lodge," from *The Prairie Traveler*, Captain Randolph B. Marcy's definitive 1859 handbook for travelers in the Trans-Mississippi West. Marcy reports that such a tepee was "warm and comfortable in the coldest winter weather."

San Sabá was the only mission in Spanish Texas to be destroyed by outright Indian attacks. It was never rebuilt.

The next year, in 1759, the Spaniards suffered another humiliating defeat at what was (and still is) incorrectly known as Spanish Fort. Located along the Red River on the Texas-Oklahoma border, this settlement was named Spanish Fort because Anglo-American pioneers found Spanish artifacts and the ruins of an old fort near the site. In fact, however, Spanish Fort was a fortified Indian village.

To retaliate for an Indian assault on the presidio of San Luis de las Amarillas, several hundred Spanish soldiers led by Colonel Diego Ortiz Parrilla attacked Spanish Fort. To their great surprise, they found it very heavily defended. It was well fortified by entrenchments, wooden stockades, and even a moat. Inside the fort were 6,000 warriors—both Taovayas (a Wichita group) and Comanches—armed with French guns and even flying a French flag. After a four-hour battle in which he lost 52 men, Ortiz had the good sense to retreat but in the process he was forced abandon his baggage train and two cannons.[89]

These back-to-back failures at San Sabá and at Spanish Fort effectively halted Spanish efforts to expand north and west of San Antonio. In the years to come, these lands would be peopled not by Spaniards but, increasingly, by Comanches.[90] Nevertheless, Spanish exploration of the Trans-Mississippi West never came to a halt.

During the winter of 1776–1777, for example, the Franciscan missionaries Francisco Domínguez and Silvestre Vélez de Escalante set out on an epic exploration of the Great Basin (Utah and Nevada), which took them through more than 1,500 miles of arid and often freezing country. Starting from Santa Fe, they rode through lands previously unknown to Europeans and explored the central Rocky Mountains, going as far north as Rangley in northwestern Colorado. They then turned west toward Provo, Utah, and found there a great salt basin, which they skirted by heading south across the Escalante Desert of southwest Utah.

They had hoped to make their way to California, but the hardships of travel forced them to cross the Colorado River near Marble Canyon and return to Santa Fe in January 1777. Their expedition must have been counted by Spanish authorities as a qualified success because the explorers returned with enticing rumors of precious metals in the canyonlands and mountains of the Southwest.[91] In his *Journal of the Escalante and Domínguez Expedition of 1776*, Escalante reported that

> The Animas River [near Durango, Colorado] flows through a canyon where there are veins of metal. Although many years ago several persons were sent out to investigate and carry away some ore, it was not learned what metal it was. The Indians and some citizens of this Kingdom [i.e., Spaniards] said they were silver mines, which caused these mountains to be called Sierra la Plata.[92]

The Escalante-Domínguez expedition also discovered the safest place to ford the Colorado River, a spot now known as the Crossing of the Fathers. Moreover, these men blazed part of what would become the Old Spanish Trail linking Santa Fe and California. Their travels gave Spanish mapmakers some new insights. For example, notations on two different maps, made by the New Mexican map-maker Bernardo Meira y Pacheco in 1777 and 1778 as a result of this expedition, reflect the growing power of the Comanches, who by then had obtained horses. The first notation read in part:

> The Cumanche nation some years ago appeared first to the Yutas [Utes]. They said they left the northern border, breaking through several nations and the said Yutas took them to trade with the Spaniards, bringing a multitude of dogs loaded with their hides and tents. They acquired horses and weapons of iron, and they have had so much practice in the management of horses and arms, they excel all other tribes in agility and spirit, making themselves lords and masters of the buffalo country....[93]

"The Needles, between Cayetano Mountains and the San Juan River — Sierra de la Plata, or Silver Mountain." (Illustration from *The Prairie Traveler* [1859] by Captain Randolph B. Marcy.)

The second notation tells us that

> This nation is very warlike and cruel. It has made itself master of the buffalo plains.... It has dispossessed the Apache Nation of all its lands, becoming master of those as far as the frontier of the provinces of our King. These two said nations are those which for many years have been in a continual state of war against this kingdom ... and have brought about such panic that they have left no town, cities or ranches of the Spaniards unattacked.[94]

Comanche warriors were able to cover great distances and could strike hundreds of miles from their starting point. By 1775 the Spanish governor of New Mexico was lamenting that, despite a constant resupply of horses from Mexico, the Comanches had stolen so many of his horses that he did not have enough left to pursue these raiders.[95]

Militarily, the Spaniards could not defeat the Comanches of Texas and New Mexico, so they decided to make peace with them instead. The Comanches were surprisingly receptive to the idea for three reasons. First, French and Spanish traders had armed the Wichitas (sedentary farmers whose villages were a center of trade on the southern Plains) with firearms and had encouraged them to attack the Apaches and the Comanches. Second, smallpox may have greatly reduced the Comanches' fighting strength, making raiding more hazardous. Finally, like other Indians, the Comanches were becoming increasingly reliant on European and American traders to supply their needs.[96]

Because the Comanches were spread out across such a huge area, it was extremely difficult for the Europeans or Americans to make a treaty with one group that other groups would respect as well. A European who understood the reasons for this was Pedro Vial.[97] Born in France in the middle decades of the eighteenth century, he became one of the most accomplished and indefatigable European explorers of the Spanish Southwest. Before the American Revolution of 1776, he had made himself familiar with the Indian cultures and lands along the Missouri River. He first attracted the attention of Spanish authorities in 1779 when, armed with this valuable knowledge, he visited Natchitoches and New Orleans. The Spaniards quickly hired him as a pathfinder, agent and interpreter.

Vial had lived among the Comanches and would later pioneer the Santa Fe Trial linking St Louis and Santa Fe, a distance of about 1,100 miles each way. In so doing, he would manage to pass safely through regions controlled by such diverse Indian groups as the Comanches, Apaches, Kansas, Osages, Arapahos, Pawnees, and Sioux. In 1785, he explained to his Spanish employers that it was the Comanches' decentralized life style that posed such a problem for foreign negotiators. He said:

> The Comanche Nation has no fixed villages because they have many horses, because of which it is necessary to find places to pasture them, and which have buffalo and deer, for that is their food, and clothing, and with which they make the tents in which they live from buffalo hides which they make white, and very strong, useful, and durable.
>
> Their *rancherías* [settlements] are organized by the captains, who, each [one] endeavoring to have his own [*ranchería*], they do not have a fixed number of subjects, but only those who can adjust to the spirit of the captain.[98]

Nevertheless, despite this problem the Spaniards were able to hammer out treaties with the Comanches of Texas in 1785 and with those of New Mexico in 1786. In New Mexico, the peace held tolerably well, probably thanks to the sound advice of Pedro Vial. Drawing on his own experiences on the Great Plains, he recommended this course of action to the Spaniards:

> From what we have learned while among this nation, theirs should be a lasting peace as long as they are treated fondly and warmly when they come to visit this Presidio and care is taken to make an annual gift to the captains and principals of the nation, without neglecting the youths; and to maintain a trader for them and have [other Indians] urge them to keep good relations.[99]

Conditions in Texas, however, were so unsettled that raiding continued there. An ironic situation developed. Comanche bands often passed through

"The Interior of the Hut of a Mandan Chief"
©2005 Alecto Historical Editions www.alectoUK.com

Texas on their raids into Mexico. They discovered that the Comancheros of New Mexico (Spanish traders whom the Comanches allowed to bring goods and wagons into their camps) would pay them well for captives and stolen goods from Texas.[100] The Texans could do very little about Comanche raids. There were not many Spaniards living in Texas; moreover, their viceroy in distant Mexico paid little attention to what he regarded as a remote and worthless backwater province. It was certainly only lightly populated: as late as 1800, there were almost 30,000 Spanish settlers in New Mexico but barely 3,000 in Texas itself.[101]

The Mandans

The Mandans lived in earth-covered, dome-shaped lodges in stockaded villages located in present central North Dakota, near Bismarck. These Indians were prosperous and peaceful. Lewis and Clark spent the winter of 1804–1805 with them. Clark reported that "The Mandans are at war with all who make war only, and wish to be at peace with all nations, Seldom the ogressors."[102]

"Bison-Dance of the Mandan Indians in front of their Medicine Lodge"
©2005 Alecto Historical Editions www.alectoUK.com

They could boast of a cultural life highlighted by elaborate religious ceremonies designed to ensure good crops, successful hunts (the buffalo dance was extremely important), and victory in battle. Only those with "medicine," that is, warriors who had purchased a bundle of sacred "medicine" objects associated with tribal mythology, could lead these ceremonies. Bundle owners had to learn the songs, stories, prayers and rituals needed for the ceremonies. These owners were also responsible for passing on this tribal lore to young initiates.[103]

The Mandans planted corn, beans, pumpkins, sunflowers, and tobacco; hunted buffalo (the summer hunt was one of the major events of the year); made baskets and pottery; and served as the hub of a far-flung trading network. In the autumn, Indians and Europeans alike made their way to the Mandan villages to trade, bringing with them a wide range of desirable items—meat, hides, tallow, horses, and even musical instruments—to barter for Mandan corn.[104]

The Europeans who played an active role trading with the Mandans included British fur traders from the Hudson's Bay Company and, later, from its rival, the Montreal-based North West Company, as well as French businessmen from St. Louis.[105] On their way up the Missouri, Lewis and

Clark jotted down the names of no fewer than 21 Euro-Americans doing business on the river and referred to at least as many others, without naming them specifically.[106]

In 1738, the last of the great French explorers of North America, Pierre Gaultier de Varennes, Sieur (an honorific equivalent to the English "Squire") de La Vérendrye, was the first European to visit the Mandan villages near Bismarck, North Dakota. He found them planting "quantities of corn, beans, peas, oats, and other grains" and described them as "very industrious." "They are sharp traders," he added, "and clear the Assiniboin [a neighboring tribe] out of everything they have in the way of guns, powder, ball, kettles, axes, knives and awls."[107] La Vérendrye left two Frenchmen with the Mandans to learn their language and to evaluate prospects for trade.

By 1781, there were nine large Mandan villages, each consisting of up to 100 lodges, with an average of ten people living in each lodge. Snug and secure as these lodges were, they immediately became death traps when smallpox and cholera epidemics broke out. The mortality rate was so high that when Lewis and Clark spent the winter of 1804–1805 with the Mandans, only two of the nine villages remained. They had a population of only about 1,250 persons.

The Mandans had a great deal of trading experience. In his journal, Lewis drew a sketch of a special type of metal war hatchet, acquired by trade, which was highly prized by the Indians.[108] The expedition's blacksmith, Private John Shields, found that he and his colleagues could make some of these hatchets by using sheet iron from a burned-out stove that was no longer of any use to the expedition. When Shields' battle-axes were finished, all that remained of the stove were a few pieces of metal about four inches square, but these, too, were much desired by the Indians.

Lewis tells us that "the Indians are extravegantly fond of sheet iron of which they form arrow-points and manufacter into instruments for scraping and dressing their buffaloe robes."[109] After some hard bargaining, the Mandans and Shields finally reached agreement on a price for the remaining pieces of sheet iron: the Mandans would give Shields seven to eight gallons of corn for each square of metal. Both parties were convinced that they had gotten the best deal. Shields deposited the corn in the expedition's commissary and Lewis wrote that

> The blacksmiths take a considerable quantity of corn today in payment for their labour. the blacksmith's have proved a happy rescuc to us in our present situation as I believe it would have been difficult to have devised any other method to have procured corn from the natives.[110]

An American historian, Stephen E. Ambrose, argued convincingly that

Working as hard as they did in such extreme cold weather, the men ate prodigiously.... It was Mandan corn that got the expedition through the winter. Had the Mandans not been there, or had they no corn to spare, or had they been hostile, the Lewis and Clark Expedition might not have survived its first winter.[111]

Here is a small but vivid illustration of the Mandans' role in intertribal trade. Shields' war hatchets became such popular trade items that after the expedition left the Mandans, Shields came across one of them 14 months later. It was then being used by the Nez Percé Indians on the western slopes of the Rocky Mountains. This meant that the war hatchet had traveled west faster than the Lewis and Clark expedition itself.[112]

The Maritime Traders of the Pacific Northwest Coast

The long, thin (50-mile maximum width) Pacific Northwest coastline stretches south from Yakutat Bay, about 220 miles northwest of Juneau, Alaska, to Cape Mendocino in northern California.[113] The Kuroshio Current, also known as the Pacific or the Japanese current, causes a heavy and frequent rainfall along this coast. Together with the mountains that block off much of the frigid air in the interior, this current also keeps most of the coast ice-free in winter.

This region contains dense forests of easily worked wood: spruce, Douglas fir, cedar and, in the south, coastal redwood. Before the coming of the Europeans and Americans, the forests supported a wealth of game animals—deer, moose, elk, bear, mountain goats, mountain sheep, and fur-bearing species—fox, minx, and beaver. Waterfowl darkened the skies during their spring and autumn migrations.

The region was also extraordinarily rich in fish and shellfish. To be had for the taking were five different kinds of salmon; herring; the oily eulachon, used to make candles; smelt; cod; quarter-ton halibut; half-ton sturgeon; shoals of herring; mollusks; seals and sea lions; porpoise; sea otters; and, for Indians with oceangoing canoes, whales as well.

These aquatic resources were essential for the Indians' survival and formed the economic basis of their impressive cultural achievements. Such achievements included superior-quality woodworking: tall totem poles, big houses made of broad planks, seaworthy dugout canoes, elaborate masks, and finely crafted storage boxes.

The first European contact with the Indians of the Pacific Northwest coast came in 1741, when the Russian explorer Chirikov sent some of his crew ashore near Sitka. Because of their rich natural environment, the

Indians of this region could develop far more complex cultures than, say, the hunter-gatherers of the Great Basin. They were thus able to sustain a large population: perhaps 129,000 to 250,000 people lived there before the coming of the Europeans and Americans. As a British scholar, Dr. John Scouler, explained in 1825,

> This numerous population is not to be wondered at when we consider the abundant means of support the country affords. The sea yields abundant supply of excellent fishes of the most agreable kind, every rivulet teeming with myriads of salmon; & the land affords an endless variety of berries & esculent roots.[114]

Trade was an important component of the Indian economy. The British explorer Lieutenant Peter Puget, for whom Puget Sound is named, wrote that "the various Tribes who inhabit the large Extent of Coast from [Juan] De Fucas Streights to the [Queen] Charlottes Islands appear to have some Commercial Intercourse with each other."[115] A well-developed competitive trade network linked the coastal Indians with those living in the interior of the country. Lewis, referring to the tribes living near the Columbia River, wrote:

> There is a trade continually carried on by the natives of the river each trading some article or other with their neighbours above and below them; and thus articles which are vended by the whites at the entrance of this river, find their way to the most distant nations.[116]

Some of this trade passed through The Dalles, i.e., the beginning of a series of falls and rapids on the Columbia River, about 80 miles east of Portland, Oregon. Indians living near Celilo Falls dried, pounded, and stacked salmon flesh in layers; thus prepared, it would keep for several years. Celilo Falls, which is now submerged by The Dales Dam, became a major trade emporium where Indians from the Pacific coast and from the Rocky Mountains exchanged their own produce for pounded salmon.[117]

Here, listed in random order, are some of the goods that flowed through informal channels of intertribal trade between the Rocky Mountains and the Northwest Pacific coast[118]:

- Sea otter pelts (the sea otter trade with Europeans and Americans will be discussed later)
- Other furs
- Goat wool and goat horns
- Bows
- Camas (lilies with edible bulbs)

- Woven hats
- Horses
- Sheep horns and sheep skin
- Bowls and spoons
- Bags
- Dried salmon
- Wappato (a starchy root)
- Eulachon fish oil (for candles)
- Sturgeon
- Shellfish
- Clamons (thick leather armor, made from elk skins, which could turn arrowheads and lance points at close range and even deflect musket and pistol balls fired at an angle or from a distance)
- Dugout canoes
- Blankets
- Whale bone, oil, and blubber
- Cedar bark
- Cedarbark packets or strings of white dentalia shells (*haiqua*), which were used as money
- Tule mats (bulrush mats) to sleep on
- Spruce roots
- Wild hemp
- Woven baskets
- Deer skins
- Copper

For their part, European and American traders ranging along the Pacific Northwest coast offered a wide range of enticing goods to the Indians. Lewis tells us that

> The traffic on the part of the whites consists in vending, guns (principally old british or American musquits) powder, balls and shot, Copper and brass kettles, brass teakettles and coffee pots, blankets from two to three point [i.e., large or small blankets], scarlet and blue Cloth (coarse), plates and strips of sheet copper and brass, large brass wire, knives, beads and tobacco with fishinghooks buttons and some other small articles; also a considerable quantity of Sailor's cloaths, as hats coats, trowsers and shirts.[119]

The physical and cultural riches of the Pacific Northwest coast were especially evident in the potlatch ceremony — an important public feast that served a variety of social and economic purposes. It marked the ascension of a new chief; celebrated rites of passage or unusual successes; expressed thanks for assistance, e.g., in building a canoe or a house; and raised the host's social status.[120]

The essence of a potlatch was *giving*: the host literally gave away or publicly destroyed almost all of his prized possessions. In the greatest potlatches of the nineteenth century, a chief might distribute to his fellow tribesmen as many as 30,000 blankets or nearly 10,000 silver and brass bracelets.[121] In such a ceremony, too, valuable whale oil might be poured onto a fire to make it burn brighter, and copper plates tossed into it to melt down and thus be destroyed.

Even less impressive potlatches had the same important objectives. They confirmed social standing, redistributed wealth and made kinsmen more dependent on each other. They also gave the host something special to look forward to, namely, the gifts that he himself he would receive in turn at future potlatches and which would begin to restore his own fortunes. A final but more speculative benefit was that potlatches may have also channeled male aggression into a harmless if extravagant social competition.[122]

The Mission Indians of California

The phrase "Mission Indians" is a generalized term referring to the many and varied linguistic groupings of the California coast. Alfred L. Kroeber and other early anthropologists reported that 11 distinct native linguistic stocks could be found within the restricted area of mission colonization, i.e., the coastal strip between San Diego and Sonoma, and the lands lying north and east of it.[123] Major Indian groups were the Chumash, Costanoan, Diegueño, Gabrielino, Juaneño, and Luiseño.

The Mission Indians were numerous and diverse. It is estimated there were 200,0000 to 250,000 of them before the Gold Rush of 1848–1849.[124] Their culture was not elaborate, however, and usually did not appeal to foreign observers. Unlike the colorful horse-mounted warriors of the Great Plains or the prosperous maritime traders of the Pacific Northwest coast, the Mission Indians made a poor impression on many European and American newcomers. For example, the *Catholic Encyclopedia* of 1908 assured its readers that

> The Indians of California constituted a culture body essentially different from all the tribes east of the Sierras. The most obvious characteristic of this culture was its negative quality, the absence of those features that dominated tribal life elsewhere.... Both mentally and physically [the Mission Indians] represented one of the lowest types on the continent."[125]

These Indians entered the history of Spanish California in 1769 only because of a perceived threat from the Russians. The Spaniards believed that the Russian settlements in Alaska, which had been established to harvest sea otters, were in fact only the opening wedge of a perfidious Russian plan to conquer California itself. In fact, ten years earlier, José Torrubia, a Spanish Franciscan, had published a book with the ominous title, *Muscovites in California*, and warned Spanish officials about this grave danger. In 1768, both the viceroy, Teodoro de Croix, and the *visitador general* (inspector general) of New Spain, José de Gálvez, told the Spanish king of their conviction that "Certain foreign Powers [i.e., Russia] ... now have an opportunity and the most eager desire to establish some Colony at the Port of Monterrey."[126] Reviewing this state of affairs from his distant vantage point in 1804, William Shaler, an American captain in the sea otter trade, summarized Spain's fears:

> In the year 1769, the court of Spain, alarmed at the progress the Russians were making on the north-west coast of America, determined to occupy Upper California, and to establish missions there for the conversion and civilization of its inhabitants.[127]

To solidify Spain's very tenuous hold on California, in 1769 *visitador general* Gálvez dispatched to California a brilliant, ascetic, indefatigable Franciscan zealot — Father Junípero Serra. Serra established the first mission at San Diego that same year. By 1823, the Franciscans would be administering a string of 21 missions stretching for more than 500 miles along the Alta (Upper) California coast from San Diego to San Francisco Solano, located in Sonoma, about 75 miles north of San Francisco.

Father Serra had previously spent 17 years as a missionary in north central Mexico and thus had considerable experience dealing with Indians. He found that the California Indians were friendly, if only because they wanted to stay on the good side of the well-armed and well-armored Spaniards. Father Juan Crespí, who chronicled the Portolá expedition of 1769, tells us:

> These gentiles [i.e., the non–Christian Indians the Spaniards hoped to convert] seem to have excellent provisions, especially all types of fish. In fact they brought so much fish to the camp that it was necessary to tell them not to bring any more because it would eventually spoil. They were not satisfied with only giving us their food, they also wanted to entertain us. It was clear that there was a rivalry between the towns. They were competing with each other to see who could give the best presents and feasts in order to win our favor.[128]

In a letter written on 3 July 1769, two days after his arrival by ship at San Diego, Father Serra justified the planned conversion of the Indians. He wrote to Father Francisco Palous, a Franciscan colleague who was later his biographer,

> My Dear Friend,
>
> Thank God I arrived the day before yesterday, the first of the month, at this port of San Diego, a truly fine one, and not without reason called famous.... The tract through which we passed is generally very good land, with plenty of water; and there, as well as here, the country is neither rocky nor overrun with brushwood.... We have seen Indians in immense numbers, and all those along this coast of the Pacific contrive to make a good subsistence on various seeds, and by fishing. The latter they carry on by means of rafts or canoes, made of tule with which they go a great way to sea. They are very civil.... We found on our journey, as well as in the place where we stopped, that they treated us with as much confidence and good will as if they had known us all their lives.[129]

This promising beginning, however, was, for the Indians at least, soon to end in tears. Needing souls to save and strong arms and backs for working the fields and raising livestock at these missions, the Franciscans recruited large numbers of coastal Indians and forced them into what amounted to penal servitude. Spanish soldiers, for their part, treated the Indians very brutally and frequently raped Indian women. One of the earliest reports along these lines dates from 1772 and comes from Father Louis Jayme at San Diego, the first mission. He wrote:

> At one of these Indian villages near this mission of San Diego, which said village is very large, and which is on the road that goes to Monterey, the gentiles therein many times have been on the point of coming here to kill us all, and the reason for this is that some soldiers went there and raped their women, and other soldiers who were carrying the mail to Monterey turned their animals into their fields and they ate up all their crops. Three other Indian villages about a league or a league and a half from here have reported the same thing to me several times.[130]

Eventually, the Indians rebelled. In 1775, Kumeyaay Indians from 15 different villages attacked and burned Mission San Diego. Father Jayme perished in this assault. Writing to Serra about the attack, Jayme's companion at the mission, Father Vincent Fuster, reported:

> If the news that [Jayme] was already dead was a blow to me, how much harder was it to bear what I saw? He was quite unrecognizable. He was disfigured from head to foot, and I could see that his death had been cruel beyond description and to the fullest satisfaction of the barbarians. He was stripped completely naked of all his clothing, even to his undergarments around his middle. His chest and body were riddled through with countless jabs they had given him, and his face was one great bruise from the clubbing and stoning it had suffered. The only way my eyes could recognize Father Luis was from the whiteness of his skin and the tonsure on his head.[131]

The Mission Indians, however, only rarely offered any resistance to the Spaniards. We may well ask why this was the case. There seem to have been a number of reasons.[132] Their communities, based on different languages and different cultures, were small and highly fragmented. Drought had destroyed many of their traditional plant foods. Climate change, due to El Niño, had ruined their fisheries. Spanish cattle and sheep devoured the acorns that had traditionally been a staple of their diet. Spanish soldiers, though few in number, were far better armed and more disciplined than the Indians. If the Indians ran away from the missions, as many of them did, they were pursued by the soldiers and punished severely if recaptured.

Moreover, the missions were so big — some spread across 100,000 acres — that they were virtually self-contained kingdoms with virtually no outside supervision. At their own discretion, the priests could have recalcitrants whipped, branded, thrown into solitary confinement, or hunted down if they fled the mission grounds. Indian women were raped by Spanish soldiers and sometimes by the missionaries themselves. The result was that few Indian recruits survived mission life for more than ten years.

Foreign visitors expressed dismay at the abuses of the missions. In 1786, the great French navigator Jean François de Galaup, Comte de La Pérouse, visited California in the course of a voyage around the world. He found that the mission at Carmel was run like a West Indian slave plantation. He reported that "The men and women are collected by the sound of a bell; a missionary leads them to work, to the church, and to all their exercises."[133] Such discipline was only possible, he said, because "The government is a veritable theocracy for the Indians; they believe that their superiors are in immediate and continual contact with God, and that they make Him descend to the altar every day."[134]

La Pérouse added:

> The friars, more occupied with heavenly than temporal interests, have neglected the introduction of the most common arts.... With pain we say it, the resemblance [to slavery] is so perfect that we have seen men and women in irons or in the stocks; and even the sounds of the lash might have struck our ears, that punishment also being admitted, though practiced with little severity. I confess that, friend of the rights of man rather than theologian, I should have desired that to principles of Christianity there might be joined a legislation which little by little would have made citizens of men whose conditions hardly differs now from that of the negroes of our most humanely governed colonies.[135]

In 1792, the British explorer George Vancouver found the Indians at the Santa Clara mission to be in a chronically depressed state. "All the operations and functions of both body and mind," he wrote, "appeared to be carried on with a mechanical, lifeless, careless indifference."[136]

The Franciscans understood the symptoms but not the underlying causes of the problem. One missionary lamented that the Indians "live well free but as soon as we reduce them to a Christian and community life ... they fatten, sicken, and die."[137] In fact, the Indians fared very poorly under mission life. Studies done in the late 1930s by Sherburne F. Cook, an American scholar, showed what happened, statistically, under mission rule: "The group response of the natives to the mission environment was therefore a very marked decline in numbers, referable primarily to the high mortality rate and secondarily to a reduced birth rate and altered sex ratio.[138]

Mission Indians were also hard-hit by epidemics (measles in 1769, smallpox in 1781–1782). Nine out of ten children died before reaching the age of eight. Moreover, forced to abandon their traditional hunting-gathering ways of life, the Indians became fatally dependent, both economically and culturally, on the missionaries.

The Blackfoot Indians of Alberta and Montana

Consisting of three Algonquin-speaking groups, the Blackfoot were the strongest and most assertive tribe on the northwestern plains. They lived at first in the Saskatchewan Valley east of the Rocky Mountains but by about 1750, they had acquired horses and guns. Overcoming weaker tribes, they pushed their way westward and occupied a large swath of territory. North to south, it stretched from the North Saskatchewan River in Canada to the Missouri River in Montana; east to west, from the North Dakota-Montana border to the base of the Rocky Mountains.

Alexander Mackenzie, an outstanding British fur trader and explorer, followed the river now bearing his name from the Great Slave Lake north to the Arctic Ocean. Later, he reached the Pacific Ocean by making the first transcontinental crossing of America north of Mexico. Mackenzie reported in 1790 that there were about 9,000 Blackfoot in the Alberta-Montana area but later estimates, probably covering larger regions, ran as high as 16,500 to 20,000 people.

During the summer, these hunter-gatherers lived in large camps, hunted buffalo on the open plains, and conducted the Sun Dance, their principal religious ceremony. During the winter, they broke up into small bands and lived in 10 to 20 lodges in sheltered river valleys. Blackfoot religious life centered on medicine "bundles." Together with fasting and other rituals, these were believed to help induce the visions that would subsequently guide a warrior's entire life.

By about 1725, the Blackfoot Indians had acquired horses from other

"A Blackfoot Indian on Horse-Back"
©2005 Alecto Historical Editions www.alectoUK.com

tribes. They also had firearms, which had been traded westward from the Hudson's Bay Company's post at York Factory on Hudson Bay. Horses and guns gave them the power to expand westward from their original homeland in the timber country and move out onto the open grasslands. They drove other, weaker tribes before them in the process. The fur trader Alexander Henry was impressed by the aggressive culture of Blackfoot warriors. He tells us that "war, women, horses and buffalo are all their delights, and all these they have at their command ... war was their principal occupation."[139] Another trader, Edward Umfreville, recorded that stealing horses was "their principal inducement in going to war," to the extent that some Blackfoot Indians went far into the Southwest to steal horses and mules from the Spaniards.[140]

The artist George Catlin spent eight years (1832–1839) traveling among "the wildest tribes of Indians of North America" and explains why a Blackfoot warrior was such a good fighter:

> An Indian, therefore, mounted on a fleet and well-trained horse, with his bow in his hand, and his quiver slung on his back, containing a hundred arrows, of which he can throw fifteen or twenty in a minute, is a formidable

and dangerous enemy. Many of them also ride with a lance of twelve or fourteen feet in length ... with a blade of polished steel; and all of them (as a protection for their vital parts), with a shield or arrow-fender made of the skin of a buffalo's neck, which has been smoked and hardened with glue extracted from the hoofs.... These shields are arrow-proof, and will glance off a rifle-shot with perfect effect by being turned obliquely, which they do with great skill.[141]

Despite their undoubted military prowess, the unrelenting hostility of the Blackfoot Indians toward European or American fur traders and explorers is thought to date only from 1806. It came about during the Lewis and Clark expedition. Lewis and some of his men chanced upon a band of eight young Blackfoot warriors. One of these Indians tried to steal the expedition's rifles, which were essential for its survival. Two of Lewis' men chased him for 50 yards, wrestled the rifles away from him and plunged a knife into his chest, killing him instantly.

At the same time, the other Blackfoot Indians were trying to steal the expedition's horses, which were equally essential for its survival. Lewis still had his own rifle and when one of these Indians, who was armed with a British musket, turned toward him and got ready to shoot, Lewis shot him through the belly.[142] Although fatally wounded, the Blackfoot nevertheless managed to return fire. Lewis later wrote: "being bearheaded I felt the wind of his bullet very distinctly."[143]

After this encounter with the Lewis and Clark expedition, the Blackfoot Indians effectively prevented any other Europeans or Americans from trapping along the beaver-rich tributaries of the upper Missouri River. At the same time, they were equally hostile to neighboring tribes, taking Indian scalps and running off Indian horses whenever the opportunities arose.

The Nez Percé of the Columbia Plateau

The Nez Percé were the largest, most powerful and best known of the Sahapin-speaking Indians of central Idaho and adjacent areas of Oregon and Washington. Before Lewis and Clark met them in 1805, they may possibly have had some fleeting contacts with fur traders or Northwest coast explorers. If such contacts did occur, however, they do not seem to have been recorded. Their entry into European-American history therefore appears to date from 1805.

An interpreter for the Lewis and Clark expedition mistakenly referred to the Nez Percé as the "pierced noses" but in fact other neighboring tribes were more inclined than the Nez Percé to wear nose pendants. The Nez Percé called themselves Nee-me-poo, meaning "the People." They lived in small villages located near salmon-filled streams. Indeed, salmon — fresh or, more commonly, dried — was their staple food, augmented in season by deer and smaller game, camas and other roots, and berries. Their A-frame mat-covered lodges were spacious and could shelter as many as 30 families.

After they acquired horses early in the eighteenth century and had mastered the selective breeding of horses, the Nez Percé gradually built up one of the biggest horse herds in North America. This allowed them to adopt a more mobile and ultimately a more prosperous existence. They could now hunt buffalo effectively. They could raid on horseback like the Plains Indians, targeting the Shoshones, Bannocks, Blackfoot and Piutes. They could live comfortably in tepees away while on hunting trips: horses could carry the tanned buffalo hides from which they were made. They could trade with other tribes east of the Rocky Mountains. Finally, thanks to their growing numbers (a function of their general prosperity), they could, increasingly, dominate their neighbors.

Indian Objectives, Hopes and Fears

Fundamentally, the Indians wanted to retain their own independence and their traditional ways of life. In retrospect, this was a forlorn hope but for a long time many Indians clung to it nevertheless. Their point of view was not irrational. At first, there were not many Europeans or Americans in the Trans-Mississippi West and the Indians had no prior experience competing with much stronger foreign cultures. As a result, they gravely underestimated the military might and the economic power of these cultures. The results were predictable. Over time, the Indians' worst fears were realized: they lost their freedom and gradually became wards of the state.

2

The Spaniards: Children of the Sun

AFTER COLUMBUS "DISCOVERED" THE West Indies in 1492 when looking for a western sea route from Europe to Asia, imperial competition between Spain and Portugal for mastery of newly found lands in the non–Christian world went into high gear. Spain quickly claimed the entirety of North America, under the terms of the papal bull *Inter Caetera* (1493). To divide the unexplored world between Spain and Portugal, the most powerful Catholic states of that time, the Spanish-born Pope Alexander VI drew an imaginary north-south line, pole-to-pole, running near the mid–Atlantic islands of the Azores and Cape Verde.

The pope gave the Spaniards all the lands to the west of that line and the Portuguese all the lands to the east. To quote some of *Inter Caetera*'s sonorous phrases:

> We [the Pope] have indeed learned that you [Ferdinand and Isabella, king and queen of Spain] ... have chosen our beloved son, Christopher Columbus ... to make diligent quest for these remote and unknown mainlands and islands through the sea which hitherto no one had sailed ... wherein dwell many peoples living in peace and, as reported, going unclothed and not eating flesh ... by the authority of Almighty God conferred upon us ... give, grant, and assign ... all islands and mainlands found and to be discovered toward the west and south by drawing and establishing a line from the Arctic pole, namely the north, and to the Antarctic pole, namely the south ... said line to be distant one hundred leagues [318 miles] towards the west and south of any of the islands commonly known as the Azores and Cape Verde.[1]

Portugal protested strenuously because this bull meant that it would not be able to claim Brazil. The next year, to clarify their respective boundaries for exploration and colonization, the Spanish and Portuguese drew up the Treaty of Tordesillas (1494). This agreement defined the boundary as a straight line, pole-to-pole, located 370 leagues (1,185 miles) west of the Cape Verde islands. The English, however, did not accept such papal grants: Queen Elizabeth specifically refused to recognize the pope's authority to give the New World to the Spanish as a fief.

In the early 1500s, a group of Spanish jurists and other learned men working with the Council of the Indies drew up a binding legal document, which the leader of an expedition was required to read aloud, in Spanish, to the Indians of the New World. This document was officially known as the *Requerimiento*, literally "requirement" or "requisition," but in practice it was really a ceremony of Indian submission and Spanish overlordship. Interpreters would try, probably with minimal success, to translate it into numerous Indian languages and convey its message to the Indians. In essence, however, the message was simple and easily grasped: this document required the Indians, on pain of death, to submit completely to Spanish rule. (See Appendix 6 — A Spanish *Requerimiento*.)

Spain's conquests of Mexico and Peru had produced such a torrent of gold and silver that the *conquistadors* confidently expected similar riches were awaiting them in North America. They therefore launched a number of expeditions — large and small, by sea as well as by land — in pursuit of wealth and other objectives. As the historian Oakah L. Jones explained,

> The expeditions were undertaken for various motives: to search for mythical kingdoms, wealth, the Straits of Anián, slaves, and runaway Christian natives; to establish Catholic missions in which to convert Native Americans to Roman Catholicism and westernize them; to defend Spain's far-flung holdings from European rivals, such as the French, British, and Russians; to explore and reveal the geography and inhabitants of many *tierras desconocidas* (unknown lands); to provide economic gain for both individuals and the king; and to locate sites for future expansion and settlements. These ventures numbered in the hundreds when one considers all those made for exploration as well as the numerous punitive campaigns.[2]

Only a handful of such expeditions was sent into the Trans-Mississippi West between 1519 and 1605. The biggest and best equipped of them were known as *entradas*, a word which literally means "entrances" or "openings" but, as used by the Spaniards, connotes a formal penetration of unknown and potentially hostile lands. A condensed account of some of these expeditions, covering only their high (or low) points, is offered here. It will provide useful insights into the importance that the Spaniards attached to this region.

The first European to explore the Gulf Coast by sea from the Florida

Keys to just above Veracruz, Mexico was the Spaniard Alonso Álvarez de Pineda. It is clear that he commanded an expedition that sailed along the coast in 1519 but today he is still a shadowy figure because no account of his voyage has survived. The only original source which links his name to a reconnaissance ordered by 1519 by Francisco de Garay, Spanish governor of Jamaica, is a reference in a royal *cédula* (royal decree) of 1521, which granted to Garay the territory, called Amichel, which Álvarez de Pineda had explored in his name.[3]

The *cédula* suggests that Álvarez de Pineda was the first to record the strong outflow of the Mississippi River into the Gulf. He christened it the Río del Espíritu Santo (River of the Holy Spirit) because he crossed it on or about Pentecost. Pineda did not go ashore on the American portion of the Gulf Coast. Instead, he spent 40 days overhauling his ships in Mexico on the banks of the Pánuco River near Tampico.

Between 1528 and 1536, "four ragged castaways"—the *conquistador* Álvar Núñez Cabeza de Vaca and his three surviving companions—spent eight years wandering through the deserts of the Southwest. He would later write one of the earliest and perhaps the most dramatic first-hand account of the Trans-Mississippi West before 1803. It is truly one of the greatest adventure and survival stories of North American history and is worth recounting here.

Cabeza de Vaca's name means "cow's head" in Spanish. Legend has it that one of his ancestors helped win victory for Christian forces at Spanish battle against Muslim invaders by marking an unguarded but strategic mountain pass with the skull of a cow. In gratitude, King Sancho of Navarra bestowed this name on Cabeza de Vaca's matrilineal progenitors.[4]

Cabeza de Vaca himself was a career soldier. His military experience in Italy won him the position of treasurer in an ill-fated 1527–1528 expedition led by Pánfilo de Narváez, who set out to explore and colonize La Florida. Despite Cabeza de Vaca's strong protests, Narváez left his ships on the west coast of Florida and with a force of about 250 men began to march inland. Food shortages and hostile Indians, however, soon forced his expedition to retreat. They built five crude, shallow draft barges from horsehides and the limbs of trees. After dragging these vessels through marshes for a week, the Spaniards finally reached the sea and set sail in hopes of finding safety at Pánuco.

Near the mouth of the Mississippi River, however, a gale scattered the barges. Two of them, carrying 80 Spaniards, were driven ashore farther west. Here we will let Cabeza de Vaca tell the story of what happened to his own boat when he was off the east Texas coast:

> Near daybreak I fancied that I could hear the sound of breakers.... Sounding, we found ourselves at seven fathoms [42 feet], and [the captain] was of the opinion that we should keep offshore till dawn. So I took the oar and rowed along the coast, from which we were one league away, and turned the stern seaward. Close to shore a wave took us and hurled the boat a horseshoe's throw out of the water. With the violent shock nearly all the people who lay in the boat like dead came to themselves, and, seeing we were close to land, began to crawl out on all fours. When they got out they climbed to a rocky area, where we built a fire and toasted some of our corn. We found rainwater, and with the warmth of the fire people revived and began to cheer up. The day we arrived there [they were near the western tip of Galveston Island] was the sixth of the month of November [1528].[5]

This landfall marks the beginning of Cabeza de Vaca's eight years of wanderings across Texas, perhaps into New Mexico and Arizona, and then through Mexico's northern provinces. He managed to survive this ordeal by becoming a trader in Indian produce and artifacts. Perhaps even more importantly, he enjoyed astounding success as a faith healer. He writes:

> We remained with the Avavares [a Texas tribe] for eight months, according to our reckoning of the moons. During that time people came to us from far and wide and said that we were truly children of the sun. Until then Dorantes [another *conquistador*] and the Negro [the North African slave Estevánico] had not cured anyone, but we found ourselves so pressed by the Indians coming from all sides that all of us had to become medicine men.... We never treated anyone that did not afterward say he was well, and they had such confidence in our skill that they believed that none of them would die as long as we were among them....[6]
>
> They all came to us so we might touch and make the sign of the cross over them. They were so obtrusive that they made it difficult to endure since everyone, sick and healthy, wanted to be blessed. It happened frequently that women of our company would give birth to children and immediately bring them to us to have the sign of the cross made over them and have us touch the babes. They always accompanied us until we were again in the care of others. Among all these people it was believed that we came from Heaven. What they do not understand or is new to them they are wont to say comes from above.[7]

Cabeza de Vaca explains how he ministered to the Indians:

> The way we treated the sick was to make the sign of the cross over them, while breathing on them, recite a Pater Noster and Ave Maria and pray to God, our Lord, as well as we could to give them good health and inspire them to treat us well ... all those for whom we prayed told the others they were cured and felt well again.[8]

In the end, eight years after their shipwreck, only what Cabeza de Vaca called the "four ragged castaways" survived: Cabeza de Vaca himself, Alonso del Castillo Maldonando, Andrés Dorantes de Carranza, and the slave Estevánico. They were the only remnants of the 250 men who set out across Florida on the Narváez expedition. In 1536, these four men finally managed to make contact with a band of Spaniards near Culiacán on the west coast of Mexico, who were hunting for Indians to enslave.

Cabeza de Vaca tells us that, upon seeing him, the slave hunters were mightily astonished:

> Having seen positive traces of Christians and being satisfied they were very nearby ... I took the Negro and eleven Indians with me and ... went in search of the Christians.... The next morning I came upon four Christians on horseback who, seeing me in such strange attire and in the company of Indians, were greatly startled. They stared at me quite a while, speechless. Their surprise was so great that they could not find words to ask me anything. I spoke first, and told them to lead me to their captain, and together we went to Diego de Alcazar, their commander.[9]

The slavers were soon casting covetous eyes on the 600 Indians who formed Cabeza de Vaca's entourage, telling them through an interpreter that Cabeza de Vaca and his companions "were of their own race but had gone astray for a while, and were people of no luck and little heart, whereas they [themselves] were the lords of the land, whom [the Indians] should obey and serve."[10]

"The Indians," Cabeza de Vaca tells us, "paid little attention to all this talk." Instead,

> They talked among themselves, saying that the Christians lied, for we had come from sunrise, while they had come from where the sun sets; that we cured the sick, while they had killed those who were healthy; that we went naked and barefoot, whereas they wore clothes and went on horseback and carried lances. Also, we asked for nothing, but gave away all we were presented with, while they seemed to have no other aim than to steal what they could, and never give anything to anybody.... In the end, we could never convince the Indians that we belonged to the other Christians, and only with considerable trouble could we prevail on them to go home.[11]

Cabeza de Vaca returned to Spain in 1537, where he published the story of his epic adventure and urged a more compassionate policy toward the Indians. His account is noteworthy for its sympathetic descriptions of the Indians he encountered (23 tribes in Texas alone), as well as for his generally accurate descriptions of the unknown lands, flora, and fauna, especially the buffalo, of the region.[12]

In the early 1540s, Cabeza de Vaca served as governor of Paraguay but was accused of corruption, a charge that may have arisen from his lenient pro–Indian policies. Recalled to Spain, he was tried, convicted and temporarily banished to North Africa. Later, however, he was pardoned and was restored to favor. At the time of his death in 1556 or 1557, he was serving as a judge in Seville.

The next Spanish explorer we shall consider — Hernando de Soto — was a seasoned warrior. He had fought alongside the *conquistador* Pizarro, who in a campaign beginning in 1531 had overwhelmed the Inca empire of Peru and had seized the great silver mines of Potosí in Bolivia. De Soto was one of the first Europeans to meet the Inca ruler Atahualpa and later helped capture him in Cajamarca in 1532. Promoted to be governor of Cuba, in this new capacity de Soto received permission to conquer La Florida.

Starting from Tampa Bay in 1539, for four years his army of more than 600 men searched for gold but found only some freshwater pearls. In the process, he cut a wide swath of destruction through Florida, Georgia, Alabama, North and South Carolina, Tennessee, Mississippi, Louisiana, Arkansas, and Texas. De Soto and his men were the first foreigners to see the Mississippi River from one of its banks, crossing it on rafts in 1541. They were quite impressed. In his 1541 account, "A True Relation of the Hardships Suffered by Don Hernando de Soto," one of de Soto's officers, identified as "a gentleman of Elvas," tells us:

> [The Mississippi] was of great depth and of very strong current. Its water was always turgid and continually many trees and wood came down on it borne along by the force of the current. It had abundance of fish of various kinds, and most of them differed from the fresh waters of Spain.[13]

De Soto and his men spent two years wandering west of the Mississippi River, looking not only for gold but also for corn to eat and an escape route that would take them away from danger. He tried to persuade the local Indians that he was a son of the sun, but Quigaltam, their chief, retorted sharply: "Let him dry up the great river [the Mississippi] and he would believe him."[14]

Continued fighting with the Indians led to the loss of some 250 Spaniards and about 150 of their horses. Finally realizing that the gold-laden, densely populated cities he was looking for simply did not exist in that region, de Soto resignedly turned away from the west. He headed southeast in hopes of eventually reaching the Gulf of Mexico, where he and his men could build boats and escape to Cuba or Mexico.

In 1542, however, De Soto died at the age of 42, probably of typhoid fever, near the confluence of the Arkansas and Mississippi Rivers. He had assured the Indians that Christians were immortal, so his men, fearing that news of his death would incite the Indians to attack, decided to sink his body in a wide, deep reach of the nearest river. Toward this end, one of the chroniclers of the expedition tells us that

> [since] there was no stone in the whole region with which to weight the body so that it would go to the bottom, they cut down a very thick oak tree and hollowed out on one side a space equal to the height of a man, into which they could put the body. On the following night they disinterred it [De Soto had initially be buried ashore] as silently as possible and put it into the cut section of the oak tree with planks nailed over the body on the other side, and thus it was as if in a coffin. With many tears and much grief on the part of the priests and gentlemen who attended this second internment, they cast it into the middle of the river's current, commending his soul to God, and they saw it sink immediately to the bottom.[15]

De Soto's chosen successor, Luis de Moscoso Alvarado, then assumed command of the expedition and decided to march overland to Mexico. After wandering through southwestern Arkansas and east Texas for six months, in 1543 the expedition managed to build seven rudimentary ships, forging into nails the chains of some of its 400 Indian slaves. The surviving Spaniards (there were only 322 of them left) thus became the first Europeans to sail down the Mississippi. They reached the mouth of the river after 17 days of skirmishes with local Indians and, 53 days later, managed to reach safety in Tampico. They had traversed nearly 4,000 miles of Indian country but had found no riches. Moreover, they had suffered very heavy losses: almost half of the original expedition had perished en route.

When Cabeza de Vaca finally reached Mexico City in 1536, his breathless accounts of emeralds in the lands he had traversed sparked more expeditions. He had written that in return for their faith healing, the Indians had presented to Dorantes

> five emeralds shaped like arrow points, the arrows of which they use in their feasts and dances. Because they seemed to be of very good quality, I asked where they got them, and they said they came from some very high mountains toward the north, where they traded feather brushes and parrot plumes for them. They also said that there were villages with many people and many houses there.[16]

These were not in fact real emeralds but only green turquoises or pieces of malachite (a green carbonate of copper). Nevertheless, many Spaniards took Cabeza de Vaca's story as convincing proof that the legendary Seven Cities of Cíbola were waiting to be found somewhere in the northern wilderness of New Spain. In 1539, Viceroy Antonio de Mendoza sent Father Marcos de Niza, guided by Estevánico, on a reconnaissance expedition to find this fabulous city.

Mendoza told Marcos: "Give the natives to understand that there is a

God in heaven and the Emperor on earth to command and govern it, to whom all have to be subjected and to serve."[17] All that the explorers found, however, was a simple pueblo called Háwikuh, which was the southernmost Zuni settlement in western New Mexico. There Estevánico, who had survived shipwreck on the Texas coast, eight years of perilous wandering through the Southwest with Cabeza de Vaca, and who was a master of Indian languages, was killed by the Zunis.

The reasons for his death remain unclear. Some historians speculate that the Zunis feared that he was a spy for or represented the advance guard of a Spanish army. A more intriguing possibility is that, relying on the enthusiastic reception as a faith healer he had received from the Indians, Estevánico may have claimed that he was a god and may have demanded too many women and too many turquoises.

In any case, when Father Marcos himself got back to Mexico City, he assured the viceroy that Háwikuh-Cíbola "had a fine appearance." It was, Marcos averred,

> the best I have seen in these regions. The houses are as they have been described to me by the Indians, all of stone, with terraces and flat roofs, as it seemed to me from a hill where I stood to view it. The city is larger than the city of Mexico.[18]

A reasonable guess is that what inspired this too-favorable opinion was the glow of the yellow-walled adobe pueblo in the clear desert sunlight. Marcos, however, threw caution to the winds and told his listeners what he knew they all wanted to hear. He fabricated an impressive and persuasive story about the enormous riches of Cíbola:

> When I showed the natives the sample of gold I had, they said there were vessels of it among their people. They wore ornaments of it hanging from their noses and ears, and they also have blades of gold to scrape the sweat from their bodies. Many of the people I saw wore silk clothing down to their feet. Of the richness of that country I cannot write, because it is so great it does not seem possible. They have temples of metal covered with precious stones—emeralds, I think. They use vessels of gold and silver for they have no other metal.[19]

Excited by Marcos's fanciful description, the viceroy organized a follow-up expedition in 1540, led by Francisco Vásquez de Coronado. This formidable force consisted of more than 1,000 men, i.e., about 300 Spaniards and about 800 Indians; 1,500 horses and mules; and sizeable herds of sheep, pigs, and cattle to feed the hungry men. In addition, two ships under Captain Hernando de Alarcón were dispatched up the coast to support the expedition by sea.

Alarcón sailed north from Acapulco to the head of the Gulf of California, and was the first European to travel (in two ships' boats) up the Colorado River. When an Indian there asked him "whether we had sprung from the water or the earth or descended from the sky," Alarcón tells us: "I gave them to understand that I came from the sun ... I am its son."[20] He sailed and rowed his boats up the Colorado as far as its junction with the Gila River near Yuma, Arizona. There he had to turn back because Coronado's expedition had already gone farther inland.

Coronado and his men were bitterly disappointed when they finally got to Háwikuh and found it to be only a typical stone-and-adobe Pueblo Indian settlement, not the golden capital that existed only in Marcos' imagination. A storm of criticism broke over Marcos' head. The chronicler of the expedition, Pedro de Castañeda de Nájera, tells us in his *Relación de la jornada de Cíbola* that "The curses that some hurled at Fray Marcos were such that God forbid they may befall him."[21] Coronado himself would report to the viceroy:

> It now remains for me to tell you about the city and kingdom of which [Father Marcos] gave Your Lordship an account. In brief, I can assure you that in reality he has not told you the truth in a single thing he said, but everything is the reverse of what he said except the name of the city and the large stone houses.... The Seven Cities are seven little villages ... it does not appear to me that there is any hope of getting gold or silver.... They are all within a radius of 5 leagues. They are all called the kingdom of Cevola, and each has its own name and no single one is called Cevola, but all together are called Cevola.... The people of the towns seem to me to be of ordinary size and intelligence, although I do not think they have the judgment and intelligence they out to have to build these houses in the way in which they have, for most of them are entirely naked except the covering of their privy parts.[22]

As the expedition approached the pueblo, 200 Zuni warriors blocked the path and sprinkled sacred cornmeal across it, thus warning the Spaniards to come no farther. Not understanding and not caring about this religious symbolism, the expedition surged forward. After some fierce fighting (stones hurled down from the pueblo knocked Coronado unconscious), the Spaniards captured Háwikuh.

Coronado then sent out detachments to scour the country. Lieutenant Pedro de Tovar's unit went into Arizona, where Lieutenant García López de Cárdenas and his men became the first Europeans to see the Grand Canyon. They spent three days looking for a way to get down the cliffs to look for a place where the Colorado River could be forded, but they failed in this attempt because the going was too difficult. The chronicler Pedro de Castañeda de Nájera reported that the lieutenant told him:

The descent was almost impossible, but, after these three days, at a place which seemed less difficult, Captain Melgosa, a certain Juan Galeras, and another companion, being the most agile, began to go down. They continued descending within view of those on top until they lost sight of them, as they could not be seen from the top. They returned about four o'clock in the afternoon, as they could not reach the bottom because of the many obstacles they met.... From the top they could make out, apart from the canyon, some small boulders which seemed to be as high as a man. Those who went down and who reached them swore that they were taller than the great tower of Seville.[23]

Although the Pueblo world was a relatively populous one — the chronicler Castañeda said that it contained 66 pueblos and about 20,000 people[24] — it held no mineral wealth the Spaniards could exploit. Thus when Coronado met an Indian delegation from Pecos whose members invited him to travel to the east to meet allegedly friendly Indians living in the buffalo country, he quickly accepted the offer. He assigned Captain Hernando de Alvarado and a small group of soldiers to go back with the Pecos delegation.

When Alvarado's expedition reached Pecos, he hired as a guide and as an interpreter an Indian slave from the Plains, whom the Spaniards dubbed El Turco (the Turk) because they thought that he resembled one. El Turco assured them he knew all about a fabulous region to the east, somewhere on the Buffalo Plains, called Quivira. In this land, he told the Spaniards,

> There was a river, flowing through the plains, which was two leagues wide, with fish large as horses and a great number of very large canoes with sails, carrying more than twenty oarsmen on each side. The nobles, he said, traveled in the stern, seated under canopies, and at the prow was a large golden eagle. He further stated that the lord of that land took his siesta under a large tree from which hung numerous golden jingle bells, and he was pleased as they played in the wind ... the common table service of all was generally wrought silver, and that the pitchers, dishes, and bowls were made of gold.[25]

Inspired by dreams of such wealth, the Spaniards then began to fight and pillage their way into the Llano Estacado (the Staked Plain), which straddles the New Mexico-Texas border. This region was so flat and so featureless that tall wooden posts had to be driven into the ground to mark the trails. The immensity of the Great Plains made a strong impression on Coronado. "The country is like a bowl," he wrote, "so that when a man sits down the horizon surrounds him all round at the distance of a musket shot."[26] There they did meet some buffalo-hunting Indians, who told about impressive settlements lying farther to the east.

In 1540, after claiming the "Kingdom of New Mexico" for their king, the Spaniards pressed on into central Kansas, where they finally reached El

Turco's Quivira. This settlement is now thought to have been located in Kansas, somewhere between Great Bend and Wichita. Instead of being the golden city of their dreams, however, it turned out to consist only of the thatched-hut villages of the Quivira (Wichita) Indians. These relatively prosperous Indians grew corn and hunted buffalo, but they had no gold or silver for the Spaniards to seize.

Realizing that El Turco had consistently lied to them, Coronado extracted a confession from him. There are two versions of it. In the first, El Turco said that the Pecos Indians had ordered him to lead the Spaniards out onto the Plains, where, he continued, "through lack of provisions, their horses would die and they themselves would become so feeble that, upon their return, the people of [Pecos] could kill them easily and so obtain revenge for what the Spaniards had done to them."[27] In the second version, El Turco is quoted as saying that he led the Spaniards astray "in order to kill them all so that they would not go to his [own] country."[28]

Coronado reacted to El Turco's confession by having the man garroted. Later, Coronado himself suffered such severe head injuries after a fall from his horse that he could only travel in a litter slung between two mules. An unrelated development — Indian uprisings in Mexico itself — urgently called for his return there. Thus in 1542 he headed back toward Mexico City, where he had to stand trial for mishandling his expedition. Probably because of his poor health, he was acquitted of these charges but was convicted on other charges, for which he was fined and lost his commission. Lieutenant Cárdenas was tried in Spain for crimes against the Indians and died in prison.

Spaniards explored the Trans-Mississippi West by sea as well as by land. In 1539, the Spanish navigator Francisco de Ulloa sailed about three quarters of the way up the western coast of Baja or Lower California but he did not get as far north as Alta or Upper California.[29] In 1542, the *conquistador* Juan Rodríguez Cabrillo became the first European to visit the Pacific shore of the United States.[30] He sailed northwest from Navidad, Mexico, to explore the coasts of the Californias. From there, he had planned to continue on to China. Cabrillo's flotilla was the first to reach San Diego Bay, which Cabrillo accurately described as "a closed and very good port."[31]

An interesting footnote here is that the name "California" comes from a Spanish novel, *Las Sergas de Esplandián* (*The Labors of the Very Brave Knight Esplandián*), published in Seville in 1510 by the Spanish author Garcí Rodríguez Ordóñez de Montalvo. This novel was well known to Spanish explorers in the New World. In the novel, Montalvo assures his readers:

> Know ye that on the right hand of the Indies there is an island called California, very near the Terrestrial Paradise and inhabited by black women without a single man among them and living in the manner of Amazons. They are robust of body, strong and passionate in heart, and of great valor. Their island is one of the most rugged in the world with bold rocks and crags. Their arms are all of gold, as is the harnesses of the wild beasts which, after taming, they ride. In all the island there is no other metal.[32]

Hernán Cortés, who in 1521 had completed the conquest of the Aztec empire of Mexico with its fabulous gold and silver mines, wrote three years later that he fully expected to find this island of Amazons somewhere off the northwest coast of Mexico. It is likely that Cabrillo hoped to discover it himself. No Amazons were found in California, but the heavy Spanish presence was not long in making itself felt there. Soon after he anchored off Point Loma in San Diego Bay, Cabrillo heard echoes of Coronado's depredations.

According to a summary of a ship's log, Indians there told him that

> in the interior men like us [Spaniards] were travelling about, bearded, clothed and armed like those of the ships. [The Indians] made signs that they carried crossbows and swords; and they made gestures with the right arm as if they were throwing lances, and ran around as if on horseback. They made signs that they were killing many native Indians, and for this reason they were afraid."[33]

Cabrillo's three ships wintered at Santa Catalina Island, where he did died after a fall. Contemporary accounts of his injury differ. One report tells us that that he broke his arm near the shoulder as the result of a fall; another says that he splintered his shinbone while leaping shore to save his men from an Indian attack. In any case, after his death the expedition proceeded north under the leadership of Bartolomé Ferrer, the senior pilot.

It is unclear precisely how far Ferrer was able to go, but in November 1542 he encountered very bad weather off Point Reyes, north of San Francisco. Either there or slightly farther north (perhaps off the California-Oregon border), he was forced to abandon his plan to sail to China. He was running low on supplies and was facing mountainous seas "so high that [his men] became crazed."[34] He therefore came about and returned to Mexico instead. He had discovered no gold or silver along the Pacific Coast but he did establish what would become a long lasting Spanish claim to this region.

Although Spanish explorers never found any exploitable amounts of gold or silver north of the present border between Mexico and the United States, in 1546 the Indians of Zacatecas in central Mexico had showed Spanish prospectors some chunks of silver ore. By the mid-1560s, the mining frontier in Mexico had pushed north into Chihuahua. Santa Bárbara became the most important silver mining center in Mexico and was soon sending out its own expeditions into New Mexico and Texas to enslave Indians to work in the mines until they died. (Today the Zacatecas Silver Belt continues to be the largest source of silver in Mexico. Two mines there have produced more than 1.5 billion ounces of silver. They are the reason why Mexico is still the world's biggest producer of silver.)[35]

In 1581, a small land expedition led by Friar Agustín Rodríguez and protected by Captain Francisco Sánchez Chamuscado and a handful of soldiers left Santa Bárbara for New Mexico. Their two-fold objective was to convert the Indians and to find new silver mines. As soon as they were in Pueblo country, the Spanish soldiers fired their muskets into the air to impress the Indians by demonstrating that the *conquistadors* were indeed "children of the sun." It was the sun itself, the Spaniards claimed, that had given them firearms for their protection.[36]

Pueblo culture impressed Hernán Gallegos, the chronicler of the expedition. "The valley [where the Zunis lived] is the best that has been discovered," he reported,

> since all of it is cultivated and not a grain of corn is lost. All the houses are of stone, which is indeed amazing. There is not a house of two or three stories that does not have eight rooms or more, which surprised us more than anything else, together with the fact that the houses are whitewashed and painted inside and out.[37]

At first, the expedition got along well with the Indians but later it proved to be a complete failure. Very few Indians were converted. No new mines were found, although returning soldiers would later claim they had seen 11 silver-bearing areas. The Indians killed a missionary who tried to get back to Santa Bárbara by himself. Over Chamuscado's strong objections, Rodríguez and another missionary, Francisco López, decided to stay on with the Indians and establish a mission north of Albuquerque. Both were killed soon after Chamuscado and his soldiers departed. On the way back to Santa Bárbara, Chamuscado himself fell ill. Since no one in the party had a lancet, his soldiers used a dirty horseshoe nail to bleed him. Not surprisingly, infection set in and he died en route.

Antonio de Espejo was a former member of the Spanish Inquisition police force who had been charged with complicity in the murder of two cowboys. Hoping to redeem his reputation, he set out overland to find the missionaries, not knowing that they were already dead. To recoup his own fortunes, he was also looking for gold and silver. For these joint purposes, he led an expedition into Pueblo country, beginning in 1582. One of the places he visited was the pueblo at Acoma, located about 50 miles west of Albuquerque.

Acoma is now the oldest continuously inhabited city in the United States: Indians were living there when Coronado entered it in 1540. Because of its dramatic location perched on top of a sandstone mesa that rises 357 feet above the valley floor, it could not be captured by other Indians. Coronado said that this fortress was "One of the strongest ever seen, because the city was built on a high rock. The ascent was so difficult that we repented climbing to the top."[38]

Espejo reported that Acoma held more than 6,000 people and that it

> is built on top of a lofty rock ... and out of the rock itself the natives have hewn stairs by which they ascend and descend from the pueblo. It is a veritable stronghold, with water cisterns at the top and quantities of provisions stored in the pueblo.[39]

At first, the expedition had good relations with the Indians but incessant Spanish demands for food gradually aroused their hostility. When the Indians of the Puaray pueblo refused to feed his expedition, Espejo had 30 of them burned alive. His expedition finally reached the confluence of the Rio Grande and Conchos Rivers on the Texas-Chihuahua border and from there made its way back into Mexico. By greatly exaggerating the economic potential of New Mexico, Espejo tried but failed to get himself put in charge of Spanish colonization in the region. That job would eventually be given to Juan de Oñate in 1595.

In the meantime, Gaspar Castaño de Sosa, lieutenant governor of Nuevo Léon (New Spain's most northeasterly province), decided to found a Spanish colony in the Pueblo country. He therefore led a party of 170 colonists to the Pecos pueblo in 1590. After capturing the pueblo, he, like other Spaniards, was much impressed by its architecture and abundant stock of corn, beans and flour. He pressed on to the Rio Grande Valley, which Espejo had recommended as a good site for settlement.

However, because Castaño de Sosa had defied the viceroy's order by mounting an expedition without official permission, it was soon recalled to Mexico. Castaño de Sosa traveled with it, "laden with a stout pair of leg irons and a chain that is very thick and heavy." After reaching Mexico City, he was sentenced to six years of exile in the Philippines for invading the "lands of peaceable Indians."[40] On the voyage to Manila, however, he was killed by rebellious slaves.[41]

The Spaniards (and the Portuguese) relied on treasure galleons—big, full-rigged ships—for their international trade. For more than 250 years, Spain's famous Manila galleons made an annual voyage between Acapulco (Mexico) and the Philippines. They carried gold and silver from Central and South American mines to Manila. They brought back Chinese trade goods, primarily silk, spices, beeswax and porcelain. These were shipped across Mexico to Veracruz and then on to Spain.

The Spaniards had failed in two earlier attempts (in 1584 and 1587) to find a suitable port on the California coast for their Manila galleons. In 1595, Spain made another effort, instructing Captain Sebastián Rodrigo Cermeño, commander of the galleon *San Agustín*, to survey the California-Oregon coast down to Mexico during the return leg of his passage from the Philippines.[42] This plan had two major advantages. By using a galleon already in these waters, it saved the cost of financing a separate expedition. By approaching the Pacific coast from the Philippines, the ship could take advantage of favorable winds and currents.

Cermeño successfully made landfall off the California-Oregon border, turned south, and headed down the coast. At Drake's Bay, north of San Francisco, he formally took possession of the land for Spain — not knowing that Sir Francis Drake had landed there sixteen years earlier and had already claimed it for England. (Drake's voyage will be described in Chapter 4.)

Galleons were built with beaked prows; high, square forecastles behind the bows; three or four thick masts; and raised sterns. Consequently, they had a great deal of windage (wind resistance). Because so much woodwork was exposed to the wind, a strong wind could easily push the ship sideways. Unlike San Francisco's well-sheltered bay, Drake's Bay is not a secure anchorage because it offers no protection from storms. In November 1595, a storm came up while *San Agustín* was anchored off Drake's Bay. The galleon was driven ashore and was broken up by powerful waves. The valuable cargo of beeswax, silk, and porcelain was lost. Much of it washed ashore and was salvaged by the Coast Miwok Indians.

Since all but the porcelain was perishable, the full extent of the galleon's cargo can never be determined. However, over 800 shards have been recovered from excavations in nearby Indian villages and gravesites. In addition, some pieces of porcelain were shaped by the Miwoks into beads, pendants and scrapers. These artifacts provide physical evidence of one of the earliest European-Indian contacts in the New World.[43]

Cermeño was a determined explorer. Undeterred by the loss of his ship, he promptly loaded his 70 sailors and passengers onto a small vessel, the bark *Santa Buenaventura* (which he had either carried, disassembled, aboard the galleon, or which his men built ashore), and continued to explore the coast. The health of his men, however, gradually declined to the point where he was forced to abandon his explorations and return to Mexico as soon as possible. This he did in 1596. The loss of *San Agustín* and its valuable cargo showed the risks involved in using Manila galleons to explore the little known and therefore dangerous California coast. This practice was therefore abandoned.

The Spaniards' permanent occupation of Pueblo lands, as distinct from their transitory explorations of these lands, did not officially begin until 1598. That year, Juan de Oñate led about 560 colonists, 80 wagons and carts, and 7,000 head of livestock into northern New Mexico through El Paso *del Norte* (the Pass of the North). This natural gateway lies between what are now the cities of Cuidad Juárez, Chihuahua, and El Paso, Texas. He crossed the Rio Grande at El Paso and established the capital of his colony at San Juan Pueblo, 25 miles north of Santa Fe. (In 1610, the new governor, Don Pedro de Peralta, would move New Mexico's capital to Santa Fe itself.) Thanks to Oñate's expedition, Spain's El Camino Real (the Royal Highway) was effectively extended an additional 600 miles.

One of the new settlers recorded the celebrations that took place when the expedition finally reached the Rio Grande after a difficult three-month journey:

> On 30 April 1598, day of the Ascension of our Lord, at this Río del Norte, Governor Don Juan de Oñate took possession of all the kingdoms and provinces of New Mexico, in the name of King Felipe [II], our lord, in the presence of Juan Pérez de Donis, royal notary and secretary of the jurisdiction and expedition. There was a sermon, a great ecclesiastical and secular celebration, a great salute and rejoicing, and in the afternoon, a comedy. The royal standard was blessed and placed in charge of Francisco de Sosa Peñalosa, the royal ensign.[44]

Matters soon took a turn for the worse. At the end of that year, a fracas erupted between the Acoma Indians and a Spanish foraging party led by Juan de Zaldívar. There are conflicting contemporary reports of what caused the fighting, but the outcome was clear: the Acomas killed Zaldívar and ten of his soldiers, and tossed their bodies off the cliffs of the mesa. Oñate and his fellow officers decided that only prompt, decisive retaliation could make New Mexico safe for Spanish colonization. "The greatest force we possess at present to defend our friends and ourselves," he wrote, "is the prestige of the Spanish nation, by fear of which the Indians have been kept in check."[45]

Early in 1599, Sergeant Major Vicente de Zaldívar, younger brother of Juan de Zaldívar, asked for and was given permission to attack Acoma. By scaling the mesa and turning two canons on the Indians, he and his men carried the day and took their revenge. About 800 Acomas died, some by suicide. Some warriors killed their wives and children so they would not fall into Spanish hands. Five hundred Acoma women and children were taken captive. Not long thereafter, after a show trial, Oñate handed down harsh sentences.

Men over the age of 25 were sentenced to 25 years of slavery, with 24 men suffering amputation of their right foot. Young men between 12 and 25, and women between 12 and 20, were sentenced to 20 years of servitude. Girls under 12 were given to the care of the friars, and boys under 12 were given to Zaldívar himself, so that under his rule they could "attain the knowledge of God and the salvation of their souls."[46]

Acting on his orders, Oñate's men also amputated the right hands of two Hopis who happened to be visiting Acoma at the time of the attack. These hapless Indians were sent home to spread word of the consequences of opposing the Spaniards. Oñate pronounced himself very pleased with what he had accomplished. "All this," he reported, "left the land pacified and intimidated."[47]

Severe as these penalties were, we must note that, as the historian Elizabeth John reminds us,

> death or servitude was not an uncommon result of clashes between Indian peoples. Mutilation and servitude were not extraordinary penalties in sixteenth-century Spain, particularly for crimes as serious as those of which the Acomas were found guilty [e.g., premeditated treason] ... Oñate exercised relative lenience when he eschewed the capital punishment that would have befallen a Spaniard guilty of the same crime.[48]

While Oñate was off on his fruitless search for the treasures of Quivira, his colony in New Mexico was slowly falling apart. The land was not suited for Spanish crops. The Indians were hostile. There was no gold or silver. As a result, many of the colonists returned to Mexico, where they complained to the authorities about conditions in New Mexico and Oñate's harsh treatment of the Indians.

At this time (1604), Oñate set off on his last expedition but this, too, was a failure. He wanted to blaze a trail to the Pacific Ocean. Towards this end, he led 30 soldiers west from the Zuni pueblos to the Colorado River and then south to the Gulf of California, but he never reached the Pacific Coast. He found no gold or silver. Tired and disillusioned, he turned back, pausing en route only long enough to carve this message among the Indian petroglyphs on Inscription Rock at El Morro National Monument in western New Mexico, where it can still be seen:

> *Pasó por aquí el Adelantado Don Juan de Oñate al descubrimiento del Mar del Sur a 16 de abril de 1605.*
> (The Adelantado ["one who goes before," i.e., the representative of the king of Castile] Don Juan de Oñate passed by here from the discovery of the Sea of the South, the 16th day of April 1605.)[49]

Oñate resigned his office in 1607. The wheels of justice in New Spain may have ground very slowly but they never came to a complete halt. Six years later, in 1613, Oñate was tried in Mexico City for using excessive force against the Acomas; for executing Indians, mutineers, and deserters; and for adultery. He was fined, stripped of his titles, banished permanently from the colony he had founded in New Mexico, and exiled from Mexico City itself for four years. He appealed his sentence with only limited success and was never restored to high office. Oñate eventually became a mining inspector in Spain and died there in 1626.

Another intrepid Spanish adventurer was Sebastián Vizcaíno. He led a four-ship expedition north from Acapulco, Mexico, in 1602, looking for a safe harbor along the California coast. Finding such a harbor was considered to be extremely important. Treasure-laden Spanish galleons did not sail due east from Manila but instead first sailed north to pick up the Kuroshio Current off the coast of Japan. Using this current, they eventually made landfall off the northern California coast near Cape Mendocino. They then turned south and headed towards Mexico. What the galleons needed at this point was protection from English privateers. The Spaniards remembered very well that, in 1587, the English navigator and freebooter Thomas Cavendish had captured the treasure galleon *Santa Ana* off the coast of Baja California when she was returning to Mexico from the Philippines.[50]

Vizcaíno charted the California coast with such precision that his maps were still in use by 1790. Many of the place-names he bestowed are with us today. Entering San Diego Bay in 1602 on the feast day of San Diego de Alcala, he called it "a port which must be the best to be found in all the South Sea."[51] Later, he identified and named Monterey Bay, describing it, over-optimistically, as perfect for Spain's maritime needs. (Monterey Bay is in fact an open roadstead. It is much inferior to San Francisco Bay but the Spaniards would not discover San Francisco Bay until 1769 because of its narrow entrance was often blanketed by fog.)

Vizcaíno cheerfully assured his viceroy in Mexico:

> I have discovered many harbors, bays, and islands, as far as the port of Monterey, a harbor which is 37 degrees of latitude, surveying all & sounding, & noting the sailing directions ... and noting what the land and the numerous peoples dwelling therein seemingly promise ... I advise His Majesty concerning the great extent of this land and its numerous population and what promise it holds forth, and what the Indians have given me to understand concerning the people of the interior, and of how gentle & affable the people are, so that they will receive readily, as I think, the holy gospel and will come into subjection to the royal crown.[52]

In 1603, Vizcaíno sent to King Felipe III of Spain a glowing report on the port of Monterey. It reads in part:

> Among the most important ports that I discovered was one located at 37 degrees latitude, which I named Monterey. I wrote to Your Majesty from there on September 28 of this year, stating that this port is all that one could hope for. It is a convenient stopping place along the coast for ships that are coming from the Philippines. The port is sheltered from all winds, and along the shore there are many pine trees that could be used for ship masts of any size desired.... It is a pleasant place. The area is populated by people whom I considered to be meek, gentle, quiet, and quite amenable to conversion to Catholicism and to becoming subjects of Your Majesty. The Indians have strong bodies and white faces. The women are somewhat smaller and have nice features.
>
> Their clothing is made from sealskins. They tan and dress the hides better than how it is done in Castile. Seals are found in abundance. They have a large amount of flax and hemp, from which they make fishing lines and nets for catching rabbits and hares. Their boats are made of pine and are very well constructed. They go out onto the ocean with fourteen oarsmen and they can sail with ease even during a strong storm.
>
> I traveled more than eight hundred leagues along the coast and kept a record of all the people I encountered. The coast is populated by an endless number of Indians, who said there were large settlements in the interior.... [The Indians] are very knowledgeable about silver and gold and said that these metals can be found in the interior.[53]

Despite Vizcaíno's conviction that Spain should develop Monterey as a haven for the Manila galleons, this was never done. Vizcaíno was later replaced by Juan de Mendoza y Luna, who argued that what Spain needed was not a port on the California coast but a mid-ocean station on one of two Pacific islands, Rica de Oro and Rica de Plata. These islands did not in fact exist, but it was believed they were located somewhere in the northern Pacific Ocean. Plans for Monterey were therefore shelved. In the end, the Manila galleon trade managed to flourish without either a California or a mid-ocean port.[54]

As Vizcaíno proceeded north, like Cabrillo 60 years earlier he ran into such heavy weather off the California-Oregon border that he was forced to turn back toward Mexico. A chronicler on one of his ships tells us that "the pitching was so violent that it threw both sick and well from their beds and the general [Vizcaíno] from his. He struck upon some boxes and broke his ribs with the heavy blow."[55]

Maritime expeditions were dangerous but overland travel was not free from perils, either. At the time of Vizcaíno's death, the overland route between northern Mexico and New Mexico remained hazardous at best. According to Friar Alonso de Bendvides, this trail exposed travelers to "very great risk" because it passed through lands inhabited by "very ferocious, barbarous and indomitable tribes."[56] Therefore, he explained, Europeans needed not only an armed escort but also some ruses of their own. The reasons:

> Whenever we go through [Indian] lands, if they see we are few in number, they attack us face to face and do all the damage they can. For this reason it is impossible to pass there with fewer than twelve men on horseback, all very well armed. Even then, it is necessary to proceed cautiously; and in the early part of the night a fire is lighted somewhere to divert their attention, while we advance as far as possible beyond it. Even when they see a large force, they lie in ambush by night and at least do whatever harm they can to the horses.[57]

The Spanish were always ready to believe that the French were plotting to invade Spanish lands in the Southwest. In 1678, the former governor of New Mexico, Diego Dionisio de Peñalosa Briceño y Berdugo, ran afoul of the Spanish Inquisition. Therefore, he offered his services to Louis XIV of France, promising to lead a French invasion into the Southwest. King Carlos II of Spain learned about the offer and — the geography of the region being a complete mystery to the Spanish court — asked for what we would now call an intelligence briefing on it. If, as the Spanish suspected, their lands lay vulnerable to a French attack up the Mississippi River, this was indeed cause for concern.

The task of writing the briefing fell to a Spanish missionary, Alonso de Posada, who had arrived in New Mexico in 1651 and had helped found missions at El Paso del Norte in 1659.[58] Although he was not an explorer himself, Posada drew on many contemporary documents (now lost) and produced a thorough, well-considered summary for the king in 1686. His report included unique information on the lands and Indian peoples north of the Rio Grande. Posada was the first European to mention the Great Salt Lake:

> From the Rio San Juan, which runs west for 70 leagues and is possessed by the Navajo nation, the trail passes into the land of the Yutahs, a warlike nation. Crossing this nation for 60 leagues in the same northwest direction one comes to some hills, and traveling through that country for another 50 leagues more or less, one arrives at the great lake in the land Indians of the North call Teguayo. The Mexicans call the lake Copalla, according to their ancient traditions the place where all Indians, even those of Mexico, Guatemala and Peru originated.[59]

Since Posada concluded that the domain of the Quivira Indians stretched all the way to the Mississippi, he believed that by passing through their lands the French might indeed be able to reach Santa Fe. He warned, however, that the Indians themselves were not to be taken lightly: "There must be on land defense against so many barbarous Indians with whom no arrangements can be made because ... they must try to defend their lands and liberty."[60]

Missionaries were among the most far-ranging travelers of North America. Father Eusebio Francisco Kino, for example, was a brilliant Italian Jesuit missionary, writer, and explorer working for Spain. He does not fit easily into any of the usual categories. Born in northern Italy, he was educated in Germany in mathematics and astronomy. Sent as a missionary to Mexico City, he worked in Baja California before coming to the Pimería Alta. This region, which straddled southern Arizona and northern Sonora, was the home of the O'odham, i.e., Indians who spoke dialects of the Piman language.

Kino has fared better at the hands of modern revisionist historians than most of his Spanish contemporaries. Certainly by Spanish standards and possibly by Pima standards as well, he accomplished a great deal. Moreover, he appears to have harmed no one. His successor remembered that Kino had been "merciful to others, but cruel to himself."[61] Over 25 years he established more than 20 missions and *visitas* (preaching stations). He had excellent relations with the Indians. He learned their languages and encouraged them to diversify their crops, to learn new trades, and to present a united front against the marauding Apaches. He opposed the Spanish policy of enslaving Indians to work in the silver mines of northern Mexico. He helped to end a Pima revolt in 1695.

What is perhaps of more lasting importance is that Kino also advanced contemporary geographical knowledge of the New World. He made the first of about 40 expeditions into Arizona in 1691. Kino explored the headwaters of two major rivers—the Colorado and the Gila. In 1705, by walking from New Mexico to the head of the Gulf of California and finding that while the gulf "ended completely there," land was still visible on the other side, he concluded that "California is not an island," as many European navigators and cartographers had erroneously believed.[62]

Geographic confusion about California dates at least from the 1540s, when Alonso de Santa Cruz's *Islario de Todas las Islas del Mundo* (*Atlas of All the World's Islands*) depicted California as *both* a peninsula and an island. Here is the explanation of this apparent contradiction: California is shown as a peninsula lying west of the Gulf of California, but the southern third of this peninsula is separated from the rest of by a narrow strait. It is thus an island.[63]

Kino set matters straight. He wrote:

> But now, thanks to His Divine Majesty, through various expeditions ... I discovered with all details, certainty and evidence, by means of a magnetic needle and astrolabe in my hand, that California is not an island but a peninsula

or isthmus, and that in thirty-two degrees of latitude [the head of the Gulf of California] there is a passage by land to California.[64]

Kino's last map, drawn up in 1710 and showing the California peninsula firmly attached to the mainland, is now in the Bibliothèque Nationale in Paris.[65] Nevertheless, other maps would continue, until late in the eighteenth century, to show California as an island.[66]

By the beginning of the eighteenth century, the Spaniards had recovered from the Pueblo Revolt in New Mexico and were firmly back in power there. They gradually became alarmed, however, by reports trickling in about incursions by Frenchmen from Louisiana. La Salle had claimed Louisiana for Louis XIV in 1682. The Spanish, however, never accepted this claim: they wanted Louisiana to be theirs. Nevertheless, the French began to colonize Louisiana in 1699, when Fort Maurepas was built on the eastern shore of Biloxi Bay at Ocean Springs.

In the late seventeenth century, Frenchmen from Louisiana had begun to push out onto the Great Plains and up the Missouri. As early as 1688, Indians living along the Rio Grande warned the Spanish governor that "some foreign people are in that territory ... and are trying to thrust themselves upon the natives."[67] Other Indian sources added what to the Spaniards was most unwelcome news. These newcomers, they reported, were fitted out like the Spaniards themselves. They were

> clothed and with harquebuses [heavy portable matchlock muskets] ... they [wore] coats or breastplates of steel, and helmets on their heads.... They visited these Indians many times and gave them axes, knives, beads, copper kettles, and sometimes clothing, and made gifts to women of ribbons and other little things, and for this reason they had warm friendship for them.[68]

In 1695, some Apaches trading at the Picuris pueblo near Taos warned the Spaniards that "a great number of Frenchmen came toward the Buffalo Plains, driving Apaches to this vicinity because of the many attacks they make against them."[69] The Spaniards learned that these traders had not actually *seen* the French but had only heard about them, yet even this was enough to be "a matter of great concern" to Spain: the Spaniards feared that the French planned to seize the rich silver mines of northern Mexico or establish alliances with the local Indians.

In 1700, Spaniards learned that Frenchmen had destroyed an Indian village on the eastern plains. By 1708, French traders were said to have penetrated 300 to 400 leagues up the Missouri and even to have reached the foothills of the Rocky Mountains. The Spaniards strongly suspected that France was plotting to displace Spain as the dominant power in the Trans-Mississippi West. Their suspicions were heightened when in 1716 the French built a fort on the Red River in Louisiana near the Caddo village of Natchitoches, about 210 miles northwest of New Orleans. French machinations in east Texas that year prompted a Spanish missionary, Francisco Hidalgo, to warn his viceroy: "Your Excellency can see [in] what a condition the French are placing us. They are slipping behind our backs in silence, but God sees their intentions."[70]

As if this were not enough, three years later, when Antonio Valverde y Cosío, governor of New Mexico, was leading an expedition against the Comanches and the Utes, he met an Indian who had survived a surprise attack by a joint force consisting of Frenchmen, Pawnees and Jumanos. Upon learning from this Indian that in two pueblos the French already "live together with the said Pawnees and Jumanos Indians, to whom they have given long guns which they taught them to shoot," Valverde wrote to his viceroy that "the design of the enemy is to advance little by little into the interior."[71]

In Europe, tensions between Spain and France came to a head during the War of the Quadruple Alliance (1718–1720). In this conflict, the French, the British, the Dutch, and the Austrians all declared war on Spain to prevent it from claiming Italy. The war had only a miniscule impact on the Trans-Mississippi West. All that happened was that, in 1719, a tiny French force from Natchitoches, consisting of commanding officer Philippe Blondel and six soldiers, seized the nearby Spanish mission of San Miguel de Linares de los Adaes. This was the easternmost establishment of Spanish Texas, and was manned by only one Spanish soldier and one lay brother.[72]

There were other alarms. In New Mexico, the Spaniards received an erroneous report that 6,000 French soldiers were already marching toward Santa Fe. The Spaniards did not trust the French, but Spain's capability to halt either French or Indian incursions in the Trans-Mississippi West was always minimal. It received a nearly fatal blow in 1720, moreover, when Governor Valverde sent his lieutenant, Pedro de Villasur, out on a military mission from Santa Fe.

Villasur headed for Pawnee country along the Platte River in Nebraska, more than 600 miles northeast of Santa Fe, to look for the Frenchmen reported to be living there with the Pawnees. His force was relatively strong, consisting of 45 Spaniards; 60 Pueblo Indians; Naranjo, a Pawnee prisoner brought along to scout the way; and Jean L'Archevêque, a former French explorer now working as an interpreter for the Spaniards.

Villasur foolishly set up his camp in tall grass at the confluence of the Platte and Loup Rivers. The Pawnees quietly slipped through the grass, surrounded the camp, and at dawn opened a withering fire on it with muskets and bow and arrows. Villasur, Naranjo, and L'Archevêque fell at once; 45

other Spaniards or Pueblo Indians were killed or wounded in this one battle. New Mexico's settlements were now inadequately defended: many of their best soldiers were dead. Blamed for choosing such an inexperienced officer to lead the campaign, Valverde was later sacked.[73]

In the wake of the Villasur disaster, the Spaniards looked to their defenses and at the same time reduce the cost of administering the northern reaches of New Spain. In 1721, they reoccupied the mission at Los Adaes and established a presidio there, staffed by 100 cavalry troops and a few Franciscan missionaries. The Spaniards hoped that this modest force would stop French incursions, reduce French influence with the Caddo Indians, and prevent French traders from illegally shipping goods into New Spain from Louisiana.

Understandably, the garrison at Los Adaes was unable to accomplish any of these objectives. Its own resources were far too feeble. The French had long enjoyed a stranglehold on trade in the region; in fact, Spanish officers sometimes had to travel as far as New Orleans itself to buy supplies for their garrisons. The Caddos, for their part, were delighted with the guns they could get from the French — but not from the Spaniards. They therefore remained loyal to their French traders.

The Spaniards made some efforts to strengthen their defenses. Between 1724 and 1727, Brigadier General Pedro de Rivera traveled more than 7,000 miles and inspected more than 100 presidios and missions in northern New Spain. His conclusions, issued as the Regulations of 1729, gave his superiors an accurate account of conditions in the northern provinces but his recommendations were generally ignored in the field. Only two changes were made there: Los Adaes became the capital of Spanish Texas (a position it would hold until 1770) and, as a cost-cutting measure, the number of soldiers was reduced from 100 to 60 because the Caddos were not hostile.[74]

The Spaniards were already hard-pressed to keep control of northern New Spain. Their problems increased further in 1762 when, under the terms of the secret Treaty of Fontainebleau, France ceded to Spain that portion of Louisiana west of the Mississippi River. (France did this chiefly to keep Louisiana out of British hands but also to compensate Spain for the loss of Florida because of the Seven Years' War.) The Spanish government would thereafter treat Louisiana as a buffer zone to protect New Mexico and the rich silver mines of northern Mexico from French, British and, later, American encroachments.

Because of this secret treaty, Spain now officially controlled the governmental structure of Louisiana. There were so few Spaniards on the ground, however, that most of the frontiersmen and traders hired by the military and fur-trading enterprises commanded by Spaniards were French or British adventurers who had already drifted into the Trans-Mississippi West.[75] In fact, between 1762 and the Louisiana Purchase of 1803, the Spaniards had to rely almost entirely on resident French middlemen to regulate the rapidly-growing American flatboat trade down the Mississippi River to New Orleans.

The Treaty of Paris (1763), which ended the Seven Years' War, recognized Spain as the new owner of Upper and Lower Louisiana. The formal transfer to Spain of these regions took place in 1763 and 1765, respectively, although Spanish control of the former French lands was more in name than in fact: the French did not leave the area. These transfers, however, did increase the need for Spaniards to make contact with the many Indian tribes living between the Gulf of Mexico and Canada, in what was now Spanish Louisiana.

The Spaniards hoped to win the support of these tribes and turn them against the British, who were pressing up against the Mississippi and were already traveling up the Missouri. In this case, however, the Spaniards could not use their traditional coercive mission-and-presidio policy to establish and maintain relations with these Indians. They simply lacked the men and money to do so. They were therefore forced to pursue the more humane, cheaper and ultimately more successful French policy of trying to woo the Indians with presents and trade. (The French had long ago adopted this policy for two very practical reasons: there were not enough Frenchmen to make coercive methods feasible, and more importantly, the French were always more interested in trading with the Indians than conquering or converting them.)

Governor Antonio de Ulloa and his successor, Alejandro O'Reilly, therefore had little choice but to leave the trading system in the hands of the French agents who were already conducting it so successfully in Louisiana. O'Reilly recruited Athanase de Mézières, the former French army officer who had shifted his allegiance to Spain, to be his lieutenant governor.[76] Nevertheless, the challenge of administering this new territory was far greater than Spanish resources could handle. This was what, in 1722, Spain expected its viceroy to do:

> Not only to keep those [Indian] nations quiet, subjugate the Comancha, castigate the Apache, and cause them to love us through continual intercourse, but also to prevent the invasions which are to be expected from the nations protected by the English and in time of war from the English themselves.[77]

To strengthen Spain's limited capabilities, in 1765 the Spanish king Charles III appointed the Marqués de Rubí as inspector general of frontier presidios. The king ordered him to consolidate defenses, to strengthen the frontier against Indian attacks, to reduce the government's expenses, and to correct financial abuses along the frontier.[78] Rubí was a loyal, hard working and competent officer. He began his inspection in 1766 and spent 23 months in the field, traveling some 7,600 miles from the Gulf of California to Louisiana.

When he finished in 1768, he recommended, among other things, that Spain reorganize its far northern frontier defenses by building a network of presidios, each about 100 miles apart and each garrisoned by 50 men. Despite the great distance between these posts, each would be safe, he argued, because the Indians never launched direct attacks on presidios. If they did, they would incur too many casualties. Rubí's defensive line would extend from the head of the Gulf of California to the mouth of the Guadalupe River, about 85 miles northeast of Corpus Christi, Texas. This line roughly parallels today's border between the United States and Mexico.

Two important Spanish communities—Santa Fe and San Antonio—lay well north of this line but they could not be abandoned because of Spain's obligations to its settlers and to the Christianized Indians there.[79] To prevent the Apaches from attacking these two settlements, each would have its own presidio with a detachment of 76 soldiers. Seven presidios would be closed, representing a considerable saving for Spain. Rubí's plan called for a total of 17 presidios.[80] The lands about the Rio Grande, Rubí concluded in his report, "should be given back to Nature and the Indians."[81]

Rubí also called for a war of extermination against the Apaches but, at the same time, for efforts to improve Spanish relations with the Comanches and Wichitas, who were enemies of the Apaches, too. The able frontiersman Athanase de Mézières, fluent in several Indian languages, was ordered to strengthen ties with these Indians by using French methods, i.e., giving gifts to facilitate trade. Many of Rubí's recommendations, which reflected the best and most enlightened Spanish thinking of the day, would be promulgated in a royal order of 1772 known as the New Regulations for Presidios. Some of these regulations would remain in effect in New Spain until the mid-nineteenth century.

In the meantime, by a royal order of 1768 King Carlos III directed that Upper California be occupied by Spaniards to keep it from falling into the hands of the Russians. *Visatador general* Gálvez and Viceroy de Croix drafted a plan to this effect. Their reasoning seemed persuasive:

> Many dangers can be averted which now threaten us, by way of the South Sea, from certain foreign powers who now have an opportunity and the most eager desire to establish a colony at the harbor of Monterrey, or at some of the

many harbors which have already been discovered on the western coasts of this New World.... The Russians have been gaining an intimate knowledge of the navigation of the Sea of Tartary; and ... they are, according to some very credible and well-grounded statements, carrying on the fur trade on a continent or perhaps an island which, it is estimated, lies at the distance of only eight hundred leagues from the western coast of the Californias, which run as far as Capes Mendocino and Blanco.[82]

This royal order set in motion what was called a "sacred expedition" to occupy Alta California by land and by sea before the Russians, moving south from their fur trading settlements in Alaska, could take it over themselves. However, Spaniards (and of course other men afloat) faced two maritime challenges.

The first of these was scurvy. Caused by lack of vitamin C, this disease is characterized by spongy gums, loose teeth, and bleeding into the skin and mucous membranes. On long voyages, many Spanish sailors were incapacitated or killed by scurvy. The Spaniards did not find a solution to this problem until Esteban José Martínez, who will be discussed later, successfully used anti-scorbutics on his 1789 voyage to the Pacific Northwest coast.

The other maritime challenge faced by the Spaniards "Fleurieu's Whirlpool," named after the French navigator C.P. Claret Fleurieu. This oceanic phenomenon was due to the prevailing clockwise circulation of the winds and currents along the California coast. The result of such an adverse swirl of wind and water was that it could take up to three months for a supply ship to make its way from San Blas, on the Pacific coast of Mexico, to San Diego—a line-of-sight distance of only 1,100 miles.

Miguel Costansó, a Spanish engineer who kept a diary of Spain's expedition to colonize San Diego and Monterey in 1769, explained this problem and how navigators coped with it:

> The navigation of the outer coast of California presents an unavoidable difficulty on account of the prevalence of north and northwest winds, which, with little interruption, continue throughout the year, and are directly contrary to the voyage [northward], as the coast bears northwest to southeast. This makes it necessary for all vessels to keep away from the coast and gain sea room until they encounter more variable and more favorable winds, with which, making as far north as they require, they can stand into windward of the port for which they are bound.[83]

The Spaniards never found an easy solution to this navigational problem, so their northward voyages always took a long time. The British explorer Vancouver, however, believed that their elaborate procedure—as he put it, "to stand a great distance into the ocean, until they reach far northward of the parallel of the port whither they are bound, and then steer for the land"[84]—was not really necessary. In his opinion, reliable winds blew out of the east and southeast most of the day and were often stronger than the landward breezes.[85]

Spain had learned from its ambassador in Moscow that Russia was stepping up its activities along the Pacific coast of North America. In a meeting convened at San Blas in 1768 between Gálvez and other prominent Spanish officials, it was agreed that California should be settled by founding Spanish presidios and missions there. According to the records of the meeting, Monterey was considered to be "truly the most advantageous [place] for protecting the entire west coast of California and the other coasts of the southern part of this continent against any attempts by the Russians or any other nations."[86]

Therefore, beginning in 1769, the Spaniards started to colonize Alta California, albeit very lightly, by building presidios and missions there. Four presidios were constructed to defend the province from expected Russian aggression and to protect neighboring missions from Indian attacks. These presidios were located in San Diego (1769), Monterey (1770), San Francisco (1776), and Santa Barbara (1782). Gradually, between 1769 and 1823, 21 missions, with a work force of about 30,000 Indians, would be strung out for more than 500 miles along the California coast.

Captain Gaspar de Portolá founded the California settlements of San Diego and Monterey, "discovered" San Francisco Bay, and became the first governor of Upper California. Spanish objectives in California were threefold: to counter the Russian threat, to build another mission north of San Diego and then, over time, to fill in the territory between Monterey and San Diego with additional missions.

In 1769, accompanied by the missionary Father Junípero Serra, Portolá left Baja California bound for San Diego, where the first of California's 21 missions (San Diego de Alcala) was established. The expedition then continued northward, looking for what Vizcaíno had too-enthusiastically described as the excellent harbor of Monterey Bay. The going was hard. Portolá wrote in his diary on May 11, 1769:

> I set out from Santa Maria, the last mission to the north, escorted by four soldiers, in company with Father Junípero Serra, president of the missions, and Father Miguel Campa. This day we proceeded for about four hours with very little water for the animals and without any pasture, which obliged us to go farther in the afternoon to find some. There was, however, no water.[87]

Portolá's search for Monterey Bay ended in abject failure. As Father Juan Crespi, the diarist and chaplain of this first expedition into California, tells us, Portolá and his men simply could not find "the port of Monterey so celebrated and so praised in their time by men of character, skillful, intelligent, and practical navigators [Vizcaíno] who came expressly to explore these coasts by order of the king."[88] The reason was that thick fog obscured the Santa Cruz shoreline, making the choppy waters of the bay look like the open sea itself.

Portolá decided he had not gone far enough, so he led his expedition further north. When he reached Half Moon Bay (about 25 miles south of San Francisco) in November 1769, he realized he was much too far north. This error, however, turned out to be a blessing in disguise. He sent Sergeant José Francisco Ortega and a small party of men up into the nearby mountains to see what they could find.

From Sweeney Ridge, a 1,200-foot-high summit in the hills overlooking Pacifica, Ortega and his men were the first Europeans to view San Francisco Bay. Father Crespi would record that this enormous bay—"a large arm of the sea"—was so big that "doubtless not only all the navies of our Catholic Monarch, but those of all Europe might lie within the harbor."[89] As the finest natural harbor along the Pacific coast, it offered a solid foothold for further Spanish expansion there.

It was not until six years later, however, that the first Spanish ship actually entered San Francisco Bay. This was Lieutenant Juan Manuel de Ayala's 78-foot packet (storeship) *San Carlos*, which sailed into the Golden Gate on 5 August 1775. Ayala's mission was to produce an accurate chart of the bay, which other Spanish ships could rely on. His pilot, Don Jose de Canizares, and some of the crew from *San Carlos* took the ship's launch and spent a month and a half surveying the bay. By September, their work was done and the Spaniards took their leave.

Earlier, after returning to San Diego in 1770, Portolá had headed north again and this time managed to find Monterey Bay. He established a presidio there "to occupy the port and defend us from attacks by the Russians, who are about to invade us."[90] Then, having discharged his orders successfully, Portolá returned to Mexico and eventually went back to Spain.

Juan Bautista de Anza, commandant of the presidio at Tubac (south of Tucson, Arizona), would become the most experienced and most successful officer of the Provincias Internas (Interior Provinces).[91] He is known, in fact, as "the last *conquistador*" because he played such a key role in expanding Spain's possessions in the New World and by pioneering trails connecting the central regions of New Spain with the Spanish outposts in California.[92] In 1773, he volunteered to lead an expedition from Tubac to California.[93] Blazing a trail for an overland supply route would, he reasoned, speed the Spanish colonization of California and would thus accomplish two objectives.

The first objective was of course to discourage Russian expansion into this rich but virtually undefended Spanish province. Although by 1773 there were two presidios and five missions in Alta California, the total Spanish population there was only about 70 people. The second objective was to help resupply Father Serra's missions, which were still largely dependent on food and goods coming up the Pacific coast by sea from San Blas. If the supply ships failed to arrive as scheduled, the missions would be famine-stricken.

Anza and his party of some 35 soldiers, including the chronicler Father Francisco Tomás Garcés from Mission San Xavier del Bac (southwest of Tucson), made their way to California in 1774. They forded the Gila River and then the Colorado with the help of the Yuma Indians, finally reaching the San Gabriel Arcángel Mission east of Los Angeles. After this epic journey, Father Garcés was so impressed by the overwhelming size of the Southwest that he wrote in his diary: "Oh, what a vast heathendom!"[94]

The expedition had planned to proceed to Monterey but the mission at Los Angeles could not spare enough supplies or animals to make this feasible. The expedition was therefore split into two parts. Father Garcés led most of the party back to the junction of the Colorado and Gila Rivers. Anza himself pressed on to Monterey with a small reconnaissance party and later went back to the river junction. The reunited expedition then returned to Tubac.

At Tubac, Anza was instructed by the viceroy to lead to California a much larger overland expedition, consisting of some 240 settlers and soldiers and more than 1,000 head of livestock. His objective was to build a presidio and a mission near San Francisco Bay. Anza and his party crossed rivers and deserts without major problems and camped at Monterey. With a few other men, Anza then proceeded north to San Francisco Bay to chose sites for the presidio and the mission.

He chose well. In his journal of the expedition, the Franciscan missionary Father Pedro Font recounts the story:

> The day broke clear and bright. At seven in the morning we set out from the little creek a short distance north of San Mateo creek, and at eleven, having marched about six leagues, we pitched camp at a lagoon or spring of clear water close to the mouth of the port of San Francisco [this area now known as Fort Point]. I beheld a prodigy of nature, which is not easy to describe. We saw the spouting of young whales, a line of dolphins or tuna, besides seals and otters.... This place and its surrounding country afforded much pasturage, sufficient firewood, and good water—favorable conditions for establishing the presidio or fort contemplated.[95]

Having chosen such a strategic, easily defended spot for his presidio, Anza planted the cross on the Cantil Blanco (White Cliff) on 20 March

1776. The first substantial fortification there, the Castillo de San Joaquin, would not be completed until 1794. Anza then headed south for Sonora. In recognition of his accomplishments on the frontier, he was appointed governor of New Mexico in 1777.

In the meantime, his deputy, Lieutenant Moraga, led the settlers from Monterey to San Francisco, where they built the presidio on a hill overlooking Fort Point and the mission on flat ground farther east. This mission was known as San Francisco de Asis. Both the presidio and the mission are still San Francisco landmarks today.

The trail that Anza and his men blazed was a success: it provided overland access to the struggling settlements of Alta California just long enough for them to become securely established. Although the trail itself was closed temporarily when the Yumas revolted against Spanish rule in 1781, it was later reopened and was used extensively by American soldiers, settlers, cattlemen, and gold miners. It is now commemorated as the Juan Bautista de Anza National Historic Trail.[96]

The Spaniards also sent a number of naval expeditions along the Pacific coast to check on Russian encroachments there. These forays gave Spain a legal claim to this region.[97] The first expedition was commanded by the experienced pilot Juan Pérez and set out in 1774 from San Blas aboard the 225-ton, 82-foot-long frigate *Santiago*. Although the viceroy tried to keep its destination secret, word quickly leaked out that the ship was "going to Russia," i.e., to Alaska.[98]

Pérez could not, however, comply with the viceroy's optimistic instructions that he sail to 60° N. latitude, i.e., the Bering Sea: the weather was simply too bad and the crew was in poor health. Friar Tomás de la Peña Sarvia, a missionary aboard the ship, confided to his diary:

> During the whole day the fog did not lift, nor could the sun be seen, it was quite cold and a heavy mist fell. I think the dampness is the cause of the *mal de Loanda*, or scurvy; for although during the whole voyage there have been some persons affected with this sickness, these cases have not been as aggravated as they are now, where there are some twenty men unfit for duty, in addition to which many others, though able to go about, have sores in their mouths and on their legs; and I believe that if God does not send us better weather soon, the greater part of the crew will perish from this disease, judging from the rate at which they are falling sick of it during these days of wet weather.[99]

Despite these hardships, Pérez managed to sail to about 55° N. latitude, i.e., to the Dixon Entrance between the Queen Charlotte Islands and the Prince of Wales Islands. He did not find any Russians there but his crew met some Haida Indians, who eagerly wanted to trade tanned skins, sea otter pelts, and blankets for European knives, cloth, beads, and big sheets of copper. Pérez noted in his diary that these Indians were "very adept at trading and commerce, judging by the briskness with which they dealt with us."[100]

On the return leg of his voyage, Pérez cruised south along the west coast of Vancouver Island, anchoring briefly off Estevan Point near the south entrance to Nootka Sound to trade with the Indians, whom he found already had some items of Spanish origin. He did not go ashore there or, later on, in Washington or Oregon, either, to take formal possession of the land. He was afraid of scurvy and of running aground on this ironbound (rugged) coast during stormy or foggy weather. Americans, however, would later cite his voyage to back up their own claim of "Fifty-four forty or fight!," i.e., that 54°40' (the north side of the Dixon Entrance) should be the northern boundary of the Oregon Country.[101]

Soon after returning to San Blas, Pérez sailed for the Pacific Northwest again in 1775 as pilot of the frigate *Santiago*. This time the ship was commanded by Bruno de Hezeta, a young Spanish naval officer who was under orders to defend the California coast from the encroaching Russian fur trade. The small schooner *Sonora*, captained by Juan Francisco de la Bodega y Quadra, joined the expedition, too.

Bruno de Hezeta took note of the outflow of the Columbia River but could not enter it because the current was too strong. "These currents and eddies of water cause me to believe the place is the mouth of some great river," he wrote, "or of some passage to another sea."[102] After naming a number of points along the coasts of northern California, Oregon and Washington, both ships were forced by strong winds to land at Point Grenville, Washington. In 1775, Hezeta claimed the region for Spain, recording in his diary:

> At four-thirty in the morning, I landed, accompanied by the Reverend Father Fray Benito de la Sierra, Don Cristóbal Reville, the surgeon Don González, and some armed men. I took possession at six in the morning.... Only six Indians presented themselves to me ashore ... [they] have beautiful faces. Some are fair in color, others dark, and all of them plump and well built. Their clothing consists of sea otter skins with which they cover themselves from the waist up.[103]

Bodega had a different and far more painful experience with the Indians. To get wood and water, he sent a boat ashore near the Hoh River on the Washington coast, crewed by seven men. A party of Indians attacked his men, killed all of them, and stole their boat. Bodega sadly named a nearby island Isla de Dolores (the Island of Sorrows). His experience was not unique: the Indians of this area were often bellicose. In 1787, for example, Captain Charles W. Barkley, who was the first foreigner to enter the Strait of Juan de Fuca, anchored his ship *Imperial Eagle* at the Hoh River. He sent a small boat ashore, crewed by six men, to explore the river. All six were killed by the Indians. Barkley gave this river a memorable name: Destruction River.

After leaving Point Grenville, the two Spanish ships parted. Hezeta turned back towards San Blas but Bodega and his pilot, Francisco Antonio Mourelle de la Rúa, decided to press on farther north. As Mourelle tells us in his dramatic 1775 account, *Journey of the* Sonora *in the Second Bucareli Expedition to Explore the Northwest Coast*, he and Bodega hit upon

> the daring project of separating [from Hezeta] and dying in their craft rather than return without enlightenment ... [they knew] that they would navigate unmapped seas; perhaps they would find themselves in an archipelago where it would not be easy for a small, lone boat to emerge felicitously; that any illness would put them in the ultimate risk at such an advanced season; that from the moment of separation they would have to stretch their rations to last the rest of the trip; and finally, that if they returned to port without progress worthy of consideration, at once there would be leveled against them accusations of insubordination.... But none of this could overcome the shameful feeling which they could imagine if two young men turned back toward San Blas from that latitude; and hoisting all their sails at ten that evening, by navigating towards the west, they found themselves in control of their own destiny by the following day.[104]

The schooner *Sonora* followed the coast north to beyond Mount Edgecombe (near Sitka, Alaska) and then sailed back to Monterey with most of her crew laid up by scurvy. The frigate *Santiago* was there, too. On the way back to San Blas, Pérez died at sea. He is remembered by historians today as the first European to reach the Pacific Northwest coast.[105]

Spanish exploration continued, particularly after the French explorer La Pérouse told the Spaniards that the Russians were building settlements in Alaska. Fearing that the Russians planned to expand their operations farther south, the Spaniards quickly sent other ships to the Northwest, for example, the Narváez (1789), Quimper (1790), Eliza (1791), and Galiano and Valdéz (1792) expeditions. The journals of their explorations in and near the Strait of Juan de Fuca still make good reading today.

The account of the Narváez expedition was written by Estéban José Martínez, who had been a junior pilot with the Pérez expedition in 1774 and was now in command of the small sloop *Princesa*. In 1789, while at Nootka, Martínez seized several British ships, including the 48-foot schooner *Northwest America*, and appointed José María Narváez, a young Spanish navigator, to its command. This ship — the first built by Europeans on the Pacific Northwest coast — had been launched by the John Meares, a

British naval officer turned merchant adventurer, in 1788. (Spain's seizure of British ships in these waters came very close to provoking a war between Britain and Spain: see Chapter 4.)

Narváez told Martínez:

> There is a very fine port named by the native Indians "Clayocuat" and by our people "Puerto de Narvaez." Numerous islands at the entrance and inside are to be seen which serve as shelter for vessels, it being possible to careen a ship there [to careen a ship is to heel her over on the beach so that one side of her hull is exposed and can be cleaned, caulked or repaired] and supply her with wood, water and timber for spars. There are some populous settlements in the port, all under the command of a king or chief, Huicananish. The Indians are very friendly, as they gave me to understanding when they visited me. They are addicted to trade, exchanging their sea-otter skins for copper or iron. They are accustomed to carry on war with those to the south, and they consider those of San Lorenzo as superior to them, because they always lose in their fights with those of Nuca [the Spanish word for Nootka].[106]

Martínez added for the record his own belief that the Strait of Juan de Fuca "has a communication with the Mississippi River," i.e., it might be the Passage."[107]

Manuel Quimper, an ensign in the Spanish navy, was given command of *Princesa* and sailed from San Blas together with two frigates. He explored the Strait of Juan de Fuca and had a good deal to say about it. His diary runs to 17 printed pages in an English translation. Quimper also wrote a five-page letter to the viceroy telling him about the expedition. We learn, for example, that when *Princesa* anchored near a basin at the east end of the strait,

> a little afterwards eight large canoes with fifteen and twenty Indians in each came alongside ... I succeeded in inducing them to come alongside through expressions of friendship and by showing them gifts which I made to them. These Indians by their suspicion showed manifestly that they had never seen a vessel, even though I noted that hanging from their ears, they wore some pieces of copper and beads. These I thought they had obtained in trade from the Indians at the entrance of the strait. They also wore English, Portuguese, and Chinese coins for earrings.[108]

Quimper landed at New Dungeness Bay to take formal possession of the land for Spain:

> At 5:30 [AM] having armed the longboat and the two canoes, I embarked with the second pilot in order to take possession. This I effected, planting the Holy Cross close to a pine, on which another [cross] was made by cutting the bark. At the foot of this the bottle of possession was buried, all the ceremonies which the instructions prescribe being performed.[109]

The Indians liked to trade but they were also prepared to attack the Spaniards if they saw they had a temporary advantage. One morning, for example, Quimper sent some of his soldiers and seamen ashore to wash their clothes. "One soldier had strayed away from the other men," he tells us,

> and gone into the woods to eat salmon berries and other fruits. The Indians, aware of the fact that the rest could not give him prompt help, came up to him, pretending friendship and giving him the same fruit which he craved so much. When they saw him off his guard they advanced on him, took, away his cutlass and gave him several blows with it on the head. As he sought to defend himself they fired some arrows at him until he fled, one of them striking him in the face.[110]

Quimper adds that "All these natives are warlike, treacherous, very thievish, and boast about having killed two captains of vessels which had come to trade with them."[111]

Lieutenant Francisco Eliza, the commandant of the Spanish base at Nootka, joined an expedition launched in 1791 to explore and survey the Strait of Juan de Fuca. He took command of the packet *San Carlos* with a crew of 70 men and was accompanied by the 36-foot schooner *Santa Saturnina*. In a letter to the viceroy, Eliza mentioned the hostility of some of the Indians:

> I [Eliza] ordered the longboat to be armed and dispatched it with the second pilot with an order to enter the Canal de Lopez de Haro, explore it and lay down the situation [i.e., calculate its latitude and longitude for use in making a chart] of what he might find there ... [the second pilot] came back telling me that it had not been possible to continue the task assigned to him because as soon as he had entered the Canal de Haro ... six large canoes came out with from sixteen to twenty Indians in each one. They were armed with long spears and each Indian had his bow and arrow. They began to menace our longboat, even overtook it, so it had become necessary to open fire on them to get away from them. Continuing his defense he saw numerous Indians running along on land hastily launching many canoes. Embarking in these they directed themselves towards the longboat with loud yells and shooting some arrows. The pilot, seeing that they paid little attention to the firearms and that at every moment more Indians were arriving, thought it advisable to retire in order not to endanger his men.[112]

Spain was not content to rest on its laurels of exploration. In a letter of 1788 to the officers of the Spanish Royal Navy, Alejandro Malaspina, an Italian in the service of Spain, told them that their king had approved

> a plan that we proposed [last year] and in which we propose to circumnavigate the world in two corvettes [small, fast ships mounting about 20 guns], to work on hydrographic charts of the western coast of America and of the Spanish settlements in Asia, and to reconnoitre New Zealand and various

islands of the Pacific Ocean.... In emulation of Messrs Cook and La Pérouse, we intend at the same time to carry out as many experiments as possible that can contribute to the progress of geography, navigation, and natural history, for which purpose H.M. [His Majesty] will provide appropriate ships, instruments and even personnel expert in those abilities which are unrelated to nautical science.[113]

In 1791, Malaspina was instructed by the king to sail from San Blas to 60° N. latitude and look for the Canal de Floridablanca, as the Spaniards called the mythical passage linking the Pacific and Atlantic oceans.[114] Malaspina made the voyage that same year, examining the Alaska coast as far west as Prince William Sound and spending about a month at the Spanish outpost in Nootka Sound. He did not make any new discoveries, although if heavy winds had not forced him far off the Northwest coast he might well have found the outlet of the Columbia River.[115]

Returning to San Blas, Malaspina offered to send two of his officers, Alcala Galiano and Cayetano Valdéz, back to the Northwest to explore the Straits of Juan de Fuca and of Georgia. They sailed in two small schooners— *Mexicana* and *Sútil*, each 46'10" in length and carrying a crew of 17 men and a few officers. Galiano and Valdéz reached Nootka in 1792, where they teamed up with the British explorer Vancouver, whose ships *Discovery* and *Chatham* were exploring the area, too. In the diary of the voyage, which they sent to the viceroy, the two Spanish captains had good things to say about the local Indians:

> We left this port for that of Cordova [named in honor of Luis de Córdova, captain general of the Spanish Navy; it is now known as Esquimault Harbor], taking with us the chief Tetacuí, who had voluntarily offered to go in the *Mexicana*. The conduct of this Indian during the crossing and the stay in Cordova, where we anchored ... caused us to draw very different inferences about these Indians from what voyagers have said about them. What they call ferocious treachery only seemed to us to be bold manliness.[116]

Navigation in confined tidal waters was never easy: there was always a risk of going aground. Big ships (corvettes and brigs) drew as much as 15 feet; small schooners drew about 6 feet. The narrative tells us that, due to a helmsman's error, the schooners *Sútil* and *Mexicana* anchored in such shallow water that they both went aground in the ebbing tide. This dangerous situation could have resulted in the loss of one or both vessels. They managed to reach deep water again only after taking emergency measures, almost certainly by resorting to kedging.[117] (Kedging means having a ship's boat drop an anchor some distance from a stranded ship. The ship's crew then uses a line from the anchor to winch the ship up to it.)

Malaspina was a thoughtful man who had ideas well in advance of his times. He had carefully studied the political situation of the Spanish colonies in the Pacific and concluded that, rather than conquering new lands militarily and exploiting them economically, Spain should instead create a voluntary confederation of countries. These would engage in mutually profitable international trade. Such a Pacific Rim trading bloc should, he thought, be administered by Spaniards based in Acapulco, Mexico.[118]

His novel ideas, however, greatly alarmed the conservative Spanish monarchy, which feared a spread of the radical ideas embedded in the French Revolution. Consequently, Malaspina was stripped of his rank, imprisoned for eight years, and then exiled for the rest of his life. The records of his expeditions—consisting of 300 journals, 450 notebooks, and 183 charts—were suppressed. They were not published in Spanish until 1990 and in English until 2004.[119]

Malaspina was not the only one thinking about the Spanish empire. "We ought not to be surprised," Viceroy Manuel Antonio Florez predicted from Mexico City in 1788,

> that the English colonies of America, now being an independent Republic, should carry out the design of finding a safe port on the Pacific and of attempting to sustain it by crossing the immense country of the continent above our possessions of Texas, New Mexico, and California.[120]

Other reflective Spaniards, too, were worried about foreign incursions. A decade later, in 1799, José Cortés, a lieutenant in Spain's Royal Corps of Engineers, wrote a long and carefully-considered *Report on the Northern Provinces of New Spain*. It is worth citing here at some length because it gives a very clear idea of Spanish fears about competition from the British and the Americans.

Cortés begins his discussion of these two nations with a stern warning:

> Dangers of grave importance and of difficult remedy threaten our territories in the northernmost part of America. We must be quite vigilant in its northwestern part and along the Misoury River. The nation that encroaches upon us at the aforesaid points [Britain] and the one that advances upon us from the other side [the United States] will not be satisfied: the first, with having provided clear proof of its ambitions, and the other, with the enlargement of its new boundaries and the population growth it has achieved. Once the ambitious designs of the first nation are realized, while the second proceeds to the point necessary to make its power more respectable and even fearsome, the empire of New Spain will fall into such disarray that its possessions cannot even term themselves having a shared dominion....[121]

He then highlights the fundamental challenge posed by the British:

> The English nation ... is well known for its limitless ambition, for the extreme which its pride has reached, and for its immediate passion for destroying all foreign commerce. It seeks to be the absolute master of it, to enchain the known world with its empire, and through the riches and preponderance of this system ... to oppress and subjugate the other nations, becoming the Queen of the Sea with the considerable strength and ascendancy that would naturally derive from its control.[122]

After outlining British ambitions elsewhere in North America, Cortés points out the enormous vulnerability of Alta California, which, he tells us, is defended by only about 300 Spanish soldiers, who are assigned to four or five different locations which are 50 or 60 leagues apart. "This is a negligible defense," he concludes, "and doubtless will surrender its arms whenever the enemy might appear."[123] If the British landed in San Francisco and Monterey simultaneously, he warns, "Alta California would surely be conquered by merely arriving and taking it."[124] This would be only the beginning of Spain's troubles: the British would then occupy Baja California; introduce contraband trade along the coast of Mexico; and seize Spain's silver and gold, both coin and bullion.

According to Cortés, the United States, which he terms "the Republic of the United Anglo-American Provinces," poses an even greater threat to Spanish interests in North America.[125] Its rapid population growth, economic dynamism, and expansionist tendencies all boded ill for Spain, especially when considered in light of two international agreements—the Treaty of London (Jay's Treaty) of 1794 and the Treaty of San Lorenzo del Escorial (Pinckney's Treaty) of 1795—which will be discussed later.

"Let us accept as a demonstrated fact," Cortés advises his readers, "that the Anglo-American plans are very ambitious and there is no doubt that they will be carried out."[126] He insists:

> I would also like to eradicate once and for all among many of my compatriots who are known as educated men, the notion that it matters not if we surrender or lose our territories because they are unpopulated, produce nothing, or burden the royal treasury. It matters a great deal, a very great deal. It is a very logical principle not to let one's enemies grow in strength, and all the more so when it is foreseen that such growth can bring our downfall closer, leaving the branches of our possessions as so many dead limbs.[127]

In this era, Spain seemed more worried about the Russians in California than about the British and the Americans on the Mississippi. Nevertheless, in the 1790s it did mount a remarkable but little-remembered campaign on the Mississippi to deter British smugglers and to defend Spanish possessions there: Spain began patrol the Mississippi with a little fleet of swift galleys known as galliots.

Formerly used in the Mediterranean, these handy little vessels could variously be propelled, as local conditions dictated, by three square sails hung from yardarms on a single central mast; rowed; poled; or cordelled, i.e., towed from the bank by means of a long rope.[128] A good example is the galliot *La Venganza*, which was the flagship of Governor General Gayoso de Lemos between 1795 and 1798. She was about 50 feet long, carried a crew of 28 men, and was armed with nine cannons (one 6-pounder on the bow and eight swivels on the sides and stern).[129]

The galliots were deployed on the Mississippi as far north as New Madrid (at the junction of the Ohio and Mississippi Rivers) to deter the expansionist, aggressive American frontiersmen. After the American Revolution, these intrepid individuals had begun to swarm into the Old Southwest—that is, into the lands lying west of the Appalachians, south of the Ohio, and east of the Mississippi. The Spaniards feared that such truculent, well-armed, self-sufficient men were only waiting impatiently for the opportunity to invade Spanish Louisiana.

The galliots never saw action and were probably deployed more to show the Spanish flag than to be an effective fighting force. On the other hand, the historian Abraham P. Nasatir, who studied this issue carefully, reached a conclusion that gives Spanish naval strategists the benefit of the doubt:

> Since the galleys were never put to the test of actual combat, it is difficult to evaluate their real contribution to the defense of Spain's Mississippi frontier. However, from the time of the formation of His Catholic Majesty's Light Squadron of Galleys until the execution of the Treaty of San Lorenzo el Real and later, Louisiana was constantly menaced with attack. The galleys played a major role in the Spaniards' plans for defense against their threatened aggressions, and their mere presence created a salutary effect upon the restless American frontiersmen. Since none of the attacks materialized, it may be concluded that the river squadron fulfilled its purpose of protecting Louisiana against foreign assault."[130]

At the same time, the Spaniards took steps in other areas, too, to protect their possessions from rival claimants. In 1673, the French had explored and began to settle in what they called *le Pays des Illinois*—the Illinois Country, i.e., the country of the Illinois Indians. The Illinois Country never had any clearly defined boundaries. In its most expansive form, it was held to extend east to the Alleghenies; west all the way to the Rocky Mountains; north to Peoria, Illinois; and south to the first European trading post in Arkansas—Arkansas Post, located about 85 miles southwest of Memphis.[131]

It was a desirable land. Writing in 1712, the Jesuit missionary Gabriel Marest reported that "Our Illinois [Indians] inhabit a very pleasant country

... the great rivers which water it, the vast and dense forests, the delightful prairies, the hills covered with very thick woods—all these features make a charming variety."[132] By 1763, there were seven French forts and four settlements in the Illinois Country, which was sometimes known as Upper Louisiana. The farthest west of these forts was Fort Orléans, located on the Missouri River near Brunswick, Missouri, about 80 miles northeast of Kansas City. Near the center of the Illinois Country was the region known as the American Bottom—a large and historically important floodplain near St. Louis, just south of the confluence of the Mississippi, Illinois, and Missouri rivers.

In 1794, the governor of Spanish Louisiana, Louis Héctor, who bore the title Baron de Carondelet, granted an exclusive fur trading monopoly to a select group of St. Louis merchants. These men were known collectively as the Company of Explorers of the Upper Missouri, or as the Missouri Company for short. They were authorized to explore and to trade along the upper Missouri River, the westernmost and least known part of the now Spanish Illinois Country. Baron Carondelet's goal was to stop the encroachment of British-Canadian fur traders, who, he feared, would otherwise extend their smuggling operations into New Mexico or Louisiana, or possibly even attack Spanish Upper Louisiana in time of war.[133]

Baron Carondelet hoped that, in addition to harvesting many furs, the Missouri Company would also be able to blaze a trail to the Pacific that would connect Spain's mid-continental and its western possessions and thus thwart Russian advances. He and his fellow Spaniards optimistically believed that exploring the Missouri would give them easy access—once they found that elusive Passage—to "neighboring Asia, whence, by a different route [down the Pacific Northwest coast], it is probable that the Russians are approaching."[134] One of the regulations setting up the Missouri Company explicitly authorized stern measures to be taken against any British or Russians found to be trading in the region. This regulation stated:

> May the central government be pleased to allow the members of the trade of this place [St. Louis] to make expeditions against foreigners who establish themselves on our land with merchandise to attract the trade of our savages, and also to authorize the merchants to confiscate their furs or goods, half for the profit of the members of the expedition and the other half to be the profit of the association for the expenses undertaken by the group.[135]

Furthermore, in 1795 the Baron also offered, in the name of the king of Spain, a munificent reward:

> Three thousand pesos to the one who should succeed in first reaching the South Sea, partly to arouse those people to a dangerous undertaking by greed and the reward, and partly in consideration of the fact that such a discovery

was important to the state; for it would determine its boundaries in a permanent fashion by founding a settlement with all the necessary arrangements to prevent the English or the Russians from establishing themselves or extending themselves on those coasts, remote from the other Spanish possessions and near Nootka Sound.[136]

With all these international and domestic intrigues going on, it is not surprising that the Missouri fur trade was rarely a dull business. In his *Account of Upper Louisiana* (1803), a contemporary writer, the French engineer Nicolas de Finiels, tells us that, seen from St. Louis,

> The Indian trade is an issue of great urgency and competition among the inhabitants of Illinois [the Illinois Country]. Hardly has the ice disappeared, freeing traffic on the streams, then big pirogues [heavy dugouts made from a single log], light flat-bottomed barges, and birchbark canoes are made ready. Soon they are filled with trade goods, which have become indispensable to the Indians because of their contact with white men. *Engagés* ("hired men," i.e., the common laborers of the fur trade) press around these frail vessels; they stretch their arms, which are numb from six months of inactivity, but which soon recover their suppleness, elasticity, and vigor. Farewell songs ring out; paddles whip the waves into a froth, leaving behind a long wake that is quickly swallowed up by the next; din from the splashing paddles rises in the air to mingle with joyful shouts. The frail vessels finally triumph over the waters; they soon disappear in the winding river and lose themselves in the distance among the islands that intersect their course.[137]

Beginning in the late 1780s, European traders on the Missouri were usually Frenchmen who had been licensed by the Spanish colonial government to engage in the fur trade. Their contemporaries accordingly saw them as quasi-agents for the Spaniards. For this reason, they are treated here as representing Spain rather than France, although not all of them become Spanish subjects. One of most prominent of these resourceful men was Jacques D'Eglise, described by the Spanish lieutenant governor, Zenon Trudeau, as being "so simple and from a province in France of such a peculiar language that nobody can understand it."[138]

D'Eglise may have spoken an impenetrable regional dialect that differed from conventional French, but he was also a very accomplished frontiersman. In 1792, he led an expedition that manhandled its heavy wooden pirogues up the Missouri all the way to the Mandan villages. He found eight settlements there, which totaled some 4,000 to 5,000 Indians. They were already well supplied with arms and other British goods from posts in Canada, and with Spanish bridles and saddles from settlements of New Mexico. Disappointed at not being able to do any business with them, he returned to St. Louis later that same year and reported this news to Trudeau.

With Trudeau's blessing, in the spring of 1793 D'Eglise and four companions set out again in two pirogues to reach the Mandan villages. This expedition, however, was halted by other tribes somewhere in central South Dakota and he was forced to return to St. Louis. D'Eglise remained active in the Missouri fur trade. Although he never made his way back to the Mandan villages, he never lost hope that he would somehow find the Passage and thus claim the 3,000-peso reward. Ultimately, he came to a sad end: he was "barbarously murdered" in New Mexico in 1806. His killers were later captured, sentenced to death and shot. Their bodies were hung in the public square.[139]

In 1794, the Missouri Company sent the first of three Spanish expeditions up the river. It was led by Jean Baptiste Truteau, a former St. Louis schoolteacher who was a cousin of Trudeau.[140] The party was instructed to travel up the Missouri to the Mandan villages, throw out any British traders they found there, build a trading fort, and then look for a route to the Pacific. This expedition was not a success because the upriver Indians wanted to maintain control of the trade.

Truteau complained that "The policy of the savages of this river is to prevent communication between us and the nations of the Upper Missouri, depriving them of munitions of war and other help that they would receive from us if we made our way there easily."[141] He wintered along the Missouri in South Dakota, traded with the local Indians, and sent some of his men back to St. Louis with the few furs he had been able to obtain. He never reached the Mandan villages and was back in St. Louis by the early summer of 1796.

The second expedition, led by a Frenchman named Lécuyer, was sent out in 1795 with orders to reach the Mandan villages and from there proceed to "the shores of the Sea of the West," i.e., the Pacific. This venture, too, was a failure. At an early stage of the trip, the Ponca Indians stole the trade goods he was carrying. Lécuyer returned to St. Louis in disgrace, where he was roundly criticized for wasting the Missouri Company's goods and for taking two Indian wives.

Undeterred by these two setbacks, the directors of the Missouri Company then chose a native of Scotland, James Mackay, to lead a third expedition. Mackay had immigrated to Canada at some point between 1774 and 1776. He first worked in the fur trade for Britain's North West Company but joined the rival Hudson's Bay Company in 1785. The next year he collected furs worked on the Assiniboine River along the Saskatchewan-Manitoba border on behalf of a trader named Robert Grant.

The first European known to have visited the Mandans since La Vérendrye arrived in their villages in 1738 was indeed a Mackay — not James Mackay but another Scottish fur trader, Donald Mackay. Donald was not related to James, although they had both been born in Scotland only 20 miles apart. Donald reached the Mandans in 1780 but his account was never published and is thus poorly known. Moreover, his narrative says nothing of significance about the Mandans, although his visit was reflected on a map that he co-authored in 1791.[142]

James Mackay first visited the Mandans in 1786 or 1787, walking across the snows of the northern plains with some unidentified companions for two weeks. His companions are not mentioned in his narrative but it would have been far too risky for him to make the trip alone. Via the grapevine, the Mandans heard that he was coming and, he tells us, immediately introduced him to one of their customs:

> Many of their Chiefs Came to Meet me, at some distance from their village, and would not permit me to enter the village on foot, they carried me between four men in a Buffaloe Robe, to the Chiefs tents.[143]

Mackay was favorably impressed by this tribe. He reports that

> The Mandaines, jointly with the Manitouris [or Minitarees] and Wattasoons [a related tribe] live in five Villages, which are almost within sight of each other, three of these Villages are on the South of the Missouri and two on the North Side. The Situation of those five Villages is charming they are built on an Elevated plaine, even and fertile, which extends on either Side to a considerable distance. Those Nations cultivate the Ground round about their Villages and sow Corn Beans, Pumpkins and Gourds; they also make earthen pots in which they Boil their Meats, these Pots resist fire as well as if they were made of iron.[144]

Details of Mackay's later travels are sketchy but it appears that in 1789 he went to New York, where he met Don Diego Maria de Gardoqui, a senior Spanish diplomat. Gardoqui shared the long-standing European interest in finding a passage across to China across North America and wrote to a Spanish colleagues:

> One of the many enthusiastic Englishmen who roam these western countries of the King's dominions inhabited only by Indians has arrived here today. This person [Mackay], although a young man, says he has traveled for nearly five years from the English establishment of Hudson Bay towards the west among various Indian nations, crossed the Mississippi and the Missouri and arrived at the cordillera of mountains which divide the waters, some to the ocean and others to the Pacific. He reports that the furthest nation he reached assured him that about 100 miles from that place there was a river which empties into the Pacific Ocean, and he adds that the distance to it was short.[145]

Gardoqui recommended Mackay to the Spanish officials in St. Louis as a man who was familiar with the upper reaches of the Missouri, which constituted the northern reaches of Spanish territory. Then something quite remarkable happened. When Mackay reached St. Louis in 1794, he hired a young Welshman, John Thomas Evans, to determine the truth or falsity of a long-standing rumor: that somewhere in the North American West there existed *a tribe of Welsh-speaking Indians.* This notion sprang from the belief, firmly held in some quarters, that the Welsh had discovered the New World in 1170, long before Columbus, and that Madoc, a Welsh prince, had led a group of his followers there. Madoc's descendants, it was asserted, were now Welsh-speaking Indians— perhaps the Mandans.[146] Evans, who became a highly competent backwoodsman during his western travels, would eventually conclude that this myth had no basis in fact.

Mackay himself became a Spanish subject in 1793. That same year he met Trudeau in St. Louis, who immediately hired him to be the "principal explorer and director of the Company's affairs in the Indian Country." Trudeau instructed Mackay "to open a commerce with those distant and Unknown Nations in the upper parts of the Missouri and to discover all of the unknown parts of his Catholic Majesty's Dominions through that continent as far as the Pacific Ocean."[147]

Mackay soon discovered, however, that the fur trade was being carried on so competitively in this region that traders representing different trading companies were often bartering in Indian villages at the same time. This was most unfortunate because, as Mackay tells us,

> In the Course of the Year [17]93 & [17]94 the English Traders sent from their Post they have on the River Assiniboine, several of their hireling to the Mandaine Nation on the Missouri, but as these persons were sent by different Employers or Traders, that in Consequence they found themselves on an opposition the one with the other, they paid Double the Value for their peleteries they exchanged, which made the Indians think immediately, that Goods were not of that value which they had at first imagined; the immoderate desire of those unfit traders showed, to procure themselves peleteries; convinced the Indians that it was not necessary to show so much friendship to the whites to entice them to return to them with goods, seeing that the only object that brought them there was to procure peleteries.[148]

On a 1795–1797 journey up the Missouri, Mackay and Evans benefited from a new map made in August 1795 by the Spanish surveyor general in St. Louis, Antoine Pierre Soulard.[149] This map was based on the late eighteenth century explorations of French fur traders up the Missouri to the Mandan villages. The Mackay-Evans expedition consisted of 32 men packed into four boats, i.e., berchas (barges) and pirogues, which were loaded with goods to barter to the Indians in exchange for furs. In 1795, Mackay established Fort Carlos IV (Fort Charles, named in honor of Charles IV of Spain) about a mile from the Omaha Indian village near Homer, Nebraska. The fort was well situated on a little hill. Mackay tells us that on 29 November 1795,

> the Prince [Indian chief] Blackbird came to visit the fort which was being built in a plain located between the very village of the Mahas and the Missouri River, on the shore of a small river which flows into the latter, and is fairly navigable. This plain is very extensive, the land is excellent, and never inundated by the waters. The location of the fort seems to have been prepared by nature. It is in a commanding district, which rises for a circumference of about one thousand feet. It looks on the shore of this river, as if to command the rest of the area. I have established my settlement and my fort there, although at a distance from the woods; however, the horses of the Prince are at my service.[150]

The epic travels of the Mackay-Evans expedition were, in geographic terms, the most significant European or American venture onto the northern Great Plains before Lewis and Clark. Summarizing his adventures, Mackay said that he had accomplished his assignment, which as he saw it was "to pave the way for the discovery & Commerce of that vast Country on both sides of the Missouri & across the Continent to the Pacific ocean ... as much as could be expected from the [limited] resources & support" that he had been given."[151]

Despite its geographic achievements, the expedition resulted in a severe financial loss to the Missouri Company. The Spaniards simply could not deliver enough goods to the Indians upriver to win their respect and still maintain an adequate profit margin. Ultimately, the Missouri Company, plagued by bad management, stiff competition from the British, and further losses (due in part to the inferiority of its goods), went bankrupt in 1797. It left over $100,000 in debts.

Although the Missouri Company itself collapsed into ruin, Mackay and Evans managed to land on their feet, thanks to the Spaniards' suspicions of British intentions. In 1798, Governor General Manuel Gayoso de Lemos wrote to Don Francisco de Saavedra, secretary of state in New Orleans:

> Foreseeing the importance of this matter [i.e., keeping the British out of the Missouri basin], I tried to keep to our cause the two most famous travelers of the northern countries of this continent; one Don Jayme Macay and the other Don Juan Evans, both natives of the Island of Great Britain, who, displeased with the Canadian companies, entered the services of our Missouri Company. But when this company failed due its poor management and great losses, I knew that necessity would oblige these two valuable subjects to solicit employment among the referred to Canadian Companies to our own very great loss. In order to avoid this inconvenience, after having had Macay at my

side for some time, in order to assure myself of his principles, I have decided to locate him at San Andrés, a new establishment near the entrance of the Missouri, naming him commandant of that post, under the dependency of the Lieutenant-Governor of Illinois. Not having any position to give Evans, I have preferred to maintain him at my cost, keeping him in my own house, in order to prevent his returning to his own country, or for his own convenience, to embrace another cause.[152]

From 1797 to 1798, yet another McKay — John McKay — was master at Brandon House, the Hudson Bay's Company's center of operations in Manitoba's Assiniboine River valley of Manitoba. Brandon House had been founded five years earlier. Together with the Red River valley, the Assiniboine River valley was a focal point of competition between the Hudson's Bay Company and the North West Company. It was rich in furs but rich in problems, too. Earlier, on 26 September 1793, the trader Donald Mackay had made this entry in the Brandon House Post Journal: "We keep a watch now as those Vagabonds of Canada who has abandoned themselves to live as the Indians may attempt to plunder, there is many of them now deserted & run away from their Masters & Employers."[153]

John McKay found that, to his great surprise, no one really knew which government — Spanish or British — exercised even nominal sovereignty over the region. In a journal entry of 12 November 1797, he complained: "No one is sure whether that part of the Misoures where the Mandles are, belongs to the Spaniards. Mr. Evans last year acknowledged that the little Souris River [just south of the Assiniboine River] was out of the line of the Spaniards."[154]

Ambitious Spanish plans to build forts to stop British and French encroachments came to naught, forcing the Spaniards to return to their previous but unsuccessful policy of giving individual traders monopolies to do business with individual tribes. In contrast to the North American Southwest, where the Spanish imprint is clearly visible to this day, the Spanish presence on the upper Missouri River has faded out completely. The maps that Lewis and Clark would use in 1803 to such good advantage during their first year of travel were its only legacy.[155]

In 1800, under the terms of the secret Treaty of San Ildefonso, Spain gave Louisiana back to France. This treaty of retrocession included not only the important port of New Orleans but also the strategic mouth of the Mississippi River itself. The two nations agreed to keep the treaty secret: they were afraid that either the British or the Americans would react by seizing Louisiana before the French could take possession of it. The treaty gives us a good insight into the era, demonstrating just how easily a large-scale transfer of territory and sovereignty could take place. For a diplomatic document, it is also unusually short, clear and interesting: see Appendix 7 — The Treaty of San Ildefonso.

There appear to have been three reasons for this unusual retrocession:

- Spain had declared war on Britain in 1796. This conflict, coupled with the threat of revolution within the restive Spanish empire itself, left the Spaniards with very few resources. They could not maintain their expensive alliances with both the Norteños (the Plains Indians who constituted "the nations of the North") and the Comanches.[156]
- Just as Louisiana turned out to be a money-loser for France, it proved to be a bad investment for Spain, too. The province cost a great deal to administer but produced little of value in return.
- Perhaps most importantly, Napoleon Bonaparte made the Spaniards an offer they could not refuse: if they gave him Louisiana plus "six ships of war in good condition built for seventy-four guns, armed and ready to receive French crews and supplies,"[157] he would in return create a kingdom, known as Etruria, in Tuscany (north-central Italy) for the Duke of Parma, son-in-law of the Spanish king Charles IV. Although Spain did return Louisiana to France, Napoleon reneged on the agreement: the Duke of Parma did not get any more land.

By the beginning of the nineteenth century, problems on the Mississippi were in sharp focus. American farmers, lumbermen, trappers and businessmen were using flatboats to move millions of dollars worth of goods through New Orleans each year. Although the French had reacquired Louisiana from Spain in 1800, Spanish officials continued to administer the territory. Juan Ventura Morales, the acting Intendant (governor) of New Orleans, claimed that the Americans were abusing their privileges by smuggling. In 1802, acting on secret instructions issued by King Carlos IV himself, Morales revoked the right of deposit (duty free temporary storage) there on all cargo coming from the United States. According to Arthur Preston Whitaker, a scholar who examined this issue in the 1930s, this measure was "one of the most provocative in the whole history of international rivalry in North America."[158]

The United States' right of deposit in New Orleans had been guaranteed by Spain in the 1795 Treaty of San Lorenzo del Escorial but it was valid for only three years and thus technically lapsed in 1798. Since then, however, American merchants had been allowed to continue using the port. By 1802, Farmers, trappers and lumbermen were sending sizeable amounts of goods through New Orleans each year. A formal withdrawal of the right of deposit meant that their cargoes could no longer be stored at the port, thus making them highly vulnerable to theft and decay.

This decision caused great anger and consternation among the American frontiersmen living west of the Appalachians. Rafting their produce down the Ohio and Mississippi Rivers to New Orleans for transshipment overseas was the only way for them to sell it profitably. The governor of Mississippi warned Secretary of State James Madison that

> The late act of the Spanish Government at New Orleans has excited considerable agitation in Natchez and its vicinity: It has inflicted a severe wound upon the Agricultural and Commercial interests of this Territory, and must prove no less injurious to all the Western Country.[159]

Although the right of deposit was reopened within seven months of its closure, the Spanish curtailment of this right sparked an immediate crisis. Jefferson responded to it declaring that control of the Mississippi was of crucial importance to the United States. He began negotiations with France for the purchase of New Orleans itself — a campaign that eventually culminated in the United States buying the whole of Louisiana from Napoleon in 1803.

Spanish objectives, hopes and fears

The Spaniards wanted to do six different but interrelated things: to find riches, win glory, protect the Mexican silver mines, convert the Indians, discover the Passage, and keep the Russians out of California. They hoped that achieving all or at least some of these objectives would strengthen their control of the Trans-Mississippi West. By the beginning of the nineteenth century, however, Spain had grown much weaker and much less competitive there. The American hegemony it dreaded would soon become the new North American reality.

3

The French: Lords of Rivers and Lakes

FRANCE WAS A COLONIAL POWER IN North America for nearly 300 years. Its involvement began in 1524, when Giovanni Verrazano, a Florentine navigator in the service of François I, king of France, sailed along the east coast of North America. It ended in two different phases. The first phase closed in 1763, when France lost New France, its empire in North America, after the British won the Seven Years' War. The second phase concluded in 1803, when Napoleon sold Louisiana to the United States.

To begin at the beginning: looking for the Passage, Verrazano explored the North American shoreline from the Carolinas north to Nova Scotia. His hopes were high. He reported, in fact, that at one point this coast was so narrow that he could easily see the "eastern sea," i.e., the Pacific Ocean, from the masthead of his ship. Verrazano was probably off North Carolina at this time. Looking westward across Hatteras Island, he could Pamlico Sound but could not see the low-lying mainland on the far side, which was not visible because the Sound is about 50 miles wide here. Despite its fundamental inaccuracy, however, his account fueled European hopes that a water passageway across North America did indeed exist.

Ten years later, in 1534, Jacques Cartier, a French explorer also sent out by François I, sailed up the Gulf of St. Lawrence, planted a cross on the Gaspé peninsula, and claimed *La Nouvelle-France* (New France) for his king. As Cartier's ship drew near the shore, he could see that the Indians who lived along the St. Lawrence River were very friendly. He tells us:

> Crossing the bay we caught sight of two fleets of Indian canoes, which numbered in all some forty or fifty canoes. The Indians set up a great clamour and

made frequent signs for us to come on shore, holding up to us some furs on sticks. [Thanks to their prior contacts with European cod fishermen, the Indians knew precisely what Cartier wanted. They were eager to barter their beaver furs for metal knives and other European products.] They showed a marvelous great pleasure in obtaining iron wares and other commodities, dancing and going through many ceremonies, and throwing salt water over their heads.[1]

The Indians quickly traded all the furs they were wearing to Cartier and his men—to the extent, says Cartier, that they "all went back naked without anything on them. They made signs to us that they would return on the morrow with more furs."[2] When Cartier reported to Paris that Canada's rivers and lakes teamed with beavers, French hatmakers clamored to import more of these valuable furs. Cartier's arrival in New France thus proved to be the foundation stone of a lucrative, highly competitive and international fur trade.

It is important to note that we would need several hefty volumes to discuss the colorful, turbulent history of New France itself. Only two essential points must be made here. The first is that New France was simply enormous. At its maximum extent before the Treaty of Utrecht (1713), which ended the War of the Spanish Succession and awarded the Hudson Bay Territory, Newfoundland and part of Acadia (i.e., peninsular Nova Scotia) to Britain, it extended west from Newfoundland to Lake Superior and south from Hudson Bay to the Gulf of Mexico. It was divided into five French colonies, each with its own administration: Canada, Acadia, Hudson Bay, Newfoundland, and Louisiana.

The second point is the cardinal importance of the fur trade itself. This international business needs to be discussed now, even at the risk of breaking the smooth flow of chronological events. We will pick up Cartier's story again later on. This trade was not, of course, the only factor motivating the French. The geographer Conrad Heidenreich reminds us that

> The motives that originally pushed the French into the interior and continued to do so throughout the seventeenth century were the fur trade, the missions to the more populous native groups, and the hopes of finding an easy route to the Pacific Ocean. Most often these motives were mentioned together as reasons for undertaking voyages of exploration. The French court was only occasionally interested in exploration. On those occasions, it hoped to find a western passage, discover minerals, and meet the dangers of English competition in the fur trade ... [however] *all the senior French ministers noted, with some chagrin, that journeys of exploration usually degenerated into fur-trading ventures.*[3]

A clear proof of this last point can be seen in the experiences of the Count of Frontenac, governor of New France. He had been ordered to establish more settlements in the colony and to do so where they would have easy access to France by sea. After he reached New France in 1672, however, he pushed far into the interior instead, hoping to make a large profit from the fur trade. For this and other shortcomings, he was recalled to France ten years later.

The fur trade was very big business: it was international, extensive, complex and changed over time. Limitations of space will prevent us from examining it here in great depth but the main point is evident: it was this trade that was chiefly responsible for the exploration, settlement and survival of New France. The demand in Europe and North America for felt hats effectively propped up a French colonial empire in eastern and central Canada. Eighty percent of the monetary economy in New France was based on the fur trade.[4]

The reason was that beaver fur made the best quality felt hats. These hats were so handsome and so resistant to wind and water that they remained popular in Europe and the United States until silk hats displaced them in the early 1840s. Their usefulness was due to the nature of beaver fur.

A beaver pelt consists of two layers—an outer layer of course guard hair and a soft undercoat of velvety fur known as the duvet. Seen through a microscope, the slender strands of the duvet are studded with tiny barbs. This barbed characteristic results in superior-quality felt.[5] The most desirable beaver pelts were called *castor gras* (literally "greasy beaver"). These were beaver cloaks or blankets that had been worn by their Indian owners for so long that all the long, coarse outer hair had fallen off, leaving only the supple duvet.

Beaver pelts were so valuable that an entire economy was based on them: they became the accepted unit of trade. A prime pelt—i.e., one that was large, properly de-fleshed, well stretched and nicely dried—was known as a "made beaver" or MB for short. This was the standard against which all other items were measured. A musket, for example, might cost 14 MB and a blanket 7 MB. A martin skin equaled ½ MB, while an otter skin changed hands at 1 MB. The Hudson's Bay Company bartered 1-gallon kettles at 18 MB, tobacco at 1 MB per pound, liquor at 4 MB per gallon, knives at 4 per MB, cloth between 2 and 5 MB per yard, gunpowder at 1 MB per pound, and lead shot of all types at four pounds for 1 MB.[6]

The beaver trade could be extremely profitable and, initially, there was no shortage of beavers. Before the Europeans came to Canada, it is estimated there were 10 million beavers living in the forested areas south of the timberline. In fact, the French government had to close the interior of Canada to the fur trade between 1696 and 1701 because a glut of beaver pelts on the

3. The French

"Beaver Hut on the Missouri."
©2005 Alecto Historical Editions www.alectoUK.com

European market had seriously depressed prices. (After the founding of Detroit in 1701, however, the French fur trade posts were gradually reopened.)

The trade later became so intensive that beavers nearly became extinct. However, these animals have excellent recuperative powers and have no natural predators, except for the wolf. With the fur trade now long gone (or at least strictly regulated) and relatively few wolves in beaver country, there are thriving populations of beavers in Canada and in the United States today.[7]

Rather than trying to describe the complicated evolution of the fur trade in New France and the northeastern United States decade by decade, it is more useful to jump ahead chronologically here and try to come to grips with the trade as a whole. Seen in overview, it had three overlapping phases. At some risk of oversimplification, we can think of these as (1) the Beaver Wars, (2) the international phase, and (3) the intramural phase.[8]

There were two Beaver Wars.[9] Both of them took place east of the Mississippi and therefore are not our primary focus in this book. The first war (1620 to 1666) was chiefly carried out around Lake Ontario but also extended northeast toward Quebec and south toward Maryland. It pitted Indians against Indians.

During the seventeenth century, the Five Nations of the Iroquois[10] constituted the strongest military force — Indian or European — in eastern North America. Deeply involved in the fur trade, the Five Nations eventually monopolized it by dominating or displacing all the other tribes near the eastern Great Lakes and along the St. Lawrence River. They also attacked French settlements in New France. By about 1660, the Five Nations were so successfully that they running a little empire based their military prowess and on the beaver trade. Their initial success, however, proved to be short-lived. It led, in fact, to their destruction.

The second Beaver War (1666–1700) was much wider in scope, both geographically and militarily. It was conducted along a broad swath of territory lying between Lake Michigan and Montreal. The combatants were British officers and their Indian allies, on one side, versus French officers and their Indian allies, on the other. In this struggle, the Iroquois gravely overextended themselves by fighting both the midwestern tribes and by attacking French and English villages. The French and their Indian allies struck back and eventually defeated the Iroquois. By 1700, the main villages of four of the five Iroquois Nations had been burned to the ground.

Some of the details of the international and the intramural stages of the fur trade will be discussed throughout this book. In general, it can be said that the international stage pitted French businessmen and French fur traders against their English counterparts. It began in 1670, when the English chartered the Hudson's Bay Company, and ended in 1763, when France lost the Seven Years' War and thus most of its holdings in North America.

The intramural stage came next. It was more complex. With the French out of the running after 1763, two dominant British firms — the Hudson's Bay Company and its arch-rival, the North West Company — competed directly with each other. This era began after the fall of New France in 1763 and ended in 1821, when the British government forced these two companies to merge because their competition had resulted in bloodshed. The intramural stage had pronounced international, religious, and social overtones. These came about because of the very different structures of these two companies.

The Hudson's Bay Company was staffed by English-speaking British or British-Canadian businessmen and by fur traders who were English-speaking Protestants. The North West Company, on the other hand, was more broadly based. Founded in Montreal in the 1779, it was a partnership of nine different fur-trading groups. It filled its top ranks — the clerks and the senior wintering partners (i.e., the men in charge of trading posts in the interior during the winter) — with English-speaking men of English or Scottish origin. Such men were usually Protestants.

Coat of arms of the North West Company from 1783 to 1821. The central importance of the fur trade is shown by the beaver and by the two vessels (a canoe and a York Boat) that the company used so extensively in this trade. The North West Company's motto, "Perseverance," was highly appropriate for its demanding and dangerous line of work. (Library and Archives of Canada, Acc. No. 1957–101.)

The lower rungs of the North West Company, on the other hand, were filled by French-speaking Catholic *voyageurs* ("travelers") and *engagés*.[11] Although outsiders sometimes called these men "Canadians," the Hudson's Bay Company traders usually referred to them as "the French." They, in return, labeled the Hudson's Bay Company traders as "the English."[12] French-speaking visitors often used the term "English," too.

Victor Collot, who had been a French general, describes the Canadian-Missouri River fur trade as it was conducted in about 1796:

> A few years since, the English merchants built small forts in several places on a river, called the Red River, which falls into that of the Asseniboines. The sources of this last river begin near the Missouri, towards the Mandanes country. They send their agents by land, either with horses in the autumn or spring, or with great dogs in the winter, which run with light and slender traineaux [sleds] on the snow, and traffic for bullocks' hides, wolf and fox skins, in exchange for powder, knives, glass beads, and vermilion. The passage from the Missouri to this river is reckoned by travellers who have made it several times, at a hundred of our common leagues.[13]

Finally, unlike the Hudson's Bay Company, the North West Company permitted all ranks of its men to take Indian wives *à la façon du pays*—"in the manner of the country," i.e., according to local custom. This was a wise move, given the fact that in its early years New France had a profound shortage of French women. By the early nineteenth century, the policy of racial intermarriage had resulted in a high degree of social stability and a sizeable Métis population.[14]

The fur trade extended over a dangerous, intricate 4,000-mile network of waterways, portages, trading posts, and forts. These arteries of competitive commerce stretched westward from Montreal to the Rocky Mountains; northwest from the Pembina area to Fort Chipewyan on Lake Athabasca; and northeast from the Pembina area to York Factory on Hudson Bay.

In exchange for the canoe-loads of trade goods sent west for traders to barter to the Indians for furs, return canoe-loads of rich furs—principally beaver, but also river otter, wolverine, fisher, wildcat, kit fox, and snowshoe hare—flowed east to Montreal and thence to Paris and other world markets.[15] (The Americans did not get directly involved in the western fur trade until after 1806, when Lewis and Clark returned to St. Louis with tales of the vast numbers of beaver and other fur-bearing mammals to be found in the Rocky Mountains.)

With this survey of the fur trade behind us, let us now backtrack and pick up the thread of French North American adventures after Cartier. For him and his successors, inland waterways would become France's key to the North American West. Perhaps, the French surmised, the network of Canadian rivers and lakes even extended all the way to the Pacific Ocean and would thus give them access to the China trade. Even if this were not the case, they quickly understood that canoes and pirogues were the best and, indeed, the only way to traverse the dense forests, rivers and lakes blanketing

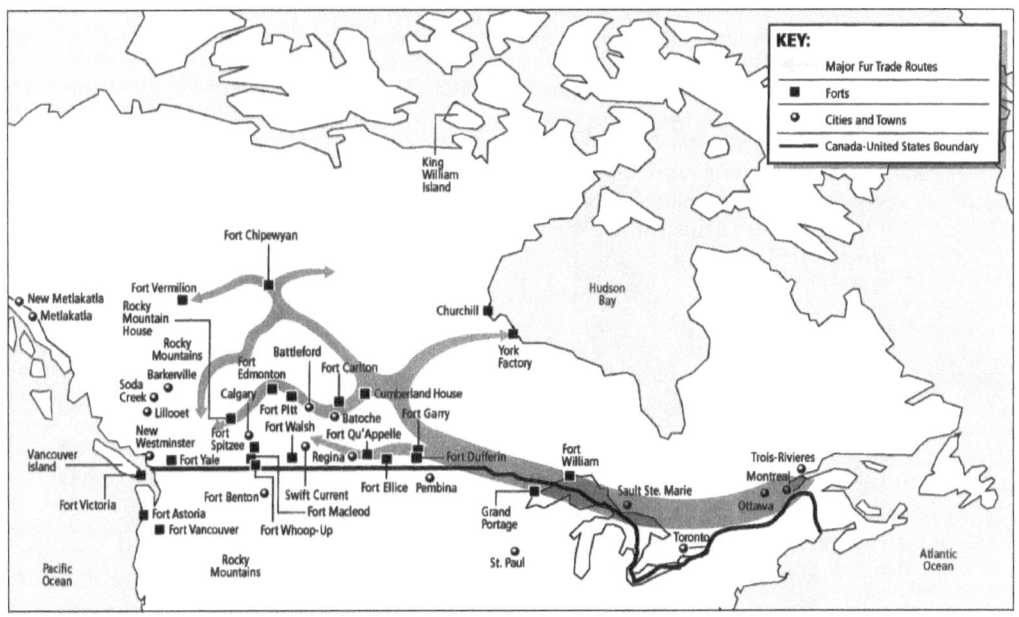

Major Fur Trade Routes. (Map by Graeme Bandeira, adapted from Time-Life Books, *The Canadians*, pp. 26–27.)

eastern North America. Traveling there on foot or on horseback was simply not feasible.

Canada contains one sixth of the world's water; in fact, 25 percent of the country is water. After Cartier, the most prominent man in the early history of New France was Jean Talon, an exceptionally able Intendant. He was in charge of justice, police, and finance and served two terms: first from 1665–1668 and again from 1670–1672. He caused thousands of settlers (hundreds of them young women) to be brought to New France during his tenure. He believed that West held great promise for France.

Talon argued that Frenchmen should build a waterway-based empire and should claim possession of Canada's fur-bearing lands before the British could. As he put it, "This country is laid out in such a way that by means of the St. Lawrence one can go anywhere inland, thanks to the lakes which lead to its source in the West and the rivers that flow into it along its shores, opening the way to the North and the South."[16]

Some of Talon's immigrants or their descendants went inland with the fur trading canoes. Many of them remained there permanently, living with Indian women and fathering an ethnic group of mixed French-Indian ancestry (the Métis). Jesuit missionaries and French explorers and fur traders also made prodigious voyages along the rivers and lakes of New France.

The French adventurer Samuel de Champlain, sponsored by Henry IV of France, arrived in New France in 1603. Describing his first trip ashore (we see here how Montreal got its name), he wrote:

> We went along, and about a league and a halfe farther, we beganne to find goodly and large fieldes, full of such Corne as the Countrey yieldeth. In the midst of these fields is the Citie of *Hochelaga*, placed heere, and as it were joyned to a great mountaine that is tilled round aboute, very fertile, on the top of whiche, you may see verye farre, we named it Mont Royall.[17]

At Montreal, the Lachine Rapids made any farther progress by sailing ship impossible. The French named these rapids La Chine ("China") because they were thought to lie athwart the route to China. The local Indians led Cartier to the top of a peak and explained to him that, very far away in the west, there were several big fresh-water seas (the Great Lakes). They told him that the biggest of these was the farthest away. It lay, they said, virtually "on the rim of the world." It was so enormous that they did not know if "there were ever man heard of that found out the end thereof."[18]

Champlain sent out some of his young men to live with the Indians to learn their languages so they could serve as interpreters. These adventuresome youths were also instructed to collect geographic information, to cultivate alliances with the Indians, and to encourage them to bring their furs directly to Quebec. Eventually, especially after the defeat of the Hurons in 1650, the French would send their own canoemen west from Montreal, paddling along the Ottawa and French rivers to obtain furs from the Indians living near the Great Lakes.

Champlain realized that the Lachine Rapids could open the door to the interior of New France. He reported:

> This current [the Lachine Rapids] extends for three or four leagues, so that it is vain to imagine that any boats could be conveyed past these rapids. But he who would pass them must provide himself with the canoes of the natives, which a man can easily carry; for to transport a boat is a thing that a cannot be done in the short time necessary to enable one to return to France to winter. And besides the first rapid, there are ten more, for the most part difficult to pass; so that it would be a matter of great toil and labour to be able to see and do by boat what a man might propose, except at great cost and expense, besides the risk of labouring in vain. But with the canoes of the natives one may travel freely and quickly throughout the country, as well as up the little rivers as up the large ones. So that by directing one's course with the help of the natives and their canoes, a man may see all that is to be seen.[19]

French canoemen would become known both as *coureurs de bois* (literally "runners of the woods") and as *voyageurs*. These terms are now used more or less interchangeably but historically there was a difference between them. Initially, both the *coureurs de bois* and the *voyageurs* worked for themselves or for small partnerships. After the fall of New France to the British in 1763 at the end of the Seven Years' War, however, the *voyageurs* tended to become the "hired paddlers" of the Montreal-based fur trading companies.[20] An entrepreneur known as a *bourgeois* ("master" in Canadian usage) would hire wage-earning *voyageurs* to paddle his trade goods west to the Indians and to bring Indian furs east back to Montreal.

Over the years, French-Canadian canoemen would paddle their way up the St. Lawrence River, through the Great Lakes and the Illinois Country, and down the Mississippi to Louisiana and the Gulf of Mexico. They made the first European contact with many of the Indian tribes along the way. Appendix 8: *Coureurs de Bois* and *Voyageurs*: The Men and Their Boats, contains some first-hand accounts of this remarkable profession.

Champlain was one of the first Europeans to understand three important facts about New France. The first was that, due to the forbidding terrain, exploration could only be undertaken by canoe. The second was that the support of the local Indians was of critical importance in this endeavor. To win and retain Indian support, traders would have to learn Indian languages and adhere rigorously to the standards of Indian diplomacy and protocol, especially by giving frequent and generous presents. These gifts were only a thinly veiled form of tribute but they were extremely important: parsimony was an unforgivable sin in Indian eyes.[21]

The third fact followed closely from this. To stay on good terms with their Indian allies, the French would not only have to refrain from selling firearms and ammunition to the enemies of these allies but also must be ready to fight shoulder-to-shoulder with the allies themselves in time of war. Huron warriors were excellent fighters: Jesuit missionaries would describe them as "all well made men of splendid figures, tall, powerful, good-natured, and able-bodied."[22] Nevertheless, when the Hurons saw two Iroquois chiefs killed outright by three musket shots fired by Champlain's men, they were so impressed by French guns that they asked Champlain if he would go "to their country, and aid them continually like a brother." Champlain confidently says: "I promised them that I would."[23]

The new French policy of expanding the fur trade westward in 1650–1660 in the wake of the Huron defeat was to have momentous consequences. The eastern tribes had served as middlemen in the fur trade and had tried to block the flow of European arms and ammunition to their enemies in the west. Now the French understood that they could make more money if they simply bypassed the eastern tribes and established direct commercial contacts with the western tribes who were actually harvesting the furs.

This sudden expansion of commercial competition damaged traditional Indian alliances and increased the rivalries between tribes. In the Northeast, the result was the Iroquois Wars of the mid-seventeenth century. During these clashes, the Iroquois, together with their English and their Dutch trading partners, decimated the Hurons—the most important middlemen of the Great Lakes region.[24]

In 1608, Champlain had founded Quebec. Its six families, totaling 28 people, constituted the first successful European settlement in New France. The young men of New France often wanted to become *coureurs de bois*. Together with Jesuit missionaries, these indefatigable canoemen helped to extend French influence among the Indians of the Great Lakes.

One of Champlain's protégés was Étienne Brûlé. He spent a year (1610–1611) among the Hurons to learn their language and then became the first interpreter for the French. He paddled his way to Lake Ontario in 1615 and was the first European to do so. In 1622, he reached Sault Sainte Marie (the Rapids of St. Mary) between Lake Superior and Lake Huron, and probably got as far as Lake Superior as well. Several reports say that, later, he was killed and devoured by the Bear clan of the Hurons, who attributed their later misfortunes to his revenge-seeking ghost. Brûlé appears to have been murdered because he tried to short-circuit the Hurons' trading monopoly with the French by establishing direct commercial relations with the Seneca Indians, who lived near Niagara Falls.[25]

During his second term as Intendant (1670–1672), Talon pressed hard for the exploration of the West, hoping to discover the Passage. He also wanted to expand New France in order to solidify the colony's position in the world and to counter the threat posed by the British. Under his direction, Simon François D'Aumont, Sieur de St. Lusson, reached the Great Lakes and Sault Sainte Marie. There D'Aumont took possession, in 1671, for New France of all "the territories from Montreal as far as the South Sea, covering the utmost extent and range possible."[26] He was formally claiming for France the entire interior of the North American continent. Although the local Indians were neither consulted nor told about this remarkable French claim, the French did work out a military alliance with some of them.[27]

In 1673, the governor of New France decided to send out a small expedition to determine the course of the Mississippi River and to find its mouth. There were two leaders of this venture into the unknown. The first was Father Jacques Marquette, a 35-year-old Jesuit missionary-explorer who was such an extraordinarily gifted linguist that he had attained fluency in six Indian languages since his arrival in Canada in 1666. His colleague was Louis Joliet, a 27-year-old philosophy student turned fur trader.[28]

In May 1673, Marquette and Joliet, together with a crew of five *voyageurs*, pushed off in two canoes from Sault Sainte. Marie, bound for Michilimackinac and points south. Michilimackinac itself was a remote outpost in *le Pays d'En Haut*, literally "the land at the top." This phrase was a French geographic concept that embraced all the territory encountered when paddling up the St. Lawrence River from Montreal, i.e., the Great Lakes and the lands and waterways beyond them. Strategically located in the Strait of Mackinac between Lakes Michigan and Huron, Michilimackinac would become the main base of France's mid-continent fur trade.[29] Later renamed Fort Mackinac, it would in turn become a center of the British fur trade.

Marquette described his *voyageurs* as "five men who were quite determined to do anything and to suffer anything for such a glorious expedition."[30] They set off in two canoes heavily laden with trade goods and paddled through Green Bay, Wisconsin; up the Fox River; crossed Lake Winnebago; and, after making a short portage, came to the hitherto-unexplored Wisconsin River. The narrative of their expedition recounts that there they "left the waters flowing to Quebeq, four or five hundred leagues from here, to float on those that would henceforth take us through strange lands."[31] These strange lands held remarkable things.

Marquette tells us in a journal entry for June 1673:

> From time to time, we came upon monstrous fish, one of which struck our Canoe with such violence that I thought it was a great tree, about to break the Canoe to pieces. [This fish may have been a blue catfish, which can weigh up to 128 pounds.] On another occasion, we saw on the water a monster with the head of a tiger, a sharp nose like that of a wildcat, with whiskers and straight, erect ears; the head was gray and the neck quite black. [This animal may have been a Florida panther, *Felis concolor coryi*, which was found throughout the southeastern United States.][32]

The explorers eventually floated out onto the Mississippi near Prairie du Chien, Wisconsin. While paddling quietly down the Mississippi, our intrepid travelers suddenly and unexpectedly found themselves at the turbulent confluence of the Missouri. Marquette tells us what they experienced:

> Sailing quietly in clear and calm water, we heard the noise of a rapid into which we were about to run. I have seen nothing more dreadful. An accumulation of large and entire trees, branches, and floating islands was issuing from the mouth of the [Missouri] with such impetuosity that we could not without great danger risk passing through it. So great was the agitation that the water was very muddy and could not become clear.[33]

Marquette added that the Missouri was a river "of considerable size, coming from the northwest, from a great distance."[34] He was convinced that it must be part of the long-sought passage towards the Far East. "Several villages of the savages are located along this river," he tells us, "and I hope by means of it to make the discovery of the Vermilion Sea [the Gulf of California] or California."[35] In fact, Joliet's map of 1675 optimistically suggested that the upper Mississippi was not very far from the *Mer Glaciale* (the Icy Sea, i.e., the Arctic). It also held out the mistaken hope that western tributaries of the Mississippi might offer navigable routes, via the Gulf of California, all the way across North America, thus helping to link the Atlantic and Pacific oceans.[36]

Making about 40 miles a day downstream, Joliet and Marquette continued along the Mississippi until they reached the mouth of the Arkansas River. There they halted and reversed course: they were worried that they would encounter hostile Indians or hostile Spaniards if they went any farther south. But they had gone far enough: their epic exploration was successful.

Although they had hoped that the Mississippi would flow into the Pacific Ocean, they had at least proved that this great river entered the Gulf of Mexico. This meant that New France could use it to establish and maintain contact with proposed French settlements on the Gulf. A French empire was thus conceivable in this part of North America. Moreover, reasoned the French, if such an empire could be established, it would also slow or even stop British expansion toward the Pacific.

To secure these lands for France, René Robert Cavelier, Sieur de La Salle, decided to explore the Ohio and Mississippi valleys. He proposed building a string of trading forts from the Great Lakes to the mouth of the Mississippi. These forts would, he thought, make it possible for the French to export furs to France, not only via the Saint Lawrence River but also through the Gulf. Moreover, such defenses would form a wedge, cutting off overland communication between the Spaniards in Florida and their countrymen in Mexico.

In 1682 he was given a royal commission and set sail for the Mississippi. His voyage down the river was not without hardship. Zenobius Membré, a Franciscan missionary who was a member of the expedition, recorded in his *Narrative of La Salle's Voyage down the Mississippi*:

> We were out of provisions, and found only some dried meat at the mouth [of the Mississippi], which we took to appease our hunger; but soon after perceiving it to be human flesh, we left the rest to our Indians. It was very good and delicate. At last, on the tenth of April [1682], we began to remount the river, living only on potatoes and alligators. The country is so bordered with canes and so low in this part that we could not hunt, without a long halt.[37]

When La Salle was on the most southeasterly reaches of the Mississippi River and could see the Gulf, he formally claimed for France all the territory between the Alleghenies and the Rocky Mountains, on the one hand, and from the Gulf of Mexico to the sources of the Missouri, on the other. La Salle named this vast new possession Louisiana in honor of Louis XIV. Marquis Jean-Baptiste Colbert Seignelay, the king's navy minister, had strongly supported the La Salle expedition. He hoped that La Salle would discover a good port on the Gulf of Mexico, around which a French settlement would grow up and would serve a base for the future conquest of Spanish lands. To this, we may add that the French also hoped to be able to control the fur trade of the entire Mississippi Valley.

La Salle returned to France and received permission to establish a colony near the mouth of the Mississippi. He then mounted an expedition to do so. This expedition, however, proved to be a complete disaster. Because La Salle did not understand the complex geography of the Gulf Coast, he could not find the Mississippi River again.[38] In 1685, he was therefore forced to establish the colony, which he named Fort St. Louis, on Spanish territory some 400 miles to the southwest—at Matagorda Bay in Texas.

Soon, however, he faced catastrophe there. With the exception of the naval vessel *Le Joly*, which took some of the disenchanted colonists back to France, he lost all of his ships. Spanish privateers captured the ketch *Saint Francis*. The storeship *L'Aimable* grounded and broke up at the mouth of Matagorda Bay. Finally, the six-gun frigate *La Belle*, given by Louis XIV to La Salle as a gift and representing La Salle's last hope of resupply or escape by sea, was wrecked on the Matagorda Peninsula during a squall.

La Salle next made several unsuccessful efforts by land to find the Mississippi. In 1685, after capturing a pirate ship that counted among its crew some deserters from La Salle's first expedition, Spanish colonial officials learned about Louis XIV's plan to establish a French presence along the Mississippi. They became greatly alarmed that this was the opening salvo of a diabolical French plan to separate the Spanish settlements in Mexico from those in Florida.

The Spaniards had never accepted La Salle's presumptuous claim in 1682 to what they considered their own territory—namely, the vast and potentially rich valley of the Mississippi River. Thus between 1685 and 1689 they launched no fewer than 11 different expeditions—five by sea and six by land—to find and uproot La Salle's ill-fated French colony at Matagorda Bay in Texas. As the Spain's Council of the Indies put it in 1686, "His Majesty's prompt action is required to pluck out the thorn that has been thrust into the heart of America."[39]

All that the Spaniards found, however, was the wreckage of *La Belle* and *L'Aimable*, the ruins of Fort St. Louis, and a handful of French survivors. La Salle himself had been ambushed and killed in 1687 by Pierre Duhaut, one of his own men. When the Indians learned of La Salle's death, they had attacked Fort St. Louis and killed almost all the remaining colonists, sparing only five children, whom they adopted into their tribe. Of all the Frenchmen who left Fort St. Louis with La Salle to look for the Mississippi, only six managed to make their way to Canada and, eventually, to France. Six others stayed with the Indians of eastern Texas.[40]

Nevertheless, as the historian Robert S. Weddle pointed out, La Salle's expedition was important because it "established in the minds of the French a claim to Texas that refused to die; thenceforth, until the French were eliminated from colonial rivalry [in 1763], virtually every Spanish move in Texas and the borderlands came as a reaction to a French threat, real or imagined."[41]

In 1686 La Salle's lieutenant, Henri de Tonti (or Tonty), an Italian who sported a metal fist covered with a glove because he had lost his right hand when fighting in Sicily, founded a trading post-and-fort known as Poste de Arkansea (Arkansas Post) near the junction of the Arkansas and Mississippi Rivers. This was the first semi-permanent French settlement in the lower Mississippi valley and the farthest outpost of French dominion. Its establishment was an early step in the long struggle between France, Spain, and England over mastery of North America. Later, in 1704, Tonti would become the first European to meet the Choctaw Indians, who would know and fear him as "the man with an iron hand." He would work out an alliance with them to offset what the French feared were Britain's efforts to increase its own influence among them.

The French missionary Louis Hennepin, a member of the Récollet Order of Friars Minor (a branch of the Franciscans), had gone to Canada with La Salle in 1675 and became his chaplain and official chronicler in 1678.[42] That year Hennepin visited Niagara Falls. Here is his account of it, the first ever printed:

> Father Gabriel and I went overland to view the great fall, the like whereof is not in the whole world. It is compounded of two great cross streams of water and two falls, with an isle sloping along the middle of it. The waters which fall from this vast height do foam and boil after the most hideous manner imaginable, making an outrageous noise, more terrible than thunder, so that when the wind blows from the south their dismal roaring may be heard above fifteen leagues.[43]

La Salle and Father Hennepin had established Fort-Crèvecoeur at what is now Peoria, Illinois, in 1680. When La Salle returned to Fort Frontenac (at Kingston, Ontario) for supplies, Hennepin and other members of the party had set out to explore the upper Mississippi River. They were captured by the Sioux in 1680 and had to accompany them on several hunting expeditions. On one of these forays, Hennepin reached what he called the Falls of St. Anthony (at Minneapolis, Minnesota), which is only about 180 miles southeast of Lake Itasca, the ultimate source of the Mississippi.

Rescued in 1680 by the French *voyageur* Daniel Greysolon, who bore the title Sieur Dulhut (or Duluth or Du Lhut), Hennepin returned to France two years later and wrote a full account of his exploits in 1683. The placename *La Louisiane* appears for the first time on his map entitled *Carte de la Nouvelle France et de la Louisiane Nouvellement découverte* (*Map of New France and of Newly-Discovered Louisiana*).

In 1697 he revised this work, entitling it *Nouvelle découverte d'un très grand pays situé dans l'Amérique* (*New Discovery of a Very Large Country Situated in America*). In it, he claimed to have explored the Mississippi to its mouth — a claim that was patently false. As the historian Bernard DeVoto put it, "Hennepin took up the literary life, creating staggering and entirely fictitious achievements for himself and trying to pass off La Salle's explorations as his own."[44]

Hennepin described the Missouri as a mighty river which was formed "from several other Rivers, which spring from a Mountain about twelve days Journey from its Mouth ... from this mountain one might see the Sea, and now and then some Great Ships."[45] Despite all their errors and exaggerations, Hennepin's books were widely read at the time and were influential in shaping contemporary views of North America, especially since they seemed to support the pyramidal height-of-land theory.

This theory, which held that all the highest mountains in the western North America were located in the same general area, dominated geographic thinking in North America in the eighteenth century. It had a major impact on the planning of the Lewis and Clark expedition. Jefferson, for example, owned copies of Hennepin's works and consulted them when writing his own *Account of Louisiana*, which he presented to Congress in 1803.

Proponents of the theory believed that the headwaters of the four major navigable rivers of North America were located there, too. These rivers were identified as the St. Lawrence; the Mississippi; the Missouri; and the Bourbon, i.e., the Nelson River, which runs from Lake Winnipeg into Hudson Bay near York Factory. The headwaters of the four rivers were so close together that, according to the theory, travelers would find it an easy matter to portage from one river system to another. Many commentators believed that traveling up the Missouri would take explorers all the way to, or at least very close to, the Columbia River, from which passage to the Pacific and thence to the Orient would be easy enough.

In the meantime, however, French fur traders bartering for hides with the Indians of the Indiana-Ohio region did not have to concern themselves with such geographical theories. They had work to do and were remarkably good at it. Their first cargo, floated down the Mississippi in 1705 by flatboat from the Indian country around the Wabash, was a load of 15,000 bear and deer hides. Using a route now closed by the Mississippi River levee system, these French boatmen passed through Bayou Manchac (just below Baton Rouge), then along the Amite River and through Lake Maurepas and Lake Ponchartrain to Biloxi, Mississippi. The hides were then sent by sea to France.[46]

By 1700, King Louis XIV had made an important decision about the English colonies east of the Appalachians: France would not tolerate their extension westward. To block any expansion by the English of the Carolinas, France would establish a new colony, Louisiana, in the lower Mississippi Valley. To give France control of the Great Lakes and to block Englishmen from using them as a springboard into the west, France would strengthen its young colony, Detroit, which was situated between Lakes Erie and Huron. It thus became official French policy to keep the Anglo-Americans penned up between the Appalachians and the Atlantic Ocean.[47]

French fur traders working around Hudson Bay suffered a serious setback in 1713 when the Treaty of Utrecht ended the War of the Spanish Succession, a complicated struggle over the balance of power in Europe. Among other things, this treaty confirmed that the Hudson Bay's drainage basin, known as Rupert's Land, belonged to Britain. (Prince Rupert of the Palatinate was the first governor of the Hudson's Bay Company, the governor of England's Mines Royal, and the cousin of King Charles II of England.) The boundaries of Rupert's land were remarkably vague but the area involved was truly gigantic — nearly 1.5 million square miles of land. East to west, Rupert's Land stretched from Labrador to Rocky Mountain House in the Canadian Rockies. North to south, it ran from the northernmost coast of Hudson Bay to the Red River of the North, which now forms the border between North Dakota and Minnesota.[48]

The Hudson's Bay Company had been incorporated by the British in 1670. Until the late 1680s it built and operated a string of trading posts in the Hudson Bay region. Most of these posts were captured by the French after 1686 and were held by them until the Treaty of Utrecht restored them to the British. The result of this treaty was that France was forced to accept British control of this fur-rich area.

Moreover, the British were now able to trade directly with the Iroquois and other tribes of the region. Ultimately, the French would begin to look for furs even farther west but in the meantime French traders still had easy access to Indian trappers around Hudson Bay. By bartering with them, they were able to get furs themselves and thus significantly reduce the flow of furs to the British.

One of the most influential colonial officers of New France was Jean-Baptiste Le Moyne, Sieur de Bienville, sometimes called the Father of Louisiana. In 1716, he founded Fort Rosalie, later known as Natchez — the first permanent European settlement on the Mississippi. The French hoped that tobacco, indigo and other commercial crops could be grown there for export. Relations between the French settlers and the Natchez Indians were friendly at first, thanks in large part to Bienville's creative if duplicitous diplomacy.

According to a contemporary source, if a certain tribe of Indians began to favor the British at the expense of the French, this is how Bienville would react:

> [He] would stir up secretly some other powerful [Indian] nations to which he would furnish powder, bullets and the greatest number of guns that he could to make war on the one that he saw was being moved by the English and especially to bring him many prisoners from the nation for whom he would give them something. He would send these prisoners back home free, sending word to their chiefs that he had done all that he had been able to do to prevent others from making war on them, but that not being able to accomplish it he had at least rescued their men whom he was sending back to them to show them that the French nation was a friend of theirs and that he himself was glad to protect them as far as it was in his power to do so, that he hoped that henceforth their nations would pay more attention to the messages that he would send them.[49]

When a tribe that had shown signs of defecting to the English did return to the French fold, Bienville would call all the warring groups together and make peace between them. He was thus able to maintain French influence with the Indians and, at least temporarily, to prevent too much fighting among them. French-Indian relations gradually took a turn for the worse. In 1729, the Natchez Indians attacked Fort Rosalie and killed more than 200 French settlers. The French, aided by the Choctaws, retaliated by killing most of the Natchez. Moreover, in the following years the French dispersed or enslaved the survivors.

Bienville had founded New Orleans in 1718 at the strategic juncture of the navigable waterways leading from the Gulf to the Mississippi and thence to the Missouri. The city began modestly enough. It consisted only of a few huts, a wooden house for Bienville himself, and a storehouse. Bienville was named governor of Louisiana that year. In 1721, New Orleans had a population of only 470 souls. The next year it became the capital of Louisiana.

Ironically, today much of the architecture of the famous Vieux Carré (the "old square," now known as the French Quarter) in New Orleans is actually Spanish, not French. In 1788, a devastating fire destroyed most of the wooden buildings built by the French. Three hurricanes and another fire inflicted further destruction in 1794.[50]

Coincident with the founding of New Orleans, the French cartographer Guillaume Delisle published in 1718 the definitive map of the area—his *Carte de La Louisiane du Cours du Mississippi* (*Map of Louisiana and the Course of the Mississippi*). This was the first detailed map of the Gulf region and one of the most useful. Covering the area from the Rocky Mountains east to the Atlantic seaboard, it showed the routes used by the explorers De Soto, Moscoso, Tonti, and St. Denis; the locations of many Indian tribes—Apaches, Padoucas (Comanches), Osages, Caddos, and others; and two trade routes—one British, the other French—that linked the Mississippi Valley with the Carolinas.[51]

Delisle's map of the Gulf region appeared at an auspicious time. The biggest influx of settlers into Louisiana came about because of the Mississippi Scheme, better known as the Mississippi Bubble. This ambitious but disastrous undertaking was the brainchild of John Law, a gifted Scottish adventurer who was an economic theorist and a mathematical wizard. Law won the confidence of Philippe II, Duke d'Orléans and regent of France, who was desperate to find an easy way to pay off the heavy debts incurred by the late Louis XIV in his endless wars.

In 1717, Law managed to obtain for his newly formed Compagnie d'Occident (Company of the West) exclusive privileges to develop the Mississippi Valley. Renamed the Compagnie des Indes (Company of the Indies) two years later, this enterprise held a complete monopoly on the colonial trade of France. Law also took over the collection of taxes in France and the minting of money, thus making himself master of both France's foreign trade and its finances.

Under the Mississippi Scheme, more than 1,800 French, German and Swiss immigrants poured into Louisiana and settled along the Mississippi River and the Gulf Coast between 1717 and 1720.[52] A John Law Concession of about 47 persons was even established as far north as Arkansas Post in 1721 and was protected by a small detachment of French soldiers.[53] Prospects for the Compagnie des Indes seemed so rosy at first that a feeding frenzy developed in France as rich and poor alike clamored to buy its stock.

Law launched one of the first modern public relations campaigns, describing Louisiana as a land overflowing with gold and silver. There was even said to be a huge emerald rock sitting in or on the banks of the Arkansas River. Because of this overblown publicity, the price of one share of the

Compagnie des Indies stock soared 36-fold, from 500 livres to 18,000 livres, far beyond what any realistic projection of earnings would justify. The French government made matters worse by printing paper money, which creditors snapped up and used to buy more shares of the stock.

The result was raging inflation. As prices soared, both paper money and *billets d'état* (promissory notes issued by the government of France) began to shed their value. Moreover, the heady profits expected from Law's investments in Louisiana failed to materialize. When the speculative bubble finally burst in 1720, most speculators were ruined. Law was forced to flee France to save his life. The John Law Concession at Arkansas Post dwindled to only 14 Frenchmen and six Negroes by 1723 and was dissolved not long afterward.

When Law, by then a poor man, died in Venice in 1729, the following epitaph made the rounds:

> Ci git cet Ecossais célèbre,
> Ce calculateur sans égal,
> Qui, par les règles de l'algèbre,
> A mis la France à l'Hôpital.[54]
> (Here lies this famous Scot,
> This arithmetician without equal,
> Who, by following the rules of algebra,
> Has put France into the poorhouse.)

Étienne de Véniard, Sieur de Bourgmont (or Bourgmond), has been called "the most colourful and intrepid of all the French explorers of the Southwest."[55] As a *coureur de bois*, he lived with the Indians of the Missouri for many years and was roundly criticized by the Jesuit missionaries at Kaskaskia for the "scandalous and criminal life" he was leading then.[56] Whatever moral lapses Bourgmont may have been guilty of (his only crime seems to have been that he fell in love with an Indian girl, lived openly with her without benefit of Christian marriage, and had a son by her), he traveled farther up the Missouri than any European before him. His detailed reports on the region helped the cartographer Guillaume Delisle work out his outstanding map of Louisiana and the courses of the Mississippi and its tributaries.

In 1712 Bourgmont turned up in Mobile and volunteered his services to French officials there. They were intrigued by his offer to make peace among the warring Indians of the Missouri and encourage them to accept an alliance with the French. Back in France, the Ministère de la Marine (the navy ministry), which was responsible for colonial affairs, liked Bourgmont's proposals.

It entertained four optimistic hopes: that French trade could be established with the silver mining towns of northern Mexico; that silver deposits would be found along the Missouri; that the Indians of the region would be converted; and that the Passage would be discovered. Moreover, reasoned the Ministry, once the French were firmly established along the Missouri they would be in a strong position, working together with their new Indian allies, to force the Spaniards out of New Mexico, Texas, and California entirely.[57]

For all these reasons, the French sent Bourgmont up the Mississippi and Missouri in 1714. During the next four years, he explored these rivers as far north as the Cheyenne River, which joins the Missouri near Pierre, South Dakota, and wrote two useful reports. The first, *Routte qu'il faut tenir pour remonter la rivière Missoury* (*Route to be followed for ascending the Missouri River*), mapped the course of the Missouri itself. The second, with the short title of *Exacte description de la Louisiane* (*Exact Description of Louisiana*), was a narrative designed to whet the Ministry's interest in supporting further exploration of the Missouri.[58]

Bourgmont assures his reader early in the narrative that "I tell you [only] what I have seen"[59] and proceeds to lay out his candid opinions about the Indians, flora, fauna and landscapes of the Mississippi and Missouri rivers. "The lower part of the Missicipi," we learn, "is the most confounded place in the world, full of drowned meadows, ... crocodiles, snakes, and other insects. It empties itself by 3 channels, in the deepest [of which] there is not more than 10 feet of depth."[60] The Indians of Biloxi are "rather rogues and rascals" but are also "great hunters and fishers and raise quantities of Indian corn, of beans, and of tobacco for their habitual use."[61]

He impresses us with the power of the Missouri and the potential wealth of its tributaries:

> Some leagues further up, on the left side as you ascend, is the great Missouris River, so famed for its swiftness. Its waters are always muddy, and especially in spring, making the Missicipi turbid for 400 leagues, and 20 leagues more towards the sea in spring at the time of the flood waters ... the Missouris ... are allies of the French. All their trade is in furs. They are not very numerous, they are of very good blood and more alert than any other tribe. From all the Missouris River can be gotten furs of every kind, very fine and good, as the climate there is very cold. Higher up is found another river which flows into the Missouris, called the Ecanzé [Kansas] River, on which there is a tribe of the same name, allies and friends of the French. Their trade is in furs. These are the most beautiful pieces of land in the world. The prairies there are like seas and full of wild beasts, especially buffalo, cows, hinds and stags, which are there in numbers that stagger the imagination. They almost always hunt with bow and arrow. They have very fine horses and are very good horsemen.[62]

In a note inserted on the margin of his narrative, Bourgmont dangles before the reader the prospect of a lucrative trade with the Spaniards, who were not very far away:

By way of the Missouris one can also find opportunity to trade with the Spanish, who are very rich in mines in this region. By all the information one can get, they are not far removed from these rivers on account of the Indians who go to them and who trade with them.[63]

Much impressed by his travels and reports, in 1722 the Compagnie des Indes appointed Bourgmont to build a long-projected fort on the upper Missouri, which would serve three purposes. It would be a military base, which could be used to bring the Comanches to terms. From it, the French could establish commercial relations with Spanish traders in Santa Fe (the French believed that following the Missouri would eventually bring them to New Mexico). Finally, it was an auspicious place from which to begin a search for the Passage.[64] Bourgmont and his expedition therefore built Fort d'Orléans on the upper Missouri, about 200 miles upstream from its confluence with the Mississippi, in 1723.

In addition to being a good outdoorsman, Bourgmont was also a good diplomat. A group of Kansas Indians paid a courtesy call at the new fort and, as custom demanded, Bourgmont offered them presents. The Indians, however, rejected his presents as wholly inadequate, indicating that they wanted gifts worth at least twice as much. Bourgmont somehow talked his way out of this impasse, only to be faced immediately by another and far more difficult one.

The Indians then presented Bourgmont with a thirteen- to fourteen-year-old girl to be his wife. Since the girl was the daughter of their chief, the match would have been a good one. It would have helped Bourgmont achieve his objectives and would have brought the Indians into a durable alliance with the French. However, he politely declined on the grounds that he already had a wife. After weighing his answer, the Indians came up with a creative compromise. They suggested that the girl be married to Bourgmont's *son* instead, but added that since they understood the boy was only ten years old, they would keep the girl for him until he was old enough to marry her. This face-saving solution pleased all the adults concerned.[65]

Later, Bourgmont set out to make peace with the Comanches. In particular, he wanted them not to prevent French explorers from making their way south to the Spanish settlements. The chief, pleased by the cornucopia of gifts that Bourgmont gave him on behalf of the king of France (these included muskets, powder and ball, cooking pots, axes, knives, awls, blankets, and trinkets for the children), agreed to keep the peace and to let the French visit the Spaniards.

As DeVoto puts it with a nice touch, the Comanches "promised to love the French and never to make war on any of their Indians. From now on, they said, the Spanish would be as the dirt and the French as the sun, but see to it that plenty of goods are sent our way."[66] Nevertheless, the chief also added, somewhat ominously, that if the French ever needed to call on him for help, he would be delighted to provide 2,000 warriors. His offer confirmed a simple fact of life along the upper Missouri: it was the Comanches, not the foreigners, who held the balance of power there.[67]

Fort d'Orléans itself was not destined to become an important military base or a vibrant trade center. After Bourgmont retired to France, the fort was ignored. Closed by the French in 1729, it then became a base for itinerant fur traders. Gradually, it faded from the historical record. Louisiana as a whole, however, fared much better.

When Louisiana became a French crown colony in 1731, it had a diverse population of about 8,000 colonists and their supporters. This mixture included French settlers, Indians, slaves, and even thousands of Germans, who settled along the Mississippi above New Orleans along what was known as the German coast. In addition, between 1764 and 1788 at least 2,639 French-speaking Acadians, originally from Nova Scotia, were added to Louisiana's international mix.[68] Their descendants, known as Cajuns, are still there.

As mentioned in Chapter 1, the French soldier, fur trader and explorer Pierre Gaultier de Varennes, Sieur de La Vérendrye, was the first European to meet the Mandans. This remarkable man has yet not received, at least in the United States, anything like the attention his exploits deserve.[69] In the course of looking for the mythical Western Sea in 1731–1744, his explorations and those of his sons extended the frontiers of New France. These frontiers would stretch west to North Dakota and northwest to Fort à la Corne near the forks of the Saskatchewan River.

Based at an exceedingly cold and isolated trading post at Lake Nipigon, La Vérendrye devoted himself single-mindedly to two tasks. First, he bartered beaver pelts from the local Indians and sent bales of these furs—some 30,000 furs per year—to his superiors in Montreal. This enriched his employers (though not La Vérendrye himself) and prevented rival British traders from getting the furs instead.

Second, he organized a careful search for the passage to the Western Sea. The historian DeVoto sets this latter scene so well in his lyrical, evocative account of La Vérendrye at Lake Nipigon in 1730 that it deserves to be quoted in full here. "The Nipigon post," DeVoto tells us,

> was on the edge of beyond. What else was it on the edge of? In a six months' winter when the temperature might not rise to twenty below zero for a month on end, there was time to inquire ... the Indians gladly bartered for his goods and gladly told him about beyond ... they told him what they knew, what they had heard, what they guessed, and what it amused them to invent. They

scratched maps on pieces of bark or hide or in the ashes of the hearth.... There were many lakes. There was a treeless country.... There was a nation of little men, three feet tall and very brave. But the tremendous news was that beyond this maze of lakes was a great river which flowed west, apparently out of Lake Winnipeg, and at its mouth was the sea. This must be the route to the Western Sea and the journey that Jacques Cartier had begun for France in 1534 could be brought to triumph in 1730.[70]

The Treaty of Utrecht (1713) had prohibited the French from harvesting furs around Hudson Bay itself, but they had adjusted to this development by trading northwest of Lake Superior instead. La Vérendrye went ever further: he established a string of eight posts in western Canada (east of the Rockies) which were known collectively as the Posts of the Western Sea. These competed with the Hudson's Bay Company's posts for control of the western fur trade. In 1738, he built Fort La Reine on the north bank of the Assiniboine River, near the modern town of Portage la Prairie, which is named for the portage between the Assiniboine River and Lake Manitoba. This would be his headquarters during his search for a route to the Western Sea.

In 1742, La Vérendrye sent two of his sons, François (known as the Chevalier) and Louis-Joseph, farther west to see if they could find the Passage. These young men spent some months traveling with the Mandan Indians, starting from Bismarck, North Dakota. The Mandans showed them odds and ends of Spanish trade goods—a bridle and a bit, a cotton shirt, and what was probably a serape. These items had come overland (not up the Missouri) by means of long established Indian intertribal trade networks with the Spanish Southwest.

The Chevalier wrote a report of his travels, which DeVoto laments as "one of the vaguest documents of exploration in American history" because it is so imprecise and lends itself to such conflicting interpretations.[71] What is clear is that the two young men got at least as far as the Black Hills in western South Dakota and conceivably may even have reached the Big Horn Range in northern Wyoming. They certainly reached the foothills of some high peaks. The Chevalier wrote:

> On January 1, 1743, we found ourselves in sight of the mountains ... I had ... a strong desire to see the sea from the top of the mountain.... Finally, [on about 20 January 1743] we reached the mountains. In general, they are well wooded, with all kinds of trees, and appear to be very high ... I was much vexed not to be able to climb the mountains as I had hoped to do. [The Indians escorting the expedition suddenly became panic-stricken at the thought that hostile tribes would attack their villages if they did not return home at once.] We then decided to return. We had come to this place in a very orderly fashion, but the return was very different: everyone fled in his own way.[72]

On their return journey, the sons passed through the Arikara villages near Fort Pierre, South Dakota. There they buried a memorial formally claiming the region for France. The Chevalier recorded: "On an eminence near the fort [Fort La Reine] I deposited a lead tablet bearing the arms and inscription of the king and placed some stones in a pyramid for the general [the viceroy — see below]."[73] By a happy stroke of luck, this seven-by-eight-inch tablet was unearthed in 1913 by a 14-year-old schoolgirl named Hattie May Foster and is now on display at the South Dakota Cultural Center in Pierre. It bears two inscriptions, one in Latin and, on the reverse side, another in French. The Latin inscription reads:

> In the twenty-sixth year of the reign of Louis XV, the most illustrious Lord, the Lord Marquis of Beauharnois being Viceroy, 1741, Peter Gaultier de La Vérendrye placed this."[74]

The French inscription, scratched on the tablet with the point of a knife, states:

> Placed by the Chevalier de la Vérendrye, witnesses Louis-Joseph, La Londette and A. Miotte, the 30th of March 1743."[75]

The La Vérendryes did their best to maintain French influence in the West but they were only marginally successful. After La Vérendrye Senior was recalled in 1744, his successor, Nicolas-Joseph de Noyelles, made no further effort to find a route to the Western Sea. Subsequently, due to the Seven Years' War, between 1758 and 1760 French trade goods no longer arrived on schedule. This shortfall forced the Indians to trade with the British rather than the French.

The Indians had only two choices: dealing with the itinerant British traders already in the West, or making the long trip back to the Hudson's Bay Company's post at York Factory to sell furs to the British there. The first option was the best choice. Thus, after the era of the La Vérendryes, the French presence in the West began to dwindle. It formally ended in 1763 when France had to surrender most of its North American holdings to the British.[76]

French traders made heroic efforts to establish commercial ties with the Spaniards of New Mexico but their overtures were rebuffed. In 1739, the two Mallet brothers, Pierre and Paul, together with seven companions made their way across the Great Plains from Fort de Chartres (near Vanadalia, Illinois) to Santa Fe. However, they had lost nine horses, laden with all their merchandise and their spare clothing, when crossing a river, so they had virtually nothing left to sell and very little left to wear.

This was lucky for them because Spain was then maintaining a strict monopoly on trade: goods that were not taxed by Spanish authorities were considered contraband and were subject to seizure. Moreover, the Spaniards suspected and not without good reason, that all foreign traders were probably spies for their competitors, France or Britain. The Mallets were therefore hauled before Spanish authorities in Santa Fe.

The Mallets kept a journal of their expedition, but it has been lost. Fortunately, a brief summary was sent to Paris and a copy of this document has survived. It shows that the Mallets were first asked "where they came from and to what purpose." They replied that

> they came from New France and that they had come with the intent to initiate a trade with the Spanish of this realm because of the intimate connection that exists between the crowns of France and Spain ... [and that despite their losses en route] they were still intent to discover this kingdom and open communication with the colonies of New Orleans and Canada, and disdainful of all sorts of troubles and of risks from the savage nations they might encounter....[77]

As classically cautious bureaucrats, however, the Spaniards decided to seek instructions from their viceroy in Mexico City—1,500 miles away—before doing anything. It took nine months for them to get a reply, during which time they treated the Frenchmen courteously, wining and dining them, but would not permit them to leave Santa Fe. When the reply finally did arrive (in 1740), it instructed the Spaniards to expel the traders and not to let any others into New Mexico unless they could prove that they had the Spanish government's permission to do business there.[78]

By then, some of the men of the Mallet expedition had married local señoritas. They decided to transfer their allegiance to Spain so they could live in Santa Fe with their new wives. The rest of the Mallet party was released and began to make its way back to French territory. Two of these men decided to return to the Illinois Country by retracing the way they had come. The Mallets and three resourceful Canadian companions, however, began by following a narrow, east-flowing stream. The historian W.J. Eccles told the rest of the story so well in a 1997 article on French exploration that we shall quote him here:

> By mid–June [1740], the stream they were following became deeper and broader, so, in a fashion typical of the Canadians of that era, with only knives for tools they cobbled together two elm-bark canoes. Turning their horses loose, they embarked in their frail craft and were swept down the Arkansas River, then on to the Mississippi and New Orleans, arriving there in March 1741. Appropriately enough, the rivulet-stream-river that they had followed through present-day New Mexico, Texas, Oklahoma, and Arkansas is still named the Canadian River.[79]

Once back in New Orleans, the Mallets told other French businessmen about the potential profits to be made trading with the Spaniards. The governor of Louisiana, Bienville, was personally eager to open up the Santa Fe trade and soon sent the Mallets back again, armed with appropriate official documents. This time their canoe overturned in the Red River and they lost all their papers, so the trip had to be abandoned. But Pierre Mallet was not one to give up easily.

In 1750, he set out for Santa Fe yet again, but Comanche warriors stole his goods and documents. His real trouble began when he finally reached Santa Fe. The Spaniards promptly arrested him and sent him first to Mexico City and ultimately to Spain for interrogation. At that point, he disappears from the historical record. It seems unlikely that he ever got back to the Trans-Mississippi West again.

The harsh treatment he received ended the immediate prospects for any French-Spanish trade in New Mexico. This trade would not begin until after the Mexican revolution of 1821. In that year, an enterprising trader, William Becknell, set off from western Missouri with a string of pack horses, hoping to sell his modest supply of calico, knives, needles and other goods to the Cheyenne Indians. He found that the Cheyennes had gone south to steal horses. Spanish soldiers he met in the Sangre de Cristo Mountains, however, told him that Mexico had just overthrown Spanish rule. Becknell accordingly made his way to Santa Fe, where he sold his goods at a fine profit in Mexican silver.[80]

French traders fared much better with the Indians. Towards the middle of the eighteenth century, French trade with the Comanches was well established, in large part because the French, unlike the Spaniards, were willing and, in fact, eager to sell firearms, powder and lead balls to the Indians. In 1748, for example, a party of 33 Frenchmen arrived at a Comanche village near Taos and offered to trade flintlock muskets for mules.[81] French traders also bartered knives and cloth in exchange for hides, horses, and slaves, i.e., Indian women and children captured by the Comanches during their raids.

This growing French influence with the powerful Comanches alarmed the Spaniards: Governor Tomás Vélez Cachupín was worried that French traders were thereby gaining "practical knowledge of the land adjacent to our settlements which they freely travel by permission of the Comanches."[82] He earnestly urged his successors to take pains

> to maintain the friendship and commerce of the Comanche tribe, diverting as much of it as possible from the French, because the Comanche tribe is the only one that could impede access to that terrain and be the ruin of New Mexico, due to its strength, use of firearms, and skill at waging war on foot or on horseback.[83]

This was good advice, because a major objective of the French was in fact to turn the Comanches solidly against the Spaniards and to encourage them to make war all along the Spanish frontier.[84]

French influence in the Trans-Mississippi West continued to grow. *Coureurs de bois* reached the foothills of the Rocky Mountains. French traders made their way to New Orleans and into East Texas. Archeological excavations of the Gilbert Site in eastern Texas have shown that by about 1750 an Indian tribe (probably the Kichais, who were linguistically related to the Caddos) had established an elaborate deer-hunting and hide-processing camp there.[85] The Indians gave French traders thousands of deer hides in return for French muskets. Many of these hides would end up as soft, sleek leather garments in Paris.

The Kichais valued firearms not only for their ability to kill game and enemies at a distance but also because they could easily trade guns for horses. A natural market soon developed in this region. The Comanches and other tribes of the southern plains had large herds of horses but relatively few firearms because Spanish traders were not allowed to sell guns to the Indians. The Indians of East Texas, on the other hand, had plenty of French guns but few horses. The Gilbert Site appears to have played a central role in the hide-gun-horse trade of the mid eighteenth century.

In 1751–1752, an expedition of 10 Frenchmen led by Boucher de Niverville reached the Rocky Mountains, looking in vain for the Mer de l'Ouest (the Western Sea). French geographic knowledge of western North America was still very vague. The best French map of 1755 could only say of the lands west of Lake Winnipeg: "*on ignore si dans cette Partie ce sont des Terres ou la Mer*" ("we don't know in this region if there are lands or the sea.")[86]

Only a handful of permanent French settlements existed beyond the little city of New Orleans. These included Natchitoches on the Red River, Arkansas Post at the junction of the Arkansas and Mississippi Rivers, and St. Genevieve and St. Louis on the Mississippi. Suddenly, the French settlements had to face a new reality in 1762: in a private agreement—the secret Treaty of Fontainebleau—unexpectedly, France ceded to Spain that huge portion of Louisiana lying west of the Mississippi River.

Why did France want to get rid of this territory? There appear to be four reasons:

- In 1762, Charles III of Spain, trying to prevent a total British victory in North America, had foolishly cast his lot with France in its war against Britain. His participation not only failed to turn the tide of the war: he also lost Florida as a result. France therefore felt it owed Spain some compensation, i.e., New Orleans and western Louisiana, for this loss.

- More importantly perhaps, the French wanted to prevent Louisiana from becoming a British possession. The next year the Treaty of Paris (1763) would end the Seven Years' War and would award most of France's holdings in North America to the British.

- Louisiana had consistently been a net drain on French finances. It would have become even more difficult for France to support after the British became the new owners of Canada, thanks to the Treaty of Paris.

- Political conditions in Paris itself nudged France into becoming only a "reluctant imperialist." As the historian Glenn R. Conrad explained, in the seventeenth and eighteenth centuries, France did not have a strong political or economic framework to run an empire in North America. This was due chiefly to the deadlock in Paris between the "internalists" and the "expansionists." The result was a "hesitant, half-hearted approach to colonialism."[87]

In 1763, the Treaty of Paris ended, simultaneously, both the Seven Years' War, which had sucked Britain, France, Spain, and Portugal into its orbit, and the French empire in North America. In a complicated minuet of diplomacy, under the terms of that treaty France ceded to Britain all its claims to Acadia, Canada, Cape Breton, and all of Louisiana east of the Mississippi. (Louisiana had expanded to include both sides of the Mississippi, but the western side was not ceded to the British — only the eastern side.) The Spaniards retained New Orleans itself. This arrangement gave Spain effective control over the mouth of the Mississippi.

France kept its fishing rights on the Grand Banks of Newfoundland Banks and was given the islands of St. Pierre and Miquelon. Britain gave back to France the islands of Guadeloupe, Martinique, Belle Isle, Maria Galante, St. Lucia, and St. Domingue (Haiti). Britain restored Havana to Spain and, in return, Spain ceded Florida to Britain. The treaty thus left Britain as Spain's only European rival in North America.

In 1764, Pierre Laclède Linguest, a French fur trader from New Orleans, founded St. Louis. Strategically located on a high bluff near the confluence of the Missouri, Illinois, and Mississippi Rivers, it would become the administrative and financial center of Upper Louisiana, part of which was also known as the Illinois Country.

We should pause here to record the remarkable achievements of René Auguste Chouteau, Linguist's exceptionally able 14-year-old stepson. Young Chouteau's first job was to direct a 30-man construction team that built the village of St. Louis. After his stepfather's death in 1778, he took over the family fur trading business and greatly expanded it. By 1794 he had a monopoly of trade with the Osage tribe and helped finance most of the other individuals and companies involved in the fur trade of the Louisiana Territory.

But this was not all. After the Louisiana Territory was sold to the United States 1803, Chouteau was appointed one of the three justices of the first territorial court. He would go on to hold a number of public offices over the rest of his life. When he died in 1829, he was the wealthiest citizen in St. Louis, the unofficial banker of the community, and the town's largest landowner.

St. Louis had been founded two years after the Treaty of Fontainebleau and was technically under Spanish rule. In 1765, Spain formally took possession of Upper Louisiana. However, the first Spanish governor, Antonio de Ulloa, resident in New Orleans, wisely permitted the highly experienced French personnel to stay on, not only in St. Louis but also at the two other former French centers for Indian trade—Natchitoches and Arkansas Post.

It was not until 1769 that Ulloa's replacement, General Alejandro O'Reilly, firmly asserted Spanish control and raised the Spanish flag over St. Louis. Even then, French merchants remained firmly in place. Louisiana would always remain Spanish more in name than in fact: despite Spanish efforts to encourage emigrants, there would always be far more Frenchmen than Spaniards on the ground.

In hopes of finding the Passage or at least profiting from the sea otter trade, in 1786 the French made a brief, one-time effort to get a permanent foothold on the Pacific Northwest coast. That year the French navigator La Pérouse landed on the southern shore of Alaska near Mount St. Elias. Although he suffered heavy casualties—a barge and two longboats carrying 21 men were lost in the strong currents of Lituya Bay—La Pérouse formally claimed the area for Louis XVI. He then continued southward and charted the coast from Alaska to Monterey Bay, California.

The Spaniards were becoming more worried about British and American intentions. In a 1798 letter to the viceroy, the governor of Louisiana, Manuel Gayoso de Lemos, offered a prescient warning about the threat of Anglo-American encroachment into Spanish lands:

> [They] introduce themselves in the thickness of the forests, like the Indians.... First they become acquainted with the Indians, trade with them, and afterwards engage in contraband trade with the natives of Mexico. Some stay in the [Spanish] territories.... They are settled in sufficient numbers so that they will establish their customs, laws, and religion. They will form independent states, aggregating themselves to the Federal Union, which will not refuse to receive them, and progressively they will go as far as the Pacific Ocean.[88]

In the secret Treaty of San Ildefonso (1800), Spain gave Louisiana back to France. This move pleased Napoleon because it opened the way for a French sugar empire in the Caribbean. His ambitious dreams of a new French empire in North America itself, however, were soon dashed by a slave revolt and an epidemic in Haiti. He decided to cut his losses and therefore sold Louisiana to the United States in 1803.

French objectives, hopes and fears

The French wanted to grow rich from the fur trade, to strengthen the competitive position of New France in North America, to convert the Indians, and to find the Passage. Their strategic hopes of displacing the British in North America were dashed by two events some 40 years apart. The first was Britain's victory in the Seven Years' War (1763). The second was France's inability to suppress a slave rebellion in Haiti (1803) — a setback that made Napoleon eager to get rid of Louisiana by selling it to the United States.

The loss of his planned sugar empire in Haiti and Louisiana did not weigh heavily on Napoleon. In fact, he subsequently went from strength to strength — establishing an empire, crowning himself emperor, and waging foreign wars for years without worrying about French public opinion.

4

The British: From Rupert's Land to the Pacific

WHEN IN 1493 THE SPANISH RULERS Ferdinand and Isabella received reports of Columbus's discoveries, they asked the pro–Spanish pope, Alexander VI, to define the regions that Spain and Portugal could legitimately explore and claim. In his bull *Inter Caetera* (1493), the pope accordingly drew an imaginary line of demarcation from pole to pole about 320 miles west of the Cape Verde Islands. Spain received the lands west of the line; Portugal, those east of the line.

This division gave all of the New World to Spain; Portugal got Africa and India. The Portuguese complained, however, that the division did not give them enough room to explore and settle the unknown regions of the world. The next year, the Treaty of Tordesillas (1494) redrew the demarcation line 1,185 miles west of the Cape Verde Islands. This revised boundary was supposed to resolve any conflict over newly discovered lands. To a certain extent, it worked. When a Portuguese explorer landed in Brazil in 1500, for example, he was able to claim it for his monarch under the terms of this treaty.

The English, however, had never accepted such papal divisions of the world and were quick to send out their own voyages of exploration and discovery. In 1496, the English navigator and explorer John Cabot received letters patent from King Henry VII authorizing him to search for unknown lands in the distant west. ("Letters patent" means any document, usually from the king or queen and open to public inspection, that confers a specific grant on a designated person.) Cabot was told to bring back to Bristol any goods he might buy in Asia and was authorized to hold a monopoly on the international trade thus established.

He sailed from Bristol in 1497 with a crew of 18 men in the little ship *Matthew*. Cabot made landfall in the New World, but the exact landing place remains unknown and is still the subject of scholarly dispute.[1] Possibilities include southern Labrador, Newfoundland, Nova Scotia, Cape Breton Island, the Gulf of St. Lawrence, and even as far south as Maine. In any case, Cabot took possession for the king of whatever land he reached. He also explored the strait, now known as Cabot Strait, between Newfoundland and Cape Breton Island. He returned to England in 1497 with glowing accounts of the New World: there are so many codfish on the Grand Banks, he said, that England would no longer have to get its fish from Iceland.

Based on his favorable reports, in 1498 Cabot received letters patent for a second expedition. He was authorized to return to his earlier landing place and from there to press on westward until he came to Cipango (Japan) or Cathay (China). This second expedition, probably consisting of five ships and some 200 men, set out in 1498. One ship was damaged and had to remain in Ireland. What happened to the four remaining ships remains a mystery today. It is unclear whether Cabot ever reached North America again: it seems more likely that his entire expedition was lost at sea.

In 1577, Sir Francis Drake, the most renowned seaman of the Elizabethan Age, set out to find the Passage by sailing north along the Pacific Coast. Francis Pretty, one of Drake's "Gentlemen at arms," was with him on this voyage. In 1580 Pretty, an able chronicler, wrote *The Famous Voyage of Sir Francis Drake into the South Sea, and therehence about the whole Globe of the Earth, begun in the year of our Lord 1577*. He tells us:

> On the fifth of June [1579], being in 43 degrees towards the pole Arctic [i.e., roughly off Cape Blanco, Oregon], we found the air so cold, that our men being grievously pinched with the same, complained of the extremity thereof; and the further we went, the more the cold increased upon us. Whereupon we thought it best to seek the land, and did so; finding it not mountainous, but low plain land, till we came within 38 degrees towards the line. In which height it pleased God to send us into a fair and good bay, with a good wind to enter the same. [Scholars continue to differ on where this bay was located. The conventional guess was Drake's Bay, about 30 miles northwest of San Francisco, but Bodega Bay, slightly farther north, is now thought to be more likely.], In this bay we anchored; and the people of the country [the Coast Miwok Indians], having their houses close by the water's side, shewed themselves unto us, and sent a present to our General [Drake].[2]

The Miwoks were friendly and the land was inviting. When the Englishmen had finished careening the ship, they were invited by the Indians to visit their villages. Pretty writes:

> We trevailed up into the Country to their villages, where we found herdes of deer by 1000 in a companie, being most large and fat of bodie.... There is no part of earth here to be taken up, wherein there is not a reasonable quantitie of gold or silver.... [The chief of the Miwoks] made several rations [gave several reasons] or rather supplications that [Drake] would take their province & kingdome into his hand and become their King, making signs that they would resign unto him their right and title to the whole land and become his subjects.[3]

Pretty added that "It seemeth that the Spaniards hitherto had never been in this part of the country, neither did ever discover the land by many degrees to the southwards of this place."[4] Drake thereupon took possession of the territory in the name of Queen Elizabeth I. Because the cliffs of white sand he found there so closely resembled the cliffs of Sussex in his native England, he christened it Nova [New] Albion, i.e., New England. Albion was a patriotic nickname for England.

Drake himself did not explain how far Nova Albion extended but he clearly had a great deal of territory in mind. A contemporary map by the Dutch cartographer Nicola van Sype, which Drake himself is thought to have revised and approved, divided North America into two parts. The first part began at the Gulf of California and extended east to the mouth of the Mississippi. This was New Spain. The second part, extending west from the St. Lawrence River, was New France. The remainder of the continent — that is, all of North America lying between New Spain and New France — was Drake's Nova Albion.[5]

Before he sailed, Drake left behind a small brass plate, nailed to a sturdy wooden post. This plate was to cause no end of scholarly controversy. Pretty recounts how

> At our departure hence our General set up a monument of our being there, as also of her Majesty's right and title to the same; namely a plate, nailed on a fair great post, whereupon was engraved her Majesty's name, the day and year of our arrival there, with the free giving up of the province and people into her Majesty's hands, together with her Highness' picture and arms, in a piece of six pence of current English money, under the plate, whereunder was also written the name of our General.[6]

A digression is justified here. Professor Herbert Bolton, an expert on Western history, taught at the University of California at Berkeley for many years. He always told his students about Drake's plate and always asked them to let him know if the plate ever turned up. In the 1930s, five of

Bolton's colleagues decided to play a joke on him. They made a copy of the plate, as much like the missing Elizabethan original as they could, and planted it in the hills of Marin County, north of San Francisco.

A chauffeur waiting for his quail-hunting employer found the plate and later discarded it in a meadow near San Quentin State Prison, a good distance from where it had been planted. In 1936, a driver had a flat tire and, as he waited for help to come, wandered around the meadow. He found the plate and, since Bolton's interest was well known, it was not long before the plate was in Bolton's hands. In 1937, the professor announced his find in print and at a meeting of the California Historical Society. The perpetrators of the hoax were too embarrassed to confess what they had done, so the plate was accepted as probably genuine.

Bolton died in 1953, never learning the truth about the hoax. In fact, it was not until 1977, when the 400th anniversary of Drake's world-circling voyage sparked renewed interest in his landing in California, that the plate was subjected to stringent metallurgical tests. These proved that the brass from which it was made had been rolled and engraved in the twentieth century.[7]

To return to the seventeenth century, the English navigator and explorer Henry Hudson had done his best, during four ocean voyages, to find the Passage. The first, in 1607, took him from Western Europe to Greenland and to Norway's Svalbard (Spitsbergen) archipelago. The second voyage, in 1608, was thwarted by the ice fields east of the Barents Sea. In 1609, he crossed the Atlantic and explored Maine, Cape Cod, the Chesapeake Bay, New Jersey, and the great river now known as the Hudson.

In 1610, Hudson set off on his last, fatal voyage aboard the 55-ton vessel *Discovery*. Earlier, another English explorer, Captain George Weymouth, had recorded that a "furious overfall" of water gushed out with each ebb tide at what is now Hudson Strait. This suggested to Hudson that a great body of water, namely, the Pacific Ocean, lay just beyond the strait. Always looking for the Passage, he sailed into James Bay (the southernmost arm of Hudson Bay). When winter came, his ship was frozen in the ice.

Hudson was a great Arctic explorer but he was a very poor leader of men, being stubborn, capricious and unfair. In the spring of 1611, once the ship was free of the ice Hudson wanted to sail northwest in hopes of finding a route to the Pacific, but his crew mutinied. Hudson, his son, and a few loyal sailors were forced into a small open boat and were set adrift. They may have managed to reach the shore and build a rudimentary shelter there, but they were never heard from again. Only a handful of the mutineers made it back to England aboard *Discovery*.

This was not only an era of active exploration: the fur trade boomed as well. In the 1660s, two *voyageurs*—Pierre Esprit Radisson and Médard Chouart des Groseilliers—became annoyed by the high cost of sending their furs back to Quebec by canoe and then having to pay a stiff tax on them. They thought there must be a better way for them to make money in the fur trade. They therefore made their way to first New England and thence to England. In London they were able to persuade a group of merchants that great riches could be gained by controlling the fur trade in the *interior* of Canada, i.e., close to the source of the furs themselves.

Consequently, in 1670, a new enterprise with the weighty title of the "Governor and Company of Adventurers of England Trading into Hudsons Bay" was incorporated in London. Known as the Hudson's Bay Company or, more commonly, as the HBC, it had four major objectives: to look for the Passage, to claim for England the entire watershed of Hudson Bay, to engage in the fur trade with the Indians, and to displace the French fur traders.

King Charles II expansively granted to this company, which was governed by his cousin,

> the sole Trade and Commerce of all those Seas Streightes Bayes Rivers Lakes Creeks and Soundes in whatsoever Latitude they shall bee that lye within the entrance of the Streightes commonly called Hudsons Streightes together with all Landes and Territoryes upon the Countryes Coastes and confynes of the Seas Bays Lakes Rivers Creeks and Soundes aforesaid that are not already possessed by or granted to any of our Subjects or possessed by the Subjects of any other Christian Prince or State with the Fishing of all Sortes of Fish Whales Sturgions and all other Royal Fishes of the Seas....[8]

In return for this generous grant, which also included control over "all Mines Royal, as well discovered as not discovered, of Gold, Silver, Gems and precious Stones, to be found or discovered within the Territories,"[9] the company was only obligated to give to the English king or queen—should they ever decide to visit Hudson's Bay (which they never did)—two elk and two black beavers.[10]

The Hudson's Bay Company received exclusive trading rights in Rupert's Land, which consisted of the entire drainage basin of Hudson Bay. It will be recalled that in 1534 Cartier had claimed New France for his king, so there were now two claimants—France and England—for the same region. As suggested earlier, Rupert's Land was enormous. It embraced what is now the provinces of Ontario and Quebec north of the Laurentians and west of Labrador; all of Manitoba; most of Saskatchewan; the southern half of Alberta; the eastern part of Nunavut Territory; and portions of Minnesota and North Dakota in the United States. All told, this came to about 1.5 million square miles, which is more than one-third of the area of Canada today. Ultimately, in 1870, the company would sell its rights in Rupert's Land to the Canadian government.

From its headquarters at York Factory, the Hudson's Bay Company's empire grew to constitute an international trading network encompassing nearly 3,000,000 square miles of North America — stretching from the Arctic Ocean to San Francisco, and from Labrador to Hawaii.[11] York Factory itself was well positioned on the Nelson River, which had been discovered in 1612 by the English explorer Sir Thomas Button and named after the sailing master of his ship. Taken together with the Bow River and the North and South Saskatchewan rivers, the Nelson formed a 1,600-mile waterway extending as far west as the Canadian Rocky Mountains. In fact, when French explorer Pierre Esprit Radisson first reached the mouth of the Nelson in 1670, he believed that this river would become a commercial route as important as the long-sought Passage.

The man who successfully undertook the first epic explorations of western Canada was a young Englishman named Henry Kelsey (c. 1667–1724).[12] He had come to the New World around 1684 as an apprentice for the Hudson's Bay Company. His first expedition took him, in about 1686, from York Factory into the Churchill River country of northeastern Manitoba. When ice barred the passage of the ship he was on (the appropriately-named *Hopewell*), he and an Indian guide went ashore and walked about 235 miles north of the river before returning to the Hudson's Bay Company's post at Churchill.

Kelsey is described as "a very active Lad, delighting much in Indian company."[13] On that first journey, he proved himself more courageous than his Indian guide. The guide did not want to go further north. He made Kelsey speak in whispers out of fear that the dreaded Inuit (Eskimos) might hear them. He berated Kelsey for being a fool who "was not sensible of dangers."[14]

Some of the details of Kelsey's most famous journey are indistinct; secondary accounts differ because his own journal was written in part in poetry and was imprecise in other aspects as well. What is clear is that his great adventure began in 1690, when he headed southwest from York Factory to open trade relations with Indian tribes in western Canada. He first made his way to Moose Lake, close to the Manitoba-Saskatchewan border. There he claimed the entire region for the Hudson's Bay Company and wintered near the Saskatchewan River. Next summer (1691), he went by canoe and on foot to the prairie grasslands southwest of The Pas (near Moose Lake) in central Saskatchewan. There he met the Assiniboin Indians and possibly the Sioux and Gros Ventre ("Big Belly") Indians as well.

During these travels, Kelsey wrote the first Canadian descriptions of the grizzly bear and the buffalo and compiled ethnographic notes on the Indians. He returned to York Factory in the summer of 1692 with a full load of furs. Thanks to King William's War (1689–1697), however, he had to surrender York Factory to the French, but eventually returned there in 1714. Appointed overseas governor of all Hudson's Bay Company settlements in 1717, Kelsey opened trade with the Inuit and, later, conducted further explorations of Inuit lands.

Despite Kelsey's achievements as an explorer — he was the first European to visit the interior plains of Canada and the first live intimately with Indians of Canada's western and northern regions — virtually nothing came of his work.[15] As DeVoto summarized the situation it with his usual felicity,

> In fact Kelsey's great feat was without issue or consequence. It shines like a shooting star in the annals of discovery and then the sky is dark again. At York Factory, he "had my labour for my travell [travail, i.e., pains]" and it was as if the first penetration of the northern plains had never been. The [Hudson's Bay] Company saw no reason to follow it up, no reason to send anyone after him — let the wild men [Indians with furs to trade] come to the Bay. The trace he had made across the void vanished completely from awareness.[16]

Although the Trans-Mississippi West is the primary focus of this book, it is now worthwhile to pause here and see what the British were doing *east of the Mississippi*.

In 1607, Jamestown — the first English colony in North America — was founded in Virginia. The English colonists, however, were much less adventurous than their continental European rivals. They doubted that the Appalachian mountain chain could ever be crossed by heavy wagons drawn by horses or oxen. They feared the unknown but surely ferocious tribes of Indians who dwelt there. They worried that, if they did manage to cross the mountains, they would then find themselves in New Spain, whose borders were undefined. If so, they told each other, the Spaniards would surely capture or kill them. For all these reasons, these colonists did not stray far from their familiar Piedmont.

It is not surprising, then, that in his definitive 400-page study on *The Explorers of North America, 1492–1806*, which was published in 1933, the historian John Bartlet Brebner could devote only 36 pages to British exploration in what is now the United States.[17] Most of these modest British expeditions have now been long forgotten, except by specialists. In contrast, the names of the great Spanish and French explorers of North America — de Soto, Coronado, Champlain, and La Salle — can still strike responsive chords with modern readers.

With the possible exceptions of John Smith of Pocahontas fame[18] and the Kentucky frontiersman Daniel Boone, the names of the early British explorers of North America are quite unknown to most of us today. Nevertheless, it is still useful to summarize the broad outlines of British exploration east of the Mississippi[19]:

- By 1700 all the major river valleys, which served as the main transportation corridor east of the Appalachians, had been found, explored and mapped. Colonial adventurers had made their way into the Deep South and had ventured out onto the trans–Appalachian waterways — onto the Ohio, the Tennessee, and the Mississippi rivers. These men had three objectives: harvesting animal pelts, chiefly deer skins and bear skins; claiming land for themselves or their sponsors; and looking for the Passage.
- In the eighteenth century, English fur traders began to filter over the Appalachian mountains and ranged westward from Pennsylvania and Virginia into the valley of the Ohio River. By 1748, there were already 300 of them on the ground. They threatened the French fur trade in the region and were in a strong position to cut off the flow of French goods between Canada and Louisiana if they so desired. Indeed, in 1748, the French commander of the Illinois Country even complained that, to add insult to injury, the Englishmen were inciting the Indians along the Mississippi to protest against French rule.[20]
- In 1750, the Virginia-based Ohio Company sent Christopher Gist to explore the 200,000 acres around the forks of the Ohio River that a British royal charter had granted to the company the year before. One of the earliest investors in the Ohio Company was George Washington. This was the first organized group to try to develop the area west of the Alleghenies. Its activities were seen by the French as a direct challenge to French claims to the region. This international rivalry helped to spark the French and Indian War.
- In 1763, the British issued a royal decree (the Proclamation of 1763) that prohibited British colonists in North America from settling west of an imaginary line extending along the crest of the Appalachian Mountains. In theory, the whole area was to be reserved for the Indians. But since this "Indian country" was a big and inviting region (the Proclamation line ran roughly from New Brunswick all the way to Georgia), many British settlers decided to move there anyway.
- In Kentucky, the famous explorer and trailblazer Daniel Boone opened the southern trans–Appalachian frontier by blazing a 200-

mile track, known as the Wilderness Road, across the mountains. Boone's first biographer was Timothy Flint, who knew Boone personally. Flint reminds us that as late as 1760,

> the country west of the Cumberland mountains was considered by the inhabitants of Carolina and Virginia, as involved in something of the same obscurity which lay over the American continent, after its first discovery by Columbus.... The real danger attending the first exploration of a country filled with wild animals and savages; and the difficulty of carrying a sufficient supply of ammunition to procure food, during a long journey, had prevented any attempt of this kind. The Allegheny mountains had hitherto stood an unsurmounted barrier between the Atlantic country and the shores of the beautiful Ohio.[21]

- It was over the Wilderness Road that Boone, in 1775, led the first party of settlers into Kentucky through the Cumberland Gap between Virginia and Kentucky. The Wilderness Road began as a narrow path but it was gradually improved. Ultimately, it would become one of the primary routes from Virginia into the Ohio River country and thence into the Trans-Mississippi West.[22]

To return now to frontier developments in Canada itself:

French influence in the interior of Canada began to decline and British influence began to increase. In 1713, the Treaty of Utrecht had awarded all of Rupert's Land to Britain. Fifty years later, Britain won the Seven Years' War. Under the terms of the Treaty of Paris (1763), France had to surrender to Britain all of Canada; all territory in North America east of the Mississippi; and, in the Caribbean, St. Vincent, Tobago, and Dominica. Spain, France's ally in the war, had to cede Florida to Britain but as compensation received the Louisiana Territory and New Orleans from the French.

France's defeat in the Seven Years' War spelled the end of the French empire in North America and a great expansion of English holdings there. One result was that the *coureurs de bois* and other French traders now worked alongside the hard-bitten Scottish immigrants who emigrated to North America to escape the rapacious landlords and other tribulations of life in rural Scotland.

The geography of the interior of North America, however, was still largely unknown. By the latter half of the eighteenth century, the pyramidal height-of-land theory was thought to offer the best explanation of likely river patterns in North America.[23] As mentioned earlier, this concept held that the headwaters of four major river systems in North America all flowed from a single pyramidal height-of-land somewhere in the West and that one of these rivers would give easy access to the Pacific.

Two British men — Robert Rogers and Jonathan Carver — were among the earliest advocates of this theory. In a petition to Parliament in 1765, Rogers, who had been a hero during the French and Indian War, asked for, but did not receive, government funding to lead an expedition westward from the Great Lakes. He hoped to find the height-of-land that was the source of the Mississippi River and of the Ouragan (Oregon) River, another name for the mythical Great River of the West.

In his *Concise Account of North America*, published in London in 1765, Rogers asserted that the mountains of the western interior were all "situated in the center, and are the highest lands in North America." From these central highlands, he claimed, the rivers flowed in every direction and "by these rivers the continent is divided into many departments, as it were from a center."[24] Although he had never been to the Trans-Mississippi West himself, Rogers did not hesitate to proclaim that "There is perhaps no finer country in the world than that which lies extended on each side of the Missouri."[25] One of Rogers' most appreciative readers was Thomas Jefferson, who recommended that the *Concise Account* be included in the roster of books for a national library.[26]

Rogers never got anywhere near the Pacific but one of his lieutenants, Jonathan Carver of Connecticut, originally a shoemaker and later a captain in the British colonial militia, managed to make his way to the upper Mississippi Valley. Carver was also looking for the pyramidal height-of-land, which, he speculated, would form the northern terminus of the Rocky Mountains. There he believed, "a number of rivers arise, and empty themselves either into the South Sea, into Hudson's Bay, or into the waters that communicate between these two seas."[27] He identified these rivers as the "four most capital rivers of the Continent of North America, *viz*. the St. Lawrence, the Mississippie, the River Bourbon [the Nelson], and the Oregan [Oregon), or River of the West."[28]

Carver was quite wrong on this particular point but he was certainly right when he predicted that one day the Mississippi itself would become a great artery of commerce. It would, he said, "enable the inhabitants to establish an intercourse with foreign climes, equally as well as the Euphrates, the Nile, the Danube, or the Volga do those people who dwell on their banks."[29]

Despite or perhaps because of his vaulting ambitions, Carver suffered a number of severe financial setbacks. The first edition of his *Travels through the Interior Parts of North America in the Years 1766, 1767, and 1768* appeared in 1778. It contained invaluable accounts of his first-hand experiences with the Sioux, with whom he wintered. Although marred by exaggerated stories and by passages plagiarized from other authors, his book soon became a bestseller and went through at least 32 editions. It has been called "the first genuinely popular American travel book."[30]

Carver himself, however, made very little money from it. He died, poverty-stricken, in 1780, probably of malnutrition. By a remarkable stroke of luck, however, in the early 1900s his original journals were discovered in the British Museum. They make it clear that it was Carver's editor, not Carver himself, who was responsible for the shortcomings of his book. It has now been well received by modern historians.[31]

Although after 1763 the French empire in Canada was taken over by the British, French influence continued in the fur trade west of the Great Lakes for many years. In 1767, for example, more than 85 percent of the traders who came to Fort Mackinac each summer to trade furs were French. The trade goods came from Britain, but they were transported and sold to the Indians by French *voyageurs*. National boundaries were notoriously vague then. In fact, when British observers looked across the Mississippi, what they saw there was "a Strange Mixture of French and Spanish Government ... so there is no knowing to whom the Country belongs."[32]

The British hoped to extend their influence all the way to the Pacific. In 1768, Sir Guy Carleton, governor of Quebec, recommended that British traders from Montreal mount an expedition to cross the continent and reach the Pacific coast. After wintering in the Great Lakes region, he explained, they could press on early in the spring and reach the Pacific well before the next winter set in. Once on the coast, he was sure that they would "find out a good port, take its latitude, longitude, and describe it so accurately as to enable our ships from the East Indies to find it out with ease, and return the year following."[33] Although nothing specific came of this proposal, it did reveal the direction of British political and commercial thought: a trans–Pacific trade headquartered in Montreal.

One of the first specific steps into the West came in 1774, when the British fur trader Samuel Hearne built Cumberland House, the first Hudson's Bay Company post located deep in the interior. Situated on Cumberland Lake (a tributary of the Saskatchewan River) about 175 miles west of Lake Winnipeg, it soon became the most important of the Company's western posts. Cumberland House competed head-to-head with the independent French traders who had been bartering with local Indians in their villages, exchanging goods with them near the source of the furs and thereby choking off the flow of furs to the Hudson's Bay Company itself.

Such itinerant peddling, known as *en dérouine*, meant that traders went out to meet the Indians in their own villages, i.e., far away from the trading posts. The sharp reduction in the supply of furs due to this new system of competition forced the Hudson's Bay Company to change its traditional "wait-by-the-Bay" strategy, which critics were denouncing as its "sleep by the frozen sea" strategy. The company soon found that it really had no choice but to expand westward, vigorously, if it hoped to compete.[34]

Well situated because it was accessible from several river systems and was close to three bands of fur-rich Indians, Cumberland House quickly became an important trading center.[35] In fact, to remain competitive the rival North West Company was forced to build a post of its own close nearby. Rivalries between Hudson's Bay Company and North West Company traders were so intense that they pushed the fur trade ever-deeper into the western interior of Canada and then over the Rocky Mountains into British Columbia.[36] Cumberland House eventually became the residence of the governor of Rupert's Land and is now preserved as part of Cumberland House National Historic Park.

In 1776, Britain's great navigator, Captain James Cook, set out on his third and final voyage with two ships: *Resolution* and *Discovery*. On his first voyage, he had surveyed Tahiti, New Zealand, and Australia; on his second, he had explored Antarctica. As stated on the title page of his celebrated book, *A Voyage to the Pacific Ocean*, which was published by the British Admiralty in 1784, this third venture was undertaken at the king's express command "for making Discoveries in the Northern Hemisphere. To determine the Position and Extent of the West Side of North America; its Distance from Asia; and the Practicability of a Northern Passage to Europe."[37]

Cook's primary mission was "to find out a Northern passage by sea from the Pacific to the Atlantic Ocean" by proceeding "Northward along the [Pacific] Coast as far as the Latitude of 65° [the Bering Strait]." He was directed "very carefully to search for, and to explore, such Rivers or Inlets as may appear to be of a considerable extent and pointing towards Hudsons or Baffins Bays."[38]

Following these instructions, he reached Cape Foulweather on the Oregon coast in March 1778. Poor visibility and the danger of running around on these uncharted shores often hampered his explorations. Cook's lieutenant, John Rickman, bemoaned "a series of the most tempestuous weather that ever blew," while a fellow seaman, surgeon's mate David Samwell, recorded

> Squally Wr [weather], with fogs & frequent Showers of Snow, Hail and Sleet, which made it very dangerous to approach this unknown Coast too near where we knew of no Shelter, we were kept cruizing off & on the Land till ... we luckily discovered a Harbour ... [this was Nootka Sound] into which we stood [sailed].[39]

Because of the consistently bad weather, Cook was forced to stand far off the coast most of the time, thus getting only a vague impression of the shoreline. For this reason, he did not notice the mouths of the Columbia or of the Strait of Juan de Fuca. He thought that Vancouver Island was the mainland of British Columbia and did not see either the Queen Charlotte Islands or the Alexander Archipelago.

Nevertheless, he expressed great pleasure with the warm welcome received from the Indians living at Friendly Cove on Nootka Sound, on the western shore of Vancouver Island. He anchored there in March 1778 and spent two months repairing his ships. Cook wrote:

> We found the coast to be inhabited and the people came off to the Ships in Canoes without shewing the least mark of fear or distrust.... They ... shewed great readiness to part with any thing they had and took whatever was offered them in exchange, but were more desireous of iron than any thing else.[40]

Cook was the first European to set foot on these shores and, as might be expected, he immediately claimed them and all the surrounding territory for Britain. His crew gave the Indians of Nootka some trinkets of little value and received 1,500 sea otter pelts in return, which were worth a fortune in China. Cook tells us that

> Amongst those who came aboard was a good-looking middle-aged man whom we afterward found to be the Chief. He was clothed in a dress made of the sea-otter's skin; and he had on his head such a cap as is worn by the people of King George's Sound [Nootka Sound], ornamented with sky-blue glass beads. Any sort of beads, however, appeared to be in high estimation of these people; and they readily gave whatever they had in exchange for them; even their fine sea-otter skins.[41]

At a time when a common laborer ashore earned less than a dollar a day, one of Cook's midshipmen traded the rim of a broken iron bucket (which could be hammered into a knife blade) for a flawless sea otter pelt, which he later sold at Canton for $300.[42] As John Ledyard, an American who sailed with Cook, tells us, "skins which did not cost the purchaser sixpence sterling sold in China for 100 dollars."[43]

The Nookas were not slow to see how valuable these pelts were to the Europeans and Americans. By 1793, Lieutenant Peter Puget could note that "taking the Sea Otter ... now engages all their Attention, that they may have a good Collection of Furs to purchase European Commodities."[44] Cook continued up the coast to the Aleutians, where he met Russian fur traders but did not find the Passage.

As one of his officers recorded,

> Captain Cook having now run along the western Coast of America till he fell in with the Coast of Asia [i.e., the Chukchi Peninsula].... He has proved that there is no passage through the Continent of America; for tho' we did not keep the Land in Sight all the way, yet the shoal water we had all along affords

a sufficient Proof of the Continuation of the Coast, & precludes the possibility of any considerable opening in that short Space of it which we did not see which lies between. We are now in Bering's Straights which divided Asia from America as high as these two Continents are known, our only hopes of a Passage now is round the Northern Extremity of America.[45]

Cook then sailed south to Hawaii, where he was at first received as a god by the natives but was then killed by them in a skirmish in November 1778. His journals survived, however, and were published in 1783-1784 when his men finally returned to England. These works, which described the rich furs to be had for the taking in the Pacific Northwest, spurred Britain, France, and the United States to join Russia and Spain in a spirited international competition there.

Cook's journals changed the course of history along the Pacific Northwest coast by calling the world's attention to the sea otter trade and by endorsing it, albeit cautiously. He wrote:

> There is no doubt but that a very beneficial fur trade might be carried on with the inhabitants of this vast coast, but unless a northern passage is found it seems rather too remote for Great Britain to receive any emolument from it. It must however be observed that the most, nay the only valuable skins, I saw amongst [the Indians] was the Sea Beaver, or Sea Otter as some call it; all other skins that I saw were of an inferior kind, the foxes and Martins in particular.[46]

> The fur of these animals [sea otters] ... is certainly softer and finer than any others we know of; and, therefore, the discovery of this part of the continent of North America, where so valuable an article of commerce may be met with, cannot be a matter of indifference.[47]

Cook was right about the fur. At 850,000 to one million hairs per square inch, sea otters have the thickest fur of any mammal. It provides excellent insulation in the cold waters of the Pacific Ocean. It works so well because a layer of air is trapped next to the skin and prevents it from getting wet. In fact, the fur of sea otter pups traps so much air that they cannot dive underwater. When their mothers leave them in order to hunt for food, they wrap the pups in a frond of kelp. The buoyant pups float on the surface of the sea like so many corks.[48]

The first expedition specifically sent out to hunt sea otters was the 1785 voyage of the 60-ton brig *Sea Otter* under the command of James Hanna. He collected 560 skins and sold them in Canton in 1786 for a goodly profit.[49] A world-circling, westerly commerce soon got underway. This was a trade in which the coastal Indians at first had the upper hand because it was they who provided the basic component — the sea otter furs.

This is how the trade worked. European and American ships laden with manufactured goods sailed around Cape Horn and exchanged their cargoes on the Pacific Northwest coast for sea otter pelts. Then they stood out to sea again, bound for China. There they sold the furs and bought silks, spices and tea with the proceeds. At last, they headed home around the Cape of Good Hope and sold their Chinese goods at American or European ports.

When he was the American ambassador to France, Thomas Jefferson owned copies of three unofficial accounts of Cook's voyage, as well as the official account published in 1784. These accounts, together with the new French interest in the Pacific Northwest — as reflected in La Pérouse's expedition of 1786 — stimulated Jefferson's interest in finding a transcontinental path to the Pacific Ocean.

The Trans-Mississippi West became much more important to the Americans after the Revolutionary War. In the Treaty of Paris (1783), Britain was forced, among other things:

- To recognize its former colonies as the independent United States of America (while retaining Canada as a British possession).
- To accept the Mississippi River as the western boundary of the new United States.
- To guarantee the right of navigation on the Mississippi. As Article 8 put it, "The navigation of the river Mississippi, from its source to the ocean, shall forever remain free and open to the subjects of Great Britain and the citizens of the United States."

Similarly, Canada became more important to the British, thanks to its lucrative fur trade. A new company appeared on the scene. Founded in 1783 to compete with the long-established and very powerful Hudson's Bay Company, the new North West Company was based in Montreal. The historian Barry Gough has aptly described Montreal at that time as

> a place of intense vitality ... an old French town that the English and Scots had flooded into after the fall of the place in 1760. The fur trade of Canada offered immense wealth, and the English and French both intended to maximize their gains in this avenue of commerce."[50]

The North West Company divided the vast territory it exploited into two major regions: the *grand nord* ("great north") and the *petit nord* ("little north"). The *grand nord* included the unexplored or only lightly explored lands west and north of Lake Winnipeg. The *petit nord* was the area bordered on the south by Lake Superior, on the west by Lake Winnipeg, on the north by the Hudson Bay lowlands, and on the east by the divide between the Albany and Moose rivers in Ontario.[51]

Staffed by Scottish merchants and French canoemen, the North West Company collected furs from Indians in the Lake Superior region and in the valleys of the Red, Assiniboine, and Saskatchewan rivers. One of North West Company's key goals was to monopolize the supply of furs close to their source. Failing to understand how successful this innovative strategy would prove to be, the more sedate men of the long-established Hudson's Bay Company looked down on these newcomers and referred to them derisively as "pedlars."

The North West Company built a trading post at Sault Sainte Marie in 1783 and would later build a lock there to handle its trade canoes and small boats. The company then spread northwest toward the shores of the Arctic. Its northernmost outpost was Fort Chipewyan, constructed at Lake Athabasca on the northern Saskatchewan-Alberta border in 1788. This area was bitterly cold, even by Canadian standards. Duncan M'Gillivray, an experienced trader, confided to his journal that in order to live there, "One ought to have his Blood composed of Brandy, his Body of Brass and his Eyes of Glass."[52]

Despite its numbing climate, however, the Lake Athabasca region proved to be so rich both in "staple fur" (beaver) and "fancy furs" (mink, marten, fisher, etc.) that ambitious traders were eager to become *hivernants*— men who spent the long, dark winters there. In fact, between 1775 and 1820, at least 23 fur trading posts were built in northern Saskatchewan and were manned year-round.[53]

The company's traders, known as Northwesters, or Nor'Westers for short, were highly competitive, aggressive men. Because canoes could not be used on frozen rivers and lakes during winter, the North West Company devised an elaborate transportation network that required two sets of canoes and crews.[54] A storage facility, initially set up on the western short of Lake Superior at Grand Portage and later moved to Thunder Bay, Ontario, was the rendezvous and turn-around point for two different canoe brigades.

The first brigade, paddling westward, brought trade goods from Montreal to Grand Portage; the second brigade, paddling eastward, brought furs from the interior to Grand Portage. The brigades met at Grand Portage in mid–May and exchanged goods and furs there. By the end of July, they were on their way home again. In this manner, furs moved east, and trade goods moved west, during the five ice-free months of the year.

The full cycle of trade, however, required up to three years to complete. This was the amount of time that elapsed between the initial shipment of trade goods from London to Montreal, on the one hand, and the final sale of Canadian furs in London, on the other. During this long period, the trade was highly vulnerable to price shifts caused by unpredictable factors. Canoes could overturn in the rapids, destroying crews, trade goods and furs alike. Indians could die from epidemics or could fail to harvest enough furs. Ocean storms or shallow-water rocks and shoals could sink big ships carrying goods and furs. High profits could be made in the fur trade when all went well, but it always remained a highly speculative business.

North West Company traders made a special point of plying their Indian customers with "high wine." This potent brew was made by stirring together brandy, dark rum, sweet sherry, tawny port, cloves, nutmeg, and cinnamon. The resulting mixture was then diluted with enough water to make it go as far as possible but not so much as to lessen its alcoholic impact too much. The historian W.J. Eccles tells us that

> Despite the efforts of the British authorities at Quebec, these traders, totally without scruples, used liquor in the trade to a degree unknown previously.... The Far West was flooded with the wine. The Indian nations became totally debauched. Once addicted, the Indians would do virtually anything to get more, including trap the animals to extinction. They refused to trade meat supplies at the trading posts for anything but liquor.[55]

Indians had a very low tolerance for alcohol and usually drank to excess whenever they had the chance. The results were predictable. A trader at a Red River post south of Lake Winnipeg made this laconic entry in his journal:

> Indians having asked for liquor, and promised to decamp and hunt well, I gave them some. Grand Gueule ["Big Mouth"] stabbed Capot Rouge ["Red Coat"], Le Boeuf ["The Ox"] stabbed his young wife in the arm, Little Shell almost beat his old mother's brains out with a club, and there was terrible fighting among them. I sowed garden seeds.[56]

A similar account comes from John Tanner, who was captured in Kentucky by the Shawnees in 1789, when he was nine years old and who grew up to become a leader of the tribe. He told a sympathetic doctor, who published his story in 1830, that

> In the course of a single day, Net-no-kwa sold one hundred and twenty beaver skins, with a large quantity of buffalo robes, dressed and smoked skins, and other articles for rum.... Of all our large load of peltries, the produce of so many days of toil, of so many long and difficult journeys, one blanket, and three kegs of rum, only remained, besides the poor and almost worn-out cloathing on our bodies.[57]

The men of the North West Company pioneered the Oregon Country, building posts in Idaho and Washington. As a result, rivalry with the Hudson's Bay Company became more intense. It would last for nearly 40 years.

During the 1790s, this competition forced the Hudson's Bay Company to develop a new type of boat, known as the York Boat, which is described in Appendix 8. Rivalry sometimes erupted into violence. This distressing state of affairs went on until 1821. At that point, the British government stepped in and forced the rivals to settle their differences peacefully. They did so, and subsequently merged under the banner and charter of the Hudson's Bay Company, which took over the fur-trading regions formerly exploited by the North West Company.

When he left the Royal Navy after the Treaty of Paris in 1783, British Lieutenant John Meares joined the merchant navy and subsequently became involved in the search for the Passage. He was one of the pioneers of the sea otter trade — a keen international interest in which had been sparked by the publication of Captain Cook's journals.[58] As Meares himself was the first to admit, "To Captain Cook ... we are indebted for the commerce of the North West Coast of America, and its profitable application to the China market...."[59]

Meares' initial trading venture on the Pacific Northwest coast in 1786-1787 was not a great success. Arriving too late in the season to trade, he had only two choices: to winter where he was (in Prince William Sound, Alaska) or to winter in Hawaii. Fearing that he would lose most of his crew to the girls and sunshine of Hawaii, he made the understandable but unfortunate decision to remain at Prince William Sound. The result was that he lost 23 sailors due to cold, scurvy, and smoke from the fires that he had to keep burning below deck for 24 hours a day to keep the ice at bay.

His second voyage (1788) was more rewarding. Meares anchored in Nootka Sound on the western coast of Vancouver Island. There he built the first ship ever constructed by Europeans on this coast (the 48-foot schooner *Northwest America*), as well as the first building erected by foreigners. He also explored southwards, taking note of the outflow of the Columbia River, which he undoubtedly would have entered had he been able to find a way through the heavy breakers guarding its mouth. Meares continued south along the coast and then sailed to China with a cargo of sea otter pelts.

One incident in what has been termed the "swirl of nations" along the Pacific Northwest coast nearly sparked a war between Britain and Spain.[60] In 1789, Nootka Sound became such a flash point of rival imperial designs that this obscure anchorage turned into an important pawn in the history of the North American continent.[61] This state of affairs arose during Meares' third voyage (1789).

The Spanish warship *Princessa* under the command of Estéban José Martínez had reached Nootka in May 1789 with orders from the viceroy of New Spain to take possession of the territory and set up a permanent colony there. The Spaniards claimed sovereignty over the whole northwestern coast of America, basing their claim on the papal bull *Inter Caetera* (1493). They asserted that sovereignty was legally established as soon as Spanish explorers had formally taken possession of an area. The British, in contrast, held that sovereignty could be established only by physical occupation of the land.

Martínez promptly seized one of Meares' ships—the 200-ton *Iphigenia Nubiana*—and charged her captain, William Douglas, with entering Spanish territory illegally. Although Martínez soon released the ship, he made Douglas sign a document that effectively transferred the title of the ship to Spain. Martínez later seized three more British ships and their crews. The ships were *Northwest America*, which he rechristened *Santa Gertrudis la Magna* and planned to use for trade and exploration; *Argonaut*, which he sent with her captain and crew to San Blas; and *Princess Royal*, renamed *Princesa Real* and sent south to Mexico as well.

News of these Spanish seizures reached London in January 1790 and official letters began to fly back and forth between London and Madrid. Meares himself arrived in London in April 1790. He claimed damages and gave a first-hand, if self-serving, account of what had happened. Although King George III's advisors asked the king to mobilize Britain for war, he did not do so. The controversy simmered along until the Spanish king Carlos IV prudently concluded that he could not win a war with Britain, especially since Prussia was backing the British. Carlos therefore saw no option but to yield.

This decision set in motion the first Nootka convention (1790). Under its terms, the Spanish agreed to release the British ships and sailors. Moreover, Spain accorded to Britain equal trading, fishing, and settlement rights (on unoccupied land), not only along the Northwest coast but also in the Pacific as well. The convention stated that

> It is agreed that the buildings and tracts of land situated on the northwest Coast of the Continent of North America, or on islands adjacent to that continent, of which the subjects of His Britannic Majesty were dispossessed about the month of April 1789 by a Spanish officer [Martínez], shall be restored to the said British subjects.... [Both British and Spanish subjects] shall have free access [to the whole region] and shall carry on their commerce without disturbance or molestation.[62]

The second Nootka convention (1793) reimbursed Meares for the damages he had suffered. A third convention (1794) provided that

> Their Majesties have further agreed that [the port of Nootka Sound] shall be free for the Subjects of both Nations to frequent occasionally the aforesaid Port and to construct there temporary Buildings.... But that neither One nor

the Other shall make any permanent establishment ... or claim there any right of Sovereignty or Territorial Dominion to the Exclusion of the Other ... [and to assist each other] to maintain to their Subjects free Access to said Port of Nootka against any other Nation which should attempt to establish there any Sovereignty or Dominion....[63]

When the Nootka Sound affair was finally settled in 1795, Spain agreed to abandon its fort there and its claim to exclusive sovereignty, but it did not thereupon relinquish its claims to other parts of the Pacific Northwest coast. Nevertheless, the Spaniards were not enamored of this region: they denounced it, privately, as a "useless territory" which had "a horrible and insufferable climate" and was inhabited only by "savage Indians."[64]

The Spanish naturalist Moziño lived at Nootka Sound for five months and seems to have shared this view. He argued that the fort there should be abandoned: it ran up "enormous expenses" and had "not produced any advantage in favor of the crown."[65] He believed that the Spaniards should retrench to San Francisco. As he put it with no little eloquence,

> The first object of our attentions should be California. There our conquest has taken roots, our religion has been propagated, and our hopes are greatest for obtaining advantages to benefit all the monarchy ... [the harbor of San Francisco] is the best of any that we have seen on the entire coast.... The landscape is very beautiful, the soil fertile, the mountains wooded, and the climate benign.[66]

Between 1792 and 1794, the celebrated British navigator and explorer George Vancouver successfully completed one of the most difficult surveys undertaken up to that time — accurately charting the Pacific coast between Point Arena (about 90 miles north of San Francisco) and Alaska. He was sent to the Pacific Northwest with three assignments: to negotiate with the Spaniards at Nootka Sound to settle the damage claims arising from the their seizures of British ships in 1789; to chart the coast between California and Alaska; and to determine whether a Passage actually existed.[67]

On this latter point, his instructions were to gain accurate information "with respect to the nature and extent of any water-communication which may tend, in any considerable degree, to facilitate an intercourse, for the purpose of commerce, between the northwest coast and the country upon the opposite of the continent."[68] In compliance with his sailing orders, he first reached the California coast off Point Arena in 1792 and from there he surveyed the coast, with the greatest care, north to Queen Charlotte Sound.[69]

Vancouver was the first European to circumnavigate Vancouver Island. He sailed through the Straits of Juan de Fuca and Georgia, threaded his way through the narrow intricate waterways north of Desolation Sound, and then returned via the west side of Vancouver Island. He was always painstaking in his efforts to disprove the existence of the Passage, using open boats for this purpose because they were shallow-draft and easily maneuverable under oars. His charts would prove to be so accurate that they were still being used by navigators in the late 1800s.

Vancouver tells us:

> I became thoroughly convinced, that our boats alone could enable us to acquire any correct or satisfactory information respecting this broken country; and although the execution of such service in open boats would necessarily be extremely laborious, and expose those so employed to numberless dangers, and unpleasant situations, that might occasionally produce great fatigue, and protract their return to the ships, yet that mode was undoubtedly the most accurate, the most ready, and indeed the only one in our power to pursue for ascertaining the continental boundary.[70]

His first landing was at Discovery Bay on the Strait of Juan de Fuca. He claimed for Britain all of the Puget Sound country, that is to say, the inland waters of Washington. His magisterial three-volume work, *A Voyage of Discovery to the North Pacific Ocean, and Round the World in Which the Coast of North-West America has been Carefully Examined and Accurately Surveyed*, was buttressed by an atlas of maps and plates. Published in 1798, it is still justly famous today.

In subsequent years, he continued the survey as far north as Cook Inlet in Alaska. In so doing, he disproved, once and for all, the existence of the fabled Passage. Captain Cook had cast grave doubt on the existence of any passage but he had not proved *conclusively* that it did not exist. For the safety of his ship and crew, Cook had usually remained well off the coast.

Vancouver was very proud of what he had accomplished, later writing that

> I trust the precision with which the survey of the coast of North West America has been carried into effect will set aside every opinion of a north-west passage. No small portion of facetious mirth passed among the seamen in consequence of our sailing ... for the purpose of discovering a north-west passage, by following up the discoveries of [earlier explorers], and a numerous train of hypothetical navigators.[71]

A word about the international background of Vancouver's voyages may be helpful here.[72] During this era, Russian fur traders were moving through the Aleutian Islands towards Alaska and its panhandle. For their part, British and American traders were actively bartering for sea otter pelts farther south along the Pacific Northwest coast. Spain, which claimed possession of the entire coast between Cook Inlet and California, was worried by these incursions. The Spaniards therefore sent expeditions north to see what was going on. Finally, in 1789 they decided to build, at Nootka Sound, a outpost known as Fort San Miguel.

This was the northernmost fort of New Spain. It was constructed at Nootka to show the Spanish flag and to establish a claim to sovereignty, not to be a formidable military asset. In fact, a visitor would report in 1792 that "Their fort is no great thing, mounted with 6 Twenty four and four and Thirty six pounders ... the platforms would not bear the weight of the metal [i.e., the cannons had to be mounted directly on the ground]."[73] Manned by a unit known as the Catalonian Volunteers, the fort consisted of six buildings of various sizes, the largest of which was said to be capable of holding 100 people and was well-built and constructed to repel the winds and cold rains of winter.

In late August 1792 Vancouver met with the Spaniards at Nootka Sound but their negotiations, although conducted amicably, failed to resolve the outstanding issues. Despite the historic rivalry between Britain and Spain in North America, their naval officers had lost none of their polished politeness when dealing with each other. For example, an entry in the diary of Spanish Commanders Don Dionisio Galiano and Don Cayetano Valdéz, who explored the Strait of Juan de Fuca in 1792 aboard the schooners *Sútil* and *Mexicana*, runs as follows:

> At 7 in the morning we saw a vessel coming toward us. She displayed the English flag and we raised the Spanish one. When she came alongside the *Sútil* permission was asked to send the boat. This was granted and a first lieutenant [Lieutenant William Broughton] came to salute the commander. He gave us to understand that Captain Vancouver, the head of the English expedition then in that port, had sent him to salute the commander of the Spanish expedition and to make known the pleasure he would have in helping us if we needed anything, and that we would find fresh water at that anchorage, something not so easily found.[74]

Thorough as his surveys were, Vancouver did make a number of errors. Perhaps the most striking was his failure to chart the Columbia River. In his journal, he explains that when he was off Cape Disappointment he noticed that

> The sea had now changed from its natural, to river colloured water; the probable consequence of some streams falling into the bay, or into the ocean north of it. Not considering the opening to be worthy of more attention, I continued our pursuit to the NW, being desirous to embrace the advantages of the now prevailing breeze and pleasant weather, so favorable to our examination of the coast.....[75]

Later, Lieutenant Broughton anchored the armed tender *Chatham* off the mouth of the Columbia. He led a boat expedition through the breakers and then up the river for one week, getting about one hundred miles upstream and taking possession of the land for Britain. Although Edward Bell, *Chatham*'s clerk, believed that "this River *might* communicate with some of the Lakes at the opposite side of the Continent," Broughton himself reached the conclusion that the Columbia "could hardly be considered as navigable for shipping."[76]

By Vancouver's time, many of the Indians of the Pacific Northwest coast were becoming used to European and American mariners. "The inhabitants," he reports, "seemed to view us with the utmost indifference and unconcern; they continued to fish before their huts as regardless of our being present, as if such vessels had been familiar to them, and unworthy of their attention."[77]

The Indians were in most cases friendly and eager to trade. Vancouver's journal tells us that

> A few of the natives in two or three canoes favored us with their company, and brought with them some fish and venison for sale. The latter was extremely good, and very acceptable, as we had not obtained any [by hunting].... Their bows and implements they freely bartered for knives, trinkets, copper, &c; and, what was very extraordinary, they offered for sale two children, each about six or seven years of age, and, being shewn some copper, were very anxious that the bargain should be closed. This, however, I peremptorily prohibited, expressing, as well as I was able, our great abhorrence of such traffic.[78]

By 1793, Vancouver had conducted surveys between Prince of Wales Island and San Luis Obispo, California. The next year he charted the coast between Cook's Inlet to San Francisco and then sailed home via Cape Horn, finally reaching Ireland in October 1795. From there, Vancouver traveled overland to London. Since leaving Falmouth in 1791, his expedition had traveled more than 65,000 miles. Out of crews totaling 180 men, only five of them died — a remarkable record for the time and one that showed Vancouver's solicitous care for his men.[79]

The first European or American to travel overland to the Pacific was the outstanding explorer and fur trader Alexander Mackenzie. Born on the west coast of Scotland, he emigrated to New York with his father when he was a boy and then went to school in Montreal. In 1779, he joined a Montreal fur trading company that later became part of the North West Company. This company ran a network of trading posts stretching west to the Canadian Rockies.

Looking back in 1801 on his long, successful and adventuresome career, Mackenzie remembered:

> I was led, at an early period of life, by commercial views, to the country North-West of Lake Superior, in North America, and being endowed by

Nature with an inquisitive mind and enterprising spirit; possessing also a constitution and frame of body equal to the most arduous undertakings, and being familiar with toilsome exertions in the prosecution of mercantile pursuits, I not only contemplated the practicability of penetrating across the continent of America, but was confident in the qualifications, as I was animated by the desire, to undertake the perilous enterprize.[80]

In 1788, with his cousin Roderick, Mackenzie set up Fort Chipewyan, a remote trading post located on Lake Athabasca in northwestern Alberta. The next year he led a death-or-glory canoe expedition, staffed by French-Canadian *voyageurs*, Indian hunters, and Indian interpreters, which successfully followed the 1,100-mile Mackenzie river from the Great Slave Lake to the delta of the river on the Arctic Ocean.

In 1793, Mackenzie set his sights on finding the elusive Passage. He set off from Fort Chipewyan, the North West Company's westernmost post, and followed the Peace River westward to its source in the Rocky Mountains of Canada. Travel was hard and unpleasant. In an entry in his "Journal of a Voyage from Fort Chipewyan to the Pacific Ocean in 1793," he tells us:

> We began our journey about twelve noon, the commencement of which was a steep ascent of about a mile; it lay along a well-beaten path, but the country through which it led was rugged and ridgy, and full of wood. When we were in a state of extreme heat, from the toil of our journey, the rain came on, and continued till the evening, and even when it ceased the underwood continued its drippings upon us.[81]

Finally, near the 55th parallel and at an altitude of only about 3,000 feet above sea level, he found, conveniently crossing the Continental Divide, "a beaten path leading over a low ridge of land eight hundred and seventeen paces in length."[82] This pass was considered to be a major discovery. As Mackenzie later told the governor general of Canada, "We carried over the height of Land (which is only 700 yards broad) that separates those Waters, the one empties into the Northern [Atlantic] Ocean, and the other into the Western [the Pacific Ocean]."[83]

Mackenzie believed that such a short, easily managed portage was all that divided the east-flowing Peace River from the west-flowing Columbia and the Pacific. In fact, however, the Peace was still a very long way from the Pacific. Mackenzie would have to follow numerous other rivers— the Finlay, Parsnip, Fraser, Dean, and Bella Coola. He succeeded in overcoming all obstacles, however, and became the first European to cross America north of Mexico. In 1793, he finally reached the mouth of the Bella Coola River at the head of the North Bentinck Arm of Burke Channel, a narrow inlet of the Pacific Ocean. Mackenzie tells us how he celebrated this achievement:

> I now mixed up some vermilion [which he had brought to trade to the Indians for use as war paint] in melted grease and inscribed, in large characters, on the South-East face of the rock on which we had slept last night, this brief memorial—
> Alexander Mackenzie, from Canada, by land, the twenty-second of July, one thousand seven hundred and ninety-three.[84]

Now recreated in red concrete, the inscription is still there today.

Mackenzie's subsequent book recounting his adventures bore a lengthy title: *Voyages from Montreal on the River St. Lawrence, Through the Continent of North America, to the Frozen and Pacific Oceans; in the Years 1789 and 1793. With a Preliminary Account of the Rise, Progress, and Present State of the Fur Trade of That Country. Illustrated with Maps.* Published in London in 1801, it was an instant success. One of the most appreciative readers was Thomas Jefferson, read this book in 1802.

Mackenzie's description of an easy crossing of the Continental Divide (it was so easy only because Mackenzie had confused the Fraser River with the upper Columbia) persuaded Jefferson that an American exploratory expedition across the continent was of critical importance and should be launched as soon as feasible. The book genuinely alarmed Jefferson because it confirmed his worst fears that the United States and Britain were about to become locked in a political and commercial power struggle in the Trans-Mississippi West.

Jefferson was especially worried by the great importance Mackenzie placed on the Columbia River. In the conclusion of the book, Mackenzie had made his views crystal clear:

> By opening this intercourse between the Atlantic and Pacific Oceans, and forming regular establishments through the interior, and at both extremes, as well as along the coasts and islands, the entire command of the fur trade of North America might be obtained, except that portion of it which the Russians have in the Pacific. To this may be added the fishing in both seas and the markets of the four quarters of the globe.[85]

To remove any possible ambiguity, in the last paragraph of his book Mackenzie wrote:

> Many political reasons, which it is not necessary to enumerate, must present themselves to the mind of every man acquainted with the enlarged system and capacities of British commerce in support of the measure which I have briefly suggested, as promising the most important advantages to the trade of the united kingdoms [England and Scotland].[86]

But Mackenzie had more in mind than just the fur trade. He wanted this new territory to be developed agriculturally and to become a British colony. He urged his government to settle it and occupy it permanently.

Jefferson was so concerned about this possibility that, to bring it unmistakably to Lewis' attention, he ordered a copy of Mackenzie's book for Lewis to take on his journey to the Pacific. Mackenzie's book was thus an important factor in Jefferson's decision to send Lewis and Clark up the Missouri.

Mackenzie also founded a new fur trading company. Formally known as the New North West Company but informally referred to as the XY Company, it competed with the old North West Company for six years (1798–1804). Competition between these two companies became ferocious. George Nelson, a young Canadian fur trader, described it as "a state of almost perpetual *Polite* war" that lasted until the XY Company was finally taken over by its rival in 1804.[87] Mackenzie himself, knighted by King George III for his outstanding work in Canada, retired to Scotland in 1808 and died there in 1820.

There is one final episode in his story. Napoleon, then languishing in exile, heard about Mackenzie's exploits and arranged for Mackenzie's book to be translated into French. After reading it, Napoleon decided that Mackenzie's precise description of the river system of Western Canada might be a lever he could use to in a campaign to re-conquer New France. He therefore ordered his military advisor, Marshall Bernadotte, to work up a plan to invade Canada by launching a surprise attack on New Orleans and then following up with a northward thrust along the Mississippi River.[88] This plan, however, was never put into operation.

While Mackenzie was blazing new trails in Canada, the self-taught British geographer and cartographer Aaron Arrowsmith was becoming the finest mapmaker of his day. Arrowsmith's first map of North America, based on data from the archives of the Hudson's Bay Company, was compiled in 1795. It shows a vestige of the long sought but non-existent Great River of the West, which here is labeled as the Great Lake River. The Missouri itself is depicted only as an isolated fragment of a river, not connected in any way to the Mississippi or to the Stony Mountains (the Rocky Mountains).

On the map, the Rockies are only low peaks, stretching from Canada in a southeasterly direction all the way to New Mexico. They are held to consist a single and, by implication, easily crossed ridge, although the map suggests that there be other ridges, too. A notation on the map states that these mountains are only "3250 Feet High Above the Level of the Base and according to the Indian account is five Ridges in some parts."[89] (The highest peak in the Rocky Mountains—Mount Elbert in Colorado—is in fact 14,333 feet high.)

A revised version of Arrowsmith's map appeared in 1802. It now shows the full length of the Missouri but still depicts the Rocky Mountains as consisting of only a single low ridge. A notation, placed near the southern part of

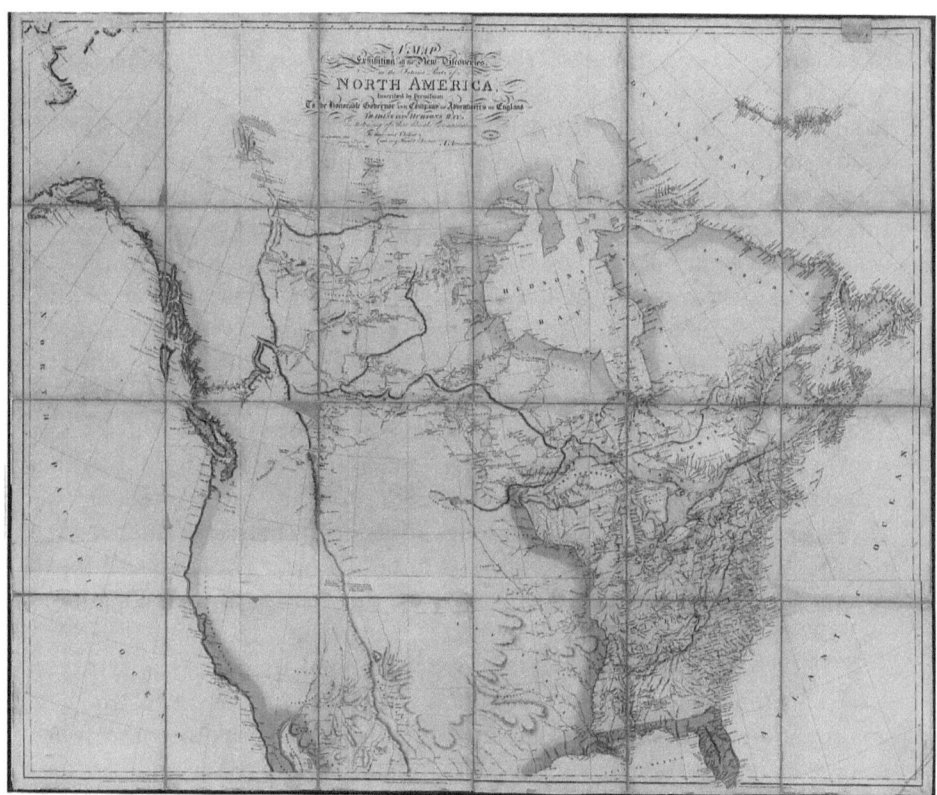

Aaron Arrowsmith's 1802 map, titled "A map exhibiting all the new discoveries of the interior parts of North America." (Library of Congress, Geography and map Division, ref. CT000584.)

the Missouri River but too small to read on the reproduction used here, mentions that "Hereabout the Mountains divide into several low Ridges."[90] This must have been very welcome news to Jefferson, who was always looking for an easy route to the Pacific Ocean to facilitate American trade with Asia.

Like Arrowsmith's 1795 map, the 1802 update left nearly blank the entire vast region between the Rockies and the Pacific coast. On the western slope of the mountains, however, Arrowsmith optimistically connects the Great Lake River with the Columbia River, using a faint dotted line. This suggested some kind of link between the two. In a note on the map, he reports that "The Indians say they sleep 8 Nights descending this River to the Sea."[91]

Arrowsmith's 1802 map was the best and most comprehensive map of the West available at that time. Thanks to the ceaseless travels of British-

Canadian and French-Canadian fur traders, Arrowsmith got the geography of eastern and central Canada right but he had to leave most of the Trans-Mississippi West blank because it had never been explored. Nevertheless, Jefferson, who owned a copy of the 1802 map, and Lewis and Clark, who used a new map based on Arrowsmith's maps, all believed that, once safely across the Rockies, reaching the Pacific would not prove very difficult. If this were indeed the case, it would certainly be feasible to export American furs to China by using this overland route.

During the autumn of 1799, two rival British-Canadian fur trading companies—the North West Company and the Hudson's Bay Company—had established fortified trading posts in the same part of western Alberta, i.e., at the foot of the Rockies, near the confluence of the North Saskatchewan and the Clearwater rivers. The North West Company had named its post Rocky Mountain House. A contemporary sketch shows that it consisted of some five wooden structures protected by tall wooden palisades. Indian hunters set up their lodges outside the palisades and bartered their furs with the traders of Rocky Mountain House. The traders shipped pelts down the North Saskatchewan River, the first leg of their long journey to Montreal and European markets.

The Hudson's Bay Company had christened its nearby post Acton House. It must have looked very much like Rocky Mountain House. The goal of these small but well defended establishments was to compete for trade with the Kootenay (or Kutenai) Indians, who lived in southeastern British Columbia, northern Idaho, and northwestern Montana. These Indian homelands, however, were so far away from Rocky Mountain House and Acton House that not many of the Kootenays went there to trade. For this reason, both posts were abandoned in 1802, although subsequently they would reopen and close again several times in response to fluctuations in the local fur trade. They are now commemorated by Canada's Rocky Mountain House National Historic Site.[92]

These posts served as a base for the British fur trader, explorer and mapmaker David Thompson, who was the greatest century surveyor in North America during the nineteenth century. His maps, compiled during his searches for the Passage, provided the first cartographic view of the far-flung western territories that later (in 1870) would became part of Canada. Thompson also surveyed parts of the northwestern United States. Some of his exploits are worth noting here.

In 1784, as a 14-year-old schoolboy at London's Grey Coat charity school, Thompson won an apprenticeship with the Hudson's Bay Company and learned surveying at its remote posts. His first achievement came in 1796, when he blazed a new trail for the Hudson's Bay Company men assigned to Lake Athabasca. Joining the North West Company in 1797, he surveyed upper Missouri in 1797–1798 to determine the latitude and longitude of the villages of the Mandans and Hidsatas and to trade with these Indians. He covered a circular course of 4,000 miles by foot, snowshoes, horseback, and canoe.

In his far-ranging travels, he came to know the French *voyageurs* well. This is what he had to say about them:

> The fact is Jean Baptiste [a colloquial name for a typical *voyageur*] will not think, he is not paid for it; and when he has a moment's respite he smokes his pipe, his constant companion and all goes well; he will go through hardships but requires a belly full at least once a day, good Tobacco to smoke, a warm blanket and a kind Master who will take his share of hard times and be first in danger. Naval and Military men are not fit to command them in distant countries, neither do they place confidence in one of themselves.[93]

Using Rocky Mountain House as a base, beginning in 1800 Thompson began looking for a route across the Rocky Mountains that would take him to the upper reaches of the Columbia. Unsuccessful at first, he finally discovered Howse Pass in 1807 and, upstream of Windermere Lake, he founded Kootenay House, the first trading post on the waters of the Columbia.

Thompson went on to explore Washington, Idaho, and Montana in 1808–1810 and in 1811 became the first European or American to travel the entire length of the Columbia by canoe — from its source high in Alberta's Rocky Mountains to the Oregon coast. The detailed map he completed in 1813–1814 became the basis for all later maps of western Canada. In addition, from 1816–1826 Thompson also surveyed the United States-Canada border from the St. Lawrence River to Lake of the Woods near the center of the continent. During his years in North America, he estimated that he had traveled over 80,000 miles by foot, snowshoes, canoes, or on horseback.[94] Summing up all these exploits before he died in 1857, Thompson took a quiet but well deserved pride in his achievements. In his *Travels in North America,* this is how he summarized his life's work:

> Thus I have fully completed the survey of this part of North America from sea to sea, and by almost innumerable astronomical Observations have determined the positions of the Mountains, Lakes and Rivers, and other remarkable places of the northern part of the continent.[95]

British objectives, hopes and fears

The British wanted to find the Passage and to establish a North American empire based on mercantilism and the fur trade. Converting the Indians was never a high priority for them. British hopes for a lasting hegemony in North America were dashed in 1776 by the successful rebellion of their American colonies. The high cost of the war to Britain (about £236 million) and the concomitant loss of one of the most profitable regions of the British Empire humiliated the British — but only temporarily. They turned adversity into opportunity by drawing a salutary lesson from their experience. This was the gradual realization that the American colonies were not in fact essential to Britain's economic survival. In fact, trade would continue to bring prosperity even in the absence of colonial rule.

Britain gradually found that it could continue to profit from trade with its former American colonies without being saddled with the high costs of governing and defending them. Moreover, in the wake of the American Revolution, the British concentrated on exploring and developing Canada, where they had been the dominant power since the fall of New France in 1763.

5

The Russians: "Soft Gold" — The Richest Fur in the World

WE HAVE ALREADY MENTIONED RUSSIA'S involvement in the sea otter trade of the Alaskan and Pacific Northwest coasts. The Russians were very good at harvesting furs. During an extended expedition to Kodiak Island in 1772–1779, for example, they gathered 9,633 pelts (including 3,838 sea otter skins), 3,457 sea otter tails, and 333 pounds of walrus teeth.[1] By 1778, there were 400 Russians working in what became known as "Russian America."[2]

Russian fur hunters beat their imperial rivals to these northwestern coasts and enjoyed four distinct advantages there:

- Alaska is very close to Russia at the Bering Strait, which was first crossed by Russian *kochas* (sturdy, flat-bottomed, shallow-draft sailing vessels) as early as 1648. The Aleutian Islands also offered convenient stepping-stones from Kamchatka (a peninsula off the northeast coast of Siberia) to Alaska.

- The Russians were in Alaska first. There was no foreign competition in these waters. The Spanish would not arrive for more than three decades; the British, for nearly four decades.

- The traditional and often conflicting objectives of North American exploration — "gold, God, and glory" — did not distract the Russians. In contrast to their European rivals, they chiefly focused on the maritime mammal fur trade. They also entertained the dream of turning the Pacific coast north of San Francisco into a Russian possession, but they never pursued this objective aggressively or successfully.

- After the Second Kamchatka Expedition (described below), Russia's later fur trading ventures along the Pacific coast were relatively small scale affairs—low key, flexible and inexpensive. Moreover, they benefited from the traditional Russian obsession with secrecy. Instructions, logs, journals, maps, reports and letters about the trade were either never printed or were published only years after the events they described.[3]

The story of the Russian fur rush into this region begins in the summer of 1732. At that time, two Russian navigators, Ivan Fyodorov and Mikhail Gvozdev, and their 39 crewmen became the first Europeans to see the northwestern coast of North America, i.e., Alaska. They could not land there, however, because of "the head wind and the shallow sea"; due to "the lateness of the season and the stormy weather," they had to return to Kamchatka.[4] Nothing came of this voyage and, in fact, the Russian authorities in St. Petersburg did not even hear about it for six years.

In the meantime, intensive preparations were well underway for the Second Kamchatka Expedition (1733–1742), also known as the American Expedition. (The First Kamchatka Expedition was sent out in 1725 by Peter the Great to explore Siberia.) The Second Expedition became the biggest exploring expedition the world had ever seen, involving about 1,000 travelers, 2,000 transport workers, and hundreds of tons of supplies and expeditionary gear.[5]

This expedition had four ambitious goals: to map the Arctic coast of Russia; to claim northwestern North America for Russia; to collect information about the islands, mainland and peoples there; and to discover the Passage. The expedition was led by two men in two ships. The senior commander was Vitus Bering, a Dane working for the Russian navy. He was the captain of the ship *St. Peter*, crewed by 78 men. The other navigator was Alexei I. Chirikov, a Russian naval officer who was the skipper of *St. Paul*, with a complement of 76 men.

Bering and Chirikov set off together in 1741 but became separated in the bad weather typical of what became known as the Bering Strait. Upon reaching Alaska, Chirikov sent a boat ashore with 11 men to reconnoiter his landfall at the southern end of the Alaskan panhandle. The boat and the men promptly disappeared without a trace.

Chirikov then sent another boat, staffed by seven men, to look for them. This boat and its crew vanished, too, either by capsizing in the freezing waters or by falling prey to the local Indians, the Tlingits. (According to a Tlingit legend, a clever warrior wrapped himself in a bearskin, pretended to be a bear, and lured the Russian fur hunters into an ambush.[6]) In addition to having lost many of his men, Chirikov had now also lost both his ship's boats. This meant he had no way to go ashore for fresh water and was therefore forced to leave Alaska. Chirikov managed to get back to Kamchatka after an arduous voyage. His only success was that he brought 900 sea otter skins back with him.

Bering and his crew, for their part, made landfall on Kayak Island at the northern end of the Alaska panhandle and then decided to return home. The weather in the Aleutians was so bad that Bering's most experienced sailor, the mate Andreas Hesselberg, said that the "indescribable gale from the west" they had endured, non-stop, for three weeks was the worst he had ever experienced in his 50 years at sea.[7] When off the Kamchatka peninsula, Bering decided to land at what is now known as Bering Island (one of the Commander Islands). His ship was later blown ashore there and was wrecked.

During the winter, Bering himself died of scurvy and many of his crew perished, too. The survivors managed to harvest more than 600 to 900 sea otter pelts, build a small ship (also named *St. Peter*) from the wreckage of the first *St. Peter*, and sail back to Russia. There they found they had stumbled onto a jackpot. Merchants in distant Kyakhta on the Siberian-Mongolian frontier, who sold goods to the Chinese market, would pay 80–100 rubles for a sea otter pelt, compared with only 20 rubles at Kamchatka.[8] This discovery triggered a Russian fur trade rush to the Pacific Northwest coast.

These traders fondly referred to sea otter pelts as "soft gold." Highly prized by Chinese mandarins as the richest and most luxurious material for their robes, the pelts—up to five feet long and two feet wide—consisted of dense, lustrous, black-and-brown fur three quarters of an inch thick. Lewis and Clark were enthralled by their beauty. Lewis wrote:

> The Sea Otter is found on the seacoast and in the salt water. This animal when fully grown is as large as a common mastive dog ... the colour is a uniform dark brown and when in good order and season perfectly black and glossey. it is the riches[t] and I think the most delicious fur in the world at least I cannot form an idea of any more so. it is deep thick silkey in the extreem and strong. the inner part of the fur when opened is lighter than the surface in it's natural position. there are some fine black and shining hairs intermixed with the fur which are rather longer and add much to it's beauty.[9]

In the wake of the Second Kamchatka Expedition, 42 Russian companies made nearly 100 voyages between 1743 and 1797 to harvest furs in the Aleutians and along the Gulf of Alaska coast. They collected nearly 187,000

Family of sea otters on a rocky Pacific coast beach, with a Russian fur trading ship in the offing. The location of this cove, which was sketched by the German artist Georg Heinrich Langsdorff between 1803 and 1807 when he was part of a Russian fur trading venture, is not known. It probably lies along the California coast between San Francisco and the Oregon border. (Honeyman Collection of Early Californian and Western American Pictorial Material. Courtesy of The Bancroft Library, University of California, Berkeley.)

furs, mainly sea otter and fur seal, worth nearly eight million rubles.[10] These fur traders, known in Russian as *promyshlenniki*, were so successful that sea otter numbers crashed. This eventually forced the Russians to sail as far south as San Francisco to find undepleted stocks of sea otters.[11]

One reason for the Russians' success was that they got experts to do the work for them. The Russians forced Aleut and Kodiak kayakers to hunt the sea otters, either by taking their women hostage or by plying the men with brandy and trinkets in return for pelts. If the Russians encountered any resistance, they retaliated savagely.

In 1763–1764, for example, the Aleuts rose against the Russians and managed to sink four of the ships' boats used by the Russians to ferry men and supplies into Alaskan harbors and along the coast. The Russians retaliated by murdering about 3,000 Aleut men. They seem to have taken pleasure in the slaughter. When a Russian hunter wanted to find out how many Aleuts could be killed by a single musket ball, he roped 12 Aleut men together in a straight line and fired at the first of them. The ball stopped in the body of the ninth man.[12]

The Aleuts and Kodiaks used light (30 pound), highly maneuverable hunting kayaks made of a thin framework of driftwood and whalebone, covered with sewn, stretched sealskins. They hunted with a two-foot-long dart (a short harpoon) tipped with a stone point, which was launched from an atlatl, the Aztec word for a spear-throwing board. An atlatl functions as an extension of the hunter's arm and gives a great mechanical advantage. In 1995, an American enthusiast using a state-of-the-art carbon fiber atlatl set a world record by hurling an aluminum dart more than 848 feet.[13]

The Russians' first settlement in California was located at Bodega Bay, about 18 miles south of their later settlement at Fort Ross. ("Ross" was an abbreviation of "Rossiya," the Russia of Tsarist days. Fort Ross is about 65 miles northwest of San Francisco.) In 1824, Antonio María Osio, a Mexican who would later write a *History of Alta California,* joined a group of Aleut kayakers who were hunting sea otters north of Bodega Bay. He recorded how a group of kayaks would surround a sea otter and force it to dive repeatedly until it was out of breath. Each kayak carried two men — a paddler and a harpooner. When the exhausted sea otter finally surfaced and could dive no longer, it would be darted. An inflated bladder, made of skin, was attached to the dart. This drag slowed the sea otter so much when it tried to dive that the kayakers could get close to it and club it to death.[14]

The Russian fur trade flourished but rivals were edging into the Pacific Northwest, too. Captain Cook visited these waters in 1776–1780. The Russian fur trader G.I. Shelikhov won financial support from his government because he could point to "evidence that the English [are] moving ... alongside the coast of America in the North Pacific, and that they anticipate considerable profit."[15] In 1787, Shelikhov warned Siberian officials that British fur traders were doing business "in our waters along the [northwest] coast of America."[16] The first British ship had sailed with 800 sea otter skins in 1785; five other British ships had arrived the next year.

In 1788, Shelikhov and his colleague Ivan Golikov drafted a report to Empress Catherine the Great calling her attention to the rapid expansion of the Russian fur trade along the Pacific Northwest coast. They could, they asserted, expand Russian rule from the Kurile Islands all way the south to San Francisco. They petitioned the empress for a grant of 250,000 rubles and a monopoly on trade. Probably wanting to save money and to avoid offending the English, who had not only commercial but also territorial claims in this region, she demurred. She deflected the explorers' requests by giving them swords, gold medals and a vague letter of encouragement.[17]

In 1790, Shelikhov hired Alexander Baranov as his manager. Baranov would keep his job for the next 28 years. He wanted to create a genuine trade empire and ruled the Russian fur trade with such an iron hand that he became known as the "Lord of Alaska." When a group of Russian Orthodox missionaries arrived at Kodiak in 1794, they were shocked by the harsh treatment being meted out to the Aleuts, who were being held in virtual slavery. The missionaries, however, found that they could do nothing to improve conditions for the Aleuts. Their efforts brought them into direct conflict with Baranov, who had the final say in all matters. His power was absolute.

By the 1780s, seven Russian fur trading companies were engaged the sea otter trade. This proved to be too many and the weaker firms gradually fell by the wayside. In 1795, Nikolai Petrovich Rezanov, a Russian diplomat, administrator and fur trader, became the chief executive of the most important firm, the Shelikhov-Golikov Fur Company. Rezanov's hidden objectives were to make the west coast of North America a Russian possession and to encourage large-scale Russian emigration there. With the support of Shelikhov's heirs, in 1799 he persuaded the Russian czar, Paul I, to charter a new Russian-American Company and to grant it a monopoly for 20 years. This company was very successful and became a reliable source of income both for Rezanov and for the imperial family.

The Russians established St. Michael's Redoubt, a trading post and fort, at New Archangel (Sitka) in 1799. This base had a flotilla of 450 two-man kayaks and could house about 300 colonists. By 1800, however, Baranov found that he was facing some intractable challenges. His ambitious plans to expand his operations south down the Pacific Northwest coast were reinforced by the unwelcome news that British, American and even a few Spanish ships were already trading for furs in Nootka Sound. Baranov believed that he had to move south quickly in order to prevent these competitors from moving north along the coast.

Baranov's Russians, however, were not only poorly paid but were often hungry, too. Their furs could be sold in Russia, but only at much lower prices than the Chinese would pay. Canton — the only Chinese port open to European and American merchants— was closed to the Russians. They therefore they had to export their furs to China through Kyakhta, that remote frontier post located on the border between Siberia and Mongolia. Prices there were low and transportation costs were high.

The Russians in North America were hunters, not farmers. Coastal rains and fog along the sea otter coasts made it difficult to grow crops.

Moreover, these men had no experience in clearing and tilling land and waiting for crops to ripen. They were not interested in learning these skills. They tried to force the Indians to become farmers but had little success: the Indians were hunters, too, and did not like farming. Consequently, not enough food was produced.

The obvious solution was to import food, but this proved to be difficult and expensive. To resolve the problem, Baranov tried to make a two-part deal with American captains. He proposed that Boston ships first bring wheat and other provisions to Russian posts on the Pacific coast and then carry Russian furs to Canton. The second (Canton) part of this deal fell through but the Boston-Pacific coast trade got underway and continued until 1839. During these years, the Russians also bought food from Spaniards in San Francisco.

Another problem faced the Russians as well. American traders had cheerfully bartered American and British firearms to the local Indians, so Russian fur traders were now in peril when the Indians turned against them. Baranov complained to the Americans but they paid no attention to him. Privately, he raged that they "before our eyes shamelessly trade powder, lead, pistols, and muskets."[18]

The Tlingits had accepted without any protest the beads, brass, bottles and other trinkets offered by the Russians to pay for their outpost at Sitka. In 1802, however, these same Indians suddenly and unexpectedly attacked this settlement when most of the Russian men had gone off hunting. Brandishing firearms acquired from American traders, the Tlingits burned down the Russian fort, destroyed the warehouse, and decapitated the men who were still there. They carried off the Aleut women as slaves.

The Russian survivors sought refuge aboard English and American ships anchored in the harbor. After this attack, the Tlingits (who numbered about 10,000 at that time) seemed so formidable that the Russians did not dare to confront them for fully two years. The Russians cautiously waited until they had amassed a small armada, consisting of the visiting 450-ton Russian frigate *Neva*, 120 Russian hunters in four small ships, and 800 Aleuts in 400 kayaks. Finally, when they were thus strongly equipped, the Russians shelled Sitka in 1804 and made one unsuccessful foray ashore, during which Baranov himself was wounded in the arm.

A military standoff then ensued. The Russians could not defeat the Tlingits without unacceptably high Russian casualties; the Tlingits could not defeat the technologically superior Russian armada. The conflict was resolved only when the Tlingits quietly slipped away from Sitka. This fracas, known perhaps too grandly as the Battle of Sitka, was the only major organized stand the Indians made against the Russians. After it, realizing the danger posed to them by massed Russian firepower, the Tlingits kept well clear of Sitka for the next two decades.[19]

Russian objectives, hopes and fears

Harvesting the pelts of sea otters and other marine mammals remained the primary Russian objective along the coastline between Alaska and California. Russia's other hopes—a lucrative, long-lasting trade with the Spanish of California and claming the Pacific coast as a Russian possession — were not to be fulfilled. Catherine the Great's fear of antagonizing the British led her to reject the expansive ambitions of Russian fur traders in that region. Her caution was probably well-founded: had she approved her traders' request for official Russian involvement in their colonial adventures, Russia might have been drawn into a war with Britain — as Spain nearly was over the Nookta Sound incident in 1789.

6

The Americans: To All Points West

THE FIRST ANGLO-AMERICAN TRADER KNOWN to have reached and crossed the Mississippi River was Thomas Welch, an entrepreneur from Charleston, South Carolina.[1] He and a colleague, Anthony Dodsworth, began by trading with the Chickasaws in northeastern Mississippi. In 1698, to shake off competition from rival traders, Welch decided to take the bold step of crossing the Mississippi into French territory. His goal was to barter guns to the Quapaw Indians living in the river valleys of Arkansas and get deerskins in return.

Welch received a great deal of help from Jean Couture, the French commandant of Arkansas Post. This was the first semi-permanent French settlement in the lower Mississippi valley and the farthest outpost of French dominion. Couture had decided to shift his allegiance from France to the British and Americans because he could no longer get French goods to sell to the Indians.

This situation came about because of a decision made by the French king. To combat a drastic fall in the price of beaver furs in European markets—caused by an oversupply of pelts from Canada—Louis XIV issued a royal decree in 1665 suspending the fur trade around the western Great Lakes. This meant that the flow of goods to French trading posts was halted, too. The result was that Arkansas Post soon ran out of trade goods and had no prospect of getting more supplies from France any time soon.

So, rather than finding himself with no French trade goods and thus no Indian customers, Couture decided to cast his lot with the British and Americans instead. He therefore led Welch to the Quapaw villages, where

Welch gave 30 muskets to the Quapaws, hoping they would use them to steal deerskins from a neighboring tribe and then trade the hides to him for more guns. Instead, they used their new weapons to drive the tribes of the Illinois Confederation out of the Quapaw hunting grounds in northeastern Arkansas. (The Illinois Confederation was a loose collection of Algonquin-speaking tribes. By the middle of the seventeenth century, competition from more powerful tribes had pushed them south along the Mississippi River.)

Welch also did his utmost to loosen French control of the region. He encouraged the Chickasaws to attack the Choctaws, who were allies of the French. He sold 150 Choctaw captives as slaves in Charleston. In 1707, he took part in a bold but unsuccessful plan to conquer the tribes of Mississippi Valley, to unite them, and then order them to attack the French bastion at Mobile, Alabama.

The Mississippi River became increasingly important to the early settlers of the western river valleys. It was the best and, in fact, often the only way for them to get their bulky or heavy products to market—for example, furs, salt, lead, lime, flour, pork and whiskey. At first, rivermen used flatboats on one-way voyages to carry farm produce and other cargoes down the river to Natchez or New Orleans and thence (by ocean-going ships) to other ports across the seas.

Early flatboats were rectangular, high-sided, flat-bottomed, wooden craft about 60 feet long and 15 feet wide. Rivermen steered these awkward slab-sided boats by means of long sweeps (oars) that were 30- to 55- feet long, one on each side of the boat.[2] Captains sold their goods at downriver ports, dismantled the flatboats, sold the lumber thus obtained, and then rode or usually walked 1,000 miles north to get back home, following a well-beaten trail known as the Natchez Trace.

In 1790, Spanish officials estimated that every year about 240 boatmen passed through Natchez on their way home. Ten years later, the Reverend Joseph Bullen estimated that "not less than one thousand" men were heading north on the Trace each year. By 1810, the ornithologist Alexander Wilson calculated that this number had doubled.[3] The Natchez Trace was not, however, a very safe route.

Although regional American folklore has delighted in exaggerated accounts of the "land pirates" infesting the Natchez Trace, some facts do emerge clearly. As early as 1786, for example, Spanish court records chronicle the rascally deeds of the "highway robbers who by force of arms strip travelers and enter the houses of citizens and plunder their most valuable effects."[4] Horse thieves, too, preyed on returning boatmen and local residents alike. Moreover, in 1801, the *Kentucky Gazette* reported that four "blacked" highwaymen, i.e., outlaws who were wearing black masks or hoods to conceal their identities, had robbed a group of boatmen heading home along the Natchez Trace.[5]

The Mississippi River itself was a primeval force that rivermen could never take for granted. The French historian and philosopher Constantin-François de Chasseboeuf Volney, who lived and traveled in the United States between 1795 and 1798, reported that the Mississippi

> rolls along a mass of yellow muddy water, a mile and a half wide, which annually lifts twenty or twenty-five feet above its banks ... forms islands and destroys them, throws trees upon one side, and uproots them on the other ... and at length overwhelms the spot which you thought most secure. The sublimity of this stream is like that of most other grand objects of nature, to be admired safely only at a distance.[6]

Zadok Cramer's pilot book, *The Ohio and Mississippi Navigator* (1802), was a bible for American rivermen. A decade later, the flatboat entrepreneur Moses Austin gave this stern advice to his son Stephen, who in 1812 was piloting a flatboat, loaded with Moses' merchandise, down to New Orleans:

> In the first place I intend to state to you some general rules to be observed in descending the Mississippi in opposition to every other advice do you observe the following rules—first never run late at Night but always make a landing under a Willow Point in time, its always better to loose a few hours than to be exposed at Night. Never land under a high bank and large timber. [A rise in the river level could undercut the bank, causing it to cave in, and could uproot trees.] When you Intend to land begin in time to pull your boat in shore and always before the boat striks turn her stern down-Stream. Never trust your boat to float unless you have a man on the look out — let this rule be always strictly observed, to much care cannot be taken in Descending this river, when you make your Boat fast at Night see yourself that the Cable is properly made fast — Never suffer any water to be in your boat a[t] Nigh[t] always put to land in Winds I advise you always to Keep out from the bend of the rivers, and guard against Points of Islands, haveing observed this much I must commit you to the Care of that being that govern us all.[7]

By 1742, keelboats—"long and narrow, sharp [pointed] at bow and stern, and of light draft,"[8] as one Ohio settler described them — had rudimentary cabins, could carry as much as 80 tons of cargo, and were able to navigate upstream. Contemporary accounts, however, made it clear that this could be done only slowly and with enormous effort — by using a combination of sailing, poling, cordelling (hauling with ropes), warping (attaching a rope to a tree and using a capstan to winch the boat up to it), or bushwhacking (simply grabbing overhanging bushes or branches and pulling the boat upstream by hand).

Keelboat on the Upper Missouri (artist Karl Bodmer's title is "Camp of the Gros Ventures of the Prairies on the Upper Missouri"). (©2005 Alecto Historical Editions www.alectoUK.com)

Britain and France vied strenuously for exclusive control of the inland commerce of the Ohio and Mississippi valleys. Their competition became so intense, in fact, that it sparked a nine-year conflict — the French and Indian War of 1754–1763. This war, which became part of a broader European struggle (the Seven Years' War, 1756–1763), arose over the question of whether the upper Ohio River valley was in fact part of the British empire. If it was, this fertile area was open for trade and settlement by Anglo-American colonists. If it was not, only French colonists were welcome there.

By 1762, France saw that it was going to lose the war. To keep Louisiana from falling into British hands, under the terms of the secret Treaty of Fontainebleau (1762) France ceded to Spain all of Louisiana west of the Mississippi River. Thus from 1762 until 1800, when Spain gave Louisiana back to France, Spain was the sovereign power from the mouth of the Mississippi to St. Louis. When Britain won the war, the Treaty of Paris (1763) accordingly recognized Spain as the new owner of Upper and Lower Louisiana.

The treaty awarded Spanish Florida to the British, who divided it into two provinces, East and West Florida. West Florida included the southern half of the state of Mississippi and the southern reaches of the river itself. It also included the old Spanish port of Pensacola and three former French settlements: Mobile, Biloxi, and Natchez.[9] What the Treaty of Paris did not resolve, however, was the basic issue of commercial supremacy in the Ohio and Mississippi valleys. On the contrary, it added two new contenders: Spain, and the American colonies, which were soon to be independent.[10]

In 1778, during the American Revolution Captain James Willing, an American adventurer living in Natchez, led a band of raiders from Pittsburgh down the Ohio and Mississippi Rivers. They seized the British trading settlement known as British Ozark, located on the east bank of the Mississippi across from the Arkansas River. After capturing Colonel Anthony Hutchins, a well-known British sympathizer living in Natchez, they forced the other inhabitants of Natchez to take an oath of allegiance to the United States. Captain Willing and his force then proceeded to New Orleans, where they hoped to get Spanish loans and military supplies for the United States. The residents of New Orleans did not welcome them, however, and their efforts failed.

After the Americans won the Revolutionary War, the Treaty of Paris of 1783 gave American rivermen the right to navigate the entire length of the Mississippi. (Spain, however, was not party to this treaty and disputed this right until 1795.) This treaty began the era of the "half-horse, half-alligator" boatmen that Mark Twain would immortalize in *Life on the Mississippi* (1883).

Twain had been a steamboat pilot on the Mississippi and knew the river well. Rivermen were great drinkers, great talkers and (sometimes) great fighters as well. Twain has left us a memorable and humorous account of a "fight" aboard a raft. One protagonist, physically a big man, shouts:

> Whoo-oop! I'm the old original iron-jawed, brass-mounted, copper-bellied corpse-maker from the wilds of Arkansas!—Look at me! I'm the man they call Sudden Death and General Desolation.... Blood's my natural drink, and the wails of the dying is music to my ear. Cast your eye on me, gentlemen!—and lay low and hold your breath, for I'm bout to turn myself loose![11]

His opponent, also a big man, replies:

> Bow your neck and spread, for the kingdom of sorrow 's a-coming! Hold me down to the earth, for I feel my powers a-working! I'm a child of sin, *don't* let me get a start! Smoked glass, here, for all! Don't attempt to look at me with the naked eye, gentlemen! ... I shake myself and crumble the mountains! ... I'm the man with a petrified heart and biler [boiler]-iron bowels![12]

Despite all their verbal posturing, neither man actually dares to *touch* his opponent. While growling stupendous threats, they edge *away* from each other. As a result, another member of the crew, Little Davy, "a little black-whiskered chap," calls out to them, "Come back here, you couple of chicken-livered cowards, and I'll thrash the two of ye!" Twain continues: "And he done it, too. He snatched them, he jerked them this way and that, he booted them around, he knocked them sprawling faster than they could get up. Why, it war'nt two minutes till they begged like dogs—and how the other lot [the other crewmen] did yell and laugh and clap their hands all the way through...."[13]

After the Treaty of Paris, American boatmen expected that the Spaniards would continue to let them do business in New Orleans itself. Spain, however, had not signed this treaty because it feared that Americans would move into and gradually take over Spanish territory. To guard against this possibility, in 1784, the Spaniards closed the lower Mississippi to non–Spanish boatmen, thereby creating a navigational and diplomatic problem that would not be finally resolved until the Treaty of San Lorenzo del Escorial of 1795.

However, the American flatboat entrepreneur and double agent James Wilkinson found a clever way for the "men of the western waters" (American rivermen) to use the Spanish part of the river legally. He himself took an oath of allegiance to Spain in 1787 and began plotting how to bring the American settlements in western Kentucky under Spanish (or his own) rule. He advised American boatmen who were heading down the river "to put on your best Bib & Tucker," to be very polite to Spanish officials and quietly offer them a bribe. He told American navigators to state their "determination to settle in Louisiana." Most importantly, he concluded, they must take "the Oath of Allegiance" and say "nothing that is not flattering & favorable to Louisiana."[14]

Wilkinson's advice proved to be so sound that hundreds of American boatmen took a nominal oath of allegiance and then sold their cargoes in Natchez or New Orleans. Moreover, the Spanish governor, Esteban Miró, quickly recognized that New Orleans could not feed itself and needed American produce. In 1788, Spain therefore allowed Americans to use the Mississippi on payment of a 15 percent duty.[15]

The Treaty of San Lorenzo del Escorial of 1795 gave further impetus to this international trade. It awarded the Natchez District to the United States, legalized American navigation of the entire Mississippi River, and granted Americans the right to store goods in Spanish New Orleans.[16] Consequently, business boomed: between 1799 and 1802, more American flour was shipped to New Orleans than in any similar period until after the War of 1812.[17]

While transport on the Mississippi was growing so dramatically, the fur trade was expanding, too. One remarkable character who deserves mention here is Peter Pond, an American fur trader, explorer, cartographer — and murderer. Born in Connecticut around 1739, he served briefly in the French and Indian War and then, in 1765, joined his father as a fur trader, operating out of Detroit.[18] He made enough money there to team up with other "free traders." (Fur trading companies advanced horses, traps and other goods to these highly independent, competitive men so that they could survive in the wilderness. The companies would then buy, at low prices, the beaver pelts and other furs harvested by the free traders at daily risk of life and limb.)

From 1773 to 1775, Pond trapped successfully in Minnesota and Wisconsin. Indian wars along the upper Mississippi, however, coupled with reports of a veritable treasure trove of furs to be had in the Lake Athabasca drainage system in northern Saskatchewan and Alberta, encouraged him to explore that remote and bitterly cold region. In 1778, he led a party of 16 canoemen in four canoes, heavily laden with supplies and trade goods, into northwest Saskatchewan. Indian hunters there showed him the La Loche (or Methy) portage — a portage so long (nearly 12 miles) and so steep that it took him fully eight days to transport his canoes, food and trade goods over it. Once he crossed it, however, he had left the hydrographic basin of Hudson Bay and was now well positioned to open the fur trade in the Athabasca country itself.

Pond may have been outstanding fur trader but according to David Thompson, a contemporary trader, cartographer and explorer, he was also "an unprincipled man of a violent character."[19] While wintering in 1781–1782 at a northern lake, Pond got into an argument with Jean-Étienne Waddens, who worked for a rival fur trading company. According to Pond, Waddens had deliberately insulted him. Although Pond claimed that he had tried to be forbearing, the insult could only be settled by a duel.

"The abuse was too grate," Pond tells us. "We met the next morning eairly and discharged pistols, in which the pore fellow was unfortenat." Waddens was shot dead. This murder occurred in a region so remote that it was beyond the reach of the law. Pond later claimed that he reported the killing but that "thare was none to prosacute me."[20]

In 1783, Pond explored the waterways around Lake Athabasca, where local Indians told him about big lakes and powerful rivers: Great Slave Lake, Great Bear Lake, and (possibly) the Peace River and the Mackenzie River. During the winter of 1784–1785, he made a detailed map of the region. It showed the major rivers and lakes stretching west of the Great Lakes and Hudson Bay to the Rocky Mountains, and west toward the Arctic.

Perhaps most importantly, it depicted the Rocky Mountains as consisting only of a single line of relatively low and, by implication, easily crossed mountains.

Pond's map also showed a (non-existent) great river, which he named the Naberkistagon. It was depicted as originating from a source somewhere on the western slopes of the Rockies and as running all the way to the South Sea, i.e., the Pacific Ocean. According to the geographical concepts current at that time, this river could only be the Oregon, or the Great River of the West. If so, it must therefore constitute the long sought Passage.[21]

In 1785, Pond submitted one copy of his map to Congress and another copy to the Lieutenant Governor of Quebec, Henry Hamilton. The map sent to Congress bore a handwritten note from Michel-Guillaume-Saint-Jean de Crèvecoeur, a famous French-American author and mapmaker, who was at the time the most widely read commentator on American life and culture. The various editions of his book, *Letters from an American Farmer*, published in 1782, 1784, 1790 and, posthumously, in 1925, are justly famous. They ask and answer a fundamental question: "What then is an American, this new man?"

Crèvecoeur wrote on Pond's map:

> Copy of a Map presented to the Congres by Peter Pond, a native of Milford in the State of Connecticut

This extraordinary man has resided 17 years in those countries & from his own Discoveries as well as from the reports of Indians, he assures himself of having at last Discovered a passage to the N.O. Sea [the northwest sea, i.e., the Arctic Ocean]; his gone again to ascertain some important observations. New York, 1st March 1785.

The original Map being incumbered with great deal of writing, I have thought it best to transcribe it separately with the references marked, by the numbers.—Copied by St. John de Crèvecoeur for his Grace of La Rochefoucault.[22]

The copy of the map sent to Quebec asked Hamilton to provide funds for Pond's project to explore the remote parts of the northwest. This request was forwarded to London, where it was turned down. In the meantime, however, Pond had become a partner in the North West Company. During the winter of 1786–1787, he was in the Peace River area, where he quarreled with John Ross, a rival fur trader. Ross was killed by a gunshot during a brawl. A witness claimed that the fatal shot had been fired by a Canadian named Pesche, who had assassinated Ross on Pond's orders.

This second murder forced the North West Company to get rid of Pond and replace him with Alexander Mackenzie, a less violent but even more able explorer. Mackenzie learned a great deal from Pond: in fact, a map that Pond drew up in 1787 provided the essential outline of the route that

Mackenzie would successfully follow to the Pacific in 1793.[23] In 1790, Pond sold all his shares in the North West Company and returned to his native Connecticut, where he died in poverty and obscurity in 1807. His maps, however, brought him international if posthumous acclaim.

In the meantime, while the Russians were the first to engage in the sea otter trade, in later decades they were surpassed by British and American traders. British ships were on the Pacific Northwest coast by 1785. American ships, however, proved to be by far most successful, mainly because they had unimpeded access to the Chinese market via Canton. (The British had access to Canton, too, but to trade there they first had to get permission from the South Sea Company and from the East India Company — a cumbersome, time-consuming process.) The Americans' competitive advantage was augmented by the high quality goods they offered for sale. The Indians were more than willing to trade prime sea otter pelts for trustworthy American guns and ammunition.

This trade was so profitable that between 1787 and 1806 about 72 American ships were harvesting furs along the Pacific Northwest coast.[24] In 1791, the French navigator C.P. Claret Fleurieu reported that

> The Americans of the United States, whose navigation and commerce are daily acquiring fresh extension, have seized with ardour, and without being discouraged by the distance, of the new support which the peltry of the northwest coast of America offers to their speculations, to their industry, and to their want of enriching themselves in order to pay the public debt: to the nations of Europe, they are becoming formidable competitors; and their activity is by no means inferior to that of the English.[25]

By 1800, American seamen were joking that the Pacific Northwest coast had become "a trade suburb of Boston." The next year, American vessels there outnumbered British ships by 22 to 1.[26] This dominance of the trade had begun in 1787, when Robert Gray, captain of the 90-ton sloop *Lady Washington*, sailed from Boston together with John Kendrick, captain of the 212-ton ship *Columbia Rediviva*. Gray collected a cargo of sea otter furs near Vancouver Island and then sailed home via Canton, thus becoming the first American to circumnavigate the globe.

He spent only six weeks in Boston, refitting the ship and loading a new cargo of trade goods. He then set sail for the Pacific Northwest in 1790, this time as captain of *Columbia Rediviva*. After wintering in Vancouver, Gray traded for sea otter skins along the coasts of Washington and Oregon. Suddenly, on 11 May 1792, his ship's lookouts saw, glittering invitingly behind two long sandbars, what seemed to be a spacious harbor. It was in fact a great river. Gray managed to thread his way through the sandbars and christened it "Columbia" in honor of his ship.

He and his men were thus the first foreigners to enter the river. As mentioned in Chapter 2, the Spanish navigator Bruno de Hezeta had commented on the outflow of the Columbia in 1775 but did not enter it because of the strong current. Gray's visit would form the basis of later American claims to the Oregon Territory—claims that would be strengthened when Lewis and Clark descended the Columbia and wintered at its mouth in 1805–1806.[27]

The rapid population growth, economic dynamism, and expansionist tendencies of the United States all boded ill for Spanish interests in North America. This was especially true in light of two international agreements that appreciably strengthened the United States by reducing the chances of war with Britain. The first of these agreements was the Treaty of London (Jay's Treaty) of 1794. Some background information may be useful here.

By the early 1790s, American leaders were worried that several long-festering disputes with the British would lead to war if left unresolved.[28] The Treaty of Paris (1783) had ended the Revolutionary War but relations between the two countries deteriorated thereafter. For example, although the British had promised to close down their string of military outposts in the Old Northwest Territory of the United States, they had not in fact done so. (The Old Northwest Territory, created by Congress in 1787, would eventually become the states of Ohio, Indiana, Illinois, Michigan, Wisconsin, and part of Minnesota.)

To negotiate a treaty resolving these and other disputes between the United States and Britain, Supreme Court Chief Justice John Jay, the senior American diplomat, was sent to London in 1794. He soon discovered that he had very little bargaining power. The British were at war with revolutionary France and were in no mood to compromise with their ex-colonists in the United States.

The best that Jay could do was to agree to a treaty that required the British to abandon their posts in the Old Northwest within two years and to offer the United States a limited commercial agreement granting it "most favored nation" status. This meant Britain would have to give to the United States the same trading privileges it accorded to a third country, and vice versa. There was no movement on any of the other outstanding issues—the United States-Canada boundary, payment of debts incurred before the Revolutionary War, and British seizures of American ships. All these were to be the subject of later arbitration.

Jay's Treaty allowed the British to seize American goods destined for France, provided that they paid for these goods. They could seize, without payment, any French goods on American ships. They could also ship furs across the American border into Canada. Because the treaty appeared to give the British so much and the Americans so little, it was extremely unpopular in the United States. Jay became one of the most hated Americans—"damned and double damned," as his critics put it, for giving in to the British. He resigned from the Supreme Court and later joked that he could have traveled the length of the United States by the light of bonfires burning his effigy.[29]

Still, there was some good news, too. The treaty gave the newly minted United States time to consolidate itself, to strengthen its defenses in case of future conflicts, and to be ready to move farther west as soon as that became feasible. The Mississippi River was declared open to both British and American shipping. A joint survey of the river near its source would be undertaken to determine precisely how far north it extended. Joint commissions would be set up to define the northwestern and northeastern boundaries between the United States and Canada. In practice, these commissions worked so well that the modern practice of international arbitration is said to date from the ratification of Jay's Treaty in 1795.

The second agreement that strengthened the United States was the Treaty of San Lorenzo del Escorial, negotiated in 1795 by Thomas Pinckney for the United States and Manuel de Godoy for Spain. This treaty is important for two reasons. First, it marks the beginning of Spain's gradual withdrawal from the Mississippi Valley. Second, for all its imperfections, Jay's Treaty did in fact ease tensions between the United States and Britain. Spain probably hoped that improving its own relations with the United States by means of Pinckney's Treaty would keep its rival, Britain, at bay.

Under the terms of this treaty, Spain, among other things, abandoned its claims to the Ohio valley and the Natchez District. The treaty legalized American navigation of the Mississippi through Spanish territory. As noted earlier, the Americans had enjoyed free use of the river since 1763. In 1784, however, the Spaniards, fearing that the aggressive Americans would gradually take over their territory, closed the lower Mississippi to non–Spanish, i.e., American, navigators. This move had infuriated the American farmers and boatmen living in the Ohio and Mississippi valleys because it threatened to deprive them of the only cheap, easy way to get their crops and products to downriver markets. The problem festered for nine years until Pinckney's Treaty finally resolved it.

Meanwhile, Americans were casting covetous eyes at Spanish lands in Louisiana and Texas. Some American men received land grants and settled down with Spanish or French wives. Others had more devious plans. One of these was Philip Nolan, an Anglo-American "mustanger" (a trader who captured and sold the wild horses of Texas), who was also a bookkeeper and shipping clerk for the double agent General James Wilkinson.

Nolan operated out of Natchitoches, Louisiana, and Nacogdoches, Texas. In about 1794, Baron Carondelet, governor of Louisiana, authorized him to round up mustangs in Louisiana as mounts for the Louisiana militia. Nolan's frequent forays into Louisiana had given him a unique knowledge of its backcountry. One of Nolan's friends was Daniel Clark, who worked in Baron Carondelet's office and whom in 1803 Thomas Jefferson would appoint as U.S. Consul in New Orleans. Clark wrote to Jefferson, stating that Nolan was a man "who will at all times have it in his power to render important services to the United States, and whom nature seems to have formed for the enterprises of which the rest of mankind are incapable."[30] Jefferson responded by writing to Nolan:

> I have understood that there are large herds of horses in a wild state, in the country west of the Missouri, and have been desirous of obtaining details of their history in that State ... I will add that your information is the sole reliance, as far as I can at present see, for obtaining your desideratum.[31]

In May 1800, it is known that Nolan was on the road to Monticello (Jefferson's home) with a present of a "fine paint stallion for Jefferson" but there is no record that the two men actually met. Nolan then decided to make yet another trip into Texas to catch mustangs. This time, however, he did not have Spanish permission to enter Texas. In October 1800 he left Natchez, leading a body of well armed men, and made his way to the Nacogdoches area and then to a tributary of the Brazos River. There he built a small fort and began to corral mustangs.

Although the exact nature of Nolan's expedition remains unknown today, it is likely the Spaniards suspected that he was spying for the Americans and that he wanted to free Texas from Spanish rule. A lesser offense was that he did not have a passport authorizing him to be in Texas. Spanish troops were sent out to arrest him. A gunfight with them erupted on 21 March 1801 and Nolan was killed. His followers were captured, tried and convicted. They spent years in Spanish prisons.[32] Nolan is said to have been the first Anglo-American to have mapped Spanish Texas. If so, his map has never surfaced. In about 1804, however, Wilkinson used information provided to him by Nolan to draw up an early map of the Texas-Louisiana frontier.

Spain had granted the United States the right of deposit in New Orleans, which stimulated the American flatboat trade. Consequently, ocean-going shipping boomed as well. In 1800, under the terms of the Treaty of San Ildefonso, Spain gave Louisiana back to France. When Pierre Clément Lassat, the new colonial *préfect* (the highest ranking French civil servant in a city), arrived in New Orleans in 1803, he reported that there were then 120 ships in port. He said that they were "French, Spanish and mostly Anglo-American, spread out like a floating forest and formed a prospect worthy of the busiest regions on the earth."[33]

The Louisiana Purchase deserves some analysis at this point. In 1803, Revolutionary War hero Horatio Gates wrote two letters to President Jefferson in which he discussed the Louisiana Purchase. In the first letter, Gates said:

> I am astonished when I see so great a business finished which but a few months since we whispered to one another about; it has the air of enchantment.... It must strike every true friend to freedom in these United States as the greatest and most beneficial event that has taken place since the Declaration of Independence.[34]

In his second letter, he congratulated Jefferson in even more poetic terms: "Let the Land rejoice, for you have bought Louisiana for a Song."[35]

Here is how the greatest land bargain in American history came about. Jefferson had felt the attraction of the West for a long time and was keenly interested in it.[36] His father, Peter Jefferson, had been one of the founding members of the Loyal Company, which was formed in 1749 to petition for grants of land west of the Allegheny Mountains. When Thomas Jefferson was ten years old, the Loyal Company planned an exploratory expedition up the Missouri but had to abandon this venture when the French and Indian War broke out in 1753.

From 1758 to 1760, Jefferson was a pupil at a school run by the Reverend James Maury, who was a member of the Loyal Company and a firm believer in the Passage. This is what, in adult terms, Maury taught his students:

> When it is considered how far the eastern branches of that immense river, Mississippi, extend eastward, how near they come to the navigable, or rather canoeable parts of those rivers which empty themselves into the sea that washes our shores to the east, it seems highly probable that its western branches reach as far the other way, and make as near approaches to rivers emptying themselves into the ocean to the west of us, the Pacific Ocean, across which a short and easy communication, short in comparison with the present route thither, opens itself to the navigation from the shore of the continent unto the Eastern Indies.[37]

When Jefferson published his *Notes on the State of Virginia* in 1781–1782, he included the Missouri and other western rivers, as well as highlights of western geography, even though the Treaty of Paris of 1763 had specifically excluded these areas from Virginia's territory. In 1783, Jefferson asked Revolutionary War hero George Rogers Clark to lead an expedition to explore the West. Clark declined and recommended his youngest brother, William, instead.

The next year, Jefferson proposed in Congress the Ordinance of 1784, which provided that new states could be formed from western territories and admitted to the United States on an equal basis with the original states. In 1786, he supported a quixotic plan to send an American explorer, John Ledyard, eastward across Siberia, alone and on foot. Ledyard was to find a ship on the Pacific coast of Russia that would take him to the west coast of North America. He was thence to travel eastward toward the Mississippi. Perhaps fortunately for Ledyard, who would probably have perished in the attempt, this plan failed: he was arrested in Russia and sent back to Europe.

Undeterred, in 1793 Jefferson and the American Philosophical Society then engaged André Michaux, a French botanist, to "find the shortest & most convenient route between the U.S. & the Pacific Ocean." Due to political intrigues, however, this expedition was aborted when it was still east of the Mississippi. Finally, as mentioned earlier, in 1802 Jefferson read Alexander Mackenzie's account of his epic journey to the Pacific. Mackenzie's report of a feasible passage to this ocean, together with his recommendation that Britain claim the Columbia river as its own, was yet a further motivation for Jefferson to send an exploratory mission into the Trans-Mississippi West.

France had ceded Louisiana to Spain in 1762. It regained this territory in 1800 under the provisions of the secret Treaty of San Ildefonso. Napoleon now wanted Louisiana again because he had developed an ambitious and theoretically lucrative plan: to use the Mississippi valley as a bread basket and trade center to supply a new French empire. This new empire would be on based the sugar-growing island of Saint Domingue (Haiti). Gail Feigenbaum, an expert on this era, tells us that "Saint Domingue may have been small, but its economic importance was large: Britain's entire colonial trade was five million pounds in 1789; France's trade with Saint Domingue alone was eleven million pounds."[38] Moreover, Napoleon also hoped that French control of Louisiana would halt the inexorable westward expansion of the United States.

In 1801, however, Haitian slaves and free blacks led by Toussaint L'Overture, who had led a slave rebellion in the 1790s, seized power from their French masters. To suppress this rebellion and restore French control, in 1802 Napoleon sent a large army to Haiti, led by his brother-in-law, Charles Leclerc. Leclerc had only limited military success and lost more than 40,000 soldiers to yellow fever. Always quick to cut his losses, Napoleon soon realized that he had to abandon Haiti and that, without it, Louisiana was of no earthly use to him. On the contrary: money earned from the sale of Louisiana could instead be used to finance his military adventures in Europe itself.

For these reasons, in 1803 he agreed to sell Louisiana to the United States for 60 million francs (about $15,000,000). The sale was financed for twenty years by the Barings Bank of London and by the Dutch firm of Hope & Co. in Amsterdam.[39] Most of this sum, i.e., $11,250,000, was to be paid immediately. The balance would be covered by the assumption by the United States of French debts to American citizens. These debts came to $3,750,000. This vast new territory virtually doubled the size of the United States. The Louisiana Purchase was at first estimated to total 909,130 square miles. When its final boundaries were drawn in 1818–1819, however, this figure was revised downward slightly, to a mere 827,192 square miles.[40]

Jefferson was ecstatic with his great bargain. He had long wanted to get title to land near New Orleans. This would have allowed American vessels to navigate the Mississippi through Spanish territory without any problems. They could then offload their goods at New Orleans for onward shipment to ports along the Atlantic coast and abroad. When Jefferson had learned about the transfer of Louisiana from Spain to France in 1800, he had sent Robert Livingston, who had been the first secretary of the Department of Foreign Affairs of the new United States, as minister to France in 1801 to try to buy New Orleans itself. At first, Napoleon refused, so Jefferson sent James Monroe, who had just completed his second term as governor of Virginia, as a special envoy to France. Spain's decision, in 1802, to revoke the Americans' right of deposit in New Orleans underscored for Jefferson the importance of getting full control of the Mississippi.

In an unexpected turn of events, just days before Monroe reached Paris, Napoleon offered to sell the United States not just New Orleans but *all of Louisiana*. The Louisiana Purchase included all the rivers, streams, lakes, plains, mountains and valleys between the Mississippi River and the Rocky Mountains. When the 6 percent loans were repaid, its final cost came of the Louisiana Purchase turned out to be $27,267,622. This was a sizeable sum for the United States, to be sure, but in retrospect, it was certainly one of the greatest real estate bargains in history. The cost to the United States was roughly three cents an acre.[41] Thirteen states would eventually be carved out of the Louisiana Purchase.[42]

All that was needed now was a flurry of paperwork in English and French to clinch the deal. Although the Constitution of the United States did not specifically authorize the Federal government to use a treaty to obtain new territory, Jefferson decided that the Louisiana Purchase was covered by the Constitutional doctrine of implied powers. The potential benefits to the nation were so great, he reasoned, that this unique opportunity should be seized immediately—before Napoleon could change his mind. The Senate agreed and ratified the treaty on 20 October 1803.

The Spaniards, who had never given up physical possession of Louisiana to the French, finally did so to the Americans at a ceremony in a lovely formal room in New Orleans, the Sala Capitular, on 30 November 1803. Spain's representatives, Governor Manuel de Salcedo and the Marqués de Casa Calvo, officially transferred Lower Louisiana to the French representative, Préfect Pierre Clément Lassat. Twenty days later, in the same room, the French turned Lower Louisiana over to its new American owners on 20 December 1803.[43] To govern lower Louisiana, Jefferson chose William Charles Cole Claiborne, former governor of the Mississippi territory and the highest-ranking civilian official in the area. A detachment of American troops under the command of General James Wilkinson occupied New Orleans on 20 December 1803.

The Spaniards were still administering Upper Louisiana when the Louisiana Purchase documents were signed.[44] Later, in the "Three Flags Ceremony" held in St. Louis on 9–10 March 1804, Upper Louisiana formally passed from Spain to France, and then from France to the United States. The Spanish commandant at St. Louis, Captain Charles De Hault Delassus, authorized the transfer to take place in front of the Government House. French authorities in New Orleans deputized an American, Captain Amos Stoddard, to accept the territory from Spain on behalf of the French Republic. The French flag was accordingly raised on 9 March 1804.

In deference to the French population of St. Louis, this flag was flown overnight. The next day, Captain Stoddard conveyed the territory from France to the American representative, Meriwether Lewis. Then the American flag was raised: the vast lands of the Trans-Mississippi West now lay open, officially, to the Americans. On 14 May 1804, Lewis and Clark left their camp at Wood River, Illinois, entered the newly acquired Louisiana Territory, and began their heroic trek to the Pacific.

One thorny problem remained: Spain and France had never defined the borders of their North American possessions with any precision. Napoleon had wanted to get rid of Louisiana; he cared nothing about its boundaries. The documents transferring Louisiana from Spain to France in 1800, and from France to the United States in 1803, described these boundaries only in ambiguous and contradictory language. The borders therefore remained extremely vague. It was unclear, for example, whether West Florida was part of Louisiana. The southwestern boundary of the Louisiana Purchase remained undefined, too. Opinions differed sharply on where these and other boundaries were or should be.

Jefferson aggressively insisted that the Louisiana Territory stretched all the way to the Rocky Mountains. It thus encompassed, in his view, the entire watersheds of the Mississippi and Missouri rivers and all their tributaries—a claim that included some parts of southwestern Canada as well. The Spaniards, for their part, argued that Louisiana was in fact very much smaller. It included, they insisted, only what the Library of Congress now describes as "a vague swath of land running from the Ohio Valley and the Alleghenies south to the Cumberland Plateau and beyond the Mississippi River."[45] In the end, the Spaniards had no way to bend the Americans to their will. Jefferson's point of view carried the day. The borders of the Louisiana Purchase would remain undefined until the Adams-Onís treaty finally settled them in 1819.

American objectives, hopes and fears

Many Americans had long wanted their country to become the sovereign power in what is now the continental United States—all the way from the Atlantic to the Pacific. As Nathanial Ames's *Astronomical Diary and Almanack* (initially published in 1726 and said to be the first almanac to join the Bible as American "household necessity") put it in the 1758 edition,

> Arts and Sciences will change the Face of Nature in their Tour from Hence over the Appalachian Mountains to the Western Ocean; Shall not then those vast Quarries, that teem with Mechnic Stone, those for Structure be piled into Great Cities, and those for Sculpture into Statues to perpetuate the Honor of [renowned] Heroes; even those who shall NOW save their Country! O! Ye unborn Inhabitants of America ... when your Eyes behold the Sun after he has rolled the Seasons round for two or three Centuries more, you will know that in Anno Domini 1758, we dream'd of Your Times.[46]

The question of territorial sovereignty was the greatest hope of many Americans. It was also the source of Jefferson's greatest fear. He worried that unless he acted quickly and decisively—e.g., by buying Louisiana and by sending out the Lewis and Clark expedition—North America might easily end up being partitioned into what would later be called competing "spheres of influence" ruled by foreign powers.

7

Epilogue
The Six Rivals:
A Summing-Up

THIS FINAL CHAPTER CARRIES THE STORY of international competition in the Trans-Mississippi West beyond the time of the Louisiana Purchase (1803) and well into the late nineteenth and early twentieth centuries. With some necessary chronological overlaps and flash-backs, it recapitulates the objectives of the six rivals—the Indians, Spaniards, French, British, Russians, and Americans—and summarizes how well or how poorly they fared in their respective quests. A final scorecard tries to show the winners and losers at a single glance.

The Indians

More than anything else, the Indians of the Trans-Mississippi West wanted to retain both their independence and their traditional ways of life. This would prove to be impossible, however, in the face of what would become the unstoppable onslaught of European and American military power and culture.

THE PUEBLO INDIANS

Many of the Pueblo Indians still live today where the Spaniards found them in 1539. These Indians were much more successful than most other tribes in preserving their cultural if not their political independence. Pueblo men were mainly farmers, not fighters. They were thus able to continue their agricultural way of life — and even to improve it by adopting European crops and livestock — regardless of which foreign government happened to be in power at the time.

Politically, the Pueblos were under Spanish rule from 1540 to 1821. They had formally pledged themselves to be vassals, that is to say, the subjects and allies, of the Spanish Crown in 1598.[1] Subsequently, Mexico ruled them from 1821 until 1846, when New Mexico became part of the United States. Two years later, under the terms of the Treaty of Guadalupe Hidalgo, the Pueblo Indians ceded 334,443,520 acres of their land to the United States.[2]

These Indians managed to retain much of their pre-conquest culture by making only superficial accommodations to the demands imposed by foreign governments, churches and schools. Discretely, they continued their age-old patterns of beliefs and practices. As a result, the underlying fabric of their social system, community organization, languages and native religion thus survived foreign occupations relatively intact.

THE APACHES

The American army defeated the Apaches during the Apache Wars in the latter half of the nineteenth century. In the process, however, the Apaches proved themselves to be masters of guerrilla warfare. Under the able leadership of such chiefs as Conchise, Mangas Coloradas, Geronimo, and Victorio, they terrorized large parts of Arizona, Colorado, Texas, and northern Mexico.

The most mobile and most combative of the Apaches living west of the Rio Grande River were the Chiricahua. Trouble erupted in their region in the wake of the 1848–1849 California gold rush.[3] Prospectors quickly flooded into Indian lands in the American Southwest, looking for gold, silver and copper. Mangas Coloradas, one of the foremost Apache leaders, courageously entered the camp of some prospectors and tried to lure them elsewhere with tales of easily accessible gold in other areas. The miners seized him, bound him and flogged him unconscious with a bullwhip. In revenge, he and his men went on the warpath.

At a meeting in 1858 at Apache Pass in the Dragoon Mountains of southeastern Arizona, the Apaches signed a peace treaty with the Americans. This truce lasted until 1861, when Conchise, Mangas Coloradas' nephew, went on the warpath himself. He did so because when he, his family, and some of his men entered Lieutenant George Bascom's tent under a flag of truce, Bascom's troops took them prisoner. Conchise drew his knife and slashed his way out through the back of the tent.

This event, known to local historians as "the Bascom Affair," triggered the killing of several American and Apache hostages. Conchise then joined his uncle in a valiant but doomed effort to expel all the foreigners from the shrunken Apache domain. Over the next 20 years, about 5,000 people would be killed and hundreds of thousands of dollars worth of damage would be done during the Apache Wars.

In 1862, an army of from 1,800 to 3,000 California Civil War volunteers marched to Apache Pass to deter any Confederate attacks. Armed with howitzers, they put the Apaches to flight and captured Mangas Coloradas. A miner remembered that

> About 9 o'clock I noticed the soldiers were doing something to Mangas. I discovered that they were heating their bayonets in the fire and burning his feet and legs. Mangas rose upon his left elbow, angrily protesting that he was no child to be played with.[4]

The soldiers then killed Mangas with four shots, scalped him, and decapitated him.

Conchise and 200 tribesmen took refuge in the Dragoon Mountains and for ten years waged unrelenting guerrilla warfare from their redoubt. The Apaches finally surrendered to General George Crook in 1865. Some warriors, however, refused to abandon their free, nomadic existence in return for permanent confinement on a reservation. They continued raiding under the leadership of Geronimo and Victorio.

Victorio had urged peace until 1877, when the U.S. Army moved his group (the Mimbres) from their native New Mexico to a bleak reservation in southern Arizona. He responded by going on the warpath, leading 250 warriors in a series of attacks that left 400 Mexicans and Americans dead. Victorio himself was killed in 1880.

The Apache Wars ended in 1886, when Geronimo and his followers surrendered. Subsequently, the Chiricahua Apaches were treated as prisoners of war and were held, successively, in camps in Florida, Alabama, and Oklahoma. Geronimo himself died at Fort Sill, Oklahoma, in 1909. In 1913, Apaches were given the choice of settling permanently either in Oklahoma or in New Mexico. About a third of them chose Oklahoma; the rest went to New Mexico.

THE CADDOS

The Louisiana Purchase was indirectly responsible for the demise of the Caddos. After 1803, American immigration into their ancestral lands increased sharply. The Caddos were pushed out and were forced to move farther south. Since it proved to be impossible for the U.S. Government to halt the influx of well-armed American pioneers into Caddo lands, the final solution was for the government to begin buying these lands.

Disease and intertribal warfare contributed to the demise of this tribe. In 1804, United States officials assumed power in Upper Louisiana. Two years later, the American explorers Thomas Freeman and Peter Custis were sent up the Red River on a voyage of exploration into the Southwest that was designed to complement Lewis and Clark's journey to the Pacific. Freeman and Custis found that while there was a great deal of game along the river, there were not many Caddos. Smallpox and wars with the Osage Indians had decimated the once-populous communities of the Caddo confederacy: there were now too few warriors to hunt the game.[5]

Freeman and Custis also discovered what became known as the Great Red River Raft, a huge logjam located just above Shreveport, Louisiana. This almost impenetrable barrier blocked direct navigation on the Red River. Consisting of fallen red cedar, cottonwood, and cypress trees covered with bushes, grass and weeds, it was so tightly bound that, as Freeman and Custis put it, "[a] man could walk over it in any direction."[6] The raft was 165 miles long and made river travel impossible, except along the shallow bayous and narrow channels that ran parallel to the river.

In 1833, the U.S. Government commissioned Captain Henry A. Shreve, an army engineer, to dynamite and break up the raft. By 1836, he had cleared a passage 71 miles long. This encouraged more immigration into Caddo lands. The raft itself reformed in 1839 and blocked travel again. It would not be permanently removed until 1900.

In the meantime, the U.S. Government had continued to buy up the lands of the Caddos. Under the terms of a treaty of 1835, the Caddos ceded all their remaining land to the United States. Although some warriors were initially unhappy about this, in the end they accepted the advice offered to them by Tsauninot, one of their chiefs. He addressed them as follows:

> My Children: For what do you mourn? Are you not starving in the midst of this land? And do you not travel far from it in quest of food? The game we live on is going farther off, and the white man is coming near to us; and is our condition not getting worse daily? Then why lament for the loss of that which yields us nothing but misery? Let us be wise then, and get all we can for it, and not wait till the white man steals it away, little by little, and then gives us nothing.[7]

The treaty provided that the United States would pay the Caddos $30,000 in goods when the treaty was signed and $10,000 in cash per year for four years thereafter. The Americans thus obtained about one million acres of land. By the early 1840s, all the Caddos had moved to the Brazos River area of Texas. They were placed in the Brazos Indian Reservation in 1855 but, four years later, threats of a massacre by white settler forced them to flee to Oklahoma. Much reduced in numbers, they were permanently settled in western Oklahoma on a reservation along the banks of the Washita River.

The Sioux

The Sioux fought valiantly to preserve their lands and their way of life, but in the end they were defeated. In the wake of the California Gold Rush of 1848–1849, prospectors invaded the territory of the Teton and Yankton Sioux. Trying to forestall trouble, in 1851 the U.S. Government forced the Sioux to agree to the First Treaty of Fort Laramie. This permitted Americans to build roads and military posts and set tribal boundaries.

The Santee Sioux surrendered most of their land in Minnesota between 1851 and 1859 and were assigned to a reservation. Treaty violations and the advance of the American frontier led them to rebel in 1862 under the leadership of Little Crow. This uprising was put down and the Santee Sioux were forced to move west to reservations in Dakota and Nebraska.

We have already mentioned U.S. Army Captain Randolph B. Marcy's definitive work, *The Prairie Traveler* (1859). Many Army officers, pioneers and settlers in the Great Plains agreed with his judgment about how to deal with Indians. Marcy's advice, which was based on 25 years of personal experience on the frontier, was as follows:

> The only way to make these merciless freebooters [the Sioux and other Plains tribes] fear or respect the authority of our government is, when they misbehave, first of all to chastise them well by striking such a blow as will be felt for a long time, and thus show them that we are superior to them in war. They will then respect us much more than when their good-will is purchased by presents.[8]

The Sioux were infuriated by the U.S. Government's plans to build the Powder River Road from Bozeman, Montana, across their favorite hunting grounds in the Big Horn Mountains. Beginning in 1865, the Oglala chief Red Cloud mounted a campaign to prevent the road from being built. In 1866, Chief High Backbone and his warriors killed more than 80 U.S. soldiers, led by a Captain Fetterman, near Fort Phil Kearny, Wyoming. This incident is now known as the Fetterman Massacre. Belatedly acknowledging defeat, the U.S. Government signed the Second Treaty of Fort Laramie in 1868, thereby agreeing to abandon the Bozeman road and to give the Sioux undisputed possession of part of South Dakota lying west of the Missouri River.

Gold was discovered in the Black Hills of South Dakota in the mid–1870s. Miners paid no attention to the treaty and flowed into Sioux lands. At the Battle of the Little Bighorn (1876), a large force of Sioux and Cheyenne wiped out Lieutenant Colonel George Armstrong Custer and more than 200 of his soldiers. This proved to be only a tactical and temporary victory for the Indians. Later that year, when 3,000 Sioux were trapped by General Alfred H. Terry's army, they had no choice but to surrender. Most of them went back to their reservations.

Chiefs Crazy Horse, Sitting Bull, and Gall initially refused to yield. Crazy Horse surrendered in 1877 and a few months later was killed in a fracas with soldiers who were trying to imprison him in a guardhouse.[9] Sitting Bull and Gall sought refuge in Canada in 1877. Conditions were so bad there that Gall abandoned Sitting Bull and surrendered to the U.S. Army in 1880. The next year Sitting Bull himself accepted a pardon and returned to the United States, where he was held as a prisoner of war for two years.

In 1890–1891, the Ghost Dance religion predicted the coming of an Indian messiah who would restore the nomadic life of earlier days. Fearing that the Ghost Dance would inflame the Sioux, government agents arrested its leaders. Sitting Bull was killed by Indian police taking him into custody. Sioux resistance came to a final, bloody end in December 1890, when U.S. troops massacred more than 200 Sioux men, women, and children at Wounded Knee.

THE COMANCHES

By 1901, the Comanches had lost almost all of their ancestral land.[10] The story of Comanche, Mexican, and American raids, counter-raids, negotiations, broken treaties, and epidemics during the nineteenth century is a sad one. It is also sufficiently complicated so that only a few highlights will be mentioned briefly here.

The Mexican Colonization Law of 1824 encouraged foreign, e.g., American, immigration into Texas. As the foreign population there grew, friction increased between the Comanches and the newcomers. In 1835, the United States signed a treaty with the Comanches and other tribes in western Oklahoma. In 1840, the Texas Rangers were formed to fight the Comanches. When Texas was annexed in 1846, the Americans inherited Mexico's longstanding problem of Comanche raiding and the lack of a boundary line between the settlements and the *Comanchería*.

American immigration across the Great Plains went into high gear after the discovery of gold in California in 1848. In 1851, the United States convened a "Peace on the Plains" conference at Fort Laramie, Wyoming, to limit intertribal warfare by drawing boundaries between the territories of rival tribes. Due to smallpox, the Comanche population dropped from about 20,000 people to only 12,000 in 1851. In 1854, the Penateka tribe (the southern branch of the Comanche) was settled on a reservation in Oklahoma but the northern section of the tribe continued to fight to protect its traditional hunting grounds.

In 1864, Colonel Christopher ("Kit") Carson was sent with a column of troops from Fort Bascom, New Mexico, into the Llano Estacado (the Staked Plain) to punish the Comanches and their Kiowa allies. He failed in this endeavor. At the end of the American Civil War in 1865, the Comanches and their Kiowa allies signed a treaty with the U.S. that gave them part of western Oklahoma. Hostilities resumed when the U.S. failed to abide by the terms of the treaty.

Under the terms of the Medicine Lodge Treaty of 1867, the Comanches and two other tribes agreed to live in a reservation in Oklahoma. The government, however, was unable to keep settlers off the land that had been promised to the Indians. Some of the most violent encounters between U.S. forces and the Comanches took place thereafter. Seeing their nomadic way of life eroding so rapidly, the Comanches, inspired by their visionary leader White Eagle, attacked Texas buffalo hunters at Adobe Walls in 1874. The Indians were defeated and the U.S. Government launched the Red River War (or Buffalo War) of 1874–1875. This campaign was the last Indian war on the Great Plains. The Comanches lost the war and were forced to settle in a reservation in Texas.

One of the most famous and respected Comanche chiefs was Quanah Parker (1845–1911), but even he could not stop the steady loss of Comanche lands. Of the 3 million acres given to them by the Medicine Lodge Treaty of 1867, the Comanches managed to keep less than 10 percent. In 1901, their reservation was broken up into 160-acre allotments and disbanded. That same year, the 90 percent of the reservation that was no longer owned by Comanches was opened up to American settlers. This set off one of the biggest land rushes in American history.

The Mandans

The history of the Mandans in the nineteenth century is short and unhappy. In 1750, there were about 3,600 Mandans. By 1800, recurrent epidemics of smallpox and cholera had forced them to abandon seven of their nine villages. When Lewis and Clark wintered with them in 1804–1805, smallpox and wars with the Sioux had cut their numbers to about 1,200. In 1837, another smallpox epidemic left only 100 to 150 Mandans alive. These survivors moved to the Fort Berthold Reservation northwest of Bismarck, North Dakota, beginning in 1845. There are only about 350 Mandans left today.

THE MARITIME TRADERS OF THE PACIFIC NORTHWEST COAST

It is a sad fact that these Indians fared poorly, too, although there were many domestic and international developments in their region. In 1810, the North West Company set up Spokane House, its first permanent inland fur trading post. In 1811–1812, the rival New York-based Pacific Fur Company established Fort Astoria near the mouth of the Columbia River as its own trading post. The British seized Astoria during the War of 1812 with the United States; after the end of the war, it was sold to the North West Company.

Following a series of negotiations in 1818–1819, Spain abandoned its claim to all lands north of the 42nd parallel, which formed the northern border of California, Nevada, and Utah. In 1818, the United States and Britain agreed to a condominium (joint occupation) of the Oregon Territory. This lasted until 1846, when, except for Vancouver Island, this region became part of the United States.

For the Indians of the Pacific Northwest coast, their earlier sea otter trade with the Europeans and Americans generated both positive and negative effects. At first, the new wealth, new goods and new ideas introduced by the foreigners stimulated Indian cultures. Before long, however, the Indians became increasingly reliant on foreign traders. Moreover, by about 1832, unregulated hunting had seriously depleted the supply of sea otters along the entire Pacific Northwest coast.

A further problem for the Indians was that, in the mid nineteenth century, American and Canadian settlers began flooding into western Washington, Oregon, Vancouver Island, and the lower Fraser River Valley. The Indians who lived there were removed and were placed in small reservations in Washington and Oregon, generally under the terms of treaties. The Indians themselves had no natural resistance to European diseases. Consequently, the Indian population of the Northwest coast fell from some 188,000 in 1774 to only about 38,000 in 1874.[11]

By the end of the nineteenth century, the surviving Indians were in dire straits. They had lost most of their land and were now dependent on imported American, British and Canadian manufactured goods. One promising development—the salmon canning industry—turned out to be a mixed blessing. Although this was a high-volume business—in 1902 alone, fisheries along the coast of Alaska produced 2.5 million cases of salmon, each one containing 48 one-pound cans—not many cannery jobs were available for the Indians themselves.

Most of workforce consisted of cheap imported labor, usually Chinese bachelors. Later, machines did much of the work. One such machine, introduced in 1903, was advertised as the "Iron Chink." It could process 60 salmon a minute, thereby replacing 15 men.[12] Another bit of bad news was that the canning industry controlled the major salmon streams, so it was no longer possible for the Indians to fish on their own if they wished to do so.

The Mission Indians

As mentioned earlier, the Mission Indians fared very poorly under mission life. Subsequently, when the Mexican government officially ended the authority of the missions in 1834, the Indians were in effect abandoned. They were promised the rights of Mexican citizenship and one-half of the mission properties, but with no protectors or advocates, they soon became easy prey for speculators.

When California was acquired by the United States in 1848, the Indians no longer had even a theoretical title to the lands they had formerly worked. The result was, as the *Catholic Encyclopedia* put it in 1908, they

> sank into a condition of homeless misery under which they died by thousands and were fast approaching extinction.... The Mission Indians of California have dwindled to fewer than one-sixteenth of their original number, and indications point to their extinction.[13]

Some of the Mission Indians managed to assimilate successfully into the agricultural or ranch life of California. One of the few success stories is that of the Agua Caliente tribe, which became prosperous because it could sell or lease its land to the upmarket resort of Palm Springs.

The Blackfoot

In 1806, two men of the Lewis and Clark expedition killed a Blackfoot who was trying to steal their rifles. This incident is traditionally held to be the reason why, for some 25 years thereafter, the Blackfoot were the sworn enemies of all trappers and effectively prevented them from trapping along the upper tributaries of the Missouri River.

The Americans signed a treaty with the Blackfoot in 1855, expecting them to settle down and become farmers. For the next 30 years, however, the Blackfoot steadfastly refused to do so. They insisted instead on remaining nomadic buffalo hunters. This was an understandable but extremely ill-advised decision. As the great buffalo herds were driven to the brink of extinction by market hunters in the early 1880s, nearly one-quarter of the Piegan Blackfoot died of starvation.

Repeated epidemics of smallpox and measles took a heavy took, too. By 1909 only 4,635 Blackfoot remained, slightly more than half of them in Alberta and the balance in Montana. The surviving Blackfoot subsequently understood the need to change their lifestyle. Many of them eventually became small-scale farmers and cattlemen in Montana or Alberta.

The Nez Percé

We noted earlier that the visit of Lewis and Clark on their westward-bound journey in 1805 spelled the beginning of the end for the powerful, prosperous culture of the Nez Percé. As the American historian John Logan Allen has remarked, "There have been few better examples of Indian-white relations in the United States where the Indians have been so consistently friendly and the white so treacherous than the long history of Nez Percé and American contacts."[14]

The Nez Percé were extremely helpful to Lewis and Clark. They described for the explorers the routes they would have to follow to reach the Pacific. In return, the explorers genuinely admired the Nez Percé. Clark says of them:

> The *Cho-pun-nish* or Pierced nose Indians are Stout likely men, handsom women, and verry dressey in their way the dress of the men are a White Buffalow robe or Elk Skin dressed with Beeds which are generally white, Sea Shells & the Mother of Pirl hung to ther hair & a piece of otter skin about their necks.... The women dress in a Shirt of Ibex or Goat Skins which reach quite down to their anckles with a girdle, their heads are not ornemented, their Shirts are ornemented with quilled Brass, Small pieces of Brass Cut into different forms, Beeds, Shells & curious bones etc. The men expose those parts which are generally kept from few [view] by other nations but the women are more perticular [in concealing their private parts] than any other nation which I have passed.[15]

The chief of the Nez Percé, Twisted Hair, seemed to Clark "a Chearfull man with apparent siencerity."[16] On their return trip eastward in 1806, Lewis and Clark stayed with the Nez Percé again. The chief again did his best to help Lewis and Clark on their journey. The explorers made this entry in their journal:

> we are anxious to procure some guides to accompany us on the different routes we mean to take from Travellers rest [one of their earlier campsites];

for this purpose we have turned our attention to Twisted hair who has several sons grown who are well acquainted as himself with the various roads in those mountains. we invited the old fellow to remove his family and live near us while we remained; he appeared gratifyed with this expression of our confidence and promised to do so.[17]

Lewis and Clark tried to get the Nez Percé to agree to the establishment of American trading posts on their lands. The Indians expressed their willingness, in principle, to permit such posts. First, however, they demanded firearms. Their enemies could get guns from British or French traders: the Nez Percé saw the absolute necessity of having guns to defend themselves and to hunt game more effectively.

The explorers willingly gave the Indians some gunpowder, lead balls and a few of their extra guns. No trading posts were established, however. By 1811, the mountain men (American beaver trappers) had reached Nez Percé lands. These hardy self-sufficient trappers were followed in the 1840s by successive waves of missionaries, homesteaders, gold miners, and settlers moving west to Oregon along the Oregon Trail.

The United States signed a treaty with the Nez Percé in 1855 that gave them a reservation of more than 7.5 million acres. In 1860, however, gold was discovered in the Salmon and Clearwater rivers, spurring an influx of miners and settlers into the reservation. The United States therefore pressured the Nez Percé into renegotiating the treaty in 1863. During this fraudulent process, 75 percent of the reservation was taken from the Indians. The tribe became increasingly split between those who accepted the new, smaller reservation and those who did not. As more homesteaders poured in, the Nez Percé lands dwindled even further. It has been asserted that, in total, 17 million acres of land were taken from the Nez Percé.[18]

Friction between these newcomers and the Indians resulted in the Nez Percé War of 1877 — and in what is arguably the most eloquent and most moving statement ever made by a North American Indian. During this war, Chief Joseph (1840–1904) sought refuge in Canada. He led 200–300 of his warriors and their families on a thousand-mile retreat across Oregon, Washington, Idaho, and Montana. When his band was finally cornered by General Nelson A. Miles in the Bear Paw Mountains of Montana, Chief Joseph was within 40 miles of the Canadian border. Seeing that there was no way to avoid defeat, he made a surrender speech that has gone down in history.

"I am tired of fighting," he said,

> Our chiefs are killed. Looking Glass is dead. Toohulhulsote is dead. The old men are all dead. It is the young men who say no and yes. He who led the young men is dead. It is cold and we have no blankets. The little children are freezing to death. My people, some of them, have run away to the hills and

have not blankets, nor food. No one knows where they are — perhaps they are freezing to death. I want to have time to look for my children and see how many of them I can find. Maybe I shall find them among the dead. Hear me, my chiefs, I am tired. My heart is sad and sick. From where the sun now stands, I will fight no more forever.[19]

In 1889, the U.S. Government began to divide the Nez Percé reservation into individual homesteads. The Dawes Act of 1893 reduced the 1863 reservation to one-tenth of its former size. Some of the Nez Percé remained on the reservation; others left to become small landowners or laborers.

The Spaniards

Spain set up four viceroyalties to govern the lands it conquered in the New World. The first and for our purposes the most important of these institutions was the Viceroyalty of New Spain (*Virreinato de Nueva España*). Established in 1535 and headquartered in Mexico City, it initially included all the territory north of the Isthmus of Panama that was under Spanish control. The Spanish conquest weighed very heavily on the Indians. Due to military losses, maltreatment, diseases, and cultural disruption, the Indian population of New Spain declined from about 25 million to 1 million during the first century of Spanish rule.[20]

New Spain eventually expanded to embrace Mexico and Central America; the Californias; the central and southwestern parts of the United States; a band of territory running east along the Gulf of Mexico to Florida; Spain's possessions in the Caribbean; and, finally, the Philippines as well. Although the frontier regions north of Mexico were only a backward and relatively unimportant part of New Spain, the Spaniards still had numerous ambitions there. The respective weight given to each of them varied with time and place but, basically, they wanted to:

- Enrich themselves by finding or confiscating gold and silver.
- Win personal and national glory.
- Use the northern frontier as a buffer to protect the rich silver mines of central Mexico.
- Convert the Indians to Roman Catholicism.
- Discover the Passage.
- Establish presidios and missions in California to block Russian encroachment south along the Pacific coast.

The Spaniards failed to achieve most of these objectives. They could not enrich themselves. The region lacked any easily exploitable deposits of valuable minerals; the Indians did not have any gold or silver themselves. Personal and national glory may have been won in the short term but it proved to be ephemeral. The silver mines of Mexico were never threatened by French, British, or American attack. The Spaniards were more successful on the religious front: virtually all the Indians under their direct control became Roman Catholics, at least nominally. It was impossible, of course, for the Spaniards to discover the non-existent Passage. On the Pacific coast, the Russians were far more interested in the sea otter trade and in buying wheat from the California missions than in trying to colonize California themselves.

In broad terms, Spain faced two fundamental and ultimately unsolvable problems in pursuit of its objectives. The first was that in the Trans-Mississippi West, as the Library of Congress puts it, "From the late eighteenth century forward, areas under Spanish control began to decrease, sometimes gradually, sometimes precipitously, as a result of pressure from the new United States that had begun to explore, colonize, and expand beyond the Appalachian Mountains."[21]

The second problem was that the turmoil of Napoleonic Europe stimulated Mexico's efforts to become independent of Spain. The Viceroyalty of New Spain officially ended when Mexico won its independence in 1821 and Spain had to recognize Mexico's independence. Later, when Spain lost the Spanish-American war in 1898, under the terms of the Treaty of Paris it was forced to renounce its claim to Cuba and to surrender the Philippines, Puerto Rico, and Guam to the victorious United States.

The French

France, for its part, had four main objectives in North America. The first and foremost of these was to maximize profits from the fur trade. As mentioned earlier, hatmakers in Paris were eager to import increasing quantities of beaver pelts, which they turned into elegant hats that resisted both rain and wind. By 1680, about 800 French traders were bartering for Indian furs in the interior and were sending them back to Montreal by the canoeload.

The secret of their success—the *en dérouine* (itinerant peddling) pattern of trade—lay in forming small partnerships, which in turn sent out small parties to do business directly with the Indians in Indian territory.[22] French traders usually took Indian wives, thus simultaneously getting a warm bedmate, a language tutor, and a host of potential customers, i.e., the relatives of these women. It is not surprising, then, that when New France finally came to an end in 1763 with Britain's victory in the Seven Years' War, the French had dominated the North American fur trade.[23]

France failed, however, to achieve its second objective — increasing its political, economic and military influence in North America to counter the numerically superior Anglo-Americans. Life in New France was so cold, harsh and uninviting that the eighteenth century French author and philosopher Voltaire is popularly but incorrectly thought to have dismissed the colony simply as *quelques arpents de neige* ("a few acres of snow").[24] Very few French men and women wanted to settle there; many of those who did died early. In 1630, only 100 colonists were living in Quebec itself.

A census of New France as a whole, conducted by Intendant Jean Talon in 1665–1668, revealed a French population of 3,215 souls, but with nearly twice as many men (2,034) as women (1,181). Hoping to make New France the center of a colonial empire, Louis XIV then took several steps to encourage population growth there. The most dramatic of these was his decision to send to New France more than 700 single women between the ages of 15 and 30. They were known as *les filles du roi* (the king's girls). Indentured servants were sent as well.[25]

By the middle of the eighteenth century, the population of New France had risen to over 50,000 inhabitants. However, Britain's American colonies, which profited from warmer climates, deeper and more fertile soils and better commercial opportunities, already had more than one million people by then. The issue of French influence was soon moot, however. When the Treaty of Paris ended the Seven Years' War in 1763, France had to surrender to Britain all of New France east of the Mississippi, except for New Orleans.

France's third objective was to convert the Indians to Roman Catholicism. At a social and personal level in settled areas, the church was the dominant institution in New France. Missionaries — the Récollets and especially the Jesuits — became firmly established. In the 1640s, Jesuits converted many of Huron Indians in the Great Lakes region. Although by 1650 both the Jesuit mission there and the might of the Hurons themselves were destroyed by Iroquois invasions, Christianity never lost its foothold in the interior of New France.

France's greatest accomplishment in this field, however, lies not in religion but in historiography. Dr. Denys Delâge, a Canadian scholar, believes that one of France's most important contributions here was its formal recognition of Indian culture as being worthy of interest and respect. What he aptly summarizes as "les écrits des missionnaires et la littérature de voyage" (the writings of missionaries and the accounts by soldiers, interpreters and *coureurs de bois*) have bequeathed to us a heritage of cultural open-mindedness in general and a defense of North American Indian cultures in particular.[26]

It is especially interesting to note that, in contrast to many of their later American counterparts, the French-Canadian *coureurs de bois* passed on to modern Canada a strong tradition of *métissage* (racial interbreeding and its accompanying cultural pluralism), rather than a culture of apartheid.

The final objective sought by the French was the Passage. When Cartier sailed up the Gulf of St. Lawrence in 1534, he thought he was heading for China. Like all the other early European explorers who tried to find the Passage, however, he ran into an unforeseen and immovable obstacle: the continent of North America.

The British

Britain had three goals in North America: to find the Passage; to profit from an economic theory known as mercantilism; and to establish an empire that would rival, and hopefully surpass, that of New France. Britain could not but fail to achieve the first goal, but it was quite successful in achieving the other two.

Mercantilism was a concept coined by the Scottish philosopher Adam Smith in 1776, but by then England and other European countries had already been putting this theory into practice for 200 years. Mercantilism held that the wealth of a nation should be measured solely by the amount of gold and silver it owned. Advocates of this theory argued that Spain had become powerful only after amassing huge amounts of bullion from its overseas possessions.

The mantra of the mercantilists was that "colonies exist only for the benefit of the mother country." Unless a given colony was earning a profit, it was of no use to the mother country. Mercantilists urged the mother country to import raw materials from its colonies and to export finished goods to them in return. Since this trade was designed to be a monopoly, no foreign competitors were tolerated. Accordingly, all the profits would flow into the mother country itself. In practice, mercantilist theory did pay good dividends for Britain when applied to its North American colonies.

During the Seven Years' War, Britain fought France and Spain in Europe, the Caribbean, Asia, and North America. This great international struggle is sometimes called "the first world war." It ended in 1763 with a total British victory: the French had to surrender New France to the British.

This seminal event marks the beginning of Britain's later imperial greatness.

With the fall of New France, English and Scottish merchants began to replace the French fur trading firms in Montreal. British (and French) trappers working for the Hudson's Bay Company penetrated deeply into the expanded Trans-Mississippi West, founding Cumberland House close to the Saskatchewan River in 1774.

The Treaty of Paris (1783) ended Britain's war with the United States. The upstart American revolutionaries had defeated Britain; many British loyalists fled to Canada. Thus just as Britain's colonial empire along the east coast of the United States came to an end, its empire in Canada was strengthened by an influx of these highly motivated English-speaking settlers. In the 1800s, moreover, thousands of newcomers arrived each year from England, Scotland and Ireland. British influence in Canada would remain dominant long after the British North America Act of 1867 established the Dominion of Canada.

The Russians

We have seen that the Russians did not try to exploit the Trans-Mississippi West for gold, God, and glory alone but focused mainly on the maritime mammal fur trade. They were so successful in this enterprise that the sea otter population of the Pacific coast between Alaska and San Francisco was severely depleted. The Russians did not immediately achieve their second objective — a commercial treaty between Russia and New Spain — but finally managed to do so in 1818. However, they failed entirely to achieve their third goal — turning the Pacific coast into a Russian possession.

The Russian fur hunters needed Spanish wheat, livestock and tallow; the California missions needed Russian tools, manufactured goods, and sea transport along the California coast. In 1806, Nikolai Rezanov, a founder of the Russian-American Company and chief of the Russian hunters on the Pacific coast, set sail from Sitka in the ship *Juno*, bound for San Francisco, the northernmost outpost of Spanish settlement in California.[27] He hoped to sign a treaty with the Spaniards so that, in return for Russian furs, they would supply his outposts along the Pacific coast.

At first, the Spanish officials in San Francisco were unresponsive: under Spanish law, it was illegal for any Spanish colony to engage in foreign trade. The Spaniards were desperately eager to trade, however, and Rezanov was a good salesman. He began by winning the backing of the son of the commander of San Francisco's *presidio*. More importantly, Rezanov, then a

42-year-old widower, became engaged to the commander's daughter, Concepción, a 15-year-old beauty said to be the prettiest girl in California.

Rezanov sailed back to Sitka with a shipload of grain and with the Spanish governor's promise to send a copy of the proposed Russian-Spanish treaty to Madrid for the king's signature. A romantic but tragic love story now began to unfold. In 1807, Rezanov set off for St. Petersburg to get Alexander I to sign the treaty and to approve his proposed Russian Orthodox-Roman Catholic wedding to Concepción. Alas, Rezanov died en route, so the treaty was not signed. After waiting in vain for Rezanov to return, Concepción rejected all other suitors and eventually became a nun.

By 1812, having harvested most of the sea otters along the Pacific Northwest coast, the Russians centered their fur trade at Fort Ross. The Spaniards continued to trade with foreign vessels, both openly and clandestinely; Russian ships were the principal players in this exchange. In 1818, the Russians worked out a trade agreement with Governor Sola of California, allowing annual trade with Sitka.[28] In its heyday, the Russian American Fur Company could boast of a string of 24 fur trading posts stretching from Alaska to San Francisco, with a trade estimated at 7 billion rubles.[29] By the end of the 1830s, however, the fur trade had dwindled to the point where Fort Ross was losing 44,000 rubles a year. It was closed in 1841.

The Americans

The Americans had two major goals in the Trans-Mississippi West and they went hand-in-hand. The first was to prevent any other nation from occupying, permanently, any part of what is now the continental United States. The second was to expand the United States all the way to the Pacific Ocean. By a combination of good luck and assertiveness, the Americans managed to accomplish both these objectives.

To prevent any other power from possessing the Trans-Mississippi West was one of the fundamental reasons why Jefferson sent Lewis and Clark to the Pacific. Jefferson knew that France, the recent owner of Louisiana, would not object. In a secret message to Congress in 1803, he asked for appropriation of $2,500 — a deliberate underestimate — to fund the Lewis and Clark expedition. (The final bill would come to more than $38,000.) He told Congress:

> While other civilized nations have encountered great expense to enlarge the boundaries of knowledge by undertaking voyages of discovery, and for other literary purposes [by "literary purposes" Jefferson means "practical knowledge"], in various parts and directions, our nation seems to owe to the same

object, as well as to its own interests, to explore this, the only line of easy communication across the continent, and so directly traversing our own part of it.... The nation claiming the territory [France], regarding this as a literary pursuit, which is in the habit of permitting within its dominions, would not be disposed to view it with jealousy, even if the expiring state of its interests there did not render it a matter of indifference.[30]

The Lewis and Clark expedition of 1804–1806 thus followed hard on the heels of the Louisiana Purchase of 1803. The most immediate and in the long run the most important result of this expedition was that it ushered in the era of the American beaver trappers and explorers known as the mountain men. These men were the greatest explorers of the Trans-Mississippi West. Their era began when Lewis and Clark were returning from the Pacific in 1806. At the Mandan villages, one of the members of the expedition asked if he could be discharged there. Clarks tells us why:

[John] Colter one of our men expressed a desire to join Some trappers who offered to become shearers [sharers] with him and furnish traps &c. the offer a very advantagious one, to him, his services could be dispenced with from this down and as we were disposed to be of service to any one of our party who had performed their duty as well as Colter had done, we agreed to allow him the privilage....[31]

Colter spent the winter of 1806–1807 trapping in the Yellowstone area. In 1807, he began to paddle, alone, down the Missouri, bound for St. Louis. At the mouth of the Platte River, however, he came across an expedition heading north for the Yellowstone. Led by the Spanish fur trader Manual Lisa, this was the first expedition sent out to exploit the treasure trove of furs in the Rocky Mountains that Lewis and Clark had described after their return to St. Lewis. Lisa promptly hired Colter to join his team.

Lewis and Clark showed Americans the way west but it was the mountain men, of whom Colter was the first to be well documented, who explored it most thoroughly. From 1807 until the late 1840s, other mountain men—Jim Bridger, Kit Carson, Tom Fitzpatrick, and Jedediah Smith are excellent examples here—would move through the Trans-Mississippi West at will. They led others across the Great Plains, the Rocky Mountains, and the Southwest and brought them safely to California, Washington and Oregon. Their encyclopedic knowledge of the region's geography, climate, and Indian cultures was instrumental in opening up the Trans-Mississippi West to American and European settlers.

The Americans' second and long-standing objective—to expand to the Pacific—can be distilled into two historically powerful words: Manifest Destiny. In the July-August 1845 edition of the *United States Magazine and Democratic Review*, the writer John L. Sullivan forecast "the fulfillment of

"Junction of the Yellow Stone River with the Missouri."
©2005 Alecto Historical Editions www.alectoUK.com

our manifest destiny to overspread the continent allotted by Providence."[32] Manifest Destiny was in essence the unilateral self-proclaimed "right" of the United States to expand all the way to the Pacific — and even beyond.

We have already mentioned some of the lands obtained by the United States from Indian tribes. Other highlights of the territorial expansion of the United States up to the middle of the nineteenth century can now be mentioned briefly as well.

France sold Louisiana to the United States in 1803. West and East Florida were ceded between 1810 and 1819. Negotiations with Britain in 1818 adjusted national ownership of some lands along the Canadian border, i.e., those west of the Mississippi and east of the Continental Divide. The Maine boundary was rectified in 1842. The Republic of Texas was annexed in 1845. The Oregon Territory was divided between the United States and Britain in 1846.

A major event was the Treaty of Guadalupe Hidalgo (1848), which ended the 1846–1848 war between Mexico and the United States. Mexico ceded nearly one million square miles of land to the United States. This vast domain would eventually become nine states: California, Nevada, Utah, New Mexico, Arizona, Colorado, Wyoming, Oklahoma, and Kansas. The Gadsden Purchase (1853) added to the United States some land south of the Gila River.

International competition in the Trans-Mississippi West must thus be counted as a clear success for the Americans. By the middle of the nineteenth century, they were the sole proprietors of a continental United States that stretched west from the Atlantic to the Pacific, and south from the 49th parallel to the Rio Grande River.

A Scorecard for the Six Rivals

1. The Indians

THEIR OBJECTIVES: To retain their independence and their traditional ways of life.

HOW THEY FARED: The Pueblo Indians managed to preserve their cultural but not their political independence. The Apaches, Sioux, Comanches, and Nez Percé were defeated militarily and were forced into reservations. The Caddos sold their land to the U.S. Government and had to enter a reservation. Decimated by disease, the Mandans had to move into a reservation. The maritime traders of the Pacific Northwest coast lost most of their land and had great difficulty finding jobs in the new economy. The Mission Indians fared very poorly under mission rule; later, some got farming or ranching jobs. The Blackfoot began to starve when the buffalo were killed off; some later became farmers or ranchers.

2. The Spaniards

THEIR OBJECTIVES: To enrich themselves, win glory, protect the silver mines of Mexico, convert the Indians, discover the Passage, and block Russian encroachment into California.

HOW THEY FARED: The Spaniards failed to enrich themselves or to win any lasting glory. Their silver mines were never threatened. The Indians were nominally converted. The Passage did not exist. The Russians made no effort to colonize California.

3. The French

THEIR OBJECTIVES: To exploit the fur trade, increase the influence of New France, convert the Indians, and find the Passage.

HOW THEY FARED: The French excelled at the fur trade. They lost New France to the British in 1763 and Napoleon sold Louisiana to the Americans in 1803. Christianity did become the dominant religion of New France but the Passage was not found.

4. The British

THEIR OBJECTIVES: To find the Passage, profit from mercantilism and the fur trade, and establish a North American empire.

HOW THEY FARED: They did not find the Passage. The mercantilist system and the fur trade did pay good dividends. At its apex, the British empire in North America included large chunks of what are now the United States and Canada. In 1776, however, the United States declared its independence. The British then turned their attention to Canada.

5. The Russians

THEIR OBJECTIVES: To exploit the marine mammal fur trade of the Pacific Northwest coast; to work out a commercial treaty with Spanish California; and to make the west coast of North America a Russian possession and encourage large scale emigration there.

HOW THEY FARED: The Russians harvested so many sea otters that the supply of these animals was drastically reduced. A treaty with California was not signed until 1818. The Pacific coast never became a Russian possession.

6. The Americans

THEIR OBJECTIVES: To prevent any other nation from possessing any part of the continental U.S., and to expand to the Pacific Ocean.

HOW THEY FARED: Both these objectives were fully achieved.

Thus ends our survey of international competition in the Trans-Mississippi West between the days of Cabeza de Vaca (1528) and the Louisiana Purchase (1803). Any work of scholarship — even a primer — is by necessity only *provisional*: old explanations must be abandoned as new facts and new interpretations come to light. Critical comments on this book are therefore most welcome. They should be addressed to the author in care of the publisher. In the meantime, readers who may wish to pursue this subject further will find some excellent primary and secondary sources listed in the bibliography.

Selected Chronology, 1492–1804

1492	First of four transatlantic voyages by Columbus opens the way for the European exploration, exploitation and colonization of the Americas.
1493	Papal bull *Inter Caetera* divides the unexplored world between Spain and Portugal, the two most powerful Catholic states of the time.
1494	Treaty of Tordesillas defines the boundary between the Spanish and Portuguese areas for exploration and colonization as a pole-to-pole line 1,185 miles west of the Cape Verde islands. The English reject this concept.
1496–1498	English navigator and explorer John Cabot receives letters patent to sail to North America and look for a passage to Asia.
Early 1500s	Spanish jurists draw up the *Requerimiento* to be used when claiming Indian allegiance and Indian lands.
1519	Spanish navigator Alonso Álvarez de Pineda sails along the Gulf coast.
1521	*Conquistador* Hernán Cortés completes the conquest of the Aztec empire of Mexico with its fabulous gold and silver mines.
1524	Giovanni Verrazano, a Florentine navigator working for France, sails along the east coast of North America from the Carolinas north to Nova Scotia, looking for the Passage.
1528–1536	"Four ragged castaways"— the *conquistador* Cabeza de Vaca and his three surviving companions— spend eight years wandering through the deserts of the Southwest.
1531	*Conquistador* Pizarro begins a campaign that will overwhelm the Inca empire of Peru and will make Spaniards the new masters of the great silver mines of Potosí, Bolivia.

1534	French explorer Jacques Cartier sails up the Gulf of St. Lawrence and claims New France for his king. Indians greet him by holding up furs on sticks, showing their eagerness to trade.
1535	Establishment of the Viceroyalty of New Spain, first of the four viceroys Spain will set up to govern its lands in the New World.
1539	Franciscan missionary Marcos de Niza and the North African slave Estevánico reach the Zuni pueblo of Háwikuh during their search for the Seven Cities of Cíbola.
1539–1543	Hunting for gold, Spain's de Soto-Moscoso expedition cuts a wide swath of destruction from Florida to west of the Mississippi. Only half of the Spanish soldiers survive.
1540–1542	Excited by the exaggerated reports coming from Father Marcos, Spain's Coronado-Alarcón expedition sets out to find Cíbola or the golden city of Quivira. In 1541, the expedition meets the Apaches on the plains of southeastern Kansas. In 1542, it meets the Caddos when it crosses their lands.
1542–1543	*Conquistador* Juan Rodriguez Cabrillo becomes the first European to visit the Pacific shore of the United States. When he dies during the voyage, his senior pilot, Bartolomé Ferrer, continues along the California coast, perhaps sailing as far north as the California-Oregon border.
1579	English explorer and navigator Sir Francis Drake claims Nova Albion (the lands north of San Francisco Bay) for Queen Elizabeth I. He leaves behind a brass plate that will later cause a long-running academic controversy.
1581	Spain's Rodríguez-Chamuscado expedition explores New Mexico but fails to convert the Indians or find new silver mines.
1582–1583	Antonio de Espejo, a Spanish explorer, leads an expedition into Pueblo country, hoping to refurbish his tattered reputation and to find gold or silver mines.
1590	Lieutenant Governor Gaspar Castaño de Sosa is sent to Mexico City in irons for leading a group of colonists to the Pueblo country without official permission.
1595	Spanish treasure galleon *San Agustín* is wrecked off Point Reyes, north of San Francisco.
1598–1601	Spanish occupation of Pueblo lands begins when Juan de Oñate leads 560 colonists into northern New Mexico. He establishes his capital at San Juan Pueblo, 25 miles north of Santa Fe. A Spanish assault on Acoma Pueblo leaves 800 Acoma Indians dead; many of the survivors suffer amputation or are enslaved.
1602–1603	Sebastián Vizcaíno, a Spanish navigator, enters San Diego Bay and then sails north to explore the California coast. Bad weather forces him to turn back off the California-Oregon border.

1604–1605	*Conquistador* Juan de Oñate tries but fails to blaze a trail from New Mexico to the Pacific coast.
1607	Jamestown, the first English colony in North America, is founded in Virginia.
1608	Samuel de Champlain, a French explorer, founds Quebec and sends young Frenchmen to live with the Indians to learn their language and customs.
1611	Mutinous crewmen cast the English navigator and explorer Henry Hudson, his son and other loyal sailors adrift in a small open boat in Hudson Bay. They are never heard from again.
1613	Juan de Oñate is tried and punished for using excessive force against the Acomas.
1660	French explorer Pierre Esprit Radisson provides the first written account of the Sioux.
1665–1668 & 1670–1672	Jean Talon, Intendant of New France, believes that French men should build a waterway-based empire in the West; find the Passage; and claim possession of the fur-rich lands of North America before the English do.
1670	Hudson's Bay Company is incorporated in London. This event marks the beginning of the first or "international" stage of the fur trade, which lasted until the fall of New France in 1763.
1671	At Sault Sainte Marie, the explorer Simon Francis D'Aumont formally claims for France the entire interior of the North American continent.
1673	French explorers Louis Joliet and Father Jacques Marquette paddle down the Mississippi to the mouth of the Arkansas River, discovering the Missouri River en route.
1680	Pueblo Indians launch a successful surprise attack against the Spanish and drive them out of Pueblo lands for 12 years.
1681	Near the mouth of the Mississippi, the French explorer La Salle claims "Louisiana" for France, i.e. all the territory between the Alleghenies and the Rocky Mountains and from the Gulf of Mexico to the sources of the Missouri.
1685	Unable to find the Mississippi again after a trip back to France, La Salle establishes a colony (Fort St. Louis) at Matagorda Bay in Texas.
1685–1689	Fearing that the French plan to take over their territory, Spain launches 11 expeditions to find and uproot La Salle's colony.
1686	Henri de Tonti, a French explorer, founds Arkansas Post, the first semi-permanent French settlement in the lower Mississippi valley, near the junction of the Arkansas and Mississippi rivers.
1688	Indians of the Rio Grande warn Spaniards that "some foreign people," i.e., French soldiers and traders, have appeared in Spanish territory.

1691–1705	Father Eusebio Kino, a Spanish missionary, explores the Southwest. By walking from New Mexico to the head of the Gulf of California, he proves that California is part of the North American mainland — not an island, as many cartographers believed.
1692	New Mexico Governor José de Vargas uses diplomacy rather than force to reassert Spanish rule over the Pueblo Indians.
c. 1695	French settlers begin to colonize the Illinois Country.
1696–1713	France temporarily closes the Canadian beaver trade: a glut of pelts on the European market has depressed prices.
1697	Father Louis Hennepin, a French missionary, publishes a map that supports the pyramidal height-of-land theory. This holds that river passage to the Pacific Ocean is feasible and relatively easy.
1698	Thomas Welch becomes the first American businessman to cross the Mississippi River and begin trade in French territory. He sells guns to the Quapaw Indians.
1700	All the major river valleys, which are the major transportation corridors east of the Appalachians, have by now been explored.
1700	King Louis XIV decides that France will not tolerate the westward extension of Britain's North American colonies: to block such expansion, France will establish a new colony in Louisiana.
1705	First flatboat cargo floats down the Mississippi. It consists of 15,000 bear and deer hides.
1706	Spanish Sergeant-Major Juan de Ulibarrí is the first European to learn about the Comanches: he hears that they are planning to raid a pueblo.
1710	Spanish officials estimate that about 240 American boatmen annually pass through Natchez on their way home. Ten years later, this number will have risen to 1,000 men a year.
1713	French fur traders suffer a setback: the Treaty of Utrecht awards Rupert's Land (the drainage basin of Hudson Bay) to Britain. This forces the French to look for furs farther west.
1716	French build a fort on the Red River in Louisiana near the Caddo village of Natchitoches.
1716	Jean-Baptiste Le Moyne de Bienville, a French explorer, founds Fort Rosalie (later known as Natchez) — the first permanent European settlement on the Mississippi.
1718	Bienville founds New Orleans and becomes governor of Louisiana.
1718	Guillaume Delisle, a French cartographer, publishes the first detailed map of the Gulf region and one of the most useful.
1720	Pawnees decimate the Villasur expedition.
1720	The Mississippi Bubble — a speculative frenzy in Louisiana — bursts, ruining French speculators.

1721	Spaniards establish a presidio at the mission at Los Adaes to stop the growth of French influence in Texas.
1722	New Orleans becomes the capital of Louisiana.
1723	French explorer Bourgmont builds Fort d'Orléans on the upper Missouri.
1729	Spain designates Los Adaes as the capital of Spanish Texas, a position it will hold until 1770.
1731	Louisiana, with a population of about 8,000 people, becomes a crown colony of France.
1731–1744	French explorer La Vérendrye searches for the route to the Western Sea. He is the first European to visit the Mandan villages near Bismarck, North Dakota (1738). In 1743, his two sons explore westward near the Rocky Mountains but do not cross them.
1732	Two Russian navigators and their crews become the first Europeans to see the northwestern coast of North America, i.e., Alaska.
1733–1742	Russia sends the Second Kamchatka Expedition to the Pacific Northwest coast. It is the biggest exploring expedition the world has ever seen.
1739	French traders Pierre and Paul Mallet make their way across the Great Plains from Illinois to Santa Fe, but are later expelled by the Spaniards.
1741	First European contact with the maritime traders of the Pacific Northwest coast: the Russian explorer Chirikov anchors near Sitka and sends two boatloads of men ashore. They never return.
1742	Keelboats can now navigate upstream on American rivers, albeit with great difficulty.
1743–1797	Forty-two Russian companies make nearly 100 voyages to harvest furs in the Aleutians and along the Gulf of Alaska, collecting nearly 187,000 furs.
1744	Spanish navigator Juan Pérez sails north from San Blas, Mexico, to the Dixon Entrance between the Queen Charlotte Islands and Prince of Wales Island.
1748	English fur traders, having ranged westward from Pennsylvania and Virginia, are now working in the Ohio River valley.
1748	Trading expedition of 33 Frenchmen arrives at a Comanche village near Taos and offers to barter firearms to the Indians in exchange for mules.
1750	French trader Pierre Mallet sets out again for Santa Fe but is arrested, sent to Spain for interrogation, and disappears from the historical record.
c. 1750	Indians of eastern Texas establish an elaborate deer hunting and hide-processing camp (now excavated as the Gilbert Site). They pro-

	vide French traders with thousands of deer hides in return for French firearms.
1750	Virginia-based Ohio Company sends Christopher Gist to explore the 200,000 acres it holds along the upper Ohio River.
1751–1752	French explorer Boucher de Niverville leads a party of 10 Frenchmen to the Rockies, but they fail to find the Mer de l'Ouest (the Western Sea, i.e., the Passage).
1755	Spanish navigators Juan Francisco Bodega and Bruno de Hezeta sail from San Blas to Point Grenville, Washington, where they take formal possession of the region. Bodega proceeds north to beyond Mount Edgecombe, near Sitka.
1758	Comanches and other Indians sack the Texas mission-fort of San Sabá.
1759	Taovayas and Comanches inflict a humiliating defeat on the Spaniards at Spanish Fort.
1762	Under the terms of the secret Treaty of Fontainebleau, France cedes to Spain all of Louisiana west of the Mississippi River.
1763	Treaty of Paris ends the Seven Years' War and brings to an end the French empire in North America. This agreement recognizes Spain as the new owner of Upper and Lower Louisiana, except for New Orleans itself. Formal transfers of these regions to Spain take place in 1763 and 1765, respectively.
1763	In the Proclamation of 1763, the British try, ultimately unsuccessfully, to prevent their colonists from settling west of the Appalachians.
1763	Fall of New France ushers in the second or intramural phase of the fur trade. This phase will last until 1821, when the British government forces the Hudson's Bay Company and the North West Company to merge.
1764	Pierre Laclède Linguest, a French fur trader from New Orleans, founds St. Louis near the confluence of the Missouri, Illinois, and Mississippi rivers. His stepson, René August Chouteau, will subsequently play a major role in the Missouri River fur trade.
1765	Marqués de Rubí is appointed inspector general of frontier presidios and reorganizes Spain's northern frontier defenses.
1765	In his *Concise Account of North America*, the British explorer Robert Rogers is an early advocate of the pyramidal height-of-land theory. This holds that the sources of major rivers of North America all lie in a central mountainous area.
1769	To head off a perceived Russian threat, Spain begins to colonize Upper California and build missions and presidios there. Father Junípero Serra establishes the first mission at San Diego; this is the earliest sustained European contact with the Mission Indians. Captain Gaspar de Portolá's men are the first Europeans to see San Francisco Bay.

1769	Governor Alejandro O'Reilly raises the Spanish flag over St. Louis but French merchants continue to dominate the economic life of the region.
1774	To discourage Russian expansion and to pioneer a supply route for California missions, the Spanish soldier Juan Bautista de Anza leads an expedition from Tubac (on the Mexico-Arizona border) to Monterey, California.
1774	Samuel Hearne, a British fur trader, builds Cumberland House, the first Hudson's Bay Company post in the western interior of Canada, on a tributary of the Saskatchewan River. It will soon become the most important of the Company's western posts.
1774–1792	Spain sends six small naval expeditions to explore the Northwest Pacific Coast and to find out what the Russians are doing there. These expeditions are led, respectively, by Pérez (1774), Hezeta (1775), Narváez (1789), Quimper (1790), Eliza (1791), and Galiano and Valdéz (1792).
1775	American trailblazer Daniel Boone leads the first party of settlers into Kentucky along the Wilderness Road and founds Boonesboro.
1775–1776	Juan Bautista de Anza, commandant of the presidio at Tubac, leads a large expedition to found a presidio and mission on San Francisco Bay.
1776	To strengthen its tenuous administrative control over northern New Spain, the Council of the Indies creates a new bureaucratic entity, the Provincias Internas (Interior Provinces).
1776–1777	Franciscan missionaries Domínguez and Escalante successfully complete an epic exploration of the Great Basin. They travel more than 1,500 miles.
1777	British explorer Jonathan Carver publishes his *Travels through the Interior of North America in the Years 1766, 1767, and 1768*. This book argues in favor of the pyramidal height-of-land theory.
1778	British Captain James Cook explores the Pacific Northwest coast. His journals will later spark a spirited international competition to collect sea otter furs there and sell them in China at great profit.
1783	Peace of Paris ends the Revolutionary War. Britain recognizes the independence of its former colonies. Canada remains a British possession. The British accept the Mississippi River as the western boundary of the new United States. American rivermen can now navigate the entire length of the Mississippi. This begins the era of the "half-horse, half-alligator" rivermen, which will later be immortalized by Mark Twain in *Life on the Mississippi*.
1783	To compete with Britain's Hudson's Bay Company, the North West Company, staffed by Scottish and French traders, is founded.
1784	Fearing that Americans will take over their lands, the Spaniards close the lower Mississippi to non–Spanish navigators. This contentious

	issue will not be fully resolved until the Treaty of San Lorenzo del Escorial of 1795 (Pinckney's Treaty).
1785	American explorer Peter Pond submits to Congress and to Quebec officials his map of the Lake Athabaska area. It shows (incorrectly) a river flowing down the western side of the Rocky Mountains into the Pacific Ocean. Some think that Pond's river must be the long-sought Passage.
1785	*Sea Otter*, a 60-ton British brig commanded by the maritime fur trader James Hanna, is the first ship sent to the Pacific Northwest coast specifically to hunt sea otters.
1785–1786	Spaniards negotiate treaties with the Comanches of Texas and New Mexico.
1786 or 1787	Scottish explorer James Mackay visits the Mandans.
1786	While exploring the southern shore of Alaska, the French explorer La Pérouse claims the territory for Louis XVI. Later, La Pérouse warns the Spaniards in California that the Russians are building settlements in Alaska.
1787	British Captain Charles W. Barkley anchors his ship *Imperial Eagle* at the Hoh River on the Washington coast and sends a small boat ashore, crewed by six men. All six are killed by the Indians.
1787	James Wilkinson, an American flatboat entrepreneur and double agent, takes a nominal oath of allegiance to Spain. He advises American rivermen to follow suit so they can use the Mississippi. Hundreds of them do so and are thus permitted to sell their cargoes in Natchez and New Orleans.
1787–1806	Displacing their British rivals, 72 American ships harvest sea otter furs along the Pacific Northwest coast.
1788	British-Canadian fur trader Duncan M'Gillivray establishes Fort Chipewyan at Lake Athabasca. This is the northernmost outpost of the North West Company.
1788	John Meares, a former British Navy officer, helps pioneer the sea otter trade by building the first ship constructed on the Pacific Northwest coast and putting up the first European building there.
1789	Spanish commander at Nootka Sound seizes three British ships, pushing Britain and Spain to the brink of war.
1790s	To deter British smugglers, Spain patrols the Mississippi with galliots (light galleys about 50 feet long).
1790	Scottish explorer Alexander Mackenzie estimates that there are about 9,000 Blackfoot Indians in the Alberta-Montana area.
1790	Alexander Baranov becomes manager of Russian fur trading operations along the Pacific coast. Ruling with an iron hand for 28 years, he is known as the Lord of Alaska.

Selected Chronology, 1492–1804

1791	Alejandro Malaspina, a Spanish explorer, is instructed to sail from San Blas to 60° north latitude and look for the Canal de Floridablanca linking the Pacific and Atlantic oceans. He examines the Alaska coast as far west as Prince William Sound and spends a month at the Spanish outpost in Nootka Sound.
1792	American Captain Robert Gray is the first foreigner to sail into the Columbia River.
1792–1793	Jacques D'Eglise, a French explorer, leads two expeditions up the Missouri River to the Mandan villages.
1792–1794	British navigator and explorer Captain George Vancouver charts the Pacific coast between Point Arena and Alaska.
1793	Scottish explorer Alexander Mackenzie becomes the first foreigner to cross North America by land and reach the Pacific Ocean.
1793–1794	Fur trade becomes so competitive in North Dakota and southern Canada that rival traders are often bartering in the same Indian villages at the same time.
1794	Under the terms of the Treaty of London (Jay's Treaty), the British agree to evacuate their fortifications in the Old Northwest. The Americans agree to allow the British to trade furs across their northern border into Canada. The Mississippi is declared open to both American and British shipping.
1794	Baron Carondelet, governor of Spanish Louisiana, opens the Illinois Country to fur traders and grants a monopoly to the Missouri Company.
1794–1796	An expedition led by Jean Baptiste Truteau tries but fails to reach the Mandan villages.
1795	An expedition led by the French frontiersman Lécuyer is sent toward the Mandan villages and thence to "the shores of the Sea of the West," i.e., the Pacific, but it fails at an early stage of travel.
1795	In the name of the king of Spain, Baron Carondelet offers a reward of 3,000 pesos to "the one who should succeed in first reaching the South Sea [the Pacific]."
1795	Treaty of San Lorenzo del Escorial (Pinckney's Treaty) marks the start of Spain's gradual withdrawal from the Mississippi Valley. Spain legalizes American navigation of the Mississippi and grants the United States the right of deposit in New Orleans.
1795	Nikolai Petrovich Rezanov becomes chief executive of the Shelikhov-Golikov Fur Company. He wants to make the west coast of North America a Russian possession and encourage large-scale Russian emigration there.
1795	After three bilateral conventions, Britain and Spain finally settle their differences over Nootka Sound in the Pacific Northwest.

1795–1797	Scotsman James Mackay and Welshman John Thomas Evans travel up the Missouri. Evans is looking for but fails to find a tribe of Welsh-speaking Indians.
1798	Nearly buried by snowdrifts during a snowshoe expedition on the Great Plains, British-Canadian fur trader David Thompson records in his journal: "It is without Doubt the worse day I ever saw I my life.'
1798	Spanish governor of Louisiana warns his viceroy about the threat of Anglo-American encroachment into Spanish lands.
1799	Czar Paul I charters the Russian-American Company and grants it a 20-year monopoly in the sea otter trade. This company becomes a reliable source of income for the imperial family.
1799	Russians establish St. Michael's Redoubt, a trading post and fort, at Sitka.
1799	In his *Report on the Northern Provinces of New Spain*, Lieutenant José Cortés gives good reasons why Spain should fear competition from the British and Americans.
1799	Rival British-Canadian fur trading companies establish two fortified trading posts in western Alberta at the foot of the Rocky Mountains. These are known respectively as Rocky Mountain House and Acton House.
1800	Using Rocky Mountain House as his base, the Canadian surveyor David Thompson begins looking for, and will later find, a route that will take him across the Rocky Mountains and into the upper reaches of the Columbia River.
1800	Under the terms of the secret Treaty of San Ildefonso, Spain returns Louisiana to France.
1801	Philip Nolan, an Anglo-American "mustanger" who probably wanted to free Texas from Spanish rule, is killed in a gunfight with Spanish troops.
1801	Slaves rebel in Haiti; 40,000 French troops there succumb to yellow fever. Napoleon decides to cut his losses by abandoning Haiti and by selling Louisiana to the United States.
1802	British geographer and cartographer Aaron Arrowsmith's revised *Map Exhibiting all the New Discoveries in the Interior Parts of North America* is the best and most comprehensive map of the West. It encourages the belief that the Rockies are only a low ridge that is easy to cross.
1802	Tlingits attack and destroy St. Michael's Redoubt at Sitka.
1802	Zadok Cramer's pilot book, *The Ohio and Mississippi Navigator*, becomes a bible for beginning rivermen.
1802	Spain revokes the right of deposit on all cargo coming to New Orleans from the United States. This sparks a political crisis that leads to

	urgent American negotiations with France for the purchase of New Orleans.
1802	Thomas Jefferson reads Alexander Mackenzie's 1801 book, *Voyages from Montreal*. It strengthens his belief that the Lewis and Clark expedition should immediately be sent overland to the Pacific to ward off British encroachment there.
1803	In his *Account of Upper Louisiana*, a French engineer Nicholas de Finiels explains why the Missouri fur trade is rarely a dull business.
1803	Jefferson presents to Congress his *Account of Louisiana*.
1803	Louisiana Purchase: In April, Napoleon sells the whole of Louisiana to the United States. In November, Spain transfers Lower Louisiana, including New Orleans, to France. In December, France transfers Lower Louisiana to the United States.
1803	Pierre Clément Lassat, the senior French official in New Orleans, describes the 120 French, Spanish and Anglo-American ships then in port as "a floating forest ... a prospect worthy of the busiest regions on the earth."
1804	In March, at the Three Flags Ceremony at St. Louis, Spain transfers Upper Louisiana to France; France then transfers it to the United States.

Appendices

1. The Lewis and Clark Expedition

LEWIS AND CLARK HAVE BEEN mentioned frequently in this book thus far to make specific points. It is now time to look at their epic 8,000-mile journey as a whole.

The routes, adventures and achievements of their expedition, which went on for 28 months, are very well documented, thanks in large part to the extensive journals kept by the explorers themselves. Lewis and Clark used small notebooks, bound in red Morocco leather, brown suede, and marbled cardboard, to record their comments. Remarkably, these have survived in good condition. Modern editions of them give us an unparalleled insight in the Trans-Mississippi West of 1804–1806. These journals still repay careful reading.

Because of its intrinsic interest and because the journals and other contemporary documents have survived, the Lewis and Clark expedition has been the subject of a great many learned and popular works. On the scholarly front, four major bibliographic landmarks stand out today.

The first is Nicholas Biddle's one-volume work, *The History of the Expedition Under the Commands of Captains Lewis and Clark*, which was not published until 1814. The second is Reuben Gold Thwaites's eight-volume set, the *Original Journals of the Lewis and Clark Expedition*, which appeared in 1904-1905. The third is Donald Jackson's two-volume work, *Letters of the Lewis and Clark Expedition* (1978). The last and so far the definitive work is Gary Moulton's magisterial eight-volume set, *The Journals of the Lewis and Clark Expedition*, which was published between 1987 and 1993.[1]

At the more popular level, there have been so many books that it is difficult to choose among them. Three of the best are Carolyn Gilman's *Lewis and Clark: Across the Divide* (2003); Stephen E. Ambrose's *Undaunted Courage: Meriwether Lewis, Thomas Jefferson, and the Opening of the American West* (1996); and John Logan Allen's *Lewis and Clark and the Image of the American Northwest* (1991).

Turning to the expedition itself, we have already noted that, for a long time, Jefferson had wanted Americans to explore the Trans-Mississippi West. In his secret message of 18 January 1803, he brought matters to a head, telling Congress:

> The river Missouri, and the Indians inhabiting it, are not as well known as is rendered desirable by their connection with the Mississippi, and consequently with us. It is, however, understood, that the country on that river is inhabited by numerous tribes, who furnish great supplies of furs and peltry to the trade of another nation [Britain], carried on in a high latitude, through an infinite number of portages and lakes, shut up by ice through a long season. The commerce on that line could bear no competition with that of the Missouri, traversing a moderate climate, offering according to the best accounts, a continued navigation from its source, and possibly with a single portage, from the Western Ocean.... An intelligent officer, with ten or twelve chosen men, fit for the enterprise, and willing to undertake it ... might explore the whole line, even to the Western Ocean....[2]

Congress approved the President's request and, by a happy coincidence, France unexpectedly decided to sell the Louisiana Territory to the United States late in 1803. To solidify possession of this enormous region so newly acquired, in 1804 Jefferson sent out from St. Louis, Missouri an exploratory expedition headed by U.S. Army Captain Meriwether Lewis and Lieutenant William Clark.

Very few Americans had ever traveled extensively in French Louisiana. In fact, as Henry Marie Brackenridge, a St. Louis journalist and lawyer who joined a fur trading expedition in 1811, wrote in his *Journal of a Voyage up the River Missouri; Performed in Eighteen Hundred and Eleven*:

> Before the memorable expedition of Lewis and Clark, none was found adventurous enough to penetrate that extensive portion of our continent more than a few hundred miles. *It was almost as little known to us, as the interior of New Holland [Australia], and the deserts of Africa.*[3]

Officially designated as the Corps of Discovery, the Lewis and Clark expedition initially included about 48 men. A quick chronology of its journey can be sketched out as follows[4]:

1803

- October: The expedition assembles at Clarksville on the Ohio River. It proceeds down the Ohio to the Mississippi, and then goes upstream as far as Wood River, just north of St. Louis. The winter of 1803-1804 is spent at Wood River.

1804

- May: In spring, heading up the Missouri in a slow, heavy 55-foot-long keelboat and in two big pirogues, the expedition passes the riverside village of Saint Charles, Missouri. This marks the formal beginning of the journey.
- August: The expedition reaches the mouth of the Platte River in Nebraska and

sees the first of the huge buffalo herds that roamed the Great Plains. At Council Bluffs, Missouri, the expedition meets its first Indians—250 members of the Otoe and Missouri tribes.

- October: The expedition arrives at the Mandan and Arikara villages at Great Bend of the Missouri, north of Bismarck, North Dakota. The winter of 1804-1805 is spent near these villages.

1805

- April: When spring comes, Lewis and Clark send the keelboat downstream back to St. Louis, laden with the biological specimens and Indian artifacts collected thus far. These will be forwarded to Jefferson. The expedition continues up-river in two pirogues and six small canoes. It reaches the junction of the Missouri and the Yellowstone rivers by the end of the month. Lewis, who himself was later chased into a river by a bear, records the dangers posed by what the explorers called the "white bear," i.e., the grizzly bear:

    the Indians give a very formidable account of the strength and ferocity of this animal, which they never dare attack but in parties of six or eight persons; and are even then frequently defeated with the loss or one or more of their party. the savages attack this animal with their bows and arrows and the indifferent guns with which the traders furnish them, with these they shoot with such uncertainty and at so short a distance, that [unless the bear is fatally shot through the head or the heart] they frequently mis their aim & fall a sacrefice to the bear. two Minetaries were killed during the last winter in an attack on a white bear. this anamall is said more frequently to attack a man on meeting with him, than to flee from him.[5]

- May: Lewis climbs a bluff above the Missouri and sees, for the first time, the high peaks of the Rocky Mountains.
- July: In Montana, just above the Great Falls of the Missouri, the expedition builds canoes out of hollowed cottonwoods and begins to paddle and pole them up-river into the mountains.
- August: Lewis drinks from what he mistakenly believes is "the most distant fountain [source] of the Mighty Missouri in surch of which we have spent so many toilsome days and wristless nights."[6] He climbs a short distance to the top of a pass and reaches the Continental Divide. Spread out before him, however, is not the easy descent to the Colombia River that he had hoped for, but the Bitterroot Mountains. It is the first evidence that there is no navigable Passage to the Pacific. The Shoshone Indians confirm this: a hard march of several days, they say, is needed to reach the headwaters of the Columbia.
- September: After getting horses and a guide from the Shoshones, the expedition crosses Lemhi Pass on the Montana-Idaho border and enters the Bitterroots. There is heavy snow; game is scarce; horses have to be killed for meat. After 11 days and 160 miles of forced marches over the mountains, the men arrive at a Nez Percé village on Weippe Prairie in Idaho. Nez Percé hospitality saves the expedition from failing due to exhaustion and lack of food and supplies.

"Hunting of the Grizzly Bear."
©2005 Alecto Historical Editions www.alectoUK.com

- October: Embarking in canoes, the expedition descends the Clearwater and the Snake rivers, finally reaching the Columbia.
- November: The men pass Beacon Rock, marking the beginning of the tidewater. Soon Clark sees the Pacific itself. "Ocian in view," he writes. "O! The joy."[7] He calculates that they have come 4,192 miles from the mouth of the Missouri. The expedition spends the winter of 1805-1806 at a wet, miserable camp near Astoria, Oregon, which they name Fort Clatsop in honor of the local Indians.

1806

- March: With the coming of spring, Lewis and Clark begin to retrace their route back to St. Louis.
- July: Lewis and Clark divide their party into two groups, for explorations north and south of the main route home. Blackfoot Indians attack Lewis's camp near the Marias River in Montana; one Indian is killed and another is fatally wounded. This is the only armed clash.
- August: The divided exploring parties join again at the mouth of the Yellowstone and head down the Missouri.

- September: At the village of La Charette, not far from St. Louis, the explorers are warmly greeted by the local inhabitants. Clarks records that "every person, both French and americans seem to express great pleasure at our return, and acknowledged themselves much astonished at seeing us return. they informed us that we were supposed to have been lost long sence, and were entirely given out by ever person &c."[8] The expedition reaches St. Louis on 23 September. Two days later, Clark makes a final, one-line entry in the journal, ending the trip on the same factual, positive note that characterizes the *Journals* as a whole: "a fine morning we commenced wrighting &c."[9]

Today, when we take stock of the achievements of the Lewis and Clark expedition, it is clear that its successes outweighed its failures. The explorers brought back a wealth of detailed knowledge about the hitherto unknown Trans-Mississippi West. The *Journals* are full of well-considered and often well illustrated accounts of the region's topography, climate, animal and plant life, and Indian tribes. Lewis and Clark also produced the first accurate maps of the vast uncharted lands between the Mississippi and the Pacific Northwest coast. Finally, their expedition permanently tied the fortunes of the Louisiana Territory and the Pacific Northwest with those of the United States as a whole.

Against these achievements can be set only two failures. First, the explorers did not find a useable route to the Pacific: the Passage did not exist, and the route they so arduously followed was impassable for wagons and thus could never be used for large-scale immigration. Second, they could not turn the proud, self-sufficient Sioux and Blackfoot into trade partners for the Americans.

The Lewis and Clark expedition is now the stuff of American legend but this has been a relatively recent development. In their own day, the successes of the expedition passed unnoticed on the wider national stage. Lewis, suffering from what Jefferson called "hypocondriac affections" (we would call it a manic-depressive syndrome), committed suicide in 1809.[10] Clark went on to become superintendent of Indian affairs. There was not much interest in the expedition itself and Biddle's edition of the journals sold only slowly. In fact, when the American historian and man of letters Henry Adams wrote a multi-volume of the Jefferson administration in 1889–1891, he barely mentioned Lewis and Clark. It was not until the outstanding eight-volume edition by Thwaites appeared, 100 years after the expedition had set out, that their fame began to spread.[11]

Where do matters stand today? Lewis and Clark are now solidly established in the pantheon of American heroes. The historian James P. Ronda has captured their memory so well that we cannot do better than to quote him here. Ronda asks rhetorically, "Why has the Lewis and Clark Expedition captured our imagination while others have faded from memory?" This is his answer:

> The essential American experience has been the journey, the trek, the quest.... The Lewis and Clark Expedition has come to represent all American journeys. In the Corps of Discovery's progress across the continent, Americans see reflected thousands of individual passages into a new world.[12]

2. Mirrors of the Trans-Mississippi West: George Catlin and Karl Bodmer

THESE TWO ARTISTS ARE IMPORTANT because they have given us the best visual records of the Trans-Mississippi West at an apogee of Indian power and glory. Their portraits suggest that the Plains Indians of that time and place were well able to hold their own against the first ripples of what would later become a tidal wave of Euro-American technology and culture.

George Catlin (1796–1872) was educated as a lawyer but first earned his living as a self-taught miniaturist, that is, a portraitist who painted tiny portraits on ivory, which clients carried in lockets. He had long been interested in Indians because they had once captured his mother. In 1831, he set off from Philadelphia to visit General William Clark, now Superintendent of Indian Affairs, in St. Louis. Catlin would spend the years 1832 through 1839 recording the character and customs of the North American Indians, just before their traditional ways of life disappeared forever.

In 1832, Catlin took the steamer *Yellow-Stone* up the Missouri to its juncture with the Yellowstone River. He passed three weeks with the Mandans in the summer of 1832, painting portraits of their chiefs, village life, religious ceremonies, and games and dances. One quarter of his best work on the Indians was devoted to this friendly and hospitable tribe. Catlin later tried to persuade Congress to buy some of his oil paintings (he produced a total of more than 500 paintings of the 48 different tribes he visited) but he failed to interest Congress in this proposal.

He was more successful when he toured the United States and Europe with what he billed as "Catlin's Indian Gallery." This show consisted of 310 oil paintings of Indians and 200 oils on other subjects, together with a large number of ornamental shirts, robes, drums, headdresses, and other items. He published his extensive journals in the two volumes of his *Manners, Customs, and Conditions of the North American Indians* (1841). When he was in his late fifties, he traveled throughout South America and in the Rockies of North America. He described these journeys in his book, *Last Rambles Amongst the Indians of the Rocky Mountains and the Andes* (1867).[1]

Catlin was a better writer than an artist. He was in fact an excellent illustrator, not an accomplished painter. His depiction of the Mandan chief Mah-to-toh-pa, or Four Bears, for example, is not as satisfying as Bodmer's portrait of the same man, whom Bodmer calls "Mató-Tópe." Both artists show the chief in the same regalia (see below) but Bodmer's portrait has a compactness, depth and solidity that Catlin's lacks. Because of Bodmer's much greater skill, it is his work — and not Catlin's — that is used in this book.

Despite any shortcomings in Catlin's portraits, however, when we turn to his journals we are treated to an enormous wealth of colorful detail that immediately brings this chief to life as a charismatic leader. Catlin writes:

The next and second chief [second to Wolf Chief, the head-chief] of the tribe is Mah-to-toh-pa (the four bears). This extraordinary man, though second in office is undoubtedly the first and most popular man in the nation. Free, generous, elegant, and gentlemanly in his deportment — handsome, brave and valiant; wearing a robe on his back, with the history of his battles emblazoned on it; which would fill a book of themselves, if properly translated. This, readers, is the most extraordinary man, perhaps, who lives at this day, in the atmosphere of Nature's noblemen; and I shall certainly tell you more of him anon.[2]

Catlin had an intuitive, sympathetic understanding of Indian life that was unusual for his age. Summing up his own experiences at a time when the Indians of the Trans-Mississippi West were either feared or held in contempt by most Europeans and Americans, he concluded that "the North American Indian in his native state is an honest, hospitable, faithful, brave, warlike, cruel, revengeful, relentless, — yet honourable, contemplative and religious being."[3]

The Swiss artist Karl Bodmer (1809–1893) accompanied the Prussian Prince Maximilian of Wied-Neuwied on the latter's travels up the Missouri River in 1833–1834. Bodmer's work is by far the best depiction of Indian life and western landscapes of that time. Trained in Paris as a landscape painter, he could paint dramatically in what was known as "the sublime mode." This was a way of showing Nature in its most threatening, overpowering and stormy manifestations, rather than simply as a well-ordered landscape carefully tailored to fit human proportions.[4] Bodmer had what Catlin lacked: painterly grace.[5]

Bodmer and Maximilian left St. Louis in 1833 aboard the steamer *Yellow-Stone*, bound for the same regions Catlin had visited the previous year. At Fort Pierre, South Dakota, they transferred to another vessel, the steamer *Assiniboine*, and finally arrived at Fort Union on the North Dakota-Montana border. During the trip, while Bodmer painted portraits of the Indians, the Prince took detailed notes, later publishing a scientific account of the trip in successive German, French, and English editions between 1839 and 1843. Cost overruns on these books led to losses, however, so a less expensive edition of selected images was published in 1846 under the title of *Nord-America in Bildern* (*North America in Pictures*).[6]

The literary quality of the Prince's books would be overshadowed by their illustrations. These consisted of Bodmer's 81 copperplate engravings, which were based on his watercolor paintings. The Prince's accounts are now read only by specialists, but Bodmer's work still appears frequently in modern books and articles about the Trans-Mississippi West — such as this one.

In 1986, the Joslyn Art Museum in Omaha, Nebraska acquired the Maximilian-Bodmer collection as a gift from an American corporation. David C. Hunt, a curator there, gave this lucid description of Bodmer's engraving of Mató-Tópe:

> In the first of two portraits he made of Mató-Tópe Bodmer shows him formally attired in a shirt of bighorn sheepskin elaborately trimmed with ermine tails, locks of hair, and strips of quillwork outlined in beads. Mató-Tópe's headdress, with its long trailer of eagle feathers, probably signified the combined battle coups of a war party or men's warrior society. The lance held in his right hand was said to have been used to kill an Arikara who had murdered his brother, its shaft afterward decorated with the enemy's scalp stretched on a hoop.[7]

"Mato-Tape, a Mandan Chief."
©2005 Alecto Historical Editions www.alectoUK.com

3. The Coming of the Horse

THE HORSE HAD AN ENORMOUS impact on military, economic and cultural life in the Trans-Mississippi West. International competition increased markedly thanks to it. Horsemen were more competitive, i.e., more successful in battle and in hunting buffalo, than men hunting on foot. The Indians were now better equipped to fight each other and posed a much graver threat to Europeans and Americans. The colorful culture of the Plains Indians, which has been celebrated so extensively in print, movies, advertising, and television that it is instantly recognized in most parts of the world today, can truly be called "the child of the horse."

Small horses (*Equus conversidens*) had lived in prehistoric North America. They ate fruit and leaves, and were in turn eaten by the Paleo-Indians. In 2001, Canadian scientists discovered the first unequivocal evidence that prehistoric North American hunters butchered these pony-sized horses. The skeleton of one of these little creatures, unearthed in southern Alberta, has butcher marks on some of its bones.[1] About 10,000 years ago, however, the climate started to change, hunting pressures increased, and the prehistoric horses became extinct.[2]

The Spaniards introduced the first "modern" horses in 1519, when the *conquistador* Hernán Cortés brought 10 stallions and 6 mares to mainland America. These horses originally came from Barbs and Arabians bred in Andalusia, Spain. Mounted Spaniards terrified the Indians, who had never seen horses before. A Spaniard on a horse could travel long distances quickly and could ride down Indian warriors who were afoot. Standing up in his stirrups and raising a long sword high above his head, he could deliver skull-splitting downward strokes that were difficult to dodge. Couching his lance, he could kill men before they could get very near him. One of Coronado's soldiers caught the essence of the matter. "The most essential thing in new lands is horses," he wrote. "They instill the greatest fear in the enemy and make the Indians respect the leaders of the army."[3]

Spaniards in North America used very large numbers of horses both in war and in peace: by the 1550s, there were already tens of thousands of horses in Mexico.[4] Spanish ranches near Santa Fe and Taos alone had thousands of horses. The Spanish government decreed that Indians should not own or ride horses but the Indians working on these ranches perforce had to learn how to handle horses. When the Pueblo Indians drove the Spaniards out of their lands during the great rebellion of 1680, many Spanish horses were left behind. These soon were traded to, or were stolen by, other tribes.

Horses multiplied very quickly on the Great Plains and became an important item of trade. Santa Fe became a major distribution center for the diffusion of horses. Oral tribal histories confirm that northern tribes, such as the Blackfoot, Nez Percé, and Flathead Indians, got their first horses from more southerly Shoshones traders.[5] By 1754, Anthony Henry, an employee of the Hudson's Bay Company, would encounter Indians in Saskatchewan who were already highly skilled at hunting buffalo from horseback.[6]

Natural selection and rider preferences resulted in the Plains Indian horse. This was a small (13.2 to 14 hands), light (700 pounds), and very sturdy horse, known colloquially as the mustang, which could survive on little food and no care. It was a godsend for the Indians. Mounted Indians could defeat rival tribes that had not yet mastered the horse. Before they had horses, the Plains Indians migrated on foot. Some of their possessions were carried on the backs of women; other goods were dragged by dogs pulling travois. In contrast, a horse could pull more than four times as much as a dog and could do so more rapidly. The Plains Indians were so impressed by this fact that they referred to horses as "big dogs," "elk dogs," or "sacred dogs."

Most importantly, mounted Indians could search for, find, follow, and attack the huge herds of buffalo that were nearly impregnable to Indians on foot. These animals ran faster than men did, so the Indians had resorted to various stratagems. Sometimes they donned the skins of white wolves and slowly inched close enough to a grazing herd to shoot a few buffalo with their bows and arrows before the rest panicked and ran off. In winter, hunters on snowshoes could spear buffalo mired in the deep snow. More rarely, warriors could stampede a buffalo herd over a high cliff and then finish off the survivors on the ground. In any case, before they had horses, it was impossible for the Indians to be sure of killing large numbers of buffalo consistently.

Hunting conditions changed dramatically with the coming of the horse. Astride his specially trained "buffalo horse," a warrior could range alongside a buffalo that was running at top speed. For ease of handling, the bows of the Plains Indians were short but they were so powerful that they could drive an arrow deep into a buffalo's body. The French frontiersman Étienne de Véniard, Sieur de Bourgmont, tells us that the Comanches "choose the fattest ones and shoot arrows into them which penetrate a foot into the animals' bellies" and by this means "kill all that they want."[7]

Writing in 1847, the Irish-Canadian artist Paul Kane reported that the Assiniboine Indians used their ash bows, which were backed with buffalo sinews, "with great dexterity and force; I have known an instance of the arrows passing through the body of the animal, and sticking in the ground at the opposite side."[8] This newfound ability to harvest large numbers of buffalo gave the Plains Indians a nearly inexhaustible supply of food — and of all other essential items made from the buffalo.

Historians believe that the Pueblo Indians were the first tribe to learn how to handle horses. The Apaches were probably the next. The Apaches traditionally came to the pueblos to trade. The Spaniards, however, discouraged this trade and forced the Pueblo Indians to work only for them. The Apaches adapted to the loss of their Pueblo trade by using their newly acquired equestrian skills to obtain horses and supplies by raiding.[9]

It was the Comanches, however, who came to represent the essence of the horse culture of the Plains Indians. They were middlemen in a brisk trade in horses between the Plains Indians and the small French settlements east of the Mississippi River. They became some of the best light cavalrymen in the world. The Texas folklorist J. Frank Dobie recorded this nineteenth-century frontier saying:

> The white man will ride the Mustang until he is played out. The Mexican will take him and ride him another day until he thinks he is tired. The Comanche will get on him and ride him to where he is going.[10]

We have already quoted the artist and author George Catlin. Writing from first-hand observation in 1832, Catlin had much to say about horses and Indians.

Among other things, this is what he tells us:

> The horses which the Indians ride in this country are invariably the wild horses, which are found in great numbers on the prairies; and have, unquestionably strayed from the Mexican borders, into which they were introduced by the Spanish invaders of that country; and now range and subsist themselves, in winter and summer, over the vast plains of prairie that stretch from the Mexican frontiers to Lake Winnipeg on the north, a distance of 3000 miles. These horses are small of stature, of the pony order; but a very hardy and tough animal, being able to perform for the Indians a continual and essential service. They are taken with the *lasso*, which is a long halter or thong made of raw-hide, of some fifteen to twenty yards in length, and which the Indians throw with great dexterity; with a noose on one end of it, which drops over the head of the animal they wish to catch, whilst running at full speed — when the Indian dismounts from his own horse and, holding to the end of the lasso, chokes the animal down, and afterwards tames and converts him to his own use.
>
> Scarcely a man in these regions is to be found, who is not the owner of one or more of these horses; and in many instances of eight, ten, or even twenty, which he values as his own personal property.[11]

John C. Ewers, a scholar of life on the Great Plains, has estimated that two Blackfoot riders "could kill enough buffalo to provide for over a ton of meat in a matter of minutes in a single chase."[12] Some of this meat was sun-dried into jerky or was pounded with fat and berries and made into pemmican. Thus prepared, it would last nearly indefinitely. The Plains Indians used horses to carry jerky and pemmican to their winter camps. They also traded these items, as well as buffalo hides, to more sedentary tribes living on the fringes of the plains, receiving corn, cotton, and other staples in return. The net result was a unique, vibrant Plains Indian culture — based chiefly on the horse — that reached its peak in about 1800 and then went into a slow but inexorable decline.

4. Firearms on the Early Frontiers

FIREARMS, LIKE HORSES, LED TO much greater international competition in the Trans-Mississippi West. Their rifles, muskets, and pistols gave Europeans and Americans the upper hand when dealing with the Indians. A Spanish priest in New Mexico reported: "God hath caused among the Indians so great a fear of [Spanish soldiers] and their arquebuses [muskets] that only with hearing it said that a Spaniard is going to their pueblos they flee."[1] Another Spanish priest, this one in Florida, said: "Gunpowder frightens the most valiant and courageous Indian and renders him slave to the White man's command."[2]

The Indians, for their part, gradually armed themselves with simple but deadly muskets obtained, directly or indirectly, from European or American traders. They could then compete more effectively with each other and with the Europeans and

Americans. On the frontier, men without guns were at an enormous and often fatal disadvantage. We learn from Lewis just what the Shoshone chief Cameahwait thought about the Spanish traders who refused to sell guns to his tribe:

> I [Lewis] can discover that these people [the Shoshones] are by no means friendly to the Spaniards. their complaint is, that the Spaniards will not let them have fire arms and ammunition, that they put them off by telling them that if they suffer [permit] them to have guns they will kill each other, thus leaving them defenceless and an easy prey to their bloodthirsty neighbours to the East of them, who being in possession of fire arms hunt them up and murder them without rispect to age or sex and plunder them of their horses on all occasions. they [the Shoshones] told me that to avoid their enemies who were eternally harassing them that they were obliged to remain in the interior of these mountains at least two thirds of the year where the[y] suffered as we saw then great hardships for the want of food sometimes living for weeks without meat and only a little fish roots and berries. but this added Cameahwait, with his ferce eyes and lank jaws grown meager for want of food, would not be the case if we had guns, we could then live in the country of buffaloe and eat as our enimies do and not be compelled to hide ourselves in these mountains and live on roots and berries as the bear do. we need not fear out enimies when placed on an equal footing with them.[3]

Europeans and Americans in the field either went about well armed or could quickly lay their hands on a firearm if the need arose. Jefferson told a delegation of chiefs from Missouri River tribes: "We are strong, we are as numerous as the stars in the heavens, & *we are all gun-men*."[4] It is therefore instructive for us to look at some of the firearms used on the early frontiers.

Writing in 1957, the American firearms expert Carl P. Russell began his authoritative work, *Guns on the Early Frontiers: A History of Firearms from Colonial Times Through the Years of the Fur Trade*, with this preface:

> The gun had a greater influence in changing the primitive ways of the Indian than any other object brought to America by the white man. It is true also that firearms became the decisive factor in subduing the Indian, and in settling the quarrels between white men during their early occupation of the New World. By the beginning of the seventeenth century the gun had become an institution in America and there were definite patterns of procedures in procuring and distributing arms and ammunition.... Efforts were made by several governments to prohibit the trading of guns to Indians, but for the most part the prohibitions had little effect.... White politicians of the day made all-out efforts to keep the gun and its powder and ball always available to the tribesmen.[5]

It may be useful to define a few technical terms here. There were three basic kinds of early single shot firearms: rifles, muskets, and pistols. Rifles have spiral rifling (lands and grooves) cut inside the bore (the barrel). Rifling imparts a spin to the ball (a round lead bullet), which stabilizes it in flight. A muzzleloading Kentucky rifle could be extremely accurate.

Using the small-bore (.36 caliber) Kentucky rifle that he called his "small rifle" or "small gun," Clark amazed the Clatsop Indians by killing two ducks at a distance of 40 yards. The Indians inspected his rifle carefully. They were used to clumsy big-bore muskets and had never seen an elegant small-bore Kentucky rifle before. Clark tells us that they said in their own language: "a good Musket do not under

Stand this kind of Musket &c."[6] Later, on their way back to St. Louis, Clark was probably using this same rifle when he tells us that he "shot at a mark with the Indians [the Nez Percé], struck the mark with 2 balls distce. 200 yds."[7]

Colonel George Hanger, a British firearms expert who had fought in the Revolutionary War, said that an expert American rifleman could hit the head of a man at 200 yards and that "provided an American rifleman were to get a perfect aim at 300 yards at me, standing still, he most undoubtedly would hit me, unless it was a very windy day."[8]

During the Revolutionary War, the backwoodsmen from Pennsylvania, Maryland, and Virginia who joined George Washington's forces could often hit a mark seven inches in diameter at a distance of 250 yards.[9] A further proof of the inherent accuracy of the Kentucky rifle comes from trials conducted in 1922. At that time, an original late eighteenth century Kentucky rifle put five shots into a 2.1-inch group when fired from a rest at a range of 100 yards.[10] This is excellent shooting: indeed, many modern hunting rifles will not do as well today.

A rifle ball had to be patched (wrapped in a small piece of soft cloth, leather, or paper) so that the rifling would bite into the patch and thus impart the stabilizing spin to the ball. Because of the tight fit of the patched ball in the bore, the ball had to be carefully forced down the bore with a ramrod. Loading a rifle was a more time-consuming process than loading a musket, which did not need patched balls.

Muskets are smoothbores, i.e., they have no rifling. They were much less accurate than a rifle but much faster and easier to reload. For this reason, muskets were issued to soldiers. Indians generally preferred them, too, for the same reason. A good man with a musket could get off three or four shots every minute. The lead ball fired by a musket weighed about one ounce and caused terrible wounds if it hit a man.

The musket had one added advantage: it could be loaded with either a ball or with shot (small lead pellets). Its accuracy was satisfactory at close range. In the hands of an expert—firing from a rest and using a patched ball—a good musket would keep its shots within a 6-inch circle at 45 yards and could hit a man at 80 yards.[11] (A patched ball could be used in a musket not to grip the non-existent rifling but to make the ball fit more snuggly in the bore.) When loaded with shot, a musket could kill birds, rabbits and other small game at up to 30 yards.

European and American frontiersmen (but rarely Indians) often carried one or two pistols as backup weapons. These ranged from small handguns so light that could be slipped into pockets to big "horse pistols" that were so heavy they had to be carried in leather holsters strapped to the saddle. Pistols were generally used only at point-blank range in case of dire necessity, i.e., when there was imminent danger and not enough time to reload a rifle or a musket.

Frontiersmen on horseback, however, sometimes used horse pistols to kill running buffalo. Writing in 1804, François-Antoine Larocque, a fur trader working for the North West Company, recorded in his "Missouri Journal" that "We saw Hills that are on the side of the Missouri River at 3 P.M. Mr. McK [Charles McKay, another Canadian fur trader] killd' a Bull, Running, with a pistol."[12]

Lewis paid $10, out of his own pocket, for a brace of pistols of his own—"1 Pair Pocket Pistols, Secret [folding] Triggers." These small pistols were made by Barnhill, very probably a British firm. Their triggers folded into recesses under the locks, making it easier to draw and fire the pistols from pockets without their catching on clothing.[13]

Lewis also bought for use by other members of the expedition "1 pr. Horsemans Pistols."[14] He had requisitioned them from a U.S. arsenal, so they were probably .69 caliber U.S. Army pistols, Model 1799. If so, they were excellent weapons for a last stand. Other experienced frontiersmen valued heavy pistols, too. The trapper Osborne Russell was at Pierre's Hole, west of Grand Teton National Park, in 1835, when his party was attacked by Indians. He recorded: "I kept a large German horse-pistol loaded by me in case they should make a charge when my gun [rifle] was empty."[15]

A flint, gripped in a mechanism known as a lock, ignited the powder charge in these early rifles, muskets, and pistols. Upon striking a metal plate (the frizzen), the flint threw a spark into the priming pan, which held a small quantity of gunpowder. When this ignited, its flame instantly passed through a small priming hole and set off the main charge in the bore.

If the flash in the priming pan failed to ignite the main charge, this was called "a flash in the pan"—an expression still in use today. Once ignited, the main charge burned with extreme rapidity and generated such high pressure that the ball or the shot was forced down the bore at tremendous speed. The Lewis and Clark expedition brought along 500 rifle flints, 125 musket flints, 176 pounds of gunpowder, 50 pounds of the "best rifle Powder," and 420 pounds of sheet lead to be melted down and cast into balls.[16]

At first, the French were the biggest arms suppliers to the Indians. By the time New France fell to the British in 1763, some 200,000 muskets had already been shipped from French factories to the Indians of New France.[17] In the southwest, the Spaniards tried, with very limited success, to keep Spanish guns out of the hands of the Indians, but French traders eagerly sold to the Indians a Spanish flintlock musket known as the *escopeta*.

A Spanish cavalryman would carry this relatively light, inexpensive .69 caliber weapon across his saddlebow, protecting it from the elements by use of a soft leather sheath. The Texas Ranger John C. Duval, who used both a rifle and an *escopeta*, tells us that the *escopeta* was "a short bell-mouth, bull-doggish looking musket, carrying a very heavy ball, which is 'death by law' when it hits, but that is seldom, for they shoot with little accuracy. They are good for nothing except to make a noise."[18] Spanish Brigadier Pedro de Rivera candidly admitted, "French firearms are effective from a long range, whereas our arquebuses have only short-range capability."[19]

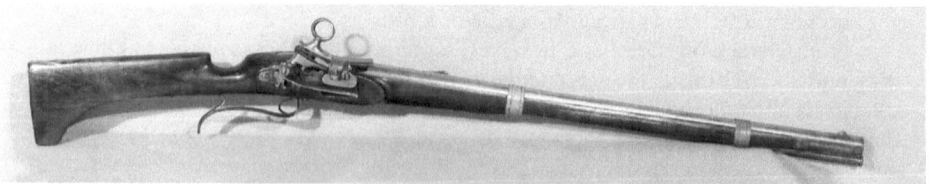

A Spanish .69 caliber flintlock *escopeta* of the laste seventeenth century. (Courtesy of the Arizona Historical Society).

APPENDIX 4: FIREARMS ON THE EARLY FRONTIERS

"Skin Lodge of Assiniboin Chief."
©2005 Alecto Historical Editions www.alectoUK.com

The British hold the world record for selling muskets to the North American Indians: they began this trade in 1623 and continued it until as late as the early 1950s.[20] During the last decade of the seventeenth century, English traders from Hudson Bay (and French traders from along the Assiniboine River and the upper Mississippi) bartered arms and ammunition to Indian middlemen living in the west, i.e., to the Cree, Assiniboin, Chippewa, and Sioux. These tribes, in turn, traded guns and munitions to the Plains Indians.

By 1750, the Sioux were especially active in this trade. Thirty years later, American, French, and British traders were all selling firearms, powder, ball and shot to the Indians of the upper Missouri — in what was technically Spanish territory.[21] On one occasion in 1791, a group of Indians armed with guns even ordered Spanish traders to cease doing business there. The Indians told the Spaniards that the British were now supplying all their needs and that, consequently, the Spaniards were no longer welcome.[22]

Selling firearms to the Indians was a sufficiently profitable calling so that well before 1805 a standardized trade gun had evolved.[23] It was variously known as the North West trade gun; the Hudson Bay fusil, fusee, or fuke; the Mackinaw gun; or the Barnett trade gun. It was a musket of about .66 caliber, with a distinctive serpentine brass ornament screwed onto the wooden stock opposite the lock. The trigger guard was made big enough so that the musket could be fired in winter while wearing a glove.

"Fort Mackenzie, August 28th 1833."
©2005 Alecto Historical Editions www.alectoUK.com

The Indians rarely took good care of their guns and were usually not good shots. Accurate shooting requires practice, which is not feasible when ammunition is scarce and expensive. (For this reason, most European and American soldiers on the frontier were poor shots, too.) Indians hoarded their ammunition, expending it only on their enemies or on game, never at targets. When they fired at each other it was usually at very close range. Bodmer's painting of a fight between Indians in 1833, just outside Fort Mackenzie in western Montana, makes this clear.

The hammer of the North West gun did not have a half cock notch in the tumbler, so the full cock notch had to be cut especially deep for safety. This meant that a very heavy trigger pull of 10 to 15 pounds seems to have been needed to fire the musket. Accurate shooting is nearly impossible with a trigger pull this heavy: today, a good quality hunting rifle has a trigger pull of about three pounds.

Despite their shortcomings as crack shots, the Indians were discerning customers nevertheless. In 1808, the fur trader John Jacob Astor formed the American Fur Company to break his dependence on British-Canadian traders. At first, he tried to sell inferior fukes to the Indians. These weapons were rejected, so he had to offer better quality muskets instead.

Writing in 1809, the Superintendent of the Indian Trade Office in Washington, D.C. had to explain carefully to Thomas Waterman, a Philadelphia gun maker, precisely what Indian customers wanted:

> I fear from the description and price that the guns you have bought are not as described by me — the real North West Gun. They cost in England 21 shillings to

22 shillings 6 pence, Sterling; they are to be known by the large guard of iron, by three screw pins to the lock, by one screw only (which passes quite through the stock) being used to secure the upper part of the guard and the lower part of the barrel; and above all by a brass mounting opposite to the lock [i.e., the dragon ornament].... If those bought by you are not of this kind they will not answer any purpose and need not be sent.[24]

The best description of how Plains Indians on horseback actually used their muskets in practice comes from Rudolph Friederich Kurz. This young Swiss artist kept a journal about his experiences among fur traders and Indians on the Mississippi and upper Missouri. He was with them between 1846 and 1852 but his comments on the use of the musket in a buffalo hunt are fully applicable to Indian hunts of an earlier day. Writing from Fort Union, near the mouth of the Yellowstone River, Kurz reported that:

> When running buffaloes the hunters do not use rifle-patches, but take along several balls in their mouths; the projectile thus moistened sticks to the powder when put into the gun. In the first place on buffalo hunts, they do not carry rifles, for the reason that they think the care required in loading them takes too much time unnecessarily when shooting at close range and, furthermore, they find rifle balls too small [i.e., they lacked stopping power]. The hunter chases buffaloes at full gallop, discharges his gun, and reloads without slackening speed. To accomplish this he holds the weapon close within the bend of his left arm and, taking the powder horn in his right hand, draws out with his teeth the stopper, which is fastened to the horn to prevent its being lost, shakes the requisite amount of powder into his left palm, and again closes the powder horn. Then he grasps the gun with his right hand, holding it in a vertical position, pours the powder down the barrel, and gives the gun a sidelong thrust with the left hand, in order to shake the powder well through the priming hole into the touchpan....
>
> Now he takes a bullet from his mouth, and with his left hand puts it into the barrel, where, having been moistened by spittle, it adheres to the powder. He dares never hold his weapon horizontal, that is, in the position taken for firing, for fear that the ball may stick fast in its course, allowing sufficient air to intervene between powder and lead to cause an explosion and splinter the barrel. So long as the ball rolls freely down the barrel there is no danger. Hunters approach the buffaloes so closely that they do not take aim but, lifting the gun lightly in both hands, point in the direction of the animal's heart and fire. They are very often wounded in the face and hands by the bursting gun barrels, which, especially when the weather is extremely cold, are shattered easily as glass.[25]

Many frontiersmen used the same kinds of guns they sold to the Indians. Other men preferred better quality weapons from Britain or from continental Europe. Some liked heavy military models, such as the nearly-indestructible British "Brown Bess" musket, while others were partial to the more delicate but highly accurate Kentucky rifle. Some frontier firearms are early examples of globalization. For example, a .68 caliber musket that British fur traders carried overland in 1811 from St. Louis to the mouth of the Columbia River has a barrel made in London. Its lock and other parts, however, were made by the American firm of McKim and Brother of Baltimore, Maryland.[26]

5. Protecting Northern New Spain from the Apaches

In 1777, Teodoro de Croix, commandant general of New Spain's Provincias Internas, drew up a detailed 16-point questionnaire for discussions with Spanish officers in Mexico City, San Antonio and Chihuahua.[1] To deal with the Apache menace, he wanted answers to some difficult questions. His questions, which have been lightly edited, were as follows:

1. How long has the Apache tribe of Indians been known on these frontiers, and since when have they made war on us?

2. What victories have we had over them, and especially in the last five years?

3. What, by prudent calculation, is the number of warriors composing each one of the branches or congregations [of these Indians], and what friendship and bond of relations do these Indians have among themselves?

4. What arms do they use, where do they live, how do they support themselves, and how do they make war upon us and in what provinces and places?

5. What declared enemies do the Apaches have among the heathen nations bordering upon their land, *rancherías*, and villages?

6. What interpretation does the peace which the Lipans [an Apache tribe] have in this province merit; in what terms was it drawn up; what advantages have flowed from them; and what conveniences or inconveniences can the conservation of this peace or the declaring of war upon them produce?

7. What favorable or adverse results ought to be inferred from [a recent surrender of five Apaches and two *rancherías*]?

8. Concerning the Comanches [and the other Indian "nations of the north"], each of the [Spanish participants in the discussions] will state what he understands and may know and what may have come to his notice, distinguishing the reports and opinions in accord with the first six points.

9. Which nations of the north are nomadic and which live in settlements, plant crops, and so on?

10. What benefits will be achieved by making war upon these tribes, allying ourselves with the Lipans, or the opposite?

11. Whether the number of troops who at present guard our frontiers will be sufficient to undertake the hostile operations either against the Lipan and the rest of the divisions of the Apaches, or against the Indians of the north?

12. If an increase in forces is considered necessary, how much will be sufficient against the Apaches and how much against the Indians of the north?

13. If against the Apaches, especially of the east, [the Spanish participants] will state whether it will be possible to undertake one or several actions or particular

ones; how, in what terms, at what seasons, places, or spots, supposing ourselves allied with the Indians of the north.

14 and 15. If against the Indians of the north, each [participant] should state his opinion with regard to the lands they occupy, those of ours which they attack, and how to secure fortunate results from the operations; which Indians will be the ones most suitable to guarantee the good faith of the alliance of the Lipans against those of the north, or that of the latter against the former.

16. Finally, what measures ought to be taken with the present troops for the defense of each one of the provinces and what operations will be the most useful ones for this purpose and for the general pacification of the territory, if the proposed increases of forces comes about?

6. A Spanish Requerimiento

THIS IS AN EDITED VERSION of a *Requerimiento* written in about 1512, designed to be delivered orally by the leader of a Spanish expedition.[1] It is extremely unlikely that translators could convey accurately to the local Indians all the complex theological points embedded in this document. The Indians, however, would very soon understand the main point of the message: either they did what the Spaniards wanted them to do, or the Spaniards would kill them.

The text is as follows:

> God our Lord created the heaven and earth, and one man and one woman of whom we and you [the Indians] all men in the world have come ... but because of the infinity of offspring that followed in the five thousand years and more since the world was created, it has become necessary that some men should go in one direction and others in another.... All these nations God our Lord gave in charge to one person, called Saint Peter, that he might be Master and Superior over mankind.... And He commanded him to place his seat in Rome ... him they call Pope.... One of the popes who succeeded him to that seat ... made a gift of these islands and the main of the Ocean Sea to the said Emperor and Queen.... Wherefore, as best you can, I entreat and require you to understand this well ... that you recognize the church as Mistress and Superior of the Universe ... and [the Spanish monarch] as sovereign.... If you shall do so you will do well in what you are held and obliged; and their Majesties and I, in their royal name, will receive you with love and charity.
>
> If you do not do this, and of malice you be dilatory, I protest to you that, with the help of Our Lord, I will enter with force, making war upon you from all directions and in every manner that I may be able, when I will subject you to obedience to the Church and the yoke of their Majesties; I will take the persons of yourselves, your wives and your children to make slaves, and shall dispose of you, as their majesties shall think fit, and I will take your goods, doing all the evil and

injury that I may be able ... and I declare to you that the deaths and damages that arise therefrom, will be your fault and not that of his Majesty, nor mine, nor of these cavaliers who come with me. And so I proclaim and require this, I ask of the Notary here that he give a certificate, and those present I beseech that they will hereof be the witnesses.

7. *The Treaty of San Ildefonso*

IN 1800, UNDER THE TERMS of the secret Treaty of San Ildefonso, Spain gave Louisiana back to France. This treaty was flawed in several ways. Spain was under pressure from Napoleon and thus had to negotiate against its own inclinations. The treaty also raised two potentially serious problems. First, although it took some time for the United States government to learn about the treaty, the *fait accompli* of having the lower Mississippi suddenly controlled by powerful Napoleonic France, rather than by enfeebled Spain, posed a real threat to American farmers. They depended on free navigation of the river to get their crops and goods to market.

Second, the treaty did not define the boundaries of the lands that Spain was giving back to France. Consequently, after Napoleon sold Louisiana to the United States in 1803 (thereby violating a pledge he had made to Spain that Louisiana would never be turned over to another power), these vague boundaries would cause tension between Spain and the United States.

This is the full text of the treaty.[1]

> Preliminary and Secret Treaty between the French Republic and His Catholic Majesty the King of Spain, Concerning the Aggrandizement of His Royal Highness the Infant Duke of Parma in Italy and the Retrocession of Louisiana.
>
> His Catholic Majesty having always manifested an earnest desire to procure for his Royal Highness the Duke of Parma an aggrandizement which would place his domains on a footing more consonant with his dignity; and the French Republic on its part having long since made known to His Majesty the King of Spain its desire to be again placed in possession of the colony of Louisiana; and the two Governments having exchanged their views on these two subjects of common interest, and circumstances permitting them to assume obligations in this regard which, so far as depends on them, win mutual satisfaction, they have authorized for this purpose the following: the French Republic, the Citizen Alexandre Berthier, General in Chief, and His Catholic Majesty, Don Mariano Luis de Urquijo, knight of the Order of Charles III, and of that of St. John of Jerusalem, a Counselor of State, his Ambassador Extraordinary and Plenipotentiary appointed near the Batavian Republic, and his First Secretary of State ad interim, who, having exchanged their powers, have agreed upon the following articles, subject to ratification.

Article 1

The French Republic undertakes to procure for His Royal Highness the Infant Duke of Parma an aggrandizement of territory which shall increase the population of his domains to one million inhabitants, with the title of King and with all the rights which attach to the royal dignity; and the French Republic undertakes to obtain in this regard the assent of His Majesty the Emperor and King and that of the other interested states that His Highness the Duke of Parma may be put into possession of said territories without opposition upon the conclusion of the peace to be made between the French Republic and His Imperial Majesty.

Article 2

The aggrandizement to be given to His Royal Highness the Duke of Parma may consist of Tuscany, in case the present negotiations of the French Government with His Imperial Majesty shall permit that Government to dispose thereof; or it may consist of the three Roman legations or any other continental provinces of Italy which form a rounded state.

Article 3

His Catholic Majesty promises and undertakes on his part to retrocede to the French Republic, six months after the full and entire execution of the above conditions and provisions regarding His Royal Highness the Duke of Parma, the colony or province of Louisiana, with the same extent that it now has in the hands of Spain and that it had when France possessed it, and as such as it ought to be according to the treaties subsequently concluded between Spain and other states.

Article 4

His Catholic Majesty will give the necessary orders for the occupation of Louisiana by France as soon as the territories which are to form the aggrandizement of the Duke of Parma shall be placed in the hands of His Royal Highness. The French Republic may, according to its convenience, postpone the taking of possession; when that is to be executed, the states directly or indirectly interested will agree upon such further conditions as their common interests and the interest of their respective inhabitants require.

Article 5

His Catholic Majesty undertakes to deliver to the French Republic in Spanish ports in Europe, one month after the execution of the provision with regard to the Duke of Parma, six ships of war in good condition built for seventy-four guns, armed and equipped and ready to receive French crews and supplies.

Article 6

As the provisions of the present treaty have no prejudicial object and leave intact the rights of any power, it is not to be supposed that they will give offense to any power. However, if the contrary shall happen and if the two states, because of the execution thereof, shall be attacked or threatened, the two powers agree to make common cause not only to repel the aggression but also to take conciliatory measures proper for the maintenance of peace with all their neighbors.

ARTICLE 7

The obligations contained in the present treaty derogate in no respect from those which are expressed in the Treaty of Alliance signed at San Ildefonso on the 2nd Fructidor 4 (August 19, 1796); on the contrary they unite anew the interests of the two powers and assure the guaranties stipulated in the Treaty of Alliance for all cases in which they should be applied.

ARTICLE 8

The ratifications of these preliminary articles shall be effected and exchanged within the period of one month, or sooner if possible, counting from the day of the signature of the present treaty.

In faith whereof we, the undersigned Ministers Plenipotentiary of the French Republic and of His Catholic Majesty, in virtue of our respective powers, have signed these preliminary articles and have affixed thereto our seals.

Done at San Ildefonso the 9th Vendemiaire, 9th year of the French Republic (October 1, 1800).

[Seal] Alexandre Berthier
[Seal] Mariano Luis de Urquijo

8. Coureurs de Bois and Voyageurs: The Men and Their Boats

The Men

There was not much room in canoes for the paddlers themselves, so Canadian canoemen tended to be short, wiry men with broad chests and muscular arms and shoulders. Thomas McKenney, an American who traveled with them in the 1820s, reported that

> A Canadian, if born to be a labourer, deems himself to be very unfortunate if he should chance to grow over five feet five, or six inches; — and he shall reach five feet ten or eleven, it forever excludes him from the privilege of becoming *voyageur*. There is no room for the legs of such people, in these canoes. But if he shall stop growing at about five feet four inches, and be gifted with a good voice, and lungs that never tire, he is considered as having been born under a most favourable star.[1]

Coureurs de bois led a life of extremes. A good example is this account, taken from a letter of 10 August 1688 from Governor Jacques-René de Brisay de Denonville to the navy minister, the Marquis of Seignelay. The governor wrote:

> This Memoir, in which I report to Monseigneur the current state of affairs in this country, contains an article where I tell Monseigneur that I must report to him one of the greatest ailments of Canada. It is, Monseigneur, the abuse of alcohol, which is so excessive that I fear the country will be lost....
> I have noticed that, faced with the strain of crossing rapids, it is common for our tired Canadian men to drink up to a pint of alcohol directly from the barrel, in order to regain some strength. Those who hold back still drink a half-septier, often on an empty stomach. Afterwards, feeling strong, they cross the rapids and then fall asleep, without a thought for food, having no appetite until the evening, when the vapors of alcohol have dissipated. In the drinking establishments, Monsignor, all the drinkers, of whom there are many, especially among the *coureurs de bois*, usually drink a pint or a quart of alcohol after drinking wine.... What ravages these mixtures can do to a stomach! And how can a man stand up to the slightest bout of illness after this manner of abuse? Indeed, many have died this year.[2]

The next account comes from a memoir written in Quebec by Jean Bouchart de Champigny, sixth Intendant of New France, in 1691. He did not want his young men to become fur traders in the west for two reasons. First, this constant drainage of manpower drastically reduced the supply of labor needed for farming. Second, to make matters even worse, *coureurs de bois* never paid the tithes or seigniorial dues levied on farmers, thus reducing the income of both civil and religious authorities in New France.

Bouchart writes:

> It is regrettable that our vigorous, never-tiring Canadian youth are attracted to nothing but these kinds of journeys, where they live in the woods like savages, spending two or three years without receiving the sacraments, in idleness and often extraordinary misery. Once accustomed to this life, they find it hard to dedicate themselves to cultivating the land, and they live in extreme poverty because they spend much upon their return.
> On the other hand, those who settle and add value to the land are rich or, at least, live very comfortably with their fields and fish ponds around their houses, as well as considerable numbers of cattle. This situation will change in the future, as there will be a lack of Frenchmen to settle this country, since they are essentially the ones who do this work, while most of their children spend all their time in journeys, a situation that is not consequential to any measure of sternness....[3]

Despite its hardships and dangers, life as a *coureur de bois* was certainly more exciting than farming. A final account here comes from Alexander Ross, author of *The Fur Hunters of the Far West* (1855), who tells us:

> One day while in a jocular mood the old man [a retired *coureur de bois*] began to talk over his past life. It was full of adventure, and may appear amusing to others as it did to us. I shall give it as nearly as I can in his own words.
> "I have now," said he, "been forty-two years in this country [i.e., along the Red River of the North, which forms part of the boundary between Minnesota and

North Dakota]. For twenty-four I was a light canoeman. I required but little sleep, but sometimes got less than I required. No portage was too long for me; all portages were alike. My end of the canoe never touched the ground until I saw the end [of the portage]. Fifty songs a day were nothing to me. I could carry, paddle, walk and sing with any man I ever saw. During that period I saved the lives of ten *bourgeois* [leaders of canoe expeditions], and was always the favorite because the others stopped to carry at a bad step and lost time. I pushed on — over rapids, over cascades, over chutes; all were the same to me. No water, no weather ever stopped the paddle or the song. I have had twenty [Indian] wives in the country; and was once possessed of fifty horses and six running dogs [sled dogs] trimmed in the first style. I was then like a *bourgeois*, rich and happy. No *bourgeois* had better-dressed wives than I; no Indian chief finer horses; no white man better harnessed or swifter dogs. I beat all the Indians at the race, and no white man ever passed me in the chase. I wanted for nothing; and I spent all my earnings in the enjoyment of pleasure. Five hundred pounds have twice told passed through my hands, although now I have not a spare shirt to my back nor a penny to buy one. Yet, were I young I should glory in commencing the same career. I would spend another half-century in the same fields of enjoyment. There is no life so happy as a voyageur's life; none so independent; no place where a man envoys so much variety and freedom as in the Indian country. Huzzah, huzzah pour le pays savage!" ["Hip, hip, hurray for the wild country!"]

After this *cri de joie* [joyous outburst], he sat down in the boat and we could not help admiring the wild enthusiasm of the old Frenchman. He had boasted and excited himself till he was out of breath and then sighed with regret that he could no longer enjoy the scenes of his past life.

Their Boats

During the heyday of the Canadian fur trade from the 1650s to the late nineteenth century, two kinds of vessels were in constant use — birchbark canoes and wooden York Boats.[4]

The most colorful craft was the big *canot de maître* ("canoe of the leader," also known as a Montreal canoe). Designed for use on the broad rivers and wide lakes lying west of Montreal, this canoe was built as large as possible with birchbark technology. Size was necessary for safety's sake. On the Great Lakes, storms could come up suddenly. Capsizing far from shore in cold, windswept, open waters meant certain death for the crew and certain destruction of the cargo. A *canot de maître* would typically be about 36 feet long and six feet wide. Crewed by eight to ten men, it could carry a three-ton payload, plus the personal baggage of the men, which was limited to 40 pounds per man.

For travel along the more confined waterways west of the Great Lakes, a smaller and handier canoe was needed. This was the *canot du nord* ("canoe of the north"). It was about 25-feet long and four to four and a half feet wide. It carried a 1.5 ton payload and was paddled by five or six men. Because of the number of portages that had to be crossed, the *canot du nord* had to be light enough so that, unloaded, it could be carried short distances by two men.

The Hudson's Bay Company hired men from Orkney for its fur trade. Although

APPENDIX 8: COUREURS DE BOIS AND VOYAGEURS

Brigade of Boats of the Fur Trade. Painted in Canada in 1846 by Paul Kane (1810–1871), this shows a fleet of York Boats scudding up the Saskatchewan River. Here is the caption Kane used for the picture: "On the Saskatchewan with a fair breeze, crowding on all sail to escape a thunder storm rolling fast after them." (Courtesy of the Royal Ontario Museum, ROM2003_815_4).

highly skilled at handling small wooden boats along their native coast, Orkneymen were not comfortable in the less stable and more fragile canoes. The Hudson's Bay Company therefore developed a new kind of boat in about 1774 to compete with the canoes of the North West Company, whose French-Canadian crews were entirely at home in canoes.

Known as the York Boat because it was built at York Factory, the Hudson Bay's Company's headquarters on Hudson Bay, this was a sturdy clinker-built (overlapping plank) boat with an overall length of between 24 and 28 feet with a beam of four feet. It could be paddled, rowed, poled, or sailed. By raising its single square sail, it could run before the wind. The Irish-born painter Paul Kane (1810–1871) has left us a dramatic painting of a fleet of 19 York Boats with their sails set, laden with furs and scudding up the Saskatchewan River in front of a gathering storm in 1846.[5]

Kane explains that the brigade of boats he saw was unusual because it was

> entirely devoted to the carriage of furs paid annually by the Hudson's Bay Company to the Russian Government, for the privilege of trading in their territory. [The cargo] consisted of seventy pieces or packs, each containing seventy-five [river] otter skins of the very best description. They are principally collected on the Mackenzie River, from whence they are carried to York Factory, where they are culled and packed with the greatest care; they then have to be carried up the Saskatchewan, across the Rocky Mountains, down the Columbia River, to Vancouver's Island, and then shipped to Sitka.[6]

Normally, however, as Kane tells us later in his book,

> The boats [25 of them, crewed by more than 130 men] are all loaded with the furs and pemmican of the Saskatchewan district. The furs are taken down to York Factory, in the Hudson's Bay, where they are shipped to Europe; the pemmican is intended for those posts where provisions are difficult to be procured.[7]

A York Boat carried five to eight tons of cargo and was crewed by six to nine men.[8] Larger, more stable and more durable than a canoe, it was also slower and much heavier. It could not, for example, be carried by hand over portages but instead had to pulled on top of rollers made of logs.[9]

Chapter Notes

Introduction

1. Cabeza de Vaca was not the first European to explore the Trans-Mississippi West: an earlier explorer was Alonso Álvarez de Pineda, who sailed along part of the Gulf Coast in 1529. However, he did not leave any account of his voyage and did not go ashore in what is now the United States. This book therefore begins with Cabeza de Vaca, who did both.

2. In 1707, the Union of the Crowns united the separate kingdoms of England and Scotland into a single kingdom known as Great Britain. Properly speaking, before 1707 one should refer to "the English"; after 1707, to "the British." The two terms, however, are sometimes used interchangeably in this book.

3. Allen, *North American Exploration*, vol. 3, p. 77.

4. Ronda, *Lewis and Clark*, p. 1.

5. Gilman, *Lewis and Clark*, p. 55.

6. Columbus was not, of course, the first European to visit the New World. In about the year 1000, the Vikings had established a colony called "Vineland" (meaning a fertile region) in Newfoundland. From there they sailed along the coast of North America, observing the Indians, the flora, and the fauna. For reasons now lost, Vineland was abandoned after a few years. The Vikings never returned to North America.

7. Private communication of 29 March 2005 from the Reference Desk at McGill University's Humanities and Social Sciences Library.

8. Quoted in Wood and Thiessen, *Early Fur Trade*, Table 1, no page number given.

9. "North America: Physical Geography," p. 1.

10. After "Physical Geography," pp. 1–3.

11. The provinces of northern New Spain were Pánuco, Sinaloa, Sonora, Pimería Alta, Baja (Lower) and Alta (Upper) California, Nueva Vizcaya, New Mexico, Nuevo León, Coahuila, Texas, and Nuevo Santander.

12. In the eighteenth century, France and Spain divided their territorial claims along the 42nd parallel. This now forms the northern border of California, Nevada, and part of Utah. When France lost the Seven Years' War in 1763, its claim to the area ended. Spain gave up its claims in international agreements of 1790 and 1819. Russia surrendered its own, weaker claims in treaties with the United States in 1824 and with Britain in 1825. In the meantime, the United States and Britain had signed an Anglo-American convention in 1818 that extended the boundary between their territories west along the 49th parallel to the Rocky Mountains. The two countries had joint occupancy of the Oregon Country between 1818 and 1846.

13. Quoted in Bergon, *Journals of Lewis and Clark*, p. xxiv.

14. In *The Course of Empire* (p. 73), the historian Bernard DeVoto tells us: "The historian Hubert Howe Bancroft used the excellent phrase 'Northern Mystery' to designate the portion of the Pacific coast above San Francisco Bay that resisted knowledge and bred error for so long a time. It will be used here [in *The Course of Empire*] to designate as the Northwestern Mystery an area that provided one of the climaxes of the imperial struggle for the continent and that contained the key features of continental geography that were the last to be discovered and understood. This area begins with the Upper Missouri River."

15. Hakluyt, *Voyages*, p. 188.

1. The Indians

1. In a private communication of 28 June 2004, Ian McLeod, Bilingual Communications Officer of the Assembly of First Nations (a national organization representing First Nations citizens in Canada), explained that Canada's Constitution recognizes three distinct aboriginal peoples. These are the "treaty Indians" or "First Nations"; the Inuit, e.g., the Eskimos; and the Métis, i.e., those of mixed aboriginal–Caucasian parentage. The Inuit and Métis are included in the term "first peoples" but not in the term "First Nations."
2. Quoted in Calloway, *Winter Count*, pp. 25–26.
3. After Calloway, *Winter Count*, pp. 26–27.
4. Private communication of 1 September 2004 from Olivia Littles of the D'Arcy McNickle Center for American Indian History.
5. Sultzman, "Comanche History," p. 1.
6. Quoted in Time-Life, *Indians*, p.
7. Quoted in Bergon, *Journals of Lewis and Clark*, p. 323.
8. Private communication of 25 April 2004 from Dr. Kathryn Abbott.
9. Columbus called the dark-skinned native peoples of the New World "Indians" because he thought he was sailing in the Indian Ocean. Technically, then, "Indians" is not an accurate term. Nevertheless, long usage has hallowed it and for this reason I prefer it to the more recent and politically correct "Native Americans."
10. Mary Crow Dog, a Sioux woman, tells us that "The Sioux used to keep winter counts, picture writings on buffalo skin, which told our people's story from year to year." Quoted in Calloway, *Winter Count*, p. 1.
11. Quoted in Gutiérrez, *When Jesus Came*, p. 44.
12. Quoted in Kavanagh, *Comanche Political History*, p. 87.
13. As Jenkins and Keal put it in their *Adirondack Atlas* (p. 69), "First, Indians fought Indians, then and Indians and Europeans fought other Indians and Europeans, and finally the Europeans, having used up the supply of Indians, fought one another."
14. Richter, *Facing East*, pp. 39–40.
15. "Historical Background," p. 1.
16. Quoted in Calloway, *Winter Count* p. 337. See also Dictionary of Canadian Biography, "Tanaghrisson," p. 1.
17. These comments are drawn from Brigham Young University's "Template" on the Pueblos, p. 3; and Calloway, *Winter Count*, p. 92.
18. After Calloway, *Winter Count*, pp. 114, 158–159.
19. After Handbook of Texas Online, "Seven Cities of Cíbola," p. 1.
20. Quoted in Knaut, *Pueblo Revolt*, p. 174.
21. Quoted in Weber, *Spanish Frontier*, p. 136.
22. Quoted in Brooks, *Captives*, p. 54.
23. The following opinions about the causes of the Pueblo Revolt have been adapted from Weber, *Pueblo Revolt*, pp. 9–16.
24. Quoted in Kessell, *Spain in the Southwest*, p. 117, and in Knaut, *Pueblo Revolt*, pp. 158–159.
25. After Calloway, *Winter Count*, p. 170.
26. Quoted in Weber, *Pueblo Revolt*, pp. 9–10.
27. Quoted in Weber, *Pueblo Revolt*, p. 10.
28. Quoted in Weber, *Pueblo Revolt*, p. 10.
29. Quoted in Weber, *Pueblo Revolt*, p. 10.
30. Weber, *Pueblo Revolt*, p. 10.
31. Quoted in Weber, *Spanish Frontier*, pp. 117–118.
32. Quoted in Kessell, *Spain in the Southwest*, p. 159.
33. Quoted in Calloway, *Winter Count*, p. 200.
34. Subgroups for the Eastern Apache include the Mescalero, Jicarilla, Chiricahua, Kipan, Lipan, and Kiowa. Subgroups for the Western Apache include the Cibecue, Mimbreño, Coyotero, and Northern and Southern Tonto (or Mogollon).
35. Private communication of 2 February 2005 from Dr. Paul Brand.
36. After Handbook of Texas Online, "Apache," p. 1.
37. Quoted in Knaut, *Pueblo Revolt*, p. 162.
38. Calloway, *Winter Count*, p. 162.
39. "Apaches," p. 1.
40. After Calloway, *Winter Count*, p. 206.
41. Quoted in Kessell, *Spain in the Southwest*, pp. 292–293.
42. After Weber, *Spanish Frontier*, p. 233.
43. Handbook of Texas Online, "Apache Indians," p. 4.
44. Calloway, *Winter Count*, p. 251.
45. Catholic Encyclopedia, "Caddo Indians," pp. 1–2.
46. Weber, *Spanish Frontier*, p. 153.
47. Douay's account is quoted in Calloway, *Winter Count*, pp. 250–251.
48. Weber, *Spanish Frontier*, p. 153.
49. The name "bull" comes from the lead seal (*bulla* in Latin) which was attached to such documents to prove their authenticity.
50. After Calloway, *Winter Count*, p. 251.
51. After Calloway, *Winter Count*, p. 253.
52. After Fehrenbach, *Comanches*, pp. 189–190.
53. After John, *Storms*, p. 158.
54. Handbook of Texas Online, "St. Denis," p. 1.
55. Some of the following comments are drawn from Weber, *Spanish Frontier*, pp. 186–187.

56. Quoted in Weber, *Spanish Frontier*, p. 186.
57. After Weber, *Spanish Frontier*, p. 186.
58. Private communication of 30 August 2004 from Dr. W. Raymond Wood.
59. Radisson is quoted in Calloway, *Winter Count*, p. 241.
60. The citations and information used here are from Calloway, *Winter Count*, p. 241, and Adams, *Radisson*, p. 134.
61. Quoted in Golay and Bowman, *North American Exploration*, p. 269.
62. Quoted in Calloway, *Winter Count*, p. 309. These quotes are from the explorers La Vérendrye, Alexander Henry, and Jonathan Carver, respectively.
63. Quoted in Wood and Thiessen, *Early Fur Trade*, pp. 79, 80.
64. Quoted in Bergon, *Journals of Lewis and Clark*, p. 39.
65. Quoted in Ambrose, *Undaunted Courage*, p. 163.
66. Quoted in Bergon, *Journals of Lewis and Clark*, pp. 40–41.
67. Quoted in Ambrose, *Undaunted Courage*, p. 163.
68. Quoted in Gilman, *Lewis and Clark*, p. 106.
69. Quoted in Calloway, *Winter Count*, p. 310.
70. Quoted in Calloway, *Winter Count*, p. 310.
71. Adapted from Gilman, *Lewis and Clark*, p. 94.
72. PBS, "Teton Sioux Indians," p. 1.
73. Marcy, *Prairie Traveler*, pp. 196–197.
74. Marcy, *Prairie Traveler*, pp. 205–206.
75. Marcy, *Prairie Traveler*, p. 206.
76. Catlin, *North American Indians*, vol. 1, p. 233.
77. Some of the following comments are drawn from Sultzman, "Comanche History," pp. 1–7.
78. After a map in Fehrenbach's *Comanches*, p. 143.
79. Quoted in Troccoli, *First Artist of the West*, p. 142.
80. Quoted in Calloway, *Winter Count*, p. 291.
81. Quoted in Calloway, *Winter Count*, p. 284.
82. Quoted in Calloway, *Winter Count*, p. 274.
83. After Kavanagh, *Comanche Political History*, p. 63.
84. Quoted in Kavanagh, *Comanche Political History*, pp. 66–67.
85. Quoted in Kavanagh, *Comanche Political History*, p. 73.
86. Quoted in Calloway, *Winter Count*, p. 289.
87. Quoted in Weber, *Spanish Frontier*, pp. 189–191.
88. Quoted in Kessell, *Spain in the Southwest*, p. 245.
89. Handbook of Texas Online, "Spanish Fort," p. 1.
90. After Weber, *Spanish Frontier*, p. 191.
91. One of the earliest legends about the inexhaustible mineral riches of the Southwest comes from the credulous Spanish missionary Friar Alonso de Benavides, who was chief administrator of the Spanish missions in New Mexico from 1626 to 1629. He claimed there were veins of silver "which run from north to south more than fifty leagues" in the Socorro Mountains of central New Mexico, adding that "the ease with which the silver can be taken out from this hill is the greatest and best in all the Indies." Quoted in Hillerman, *Best of the West*, pp. 25–26.
92. Quoted in Golay and Bowman, *North American Exploration*, p. 210.
93. This is from a map of 1778 and is quoted in Kavanagh, *Comanche Political History*, p. 89.
94. This is also from the 1778 map and quoted in Kavanagh, *Comanche Political History*, p. 87.
95. Quoted in Sultzman, "Comanche History," p. 5.
96. After Kessell, *Spain in the Southwest*, pp. 300–301, and Weber, *Spanish Frontier*, p. 283.
97. Some of the following discussion is drawn from Handbook of Texas Online, "Vial, Pedro," pp. 1–2.
98. Quoted in Kavanagh, *Comanche Political History*, p. 102.
99. Quoted in Kavanagh, *Comanche Political History*, p. 103.
100. After Fehrenbach, *Comanches*, p. 231.
101. After Kavanagh, *Comanche Political History*, p. 148.
102. Quoted in National Geographic, "Mandan Indians," p. 2.
103. "Mandan," p. 2.
104. PBS, "Mandan Indians," p. 1.
105. Ambrose, *Undaunted Courage*, p. 182.
106. Gilman, *Lewis and Clark*, note 14, p. 400.
107. Quoted in Calloway, *Winter Count*, p. 301.
108. This account follows Ambrose, *Undaunted Courage*, p. 199.
109. Quoted in Bergon, *Journals of Lewis and Clark*, p. 87.
110. Quoted in Ambrose, *Undaunted Courage*, p. 200.
111. Ambrose, *Undaunted Courage*, p. 200.
112. Calloway, *Winter Count*, p. 303.
113. This section draws on the *Encyclopaedia Britannica*'s excellent article, "Northwest Coast Indian," pp. 1–13.
114. Quoted in Gibson, *Otter Skins*, p. 3.
115. Quoted in Gibson, *Otter Skins*, p. 3.
116. Quoted in Gilman, *Lewis and Clark*, p. 238.

117. Allen, *Lewis and Clark*, note 18, p. 313.
118. After Gilman, *Lewis and Clark*, pp. 224, 227, 238, 240.
119. Quoted in Bergon, *Journals of Lewis and Clark*, pp. 345–346.
120. "Northwest Coast Culture Area," p. 7.
121. Time-Life, *Canadians*, p. 76.
122. "Northwest Coast Culture Area," p. 7.
123. *Catholic Encyclopedia*, "Mission Indians," p. 2.
124. Private communication of 1 September 2004 from Olivia Littles of the D'Arcy McNickle Center for American Indian History.
125. *Catholic Encyclopedia*, "Mission Indians," p. 7.
126. Quoted in Weber, *Spanish Frontier*, p. 236.
127. Quoted in Gibson, *Otter Skins*, p. 12.
128. Quoted in Beebe and Senkewicz, *Lands of Promise*, p. 126.
129. Quoted in San Diego Historical Society, "Serra," p. 3.
130. Quoted in Beebe and Senkewicz, *Lands of Promise*, p. 156.
131. Quoted in Beebe and Senkewicz, *Lands of Promise*, p. 191.
132. Some of the following discussion is drawn from Calloway, *Winter Count*, p. 396.
133. Quoted in Calloway, *Winter Count*, p. 397.
134. Quoted in French in Galaup, *Voyage*, vol. 2, p. 275.
135. Quoted in Golay and Bowman, *North American Exploration*, p. 221.
136. Quoted in Calloway, *Winter Count*, p. 397.
137. Quoted in "Junipero Serra," p. 2.
138. Cook, *Conflict*, p. 12.
139. Quoted in Calloway, *Winter Count*, p. 297.
140. Quoted in Calloway, *Winter Count*, p. 297.
141. Catlin, *North American Indians*, vol. 1, p. 38.
142. After Janin, *Fort Bridger*, p. 21.
143. Quoted in Allen, *Lewis and Clark*, p. 356.

2. The Spaniards

1. Quoted in Golay and Bowman, *North American Exploration*, p. 109.
2. Jones, "Spanish Penetrations," pp. 63–64.
3. Handbook of Texas Online, "Álvarez de Pineda," p. 1.
4. Handbook of Texas Online, "Cabeza de Vaca," p. 1.
5. Cabeza de Vaca, *Chronicle*, p. 30.
6. Cabeza de Vaca, *Chronicle*, pp. 60–61.
7. Cabeza de Vaca, *Chronicle*, p. 87.
8. Cabeza de Vaca, *Chronicle*, pp. 40–41.
9. Cabeza de Vaca, *Chronicle*, p. 93.
10. Cabeza de Vaca, *Chronicle*, p. 96.
11. Cabeza de Vaca, *Chronicle*, p. 96.
12. After Golay and Bowman, *North American Exploration*, p. 64.
13. Quoted in Golay and Bowman, *North American Exploration*, p. 186.
14. Quoted in Kessell, *Spain in the Southwest*, p. 3.
15. Quoted in Clayton, Knight, and Moore, *De Soto Chronicles*, vol. 2, p. 450.
16. Cabeza de Vaca, *Chronicle*, p. 87.
17. Quoted in Weber, *Spanish Frontier*, p. 14.
18. Quoted in Kessell, *Spain in the Southwest*, p. 32.
19. Quoted in Golay and Bowman, *North American Exploration*, p. 101.
20. The first quotation is taken from Weber, *Spanish Frontier*, p. 26; the second, from Calloway, *Winter Count*, p. 121; and the third, from Gutíerrez, *When Jesus Came*," p. 43.
21. Quoted in Calloway, *Winter Count*, p. 134.
22. Quoted (to varying degrees) in Golay and Bowman, *North American Exploration*, p. 75; Weber, *Spanish Frontier*, p. 47; and Calloway, *Winter Count*, p. 135.
23. Quoted in Hillerman, *Best of the West*, p. 20.
24. Quoted in Calloway, *Winter Count*, p. 136.
25. Quoted in Calloway, *Winter Count*, pp. 138–139.
26. Quoted in Morley, *Exploring North America*, p. 12.
27. Quoted in Calloway, *Winter Count*, p. 141.
28. Quoted in Calloway, *Winter Count*, p. 475.
29. See Weber, *Spanish Frontier*, p. 40.
30. Cabrillo was a hard man. He took part in the Spanish conquests of Cuba, Mexico, Guatemala, and Honduras. When Cortés ordered him to find some way to make pitch to seal the seams of small boats to be used in attack on the Aztec's island capital city of Tenochtitlán, Cabrillo used fat rendered from the bodies of dead Indians. (After Weber, *Spanish Frontier*, p. 40.)
31. Quoted in National Park Service, "Cabrillo," p. 1.
32. "Motives for Exploration," p. 2.
33. Quoted in Kessell, *Spain in the Southwest*, p. 49.
34. Quoted in Weber, *Spanish Frontier*, p. 41.
35. Western Silver Corporation, "Growth through Silver," pp. 1–2.
36. After John, *Storms*, p. 25.
37. Quoted in Calloway, *Winter Count*, p. 143.
38. Quoted in "Acoma Pueblo," p. 1.
39. Quoted in Calloway, *Winter Count*, p. 144.
40. Quoted in Weber, *Spanish Frontier*, p. 80.

41. After Golay and Bowman, *North American Exploration*, p. 66.
42. The following account is drawn from Golay and Bowman, *North American Exploration*, pp. 66–67.
43. Private communication of 12 December 2004 from Carola DeRooy, the archivist at Point Reyes National Seashore.
44. Quoted in Encinias, *Historia de la Nueva México*, p. xxviii.
45. Quoted in Calloway, *Winter Count*, p. 148.
46. The sentences and citation are from Calloway, *Winter Count*, p. 149.
47. Quoted in Calloway, *Winter Count*, p. 149.
48. John, *Storms*, p. 50.
49. Quoted in Golay and Bowman, *North American Exploration*, p. 107.
50. Weber, *Spanish Frontier*, p. 83.
51. Quoted in Swanson, *San Diego*, p. 293.
52. Quoted in Golay and Bowman, *North American Exploration*, p. 121.
53. Quoted in Beebe and Senkewicz, *Lands of Promise*, pp. 44–45.
54. After Beebe and Senkewicz, *Lands of Promise*, p. 73.
55. Quoted in Kessell, *Spain in the Southwest*, p. 92.
56. Quoted in Knaut, *Pueblo Revolt*, p. 124.
57. Quoted in Knaut, *Pueblo Revolt*, p. 125.
58. Comments on Posada are drawn from *Handbook of Texas Online*, "Posada," pp. 1–2.
59. Quoted in Golay and Bowman, *North American Exploration*, p. 234.
60. Quoted in Weber, *Spanish Frontier*, p. 204.
61. Quoted in Calloway, *Winter Count*, p. 183.
62. Quoted in Jones, "Spanish Penetrations," p. 59.
63. After Beebe and Senkewicz, *Lands of Promise*, p. 54.
64. Quoted in Kessell, *Spain in the Southwest*, p. 159.
65. After Kessell, *Spain in the Southwest*, pp. 186–187.
66. After Beebe and Senkewicz, *Lands of Promise*, p. 62.
67. Quoted in Calloway, *Winter Count*, p. 206.
68. Quoted in Calloway, *Winter Count*, pp. 206–207.
69. Quoted in Calloway, *Winter Count*, p. 207.
70. Quoted in Weber, *Spanish Frontier*, p. 162.
71. Quoted in Calloway, *Winter Count*, p. 209.
72. Situated on the northern border of Spain's empire in North America, Spanish Texas constituted only of a small part of modern day Texas. It extended north from the Nueces River, which flows into the Gulf of Mexico at Corpus Christi, to the headwaters of the Medina River northwest of San Antonio, and thence eastwards into Louisiana. Over time, Spanish Texas was part of four different provinces in the viceroyalty of New Spain. See Handbook of Texas, "Spanish Texas," p. 1.
73. The account of the Villasur disaster comes from Calloway, *Winter Count*, pp. 209–211.
74. Handbook of Texas, "Los Adaes," pp. 1–2.
75. After Allen, *Lewis and Clark*, p. 39.
76. After Calloway, *Winter Count*, pp. 361.
77. Quoted in Calloway, *Winter Count*, p. 362.
78. Handbook of Texas Online, "Rubí," p. 1.
79. Handbook of Texas Online, "New Regulations," p. 1.
80. After Weber, *Spanish Frontier*, p. 216.
81. Quoted in Fehrenbach, *Comanches*, p. 214.
82. Quoted in Gibson, "Exploration," pp. 348–349.
83. Quoted in Gibson, "Exploration," p. 350. My discussion of "Fleurieu's Whirlpool" is taken from the same page.
84. Quoted in Gibson, "Exploration," p. 350.
85. After Gibson, "Exploration," pp. 350–351.
86. Quoted in Beebe and Senkewicz, *Lands of Promise*, p. 111.
87. Quoted in Golay and Bowman, *North American Exploration*, p. 233.
88. Quoted in "MissionTour," p. 1.
89. Quoted in Weber, *Spanish Frontier*, p. 245.
90. Quoted Colasurdo, *Golden Gate National Parks*, p. 19, and in Weber, *Spanish Frontier*, p. 246.
91. To strengthen its tenuous administrative control over New Spain, in 1776 the Council of the Indies created a new bureaucratic entity, the Provincias Internas (Interior Provinces). This administrative body covered northern Spain its entirety, that is to say, Neuva Vizcaya, Coahuila, Sonora, Sinaloa, Texas, New Mexico, Baja California, and Alta California. This enormous area was not governed by the viceroy in Mexico City, who already had so many other responsibilities that he could not give it his full attention, but by a senior Spanish officer who reported directly to the king. After Calloway, *Winter Count*, pp. 376, 378, and Kessell, *Spain in the Southwest*, p. 310.
92. Golay and Bowman, *North American Exploration*, pp. 200, 202.
93. This account is drawn from John, *Storms*, pp. 557–571.
94. Quoted in Calloway, *Winter Count*, p. 1.
95. Quoted in Golay and Bowman, *North American Exploration*, p. 201.
96. National Park Service, "Juan Bautista de Anza National Historic Trail," p. 3.
97. In discussing theses voyages I have drawn freely from Blumenthal, *Early Exploration of Inland Washington Waters*.
98. Quoted in Weber, *Spanish Frontier*, p. 249.

99. Quoted in Golay and Bowman, *North American Exploration*, p. 230.
100. Quoted in Calloway, *Winter Count*, p. 399.
101. After Weber, *Spanish Frontier*, p. 249.
102. Quoted in Allen, *Lewis and Clark*, p. 31.
103. Quoted in Golay and Bowman, *North American Exploration*, p. 219.
104. Quoted in Golay and Bowman, *North American Exploration*, p. 206.
105. After Blumenthal, *Early Exploration*, pp. 17–18.
106. Quoted in Blumenthal, *Early Exploration*, pp. 19–20.
107. Quoted in Blumenthal, *Early Exploration*, p. 20.
108. Quoted in Blumenthal, *Early Exploration*, pp. 25–26.
109. Quoted in Blumenthal, *Early Exploration*, p. 28.
110. Quoted in Blumenthal, *Early Exploration*, p. 37.
111. Quoted in Blumenthal, *Early Exploration*, p. 37.
112. Quoted in Blumenthal, *Early Exploration*, pp. 49–50.
113. Quoted in Golay and Bowman, *North American Exploration*, p. 224.
114. After Blumenthal, *Early Exploration*, p. 76.
115. Wilford, "Blow off course."
116. Quoted in Blumenthal, *Early Exploration*, p. 75.
117. After Blumenthal, *Early Exploration*, p. 84.
118. "Malaspina," p. 2.
119. After Wilford, "Blown off course."
120. Quoted in Ronda, *Astoria*, p. xi.
121. Quoted in John, *Views*, pp. 34–35.
122. Quoted in John, *Views*, p. 36.
123. Quoted in John, *Views*, p. 38.
124. Quoted in John, *Views*, p. 38.
125. After John, *Views*, p. 42.
126. Quoted in John, *Views*, p. 45.
127. Quoted in John, *Views*, p. 46.
128. After "James Mackay," p. 1.
129. A sketch of this galiot can be found in Nasatir, *Spanish War Vessels*, frontispiece.
130. Nasatir, *Spanish War Vessels*, p. 143.
131. After Brown, "Illinois Country," p. 1.
132. Quoted in "Illinois Country," p. 1.
133. After Weber, *Spanish Frontier*, p. 286.
134. Quoted in Calloway, *Winter Count*, p. 393.
135. Quoted in Nasatir, *Before Lewis and Clark*, vol. 1, p. 85.
136. Quoted in Wood, *Prologue*, p. 30.
137. Quoted in Wood, *Prologue*, pp. 28–29.
138. Quoted in Wood, *Prologue*, p. 29.
139. After Wood, *Prologue*, p. 31.
140. Much of the following information on these three expeditions has been drawn from Wood, *Prologue*, pp. 31 ff.
141. Quoted in Calloway, *Winter Count*, p. 394.
142. Private communication of 30 August 2004 from Dr. W. Raymond Wood.
143. Quoted in Wood, *Prologue*, p. 38.
144. Quoted in Wood, *Prologue*, p. 39.
145. Quoted in Wood, *Prologue*, pp. 39–40.
146. After Wood, *Prologue*, p. 42.
147. Quoted in Wood, *Prologue*, pp. 41–42.
148. Quoted in Wood and Thiessen, *Early Fur Trade*, p. 14.
149. For a good discussion of this map, see Wood, *Prologue*, pp. 47–64.
150. Quoted in "James Mackay," p. 1.
151. Quoted in Briceland, "British Exploration," p. 325.
152. Quoted in Wood, *Prologue to Lewis and Clark*, pp. 152–153.
153. Quoted in Wood and Thiessen, *Early Fur Trade*, p. 51.
154. Quoted in Wood and Thiessen, *Early Fur Trade*, p. 29.
155. "James Mackay," p. 2.
156. After Calloway, *Winter Count*, pp. 290, 395.
157. Avalon Project, "Treaty of San Ildefonso," p. 2.
158. Whittier, *Mississippi Question*, p. 189.
159. Quoted in "New Orleans closed to Americans," p. 1.

3. The French

1. Quoted in PBS, "Empire of the Bay," p. 3.
2. Quoted in PBS, "Empire of the Bay," p. 3.
3. Heidenreich, "Early French Exploration," p. 147. Italics added.
4. After Delâge, "French and English Colonial Models," p. 4.
5. After "Historical Background: The Fur Trade," p. 1.
6. After "A Year in the Life," p. 14.
7. Today, beaver dams often cause difficulties for ranchers in the American Rockies. It is illegal to kill beavers there. One rancher near Fort Bridger, Wyoming, told me that the only way for him to deal with this problem is to "Shoot, shovel, and shut up."
8. The fur trade was sufficiently complex so that no short summary can hope to do it justice. The facts about the are not in dispute; the interpretations are. For an overview that differs from the one used in this book, see "The Canadian-Missouri River Fur Trade," in Wood and Thiessen's *Early Fur Trade on the Northern Plains*, pp. 3–17. Wood and Thiessen maintain

that "The fur trade of western North America consisted of two grand divisions, one Canadian and one American." They explain in detail how the Canadian system involved competing French and British merchants operating out of Montreal and posts along Hudson Bay. The American system, based in St. Louis, was dominated successively by the French, the Spaniards, and the Americans. All this is true enough, but I think the overview used here is simpler and thus more useful.

9. This discussion of the Beaver Wars is drawn from Jenkins and Keal, *Adirondack Atlas*, pp. 70–71.

10. The Five Nations of the Iroquois were the Seneca, Cayuga, Onondaga, Oneida, and Mowhawk.

11. After Nelson, *My First Years*, pp. 11, 35 (footnote 15).

12. After Wood and Thiessen, *Early Fur Trade*, p. 10.

13. Quoted in Wood and Thiessen, *Early Fur Trade*, p. 14.

14. *Canadian Encyclopedia*, "Fur Trade after 1760," p. 1.

15. After Time-Life Books, "The Canadians," pp. 24–25.

16. Quoted in Calloway, *Winter Count*, p. 217.

17. Quoted in Golay and Bowman, *North American Exploration*, p. 144.

18. Quoted in DeVoto, *Course of Empire*, p. 55.

19. Quoted in Heidenreich, "Early French Exploration," p. 76.

20. After "History of Saskatchewan Waterways," p. 7.

21. After Eccles, "French Exploration," p. 153.

22. Cited in Delâge, "Québec," p. 3.

23. Quoted in Heidenreich, "Early French Exploration," p. 81.

24. After Swagerty, "Fur Trade," p. 1.

25. Private communication of 12 May 2005 from the Canadian scholar Denys Delâge.

26. Quoted in Calloway, *Winter Count*, p. 244.

27. Private communication of 12 May 2005 from the Canadian scholar Denys Delâge.

28. Heidenreich, "Early French Exploration," p. 127.

29. The French would eventually divide *le Pays d'En Haut* into three administrative districts: La Poste du Sud, which embraced the region south of Detroit; La Baie, which included Green Bay and the headwaters of the Mississippi River; and La Mer de l'Ouest (the Western Sea), which took in everything west of Rainy Lake on the Ontario-Minnesota border. After Eccles, "French Exploration, p. 179.

30. Quoted in Nasatir, *Before Lewis and Clark*, vol. 1, p. 3.

31. Quoted in DeVoto, *Course of Empire*, p. 117.

32. Quoted in Golay and Bowman, *North American Exploration*, p. 288.

33. Quoted in DeVoto, *Course of Empire*, p. 118.

34. Quoted in Allen, *Lewis and Clark*, p. 5.

35. Quoted in Nasatir, vol. 1, p. 3.

36. After Heidenreich, "Early French Exploration," p. 129.

37. Quoted in Golay and Bowman, *North American Exploration*, p. 292.

38. In fairness to La Salle, it should be noted that the Mississippi's present delta exceeds 11,000 square miles in area. The Mississippi (to quote from "A History of New Orleans," p. 3) "is most shallow and treacherous at the sandbars crossing its mouth in the Gulf of Mexico. Where the river meets the gulf is nothing but marsh and watery muck, a desolate scene that extends so far out into the gulf [that] it created more difficulties for both seagoing and coastal vessels. With no distinguishing features except mud banks and salt marsh tufts, the river's several mouths and labyrinth of bayous made the three true entrances difficult to find."

39. Quoted in Kessell, *Spain in the Southwest*, p. 137.

40. After Handbook of Texas Online, "La Salle Expedition," pp. 1–2.

41. Handbook of Texas Online, "La Salle Expedition," p. 3. Weddle is the author of this entry in the Handbook.

42. Some of these comments on Hennepin were drawn from "Louis Hennepin," pp. 1–2.

43. Quoted in Golay and Bowman, *North American Exploration*, p. 282.

44. DeVoto, *Course of Empire*, p. 143.

45. Quoted in Allen, *Lewis and Clark*, p. 8.

46. After U.S. Army, "Mississippi River Navigation: Early Navigation," p. 1.

47. After Eccles, "French Exploration," p. 158.

48. In 1869, Canada bought Rupert's Land from the Hudson's Bay Company. Rupert's Land was about ten times the size of what was then Canada.

49. Quoted in Brown, "Certain Aspects," p. 27.

50. McNabb, "A History of New Orleans," p. 12.

51. After Calloway, *Winter Count*, p. 261.

52. After Calloway, *Winter Count*, p. 259.

53. National Park Service, "Arkansas Post: Founding," p. 1.

54. Mackay, "Extraordinary Popular Delusions," p. 24.

55. Eccles, "French Exploration," p. 165.

56. Quoted in American Journeys Collection, "Exact Description," p. 4.

57. After Eccles, "French Exploration," p. 167.

58. The full title in French is considerably longer. The English translation of it is: "Exact Description of Louisiana, of Its Harbours, Lands and Rivers, and Names of the Tribes Which Occupy It, and the Commerce and Advantages to be Derived Therefrom for the Establishment of a Colony." Cited in American Journeys Collection, "Exact Description," p. 8.
59. Quoted in American Journeys Collection, "Exact Description," p. 8.
60. Quoted in American Journeys Collection, "Exact Description," p. 11.
61. Quoted in American Journeys Collection, "Exact Description," p. 11.
62. Quoted in American Journeys Collection, "Exact Description," pp. 15–16.
63. Quoted in American Journeys Collection, "Exact Description," p. 16.
64. After Eccles, "French Exploration," p. 168.
65. After Eccles, "French Exploration," p. 169.
66. DeVoto, *Course of Empire*, p. 185.
67. After Eccles, "French Exploration," p. 170.
68. Acadian-Cajun, "Exile Destination: Louisiana," p. 2.
69. There is, however, a Verendrye National Monument. It was established in 1917 on the left bank of the upper Missouri River near the town of Sanish, North Dakota. With an area of 250 acres, it marks the spot where Vérendrye and his sons camped during their explorations in 1742. The central feature of the monument is Crowhigh Butte, which rises 565 feet above the river.
70. DeVoto, *Course of Empire*, p. 196.
71. DeVoto, *Course of Empire*, p. 213.
72. Quoted in Smith, *Explorations of the La Vérendryes*, pp. 109–110.
73. Quoted in Smith, *Explorations of the La Vérendryes*, p. 113.
74. Fort Pierre, "Verendrye Monument," p. 1.
75. "Lead Tablet," p. 1.
76. After La Vérendrye, *In Search of the Western Sea*, p. 163.
77. "Journal," p. 2.
78. After American Journeys, "Background of Extract of the Journal," p. 1.
79. Eccles, "French Exploration," p. 174.
80. Time-Life, The *Expressmen*, p. 21.
81. Calloway, *Winter Count*, p. 326.
82. Quoted in Calloway, *Winter Count*, p. 327.
83. Quoted in Calloway, *Winter Count*, p. 327.
84. After Fehrenbach, *Comanches*, p. 198.
85. This section on the Kichai Indians is from drawn two articles (with the same name) on "The Gilbert Site," pp. 1–5 and 1–11, and from "Kichai Indians," p. 1.
86. "Maps," p. 2.
87. After Conrad, "Reluctant Imperialist," pp. 637–638.
88. Quoted in Kessell, *Spain in the Southwest*, p. 325.

4. The British

1. For a judicious discussion of Cabot's 1497 voyage, see Croxton, "The Cabot Dilemma."
2. Modern History Sourcebook, "Francis Pretty," p. 10.
3. Quoted in Golay and Bowman, *North American Exploration*, p. 85.
4. Modern History Sourcebook, "Francis Pretty," p. 12.
5. Gouch, *Northwest Coast*, p. 22.
6. Modern History Sourcebook, "Francis Pretty," p. 12.
7. CNN.com, "Solved mystery," pp. 1–2.
8. Quoted in DeVoto, *Course of Empire*, p. 127.
9. Quoted in Ruggles, "British Exploration," p. 204.
10. "Hudson's Bay Company," p. 1.
11. PBS, "Empire of the Bay," p. 1.
12. Some of this section is drawn from Golay and Bowman, *North American Exploration*, "Kelsey, Henry," p. 289.
13. Quoted in Calloway, *Winter Count*, p. 246.
14. Quoted in DeVoto, *Course of Empire*, p. 162.
15. After Ruggles, "British Exploration of Rupert's Land," p. 218.
16. Devoto, *Course of Empire*, p. 164.
17. After Briceland, "British Exploration, p. 269.
18. Pocahontas, the daughter of an Indian chief, intervened to prevent Smith from being executed.
19. After Briceland, "British Exploration," p. 269 ff. I have drawn heavily on this article to sketch out British exploration east of the Mississippi.
20. After Briceland, "British Exploration," p. 312.
21. Flint, *Biographical Memoir*, p. 42.
22. After Janin, *Fort Bridger*, p. 12.
23. An excellent discussion of this theory can be found in Allen, *Lewis and Clark*, which has been drawn upon here.
24. Quoted in Allen, *Lewis and Clark*, p. 26.
25. Quoted in "Robert Rogers," p. 1.
26. "Robert Rogers," p. 1.
27. Quoted in Allen, *Lewis and Clark*, p. 123.
28. Quoted in Gilman, *Across the Divide*, p. 58.
29. Quoted in "The Adventures of Jonathan Carver," p. 1.
30. Gelb, *Jonathan Carver's Travels*, p. 1.
31. After "The Adventures of Jonathan Carver," p. 9.

32. Quoted in Calloway, *Winter Count*, p. 359.
33. Quoted in Gough, *First Across the Continent*, p. 57.
34. Quoted in "Hudson's Bay Company," p. 1.
35. "Village of Cumberland House," p. 1.
36. "Hudson's Bay Company," p. 2.
37. Quoted in Nordyke, *Pacific Images*, p. 168.
38. Quoted in Gibson, "Exploration," p. 375.
39. Quoted in Gibson, "Exploration," p. 376.
40. Quoted in Gibson, "Exploration," p. 376.
41. Quoted in Golay and Bowman, *North American Exploration*, p. 209.
42. Quoted in Gibson, "Exploration," p. 377.
43. Quoted in Kessell, *Spain in the Southwest*, p. 326.
44. Quoted in Gibson, *Otter Skins*, p. 268.
45. Quoted in Gibson, "Exploration," pp. 378–379.
46. Quoted in Gunther, *Indian Life*, p. 193.
47. Quoted in Nordyke, *Pacific Images*, plate 31.
48. Marine Mammal Center, "Sea Otter," p. 1.
49. After Blumenthal, *Early Exploration*, p. 3.
50. Gough, *First Across the Continent*, p. 41.
51. "Structure of NWC," p. 1.
52. Quoted in Time-Life, *The Canadians*, p. 38.
53. "Historical background of the village of Buffalo Narrows," pp. 4–5.
54. The following discussion is drawn from "Structure of NWC," pp. 2–3.
55. Eccles, "French Exploration," p. 201.
56. Quoted in Time-Life, *The Canadians*, p. 38.
57. Quoted in Time-Life, *The Canadians*, p. 39.
58. In this section I have drawn heavily on Blumenthal's excellent study, *The Early Exploration of Inland Washington Waters*, especially pp. 3–7.
59. Quoted in *Gibson, Otter Skins*, p. 22.
60. Nasatir, *Before Lewis and Clark*, vol. 1, p. 77.
61. After Golay and Bowman, *North American Exploration*, p. 227.
62. Quoted in Golay and Bowman, *North American Exploration*, p. 226.
63. Quoted in a private communication of 7 October 2004 from Richard W. Blumenthal.
64. Quoted in Gibson, "Exploration," p. 370.
65. Quoted in Gibson, "Exploration," p. 370.
66. Quoted in Gibson, "Exploration," p. 371.
67. After Lamb, "Captain George Vancouver," p. 3.
68. Quoted in Allen, *Lewis and Clark*, p. 36.
69. Vancouver's account of his 1792 voyage makes good reading even today. See Blumenthal, *Early Exploration*, pp. 105–194.
70. Quoted in Gibson, "Exploration," p. 383.
71. Quoted in Golay and Bowman, *North American Exploration*, p. 389.
72. After Lamb, "Captain George Vancouver," pp. 2–3.
73. Quoted in a private communication of 27 January 2004 from Bunny Fontana.
74. Quoted in Blumenthal, *Early Exploration*, p. 76.
75. Quoted in Blumenthal, *Early Exploration*, p. 107.
76. Quoted in Gibson, "Exploration," p. 385.
77. Quoted in Blumenthal, *Early Exploration*, p. 120.
78. Quoted in Blumenthal, *Early Exploration*, p. 126.
79. After Lamb, "Captain George Vancouver," p. 7.
80. Quoted in Gough, *First Across the Continent*, p. 17.
81. Quoted in Golay and Bowman, *North American Exploration*, p. 364.
82. Quoted in Allen, *Lewis and Clark*, p. 27.
83. Quoted in Ambrose, *Undoubted Courage*, p. 73.
84. Quoted in Mackenzie, *Journal*, p. 239.
85. Quoted in DeVoto, *Course of Empire*, p. 421.
86. Quoted in DeVoto, *Course of Empire*, p. 422.
87. Nelson, *My First Years in the Fur Trade*, p. 5.
88. After "Sir Alexander Mackenzie," p. 2.
89. Quoted in "Lewis and Clark: Maps of Exploration," p. 1.
90. Quoted in "Lewis and Clark: Maps of Exploration," p. 1.
91. Quoted in Allen, *Lewis and Clark*, p. 80.
92. Private communication of 27 September 2004 from Judy Lougheed, Administration Clerk, Rocky Mountain House National Historic Site.
93. Quoted in DeVoto, *Course of Empire*, p. 241.
94. After Wood and Thiessen, *Early Fur Trade*, p. 93.
95. Quoted in Golay and Bowman, *North American Exploration*, p. 387.

5. The Russians

1. Gibson, "Exploration," p. 341.
2. Gibson, "Exploration," p. 340.
3. Gibson, "Exploration," p. 341.
4. Quoted in Gibson, "Exploration," p. 333.
5. After Gibson, "Exploration," p. 334.
6. Time-Life. *The Alaskans*, p. 22.
7. Gibson, "Exploration," p. 337.
8. Gibson, "Exploration," p. 339.

9. Quoted in Bergon, *Journals of Lewis and Clark*, pp. 351–352.
10. Gibson, "Exploration," p. 340.
11. The National Biological Service estimates that there were several hundred thousand sea otters in the north Pacific region when commercial hunting began in the eighteenth century. By 1911, when the harvesting of sea otters was forbidden by an international treaty, only scattered colonies remained, each numbering less than a few hundred animals. Thanks to the ban on hunting and other conservation efforts, today there are more 100,000 sea otters living in 75 percent of their original range. See Bodkin *et al*, "Sea Otters," p. 1.
12. Time-Life, *The Alaskans*, p. 24.
13. "Atlatl," p. 1.
14. After Beebe and Senkewicz, *Lands of Promise*, pp. 317–320.
15. Quoted in Gibson, "Exploration," pp. 344–345.
16. Quoted in Gibson, "Exploration," p. 345.
17. After Ronda, *Astoria*, pp. 65–66.
18. Quoted in Ronda, *Astoria*, p. 68.
19. Some of this discussion is drawn from Time-Life, *The Alaskans*, pp. 24–35.

6. The Americans

1. After Golay and Bowman, *North American Exploration*, p. 312, and the websites "Chitimacha History" and "Houma History."
2. After Allen, *Western Rivermen*, p. 238.
3. These figures are from Allen, *Western Rivermen*, p. 79.
4. Quoted in Allen, *Western Rivermen*, pp. 80–81.
5. After Allen, *Western Rivermen*, p. 81.
6. Quoted in Allen, *Western Rivermen*, p. 42.
7. Quoted in Allen, *Western Rivermen*, p. 74.
8. Quoted in Allen, *Western Rivermen*, p. 66.
9. Mississippi History Now, "Mississippi Under British Rule," p. 1.
10. After Allen, *Western Rivermen*, p. 59.
11. Twain, *Life on the Mississippi*, p. 53.
12. Twain, *Life on the Mississippi*, pp. 53–54.
13. Twain, *Life on the Mississippi*, p. 55.
14. Quoted in Allen, *Western Rivermen*, p. 61.
15. After Weber, *Spanish Frontier*, p. 279.
16. After Allen, *Western Rivermen*, p. 61.
17. After Allen, *Western Rivermen*, p. 62.
18. Part of this section is drawn from Library and Archives of Canada, "Peter Pond," pp. 1–4.
19. Quoted in DeVoto, *Course of Empire*, p. 274.
20. Quoted in Time-Life, *Canadians*, p. 23.
21. After Allen, *Lewis and Clark*, pp. 19, 23, 24–25.
22. Quoted in Library and Archives of Canada, "Peter Pond," p. 3.
23. Ruggles, "British Exploration," p. 254.
24. Ronda, *Astoria*, p. 67.
25. Quoted in Gibson, *Otter Skins*, p. 3.
26. After Calloway, *Winter Count*, 407.
27. After Golay and Bowman, *North American Exploration*, p. 341.
28. Some of the following is drawn from U.S. Department of State, "John Jay's Treaty," p. 1
29. "Jay's Treaty," p. 1.
30. Quoted in Spanish Texas, Section 2, p. 7.
31. Quoted in Spanish Texas, Section 2, p.7.
32. After Handbook of Texas Online, "Nolan, Philip," pp. 1–2; a private communication from Linda Longoria of 18 April 2005; and Spanish Texas, Section 2, "Philip Nolan," pp. 1–8.
33. Feigenbaum, *Jefferson's America*, p. 225.
34. Letter of 7 July 1803, quoted in Kulka, *Wilderness*, p. 284.
35. Letter of 18 July 1803, quoted in National Archives, "Louisiana Purchase," p. 1.
36. Some of the following comments are drawn from "Monticello," pp. 1–2.
37. Quoted in Allen, *Lewis and Clark*, p. 60.
38. Feigenbaum, *Jefferson's America*, p. 225.
39. Napoleon was paid in United States bonds, which he sold to Hope and Co. and to Baring at a discount. Therefore, Napoleon received only $8,831,250 in cash for Louisiana. See "The United States Takes Possession," p. 2.
40. Kukla, *Wilderness*, p. 415.
41. Depending on what figures are used, calculations of the total cost to the United States of the Louisiana Purchase range from a low of about two cents an acre to a high of less than five cents per acre. About three cents an acre seems a good compromise for our purposes here. In its article on the Louisiana Purchase, the *Encyclopaedia Britannica* says the cost was "less than three cents per acre." See http://www.britannica.com/eb/print?eu=50375, accessed 8 July 2003.
42. In alphabetical order, these thirteen states are: Arkansas, Colorado (that portion of the state east of the Rocky Mountains), Iowa, Kansas, Louisiana, Minnesota (that portion west of the Mississippi), Missouri, Montana, Nebraska, North Dakota, Oklahoma, South Dakota, and Wyoming. After Kukla, *Wilderness*, p. 331.
43. Laussat's instructions were to transfer Louisiana to the United States the next day, but 20 days actually elapsed before this second transfer took place. In the meantime, Laussat became governor of Louisiana and created a new town council. See "The Cabildo," p. 3.
44. Some of the following comments are drawn from National Park Service, "The French Settlement, pp. 1–2.

45. Library of Congress, "Parallel Histories: North America," p. 2.
46. Quoted in Feigenbaum, *Jefferson's America*, p. 1. The original punctuation has been very lightly edited.

7. Epilogue

1. John, *Storms*, p. 735.
2. The main provision of the Treaty of Guadalupe Hidalgo, which ended the war between the United States and Mexico, was that Mexico had to cede 55% of its territory (i.e., present-day Arizona, California, New Mexico, Texas, and parts of Colorado, Nevada, and Utah) to the United States, in return for $15 million in compensation for war-related damages to Mexican property. See "Treaty of Guadalupe Hidalgo," p. 1.
3. Some of the following discussion is drawn from "The Chirichua Apaches," pp. 1–4.
4. Quoted in "The Great Chiefs," p. 73.
5. After Calloway, *Winter Count*, pp. 382, 425.
6. Quoted in "Red River Raft," p. 1.
7. Quoted in Glover, *Caddo Indians*, p. 26.
8. Marcy, *Prairie Traveler*, p. 211.
9. Many Indian tribes put a high premium on oratory. One of the tragedies of Indian life in the Trans-Mississippi West is that so little of this oratory has been preserved. Some of it has a timeless quality. Consider, for example, the exhortation of the Sioux chief Crazy Horse (c. 1842–1877) to his warriors in 1876 as they faced Custer and his troops at the Battle of the Little Bighorn, popularly known as Custer's Last Stand. Crazy Horse shouted out to his men: "Ho-ka hey! It is a good day to fight! It is a good day to die! Strong hearts, brave hearts, to the front! Weak hearts and cowards to the rear." (Sourced to Stephen E. Ambrose's book *Crazy Horse and Custer*, this quotation appeared on the Web at http://www.firstnationsmonday.com/1000-Tipis/ray6.htm, accessed on 29 January 2005.)
10. Some of the points made here are drawn from "Comanche History," pp. 1–9.
11. Ted Case Studies, "Hudson Bay Company," p. 2.
12. Time-Life Books, "The Alaskans," pp. 218–219.
13. Catholic Encyclopedia, pp. 9–10.
14. Logan, *Lewis and Clark*, p. 304.
15. Quoted in Bergon, *Journals of Lewis and Clark*, p. 288.
16. Quoted in Ambrose, *Undaunted Courage*, p. 299.
17. Bergon, *Journals*, p. 406.
18. "Nez Perce," p. 1.
19. Chief Joseph, "I will fight no more forever."
20. *Encyclopaedia Britannica*, "New Spain," p. 1.
21. Library of Congress, "Parallel Histories: Overview," p. 1.
22. *Canadian Encyclopedia*, "Fur Trade," p. 1.
23. Houghton Mifflin, "Fur Trade," p. 2.
24. In Voltaire's *Candide*, the phrase "a few acres of snow" actually refers not to New France as a whole but only to Acadia, a region now split between the Canadian Maritimes and New England. The full quotation from *Candide* is: "Vous savez que ses deux nations [Britain and France] sont en guerre pour quelques arpents de neige vers le Canada, et qu'elles dépensent pour cette belle guerre beaucoup plus que tout le Canada ne vaut." ("You know that these two nations are at war over a few acres of snow near Canada, and that they are spending more on this little war than all of Canada is worth.") See *Wikipedia*, "a few acres of snow," p. 1.
25. Wikipedia, "New France," pp. 2–3.
26. These comments are drawn from private communications from Dr. Delage of July 2005.
27. Some of the following discussion is drawn from Beebe and Senkewicz, *Lands of Promise*, pp. 293–294, 316–317.
28. The American writer Richard Henry Dana, Jr., author of the classic *Two Years Before the Mast* (1840), gathered and cured bullock hides in California in 1835–1836. This is what he had to say about the Russians:

Here [in San Francisco Bay], at anchor, and the only vessel, was a brig under Russian colors, from Asitka [Sitka], in Russian America, which had come down to winter and to take in a supply of tallow and grain, great quantities of which latter article are raised in the missions at the head of the bay ... and such a stupid and greasy-looking set [the Russian sailors], I certainly never saw before.... They had brutish faces, looked like the antipodes [exact opposites] of sailors, and apparently dealt in nothing but grease. They lived upon grease; eat it, drink it, slept in the midst of it, and their clothes were covered with it. To a Russian, grease is the greatest luxury.... The grease seemed actually coming through their pores, and out in their hair, and on their faces. It seems as if it were this saturation which makes they stand cold and rain so well.

Dana, *Two Years*, pp. 297–298.
29. TED Case Studies, "Hudson Bay Company," p. 2.

30. "Historical Documents," p. 4.
31. Quoted in Bergon, *Journals*, p. 471.
32. Quoted in "Manifest Destiny," p. 1.

Appendix 1: The Lewis and Clark Expedition

1. After Ambrose, *Undaunted Courage*, pp. 108, 479–480.
2. Historical Documents, pp. 1–2.
3. Brackenridge, *Journal*, p. 27. Italics added.
4. Some of the following chronology is drawn from Golay and Bowman, *North American Exploration*, pp. 354–358.
5. Quoted in Bergon, *Journals*, pp. 103–104.
6. Quoted in Bergon, *Journals*, p. 224.
7. Quoted in Golay and Bowman, *North American Exploration*, p. 357.
8. Quoted in Bergon, *Journals*, p. 485.
9. Quoted in Bergon, *Journals*, p. 486.
10. In a brief biography composed about three years after Lewis's death, Jefferson wrote: "Governor Lewis had from early life been subject to hypocondriac affections. It was a constitutional disposition in all the nearer branches of the family of his name, & was more immediately inherited by him from his father.... During his Western expedition the constant exertion which that required of all the faculties of body & mind, suspended these distressing affections; but after his establishment at St. Louis in sedentary occupations they returned upon him with redoubled vigor, and began seriously to alarm his friends...." Quoted in Ambrose, *Undoubted Courage*, p. 476.
11. After Ambrose, *Undoubted Courage*, p. 484.
12. Ronda, *Voyages of Discovery*, p. 329.

Appendix 2: Mirrors of the Trans-Mississippi West

1. After Catlin, *North American Indians*, frontispiece.
2. Catlin, *North American Indians*, p. 104.
3. Quoted in "Lewis and Clark in North Dakota," p. 2.
4. Murry, "Western Landscape," p. 2.
5. After Campbell, "At Tate Britain," p. 31.
6. Joslyn Art Museum and Editions Alecto, *Bodmer's America*, no page numbers printed in text.
7. Hunt, "Karl Bodmer," pp. 1–2.

Appendix 3: The Coming of the Horse

1. CBC News, "Alberta scientists," p. 1.
2. Some of the information in this appendix comes from "Spanish Colonial Horse," pp. 1–14.
3. Quoted in Weber, *Spanish Frontier*, p. 17.
4. After Calloway, *Winter Count*, p. 268.
5. After Encyclopedia of American Indians, "Horses and Indians," p. 1.
6. Encyclopedia of American Indians, "Horses and Indians," p. 1.
7. Quoted in Calloway, *Winter Count*, p. 272.
8. Kane, *Wanderings of an Artist*, p. 96.
9. After Handbook of Texas Online, "Apache Indians," p. 2.
10. Quoted in "Spanish Colonial Horse," p. 4.
11. Catlin, *North American Indians*, pp. 160–161.
12. Quoted in Calloway, *Winter Count*, p. 272.

Appendix 4: Firearms on the Early Frontiers

1. Quoted in Weber, *Spanish Frontier*, p. 25.
2. Quoted in Weber, *Spanish Frontier*, p. 25.
3. Bergon, *Journals*, pp. 250–251.
4. Quoted in Gilman, *Lewis and Clark*, p. 37. Italics added.
5. Russell, *Guns*, pp. vii–viii.
6. Quoted in Gilman, *Lewis and Clark*, p. 68.
7. Quoted in Bergon, *Journals*, p. 406.
8. Quoted in Gilbert, *Stalk*, pp. 8–9.
9. McCullough, *1776*, p. 38.
10. Gilbert, *Stalk*, p. 1.
11. Garavaglia and Worman, *Firearms*, p. 347, and Gilbert, *Stalk*, p. 8.
12. Quoted in Wood and Thiessen, *Early Fur Trade*, p. 136.
13. After Gilman, *Lewis and Clark*, p. 65.
14. Bergon, *Journals*, p. xli.
15. Quoted in Russell, *Guns*, p. 86.
16. After Bergon, *Journals*, p. xli.
17. After Russell, *Guns*, pp. 22–23.
18. Handbook of Texas Online, "Escopeta," p. 1.
19. Quoted in Kessell, *Spain in the Southwest*, p. 220.
20. After Russell, *Guns*, p. 40.
21. After Russell, *Guns*, pp. 34–35.
22. After Russell, *Guns*, p. 37.
23. Some of the following section is drawn from "Northwest Smoothbore Indian Trade Gun," pp. 1–11.
24. Quoted in Russell, *Guns*, p. 106.

25. Quoted in Russell, *Guns*, p. 69, and in Garavaglia and Worman, *Firearms*, p. 357.
26. Russell, *Guns*, pp. 66–67.

Appendix 5: Protecting Northern New Spain from the Apaches

1. This questionnaire is drawn from John, *Storms*, pp. 501–502.

Appendix 6: A Spanish Requerimiento

1. Quoted in Golay and Bowman, *North American Exploration*, p. 111.

Appendix 7: The Treaty of San Ildefonso

1. Avalon Project, "Treaty," pp. 1–3.

Appendix 8: Coureurs de Bois and Voyageurs

1. Quoted in Time-Life, *The Canadians*, p. 32.

2. Civilization.ca "August 10, 1688," p. 1.
3. Civilization.ca "May 12, 1691," p. 1.
4. After "History of Saskatchewan Waterways," pp. 9–16.
5. Kane's paintings are among the earliest records of life in the Canadian Northwest before European settlement. He was also the first Canadian painter to write a best-selling book — *Wanderings of an Artist Among the Indians of North America* (1859). This popular travelogue, which appeared in English, French, Danish and German editions, is still in print.
6. Kane, *Wanderings of an Artist*, p. 72.
7. Kane, *Wanderings of an Artist*, pp. 292, 293.
8. A bill of lading for a York boat in 1803 lists a great many items, not all of which would have been carried in the boat at the same time. They included tobacco, brass pots, tinned pots, ham, pork jowls, salt, grease, gunpowder, sugar, alcoholic beverages, beef, butter, tongue, sausage, barley, rice, cheese, raisins, figs, prunes, hats, knives, guns, traps, soap, pieces of iron and steel, lead balls, wheat, peas, and 200 lbs. of paper-wrapped packages of pork. After "York Bill of Lading, 1803."
9. After "York Boat," pp. 1–2.

Selected Bibliography

Acadian-Cajun Genealogy & History. "Exile Destination: Louisiana." http://www.acadian-cajun.com/exla.htm. Accessed 12 July 2004.
"Acoma Pueblo—Sky City." http:www.collectorsguide.com/ab/abfa22.html. Accessed 21 May 2004.
Adams, Arthur T. (ed.) *The Explorations of Pierre Esprit Radisson*. Minneapolis: Ross & Haines, 1961.
"The Adventures of Jonathan Carver." http://bell.lib.umn.edu/hennepin/carver.html. Accessed 16 November 2003.
"Alejandro Malaspina (1754–1810)." http://www.malaspina.com/site/person_796.asp. Accessed 3 June 2004.
Allen, John Logan. *Lewis and Clark and the Image of the American Northwest*. New York: Dover, 1991.
———. (ed.) *North American Exploration*. Vol. 3. Lincoln and London: University of Nebraska Press, 1997.
Allen, Michael. *Western Rivermen, 1763–1861: Ohio and Mississippi River Boatmen and the Myth of the Alligator Horse*. Baton Rouge and London: Louisiana State University Press, 1990.
"The Alexander Mackenzie Voyageur Route." http://www.amvr.org/. Accessed 8 October 2004.
Ambrose, Stephen E. *Undaunted Courage: Meriwether Lewis, Thomas Jefferson, and the Opening of the American West*. New York: Touchstone, 1996.
American Journeys. "Extract of the Journal of the Expedition of the Mallet Brothers to Santa Fe, 1739–1740." http://www.americanjourneys.org/aj-092/summary/index.asp. Accessed 13 July 2004.
American Journeys Collection. "Etienne Veniard de Bourgmont's 'Exact Description of Louisiana.'" Document No. AJ-093. www.americanjourneys.org. Accessed 11 November 2004.
"Apaches." http://www.texancultures.utsa.edu/mystery/apaches.htm. Accessed 15 June 2004.
"The Atlatl." http://www.flight.toys.com/atlatl.html. Accessed 4 November 2004.
Avalon Project at Yale Law School. "Treaty of San Ildefonso: October 1, 1800." http://www.yale.edu/lawweb/avalon/ildefens.htm. Accessed 25 August 2004.
Beebe, Rose Marie, and Robert M. Senkewicz. (eds.) *Lands of Promise and Despair: Chronicles of Early California, 1535–1846*. Santa Clara and Berkeley: Santa Clara University and Heyday Books, 2001.
Bergon, Frank (ed.) *The Journals of Lewis and Clark*. New York: Penguin, 2003.
"Blackfoot." http:lucy.ukc.ac.uk/EthnoAtlas/Hmar/Cul_dir/Culture.7833. Accessed 29 August 2004.

Blumenthal, Richard W. (ed.) *The Early Exploration of Inland Washington Waterways: Journals and Logs from Six Expeditions, 1786–1792*. Jefferson, NC: McFarland, 2004.
Bodkin, James L., Ronald J. Jameson, and James A. Estes. "Sea Otters in the North Pacific Ocean." http://bioloy.usgs.gov/s+t/noframe/s043.html. Accessed 7 December 2004.
Brackenridge, Henry Marie. *A Journal of a Voyage Up the River Missouri; Performed in Eighteen Hundred and Eleven*. 2nd ed. Baltimore: Cole and Maxwell, 1816. In Thwaites, Reuben Gold (ed.) *Early Western Travels, 1748–1846*, vol. VI, Cleveland: Clark, 1904, pp. 25–166.
Briceland, Alan V. "British Exploration of the United States Interior." In Allen, John Logan, *North American Exploration*. Vol. 2. *A Continent Defined*. Lincoln and London: University of Nebraska Press, 1997, pp. 269–327.
Brigham Young University. "Template: Pueblos." http://fhss.byu.edu/anthro/mopc/pages/Exhibitions/Earth/Pueblos.html. Accessed 3 May 2004.
"British Empire: The Map Room: North America: The Thirteen Colonies." http://www.britishempire.co.uk/maproom/13colonies.htm. Accessed 6 September 2004.
Brooks, James. F. *Captives and Cousins: Slavery, Kinship, and Community in the Southwest Borderlands*. Chapel Hill and London: University of North Carolina Press, 2002.
Brown, Ian W. "Certain Aspects of French-Indian Interaction in Lower Louisiane." In Walthall, John A. and Thomas E. Emerson, *Calumet and Fleur-de-Lys: Archeology of Indian and French Contact in the Midcontinent*. Washington and London: Smithsonian Institution Press, 1992, pp. 17–34.
Brown, Margaret. "Colonists and Colonizing in the Illinois Country." http://www.nps.gov/jeff/LewisClark2/TheBicentennial/Symposium2001.../Brown_Margaret.ht. Accessed 21 June 2004.
Cabeza de Vaca, Alvar Núñez. (Trans. Fanny Bandelier). *Chronicle of the Narváez Expedition*. New York: Penguin, 2002.
"The Cabildo: The Louisiana Purchase." http://lsm.crt.state.la.us/cabildo/cab4.htm. Accessed 14 August 2003.
Cabrillo National Monument Foundation. *An Account of the Voyage of Juan Rodríguez Cabrillo*. San Diego: Cabrillo National Monument Foundation, 1999.
"California as an Island." http://www.jpmaps.co.uk/spotlight.htm. Accessed 9 January 2004.
Calloway, Colin G. *One Vast Winter Count: The Native American West before Lewis and Clark*. Lincoln and London: University of Nebraska Press, 2003.
Calverley, Dorthea. "The Beaver, the Foundation of the Fur Trade." http://www.runningdeerslonghouse.com/webdoc210.htm. Accessed 5 July 2004.
Campbell, Peter. "At Tate Britain." In the *London Review of Books*, vol. 27, no. 13, 7 July 2005, p. 31.
The Canadian Encyclopedia. "Fur Trade." http://thecanadianencyclopedia.com/PrinterFriendly.cfm?Params=A1ARTA0003112. Accessed 12 March 2005.
_____. *The Canadian Encyclopedia*. "Fur Trade After 1760." http://www.thecanadianencyclopedia.com/index.cfm?PgNum=TCE&Params=A1SEC779698. Accessed 27 September 2004.
Castañeda, Pedro de. "Narrative of the Expedition to Cíbola, Undertaken in 1540, in Which Are Described All Those Settlements, Ceremonies, and Customs." In Hammond, George P. and Agapito Rey. *Narratives of the Coronado Expedition in 1540–1542*. Albuquerque: University of New Mexico Press, 1940, pp. 191–283.
Catholic Encyclopedia. "Caddo Indians." http://www.newadvent.org/cathen/03129a.htm. Accessed 16 January 2005.
_____. "Mission Indians (of California)." http://www.newadvent.org/cathen/10369a.htm. Accessed 13 May 2004.
Catlin, George. *The North American Indians: Being Letters and Notes on Their Manners, Customs, and Conditions, Written During Eight Years' Travel Amongst the Wildest Tribes of Indians in North America, 1832–1839*. Vol. 1. Scituate, MA: Digital Scanning, 2000.
Cavan, Seamus. *Daniel Boone and the Opening of the Ohio Country*. New York and Philadelphia: Chelsea House, 1991.
CBC News. "Alberta scientists find prehistoric horse." http://www.cbc.ca/story/news/?/news/2001/05/02/horseuc_aa_0110502. Accessed 16 February 2005.

Chief Joseph. "I will fight no more forever." http://www.4literature.net/Chief_Joseph/I_Will_ Fight_No_More_Forever/. Accessed 10 September 2004.
"The Chiricahua Apaches." http://www.desertusa.com/magfeb98/feb_pap/eu_apache.html. Accessed 15 January 2005.
"Chitimacha History." http:www.dickshovel.com/chi.html. Accessed 17 April 2005.
Civilization.ca. "August 10, 1688." http:www.civilization.ca/vmnf/popul/coureurs/chrono/1688htm. Accessed 18 June 2004.
Civilization.ca: "May 12, 1691." http://www.civilization.ca/vmnf/coureurs/chrono/1691en.htm. Accessed 18 June 2004.
Claton, Lawrence A., Vernon James Knight Jr., and Edward C. Moore (eds.). *The De Soto Chronicles: The Expedition of Hernando de Soto to North America in 1539–1543*. 2 vols. Tuscaloosa and London: University of Alabama Press, 1993.
CNN.com. "Solved mystery: Fake Drake plate a prank." .../cpt?action=cpt&title=CNN.com+-+Solved+mystery%3A+Fake+Drake+plate+a+prank+-+Feb.-9/20/04. Accessed 20 September 2004.
Colasurdo, Christine. *Golden Gate National Parks*. San Francisco: Golden Gate National Parks Association, 2002.
"Comanche History." Part One: http://www.tolatsga.org/ComancheOne.html. Accessed 31 January 2004. Part Two: http://dickshovel.com/ComancheTwo.html. Accessed 31 January 2004. Part III: http://www.dickshovel.com/ComancheThree.html. Accessed 19 January 2005.
Conrad, Glenn R. "Reluctant Imperialist: France in North America." In Conrad, Glenn R. (ed.) *The Louisiana Purchase Bicentennial Series in Louisiana History*. Vol. I—*The French Experience in Louisiana*. Layfayette: Center for Louisiana Studies, 1995.
Cook, Donald, and Iris Engstrand. *Quest for Empire: Spanish Settlement in the Southwest*. Golden: Fulcrum, 1996.
Cook, Sherburne F. *The Conflict between the California Indian and White Civilization*. Berkeley and Los Angeles: University of California Press, 1976.
Cook, Warren L. *Flood Tide of Empire: Spain and the Pacific Northwest, 1543–1819*. New Haven and London: Yale University Press, 1973.
Crespi, Juan (Trans. and ed. Alan K. Brown.) *A Description of Distant Roads: Original Journals of the First Expedition into California, 1769–1770*. San Diego: San Diego State University Press, 2001.
Croxton, Derek. "The Cabot Dilemma: John Cabot's 1497 Voyage & the Limits of Historiography." http://etex.lib.virginia.edu/journals/EH/EH33/croxto33.html. Accessed 20 June 2004.
Dana, Richard Henry, Jr. *Two Years Before the Mast*. New York: Penguin, 1986.
"David Thompson: Canada's greatest geographer." http://www.davidthompsonthings.com/geog1.html. Accessed 24 September 2004.
Delâge, Denys. "French and English Colonial Models in North America." An unpublished article based on a paper read at the 20 October 2001 conference of the Center for French Colonial Studies at the University of Windsor in Ontario, Canada.
_____. "Québec, 1633–1663." An unpublished article of 4 April 2003.
DeVoto, Bernard. *The Course of Empire*. Boston and New York: Houghton Mifflin, 1998.
Dictionary of Canadian Biography. "Tanaghrisson." http://www.biographi.ca/EN/ShowBio Printable.asp?BioID=35796. Accessed 6 September 2004.
Eccles, W.J. "French Exploration in North America, 1700–1800." In Allen, John Logan (ed.) *North American Exploration*. Vol. 2. *A Continent Defined*. Lincoln and London: University of Nebraska Press, 1997, pp. 149–202.
Encinias, Miguel, Alfred Rogríguez, and Joseph P. Sánchez. "Historical Overview." In Encinias, Miguel, Alfred Rodrígues, and Joseph P. Sanchez, *Historia de la Nueva México, 1610*. Albuquerque: University of New Mexico Press, 1992, pp. xxv–xliii.
Encyclopædia Britannica. "New Spain, Viceroyalty of." http://www.britannica.com/eb/print?tocId=9055514&fullArticle=false. Accessed 25 January 2005.
_____. "Northwest Coast Indian." http://www.britannica.com/eb/print?eu=127683. Accessed 11 May 2004.

———. "Sioux." http://www.britannica.com/eb/print?eu=69728. Accessed 1 April 2004.
Encyclopedia of North American Indians. "Horses and Indians." http//college.hmco.com/history/readerscomp/naind/html/na_015700_horsesandind.htm. Accessed 14 February 2005.
Engstrand, Iris H.W. "Seekers of the 'Northern Mystery.'" In Gutiérrez, Ramón A. and Richard J. Orsi. *Contested Eden: California before the Gold Rush*. Berkeley, Los Angeles, and London: University of California Press, 1998.
Fehrenbach, T.R. *Comanches: The History of a People*. New York: Anchor, 2003.
Feigenbaum, Gail (ed.) *Jefferson's America & Napoleon's France*. New Orleans: New Orleans Museum of Art, 2003.
Flint, Timothy. *Biographical Memoir of Daniel Boone*. (James K. Folsom ed.) Schenectady, NY: New College and University Press, 1967.
Fort Pierre. "Verendrye Monument." http://www.fortpierre.com/vm.html. Accessed 12 July 2004.
Foster, Lee. "Eusebio Kino's Legacy in the Sonora Desert of Mexico and Arizona." http://www.fostertravel.com/MXKINO.HTML. Accessed 2 June 2004.
"The Fur Trade in New France—Chronology: March 6, 1645." http://www.civilization.ca/vmnf/popul/coureurs/chrono/031645en.htm. Accessed 18 June 2004.
"The Fur Trade in New France—Chronology: August 10, 1688." http://www.civilization.ca/vmnf/popul/coureurs/chrono/1688en.htm. Accessed 18 June 2004.
Galaup, Jean François. *Voyage de la Pérouse autour du Monde*. 4 vols. Paris: Imprimerie de la République, 1797.
Garavaglia, Louis A., and Charles G. Worman. *Firearms of the American West, 1803–1865*. Niwot: University Press of Colorado, 1998.
Gelb, Norman (ed.) *Jonathan Carver's Travels Through America 1766–1768: An Eighteenth-Century Explorer's Account of Uncharted America*. New York: Wiley, 1993.
Gibson, James R. "The Exploration of the Pacific Coast." In Allen, John Logan (ed.) vol. 2. *North American Exploration: A Continent Defined*. Lincoln and London: University of Nebraska Press, 1997, pp. 328–396.
———. *Otter Skins, Boston Ships, and China Goods: The Maritime Fur Trade of the Northwest Coast, 1785–1841*. Montreal, Kingston, and London: McGill-Queen's University Press, 1992.
Gilbert, Adrian. *Stalk and Kill*. New York: St. Martin's Press, 1997.
"The Gilbert Site." http://www.texasbeyondhistory.net/gilbert/. Accessed 29 November 2004; and http://www.texasbyondhistory.net/gilbert/french.html. Accessed 30 November 2004.
Gilman, Carolyn. *Lewis and Clark: Across the Divide*. Washington and London: Smithsonian Books, 2003.
Golay, Michael and John S. Bowman. *North American Exploration*. Hoboken: Wiley, 2003.
Glover, William R. *A History of the Caddo Indians*. Reprinted from *The Louisiana Historical Quarterly*, Vol. 18, No. 4, October 1935. http://ops.tamu.edu/x075bb/caddo/Indians/htmsl. Accessed 16 January 2005.
Goss, John. *The Mapmaker's Art: An Illustrated History of Cartography*. Hong Kong: Rand McNally, 1993.
Gough, Barry M. *First Across the Continent: Sir Alexander Mackenzie*. Norman and London: University of Oklahoma Press, 1997.
———. *The Northwest Coast: British Navigation, Trade, and Discoveries to 1812*. Vancouver: UBC Press, 1992.
Gunther, Erna. *Indian Life on the Northwest Coast of North America As Seen by the Early Explorers and Fur Traders during the Last Decades of the Eighteenth Century*. Chicago and London: University of Chicago Press, 1972.
Gutiérrez, Ramón A. *When Jesus Came, the Corn Mothers Went Away: Marriage, Sexuality, and Power in New Mexico, 1500–1846*. Stanford: Stanford University Press, 1991.
Hakluyt, Richard. *Voyages and Discoveries*. Harmondsworth: Penguin, 1985.
Handbook of Texas Online. "Apache Indians." http://www.tsha.utexas.edu/handbook/online/articles/print/AA/bma33.html. Accessed 15 June 2004.
———. "Cabeza de Vaca, Álvar Núñez." http:www.tsha.utexas.edu/handbook/online/articles/CC/fca6.htm. Accessed 10 April 2004.

———. "Escopeta." http://www.tsha.utexas.edu/handbook/online/articles/print/EE/qvel.html. Accessed 21 February 2005.
———. "Kichai Indians." http://www.tsha.utexas.edu/handbook/online/articles/KK/bmk8.html. Accessed 30 November 2004.
———. "La Salle Expedition." http://www.tsha.utexas.edu/handbook/online/articles/print/LL/upl1.html. Accessed 8 June 2004.
———. "Los Adaes." http://www.tsha.utexas.edu/handbook/online/articles/print/LL/nfl1.html. Accessed 6 June 2004.
———. "Mallet Expeditions." http://www.tsha.utexas.edu/handbook/online/articles/print/MM/upm1.html. Accessed 13 July 2004.
———. "New Regulations for Presidios." http://www.tsha.utexas.edu/handbook/online/articles/print/NN/nfn1.html. Accessed 8 June 2004.
———. "Nolan, Philip." http://www.tsha.uteas.edu/handbook/online/articles/print/NN/fno.2.html. Accessed 18 April 2005.
———. "Posada, Alonso de." http//www.tsha.utexas.edu/handbook/online/articles/PP/fpo25_print.html. Accessed 12 August 2005.
———. "Rubí, Marqués de." http://www.tsha.utexas.edu/handbook/online/articles/print/RR/frul.html. Accessed 8 June 2004.
———. "St. Denis, Louis Juchereau de." http://www.tsha.utexas.edu/handbook/online/articles/print/SS/fst1.html. Accessed 8 June 2004.
———. "Seven Cities of Cíbola." http://www.tsha.utexas.edu/handbook/online/articles/print/SSS/uxscn.html. Accessed 30 May 2004.
———. "Spanish Fort, Texas." http://www.tsha.utexas.edu/handbook/online/articles/print/SS/hns64.html. Accessed 8 September 2004.
———. "Spanish Texas." http://www.tsha.utexas.edu/handbook/online/articles/print/SS/nps1.html. Accessed 6 June 2004.
———. "Vial, Pedro" http://www.tsha.utexas.edu/handbook/online/articles/print/VV/fvi1.html. Accessed 19 April 2005.
Heidenreich, Conrad. "Early French Exploration in the North American Interior." In Allen, John Logan (ed.), *North American Exploration. Vol. 2. A Continent Defined*. Lincoln and London: University of Nebraska Press, 1997, pp. 65–148.
Hillerman, Tony (ed.) *The Best of the West: An Anthology of Classic Writing from the American West*. New York: HarperPerennial, 1991.
"Historical Background: The Fur Trade." http://mdc.mo.gov/teacher/highered/craft4.htm. Accessed 5 July 2004.
"Historical Background of the Lewis and Clark Expedition: Lower Missouri Region." http://athena.emporia.edu/nasa/lewis_cl/history.htm. Accessed 6 September 2004.
"Historical Background of the Village of Buffalo Narrows." http://www.jkcc.com/evje/bnhistorical.html. Accessed 2 February 2005.
"Historical Documents: Jefferson's Secret Message to Congress Regarding the Lewis & Clark Expedition (1803)." http://www.historicaldocuments.com/JeffersonsSecretMessagetoCongress.htm. Accessed 24 January 2005.
"History of Saskatchewan Waterways." http://www.lights.com/waterways/history.htm. Accessed 3 April 2005.
Hosley, William. *Colt: The Making of an American Legend*. Amherst: University of Massachusetts Press, 1996.
Houghton Mifflin. "Fur Trade." http://college.hmco.com/history/readerscomp/naind/html/na_012800_furtrade.htm. Accessed 5 July 2004.
"Houma History." http://www.dickshovel.com/hou.html. Accessed 17 April 2005.
"The Hudson's Bay Company." http://www.collectionscanada.ca/explorers/h24-1502-e.html. Accessed 21 September 2004.
Hunt, David C. "Karl Bodmer." http://www.joslyn.org/permcol/west/pages/bodmer1.html. Accessed 18 February 2005.
"The Illinois Country." http://www.museum.state.il/us/muslink/nat_amer/post/htmls/ic.html. Accessed 1 November 2004.
"*Inter Caetera*." http://www.catholic-forum.com/saints/pope0214a.htm. Accessed 25 May 2004.

"James Cook: Chart of the NW Coast of America and NE Coast of Asia explored in the years 1778 and 1779." http://www.lib.virginia.edu/speccol/exhibits/lewis_clark/exploring/ch4.-25.html. Accessed 2 November 2003.
"James Mackay, the Otos & Omaha." http://www.nebraskastudies.org/0300/stories/0301_0117.html. Accessed 22 August 2004.
Janin, Hunt. *Fort Bridger, Wyoming: Trading Post for Indians, Mountain Men and Westward Migrants*. Jefferson, NC: McFarland, 2001.
"Jay's Treaty." http://www.u-s-history.com/pages/h455.html. Accessed 10 October 2004.
Jenkins, Jerry and Andy Keal. *The Adirondack Atlas: A Geographic Portrait of the Adirondack Park*. New York: Wildlife Conservation Society, 2004.
John, Elizabeth A.H. *Storms Brewed in Other Men's Worlds: The Confrontation of Indians, Spanish, and French in the Southwest, 1540–1795*. 2nd ed. Norman and London: University of Oklahoma Press, 1996.
____ (ed.) (Trans. John Wheat.) *Views from the Apache Frontier: Report on the Northern Provinces of New Spain, 1799*. Norman and London: University of Oklahoma Press, 1989.
Jones, Okah L., Jr. "Spanish Penetrations to the North of New Spain." In Allen, John Logan (ed.), vol. 2. *North American Exploration: A Continent Divided*. Lincoln and London: University of Nebraska Press, 1997, pp. 7–64.
Josephy, Alvin M. Jr. *The Nez Perce Indians and the Opening of the Northwest*. Albuquerque: University of New Mexico Press, 1940.
Joslyn Art Museum and Editions Alecto. *Bodmer's America: Karl Bodmer's Illustrations to Prince Maximilian of Wied-Neuwied's Travels in the Interior of North America, 1832–1834*. Omaha and London: Joslyn Art Museum and Editions Alecto, 1991.
"The Journal." http://www.content.wisconsinhistory.org/cgi-bin/docitemview.exe?CISOROOT=/aj&CISOPTR=5632. Accessed 14 July 2004.
Kane, Paul. *Wanderings of an Artist Among the Indians of North America*. Mineola: Dover, 1996.
Kavanagh, Thomas W. *Comanche Political History: An Ethnohistorical Perspective, 1706–1875*. Lincoln and London: University of Nebraska Press, 1996.
Kelsey, Harry. *Discovering Cabrillo*. Altadena: Liber Apertus Press, 2004.
Kessell, John L. *Spain in the Southwest: A Narrative History of Colonial New Mexico, Arizona, Texas, and California*. Norman: University of Oklahoma Press, 2002.
Knaut, Andrew L. *The Pueblo Revolt of 1680: Conquest and Resistance in Seventeenth-Century New Mexico*. Norman and London: University of Oklahoma Press, 1995.
Kukla, Jon. *A Wilderness So Immense: The Louisiana Purchase and the Destiny of America*. New York: Knopf, 2003.
Lamb, W. Kaye. "Captain George Vancouver." http://www.discovervancouver.com/GVB/captain-george-vancouver.asp. Accessed 6 October 2004.
"Lead Tablet." http:www.sd4history.com/Unit1/leadtablet.htm. Accessed 12 July 2004.
Lewis, Jon E. *The West: The Making of the American West*. London: Robinson, 2001.
"Lewis and Clark in North Dakota." http/dorgan.senate.gov/lewis_and_clark/credits.html. Accessed 18 February 2005.
Lewis and Clark Journals. The journals themselves are at http://lewisandclarkjournals.unl.edu/files/xml/1806-02-23.xml. The "most delicious fur" quote is at http://libr.unl.edu/cgi-bin/webgimpse.cgi?ID=2&query+most+delicious+fur. Accessed 5 November 2004.
"Lewis and Clark: Maps of Exploration 1507–1814." http://www.lib.virginia.edu/speccol/exhibits/lewis_clark/planning3.html. Accessed 11 October 2004.
"Lewis & Clark — Tribes— Nez Perce Indians." http//www.nationalgeographic.com/lewisandclak/record_tribes_013_12_17.html. Accessed 28 August 2004.
Library and Archives Canada. "The Jesuit *Relations* and the History of New France." http://www.collectionscanada.ca/jesuit-relationa/index-e.html. Accessed 27 January 2005.
Library of Congress. "Parallel Histories: Overview." http://international.loc.gov/intldl/eshtml/eng/cssstry.html. Accessed 28 October 2003.
____. "Parallel Histories: North America in the 18th Century." http://international.loc.gov/intldl/eshtml/eng/esam18.html. Accessed 23 January 2005.
____. "Peter Pond's Search for Fortune." http://www.collectionscanada.ca/explorers/h24-1620-e.html. Accessed 10 October 2004.

"Louis Hennepin." http://www.lib.virginia/edu/speccol/exhibits/lewis_clark/exploring/ch2-8.html. Accessed 4 July 2004.
Mackay, Charles. "Extraordinary Popular Delusions and the Madness of Crowds: The Mississippi Scheme. [1852]" http://robotics.caltech.edu/~mason/Delusions/epdatmoc.html. Accessed 11 July 2004.
Mackenzie, Alexander. (Walter Sheppe ed.) *Journal of the Voyage to the Pacific*. New York: Dover, 1995.
Maguire, James H., Peter Wild, and Donald A. Barclay (eds.) *A Rendezvous Reader: Tall, Tangled, and True Tales of the Mountain Men, 1805–1850*. Salt Lake City: University of Utah Press, 1997.
Makarova, Raisa V. (Trans. and ed. Richard A. Pierce and Alton S. Donnelly). *Russians on the Pacific 1743–1799*. Kingston: Limestone Press, 1975.
"The Mandan: Spirit and Ritual." http://members.aol.com/nacanapah/mandan.htm. Accessed 18 May 2004.
"Manifest Destiny." http://www.britannica.com/eb/print?tocId=9050542&fullArticle=false. Accessed 25 January 2004.
"Maps." http://www.collectionscanada.ca/explorers/h24-1503-e.html. Accessed 23 September 2004.
Marcy, Randolph B. *The Prairie Traveler*. Old Saybrook: Applewood Books, 1969.
Matthiessen, Peter. "Introduction." In Catlin, George, *North American Indians*, New York: Penguin, 2004.
Marine Mammal Center. "Sea Otter." http://www.tmmc.org/learning/education/mannalinfo/seaotter.asp. Accessed 7 December 2004.
McCormick, George. "Destruction Island." http://www.forks-web.com/fg/destructionisland.htm. Accessed 10 June 2004.
McCullough, David. *1776*. New York, London, Toronto, Sidney: Simon & Schuster, 2005.
McNabb, Donald and Louis E. "Lee" Madère, Jr. "A History of New Orleans." http://www.madere.com/history.html. Accessed 2 July 2004.
"MissionTour: A Virtual Tour of the California Missions." http://missiontour.org/carmel/history.htm. Accessed 19 October 2004.
Mississippi History Now. "Mississippi Under British Rule—British West Florida." http://mhistory.k12.ms.us/features/feature5/west_florida.html. Accessed 3 December 2004.
Modern History Sourcebook. "Francis Petty: Sir Francis Drake's Famous Voyage Round the World, 1580." http://www.fordham.edu.halsall/mod/1580Pretty-drake.html. Accessed 17 September 2004.
"Monticello: Jefferson's West." http//www.monticello.org/jefferson/lewisandclark/prechronology.htm. Accessed 18 June 2003.
Morley, Jacqueline, and David Antram. *Exploring North America*. Hove: Macdonald, 1996.
"Motives for Exploration: Headin' West and North." http://www.californiahistory.net/text_only/3_1.htm. Accessed 4 July 2004.
Murray, Richard. "Interview Transcript: Western Landscape." http://catlinclassroom.si.edu/interviews/wl-murray.html. Accessed 18 February 2005.
Nasatir, A.P. (ed.) *Before Lewis and Clark: Documents Illustrating the History of the Missouri, 1785–1804*. 2 vols. St. Louis: St. Louis Historical Documents Foundation, 1952.
_____. *Spanish War Vessels on the Mississippi 1792–1796*. New Haven and London: Yale University Press, 1968.
National Archives and Records Administration. "The Louisiana Purchase." http://www.archives.gov/exhibit_hall/american_originals/loupurch.html. Accessed 7 December 2004.
National Geographic. "Lewis & Clark—Tribes—Mandan Indians." http://www.nationalgeographic..com/lewisandclark/record_tribes_010_5_3.html. Accessed 20 January 2005.
National Park Service. "Arkansas Post: The Founding of Arkansas Post, 1686." http://www.nps.gov/arpo/found/chap5.htm. Accessed 6 July 2004.
_____. "Cabrillo." Washington, D.C.: Government Printing Office document number 2003-496-196/40449, 2002.
_____. "The French Settlement." http://www.nps.gov/jeff/french_settlement.html. Accessed 18 June 2004.

_____. "Juan Bautista de Anza National Historic Trail." http:www.nps.gov/juba/. Accessed 14 June 2004.

_____. "Maria de la Concepcion Marcela Arguello." http://www.nps.gov/prsf/history/bios/concep.htm. Accessed 13 March 2005.

Nelson, George. *My First Years in the Fur Trade: The Journals of 1802–1804.* (Laura Peers and Theresa Schenck eds.) St. Paul: Minnesota Historical Society Press, 2002.

"New Orleans closed to Americans." http://www2.worldbook.com/features/lewisandclark/html/pushing_purchase.html. Accessed 18 June 2004.

"Nez Perce." http://www.mnsu.edu/cultural/northamerica/nezperce.html. Accessed 28 August 2004.

"Nez Perce History." http://logos.uoregon.udu/explore/oregon/nphistory.html. Accessed 24 August 2004.

"Nez Perce Indians." http://www.pbs.org/lewisandclark/native/nez.html. Accessed 28 August 2004.

Nordyke, Elanor C. *Pacific Images: Views from Captain Cook's Third Voyage.* Singapore: Hawaiian Historical Society, 1999.

"North America: Physical Geography." http://www.harpercollege.edu/~mhealy/g101ilec/namer/nad/naphys/naphystx.htm. Accessed 4 February 2005.

"Northwest Coast Culture Area." http://www.cabrillo.cc.ca.us/~crsmith/noamer_nwcoast.html. Accessed 14 January 2004.

"Northwest Smoothbore Indian Trade Gun." http://www.thefurtrapper.com/trade_guns.htm. Accessed 19 April 2005.

Parkman, Francis. *The Discovery of the Great West.* Paulton: Eyre & Spottiswoode, 1962.

_____. (Colin G. Calloway ed.). *Pioneers of France in the New World.* Lincoln and London: University of Nebraska Press, 1996.

PBS. "Empire of the Bay: Setting Sail for North America." http://www.pbs.org/empireofthebay/broadcast1.html. Accessed 18 September 2004.

_____. "Junipero Serra." http://www.pbs.org/weta/thewest/people/s_z/serra.htm. Accessed 11 May 2004.

_____. "Mandan Indians." http//www.pbs.lewisandclark/native/man.html. Accessed 9 May 2004.

_____. "Teton Sioux Indians." http://www.pbs.org/lewisandclark/native/tet.html. Accessed 9 May 2004.

_____. "Yankton Sioux Indians." http://www.pbs.org/legisandclark/native/yan.html. Accessed 9 May 2004.

"Physical Geography." http://www.infoplease.com/ce6/A0861706.html. Accessed 4 February 2005.

"Pueblo Indians." http://www.dragonflydream.com/PuebloIndians.html. Accessed 31 January 2004.

"Red River Raft." http://www.ok-history.mus.ok.us/enc/rdrivrft.htm. Accessed 17 January 2005.

Richter, Daniel K. *Facing East from Indian Country: A Native History of North America.* Cambridge and London: Harvard University Press, 2001.

"Robert Rogers: *A Concise Account of North America.* London, 1765." http://www.lib.virginia.edu/speccol/exhibits/lewis_clark/exploring/ch4-23.html. Accessed 25 September 2004.

Ronda, James P. *Astoria & Empire.* Lincoln and London: University of Nebraska Press, 1990.

_____. "Foreword." In Wood, W. Raymond. *Prologue to Lewis and Clark: The Mackay and Evans Expedition.* Norman: University of Oklahoma Press, 2003, pp. xi–xiv.

_____. *Lewis and Clark among the Indians.* Lincoln and London: University of Nebraska Press, 1984.

_____. "Peter Pond and the Exploration of the Greater Northwest." In Schwantes, Carlos (ed.) *Encounters with a Distant Land: Exploration and the Great Northwest.* Moscow: University of Idaho Press, 1994.

_____. (ed.) *Voyages of Discovery: Essays on the Lewis and Clark Expedition.* Helena: Montana Historical Society Press, 1998.

Ross, Alexander. "The Coureur de Bois." http://www.canadahistory.com/sections/documents/docdiscription_of_coureur_de_bois.htm. Accessed 22 June 2004.

Ruggles, Richard I. "British Exploration of Rupert's Land." In Allen, John Logan (ed.), *North American Exploration*. Vol. 2. *A Continent Divided*. Lincoln and London: University of Nebraska Press, 1997, pp. 203–268.

Russell, Carl P. *Guns on the Early Frontiers: A History of Firearms from Colonial Times through the Years of the Western Fur Trade*. Lincoln and London: University of Nebraska Press, 1957.

San Diego Historical Society. "Father Junipero Serra." http://www.sandiegohistory.org/bio/serra/serra.htm. Accessed 11 May 2004.

———. "Sebastian Vizcaíno." http:www.sandiegohistory.org/bio/vizcaino/vizcaino.htm. Accessed 1 June 2004.

"Sir Alexander Mackenzie." http://www.canoe-odyssey.com/mackenzie.php. Accessed 8 October 2004.

Smith, G. Hubert. *The Explorations of the La Vérendryes in the Northern Plains, 1783–43*. (Raymond W. Wood ed.). Lincoln and London: University of Nebraska Press, 1980.

Southwestern Historical Quarterly Outline. "Early Settlement for the Annexation of California." http://www.tsha.utexas.edu/publications/journals/shq/onlilne/v018/nl/018001015-print.html. Accessed 2 November 2004.

"Spanish Colonial Horse and the Plains Indian Culture." http://www.furtrapper.com/indian_horse.htm. Accessed 14 February 2005.

Spanish Texas, Section 2. "Philip Nolan." http://users.ev1.net/~gpmoran/chap1a.htm. Accessed 18 April 2005.

"Structure of NWC." http://132.206.203.207/nwc/history/02.htm. Accessed 2 February 2005.

Sultzman, Lee. "Comanche History." http://www.tolatsga.org/ComancheOne.html. Accessed 31 January 2004.

Swagerty, William R. "Fur Trade." http://college.hmco.com/history/readerscomp/naind/html/na_012800_furtrade.htm. Accessed 5 July 2004.

Swanson, David. *San Diego 2005*. Hoboken: Wiley, 2004.

Taylor, Colin F. and Sturtevant, William C. *The Native Americans: The Indigenous People of North America*. London: Salamander, 1996.

TED Case Studies. Case Number 113: "Hudson Bay Fur Trade in 1800s." http://www.american.edu/TED/hudson.htm. Accessed 31 January 2004.

Time-Life Books. *The Old West: The Alaskans*. Alexandria: Time-Life, 1977.

———. *The Old West: The Canadians*. Alexandria: Time-Life, 1977.

———. *The Old West: The Expressmen*. Alexandria: Time-Life, 1974.

———. *The Old West: The Great Chiefs*. Alexandria: Time-Life, 1975.

———. *The Old West: The Indians*. Alexandria: Time-Life, 1973.

———. *The Old West: The Trailblazers*. New York: Time-Life, 1973.

"The Treaty of Guadalupe Hidalgo." http://www.loc.gov/exhibits/ghtreaty. Accessed 14 January 2005.

Troccoli, Joan Carpenter. *First Artist of the West: George Catlin: Paintings and Watercolors*. Tulsa: Gilcrease Museum, 1993.

Twain, Mark. *Life on the Mississippi*. New York: Penguin, 1986.

"The United States Takes Possession of the Louisiana Territory." http//www.nps.gov/Jeff/LewisClark2/Circa1804/In1804/HeadlinesLouisinaPurchase.htm. Accessed 18 June 2004.

U.S. Army. "Mississippi River Navigation: Early Navigation." http://www.mvn.usace.army.mil/PAO/history/MISSRNAV/navitgation.asp. Accessed 25 January 2004.

U.S. Department of State. "John Jay's Treaty." http://www.state.gov/r/pa/ho/time/nr/14318.htm. Accessed 12 December 2004.

Utley, Robert M. *A Life Wild and Perilous: Mountain Men and the Paths to the Pacific*. New York: Holt, 1997.

Vérendrye, La. *In Search of the Western Sea: Selected Journals of La Vérendrye*. (Denis Combet ed.). Winnipeg: Great Plains Publications, 2001.

"Village of Cumberland House." http://www.lights.com/newsask/cumberlandhouse.html. Accessed 24 September 2004.

"Visions from the Wilderness: The Art of Paul Kane." http://www.paulkane.ca/php/about_kane.php. Accessed 4 May 2005.

Voght, Lloyd. *Historic Buildings of the French Quarter*. Gretna: Pelican, 2002.
Walter, John. *The Guns That Won the West: Firearms on the American Frontier, 1848–1898*. London: Greenhill, 1999.
Weber, David J. *The Spanish Frontier in North America*. New Haven and London: Yale University Press, 1992.
_____. (ed.) *What Caused the Pueblo Revolt of 1680?* Boston and New York: Bedford/St. Martin's, 1999.
Western Silver Corporation. "Growth through Silver." http://www.westernsilvercorp.com/history.htm. Accessed 3 June 2004.
Whitaker, Arthur Preston. *The Mississippi Question 1795–1803: A Study in Trade, Politics, and Diplomacy*. New York and London: Appleton-Century, 1934.
Wikipedia. "a few acres of snow." http:www.answers.com/a+few+acres+of+snow&r=67. Accessed 28 January 2005.
_____. "New France." http://en.wikipedia.org/wiki/New_France. Accessed 26 January 2005.
Wilford, John Noble. "Blown off course from fame." In *International Herald Tribune*, 3 June 2004.
Wood, W. Raymond. *Prologue to Lewis & Clark: The Mackay and Evans Expedition*. Norman: University of Oklahoma Press, 2003.
Wood, W. Raymond and Thomas D. Thiessen (eds.). *Early Fur Trade on the Northern Plains: Canadian Traders Among the Mandan and Hidatsa Indians, 1738–1818*. Norman: University of Oklahoma Press, 1985.
"A Year in the Life of a Canoe Brigade." http://www.northwestjournal.ca/XVII2.htm. Accessed 12 March 2005.
"York Boat Bill of Lading, 1803." http://www.xmission.com/~drudy/mtman/html/yorkboat.html. Accessed 27 September 2004.
"The York Boat." http://www.mhs.mb.ca/docs/pageant/02/yorkboat.shtml. Accessed 27 September 2004.

Index

Acoma Pueblo 60–61, 63, 64, 65
Allen, John Logan 1, 191
Ambrose, Stephen E. 36–37
Anza, Juan Bautista de 76–78
Apache Indians 10, 17–18, 27, 28, 32, 33, 69, 72, 73, 114, 183–184, 201
Arrowsmith, Aaron 152–154

Baranov, Alexander 162–163
beaver fur trade 46, 87, 88, 89, 91, 97–102, 103, 104, 105, 107, 108, 112, 113, 116, 119, 125, 126, 130–131, 133, 134, 137, 138, 141, 142–143, 149, 152, 154, 155, 165, 171, 174, 192, 194, 195, 199, 201, 202
Bering, Vitus 158–159
Bienville, Jean-Baptiste Le Moyne, Sieur de Bienville 113, 122
Blackfoot Indians 11, 44–46, 47, 190–191, 201
Bodega, Juan Francisco de la 79, 80
Bodmer, Karl 8, 168
Bolton, Herbert 129–130
Bourgmont, Étienne de Véniard, Sieur de Bourgmont 115–118
Britain 2, 6, 84, 94, 97, 110, 112, 121, 123, 124, 137, 151, 156, 164, 168, 175, 178, 189, 195, 196
British 1, 2, 4, 8, 35, 38, 43, 44, 46, 49, 70, 71, 72, 81, 83, 84, 85, 87, 88, 89, 92, 93, 100, 106, 107, 108, 112, 113, 114, 120, 123, 124, 125, 126, 127–156, 157, 162, 164, 168, 169, 173, 174, 175, 182, 189, 192, 194, 196–197, 200, 201, 202
Brûlé, Étienne 106

Cabeza de Vaca 1, 50–53, 54, 55, 202
Cabot, John 127–128

Cabrillo, Juan Rodríguez 58, 59, 66
Caddo Indians 10, 70, 71, 114, 123, 184–185, 201
California 3, 6, 31, 37, 41, 56, 58–59, 62, 63, 64, 65, 66, 68–69, 73, 74, 75, 76, 77, 78, 79, 84, 85, 95, 108, 116, 129, 130, 146, 147, 149, 160, 164, 183, 186, 187, 189, 190, 193, 193, 194, 197, 198, 199, 201, 202
Calloway, Colin 3
Canada 2, 4, 5, 44, 72, 88, 92, 93, 97, 98, 99, 101–103, 105, 110, 119, 121, 124, 131, 132, 133, 134, 135, 137, 138, 141, 142, 150, 152, 154, 155, 156, 165, 172, 174, 175, 181, 189, 192, 195, 196, 197, 200, 202
Carondelet, Baron de 87–88, 176
Cartier, Jacques 96–97, 102, 103, 131, 196
Carver, Jonathan 136–137
Catlin, George 8, 26, 27, 45–46
Champlain, Samuel de 103–104, 105, 106, 133,
China 3, 7, 8, 58, 59, 61, 90, 102, 104, 128, 139, 141, 144, 154, 159, 162, 196
Chirikov, Alexei I. 32, 158–159
Chouteau, René Auguste 124–125
Cíbola (Seven Cities of) 13, 54, 55, 56
Clark, William 2, 8, 10, 24, 34, 177, 199
Comanche Indians 10, 11, 17, 18, 21, 27–34, 70, 72, 73, 94, 114, 117, 118, 122, 123, 187–188, 201
Cook, James 138–140, 141, 144, 161
Coronado, Francisco Vásques de, and the Coronado expedition 17, 55–58, 59, 61, 133
Cortés, José 84–85
Council of the Indies 16, 109

Coureurs de bois (canoemen-traders) 104–105, 106, 123, 135, 196
Coutre, Jean 165–166
Crèvecoeur, Michel-Guillaume-Saint-John de 172
Cumberland House 137, 138

D'Eglise, Jacques 88–89
Delâge, Denys 195
Deslisle, Guillaume 114, 115
De Soto, Hernando 20, 53–54, 114, 133
DeVoto, Bernard 2, 111, 117–118, 119, 133
Drake, Sir Francis 62, 128–130

Eliza, Francisco 82
Engagés (hired canoe crewmen) 101, 197
Escalante, Silvestre Vélez de 15
Estevánico 13, 51, 52, 54, 55
Evans, John Thomas 91–93

firearms 17–18, 22, 23, 29, 32, 39, 44, 45, 46, 60, 69, 70, 71, 105, 113, 117, 122, 123, 163, 165, 166, 192
flatboat and keelboat trade 94, 166–168, 170, 176
France 1, 2, 4–6, 18, 20, 21, 22, 23, 28, 29, 30, 32, 35, 36, 49, 67, 69, 70, 71, 72, 73, 80, 84, 86, 87, 88, 89, 91, 93, 94, 95, 96–126, 131, 133, 134, 135, 136, 137, 140, 141, 150, 154, 155, 165, 166, 167, 168, 169, 171, 172, 174, 178, 179, 180, 182, 192, 194, 195, 196, 197, 198, 199, 200–202

Galleons 61–63, 65, 66
Galliots 85–86
Gálvez, José de 41, 73, 75
Gilman, Carolyn 2
Gray, Robert 173–174
guns *see* firearms

Hakluyt, Richard 7
Hearne, Samuel 137
Hennepin, Louis 110–111
Hezeta, Bruno de 79, 80, 174
horses 13, 32, 39, 44, 45, 46, 47, 53, 55, 59, 103, 116, 122, 123, 166
Hudson, Henry 130
Hudson Bay 6, 45, 90, 97, 102, 111, 112, 113, 119, 130, 131, 136, 141, 171
Hudson's Bay Company 4, 5, 35, 45, 89, 93, 98, 100, 101, 102, 112, 119, 120, 131–132, 133, 137–138, 141, 142, 143, 144, 152, 154, 197

Indians 1, 4, 8, 9–47, 49, 51, 52, 53, 54, 55, 57, 58, 59, 60, 61, 62, 64, 65, 66, 67, 68, 69, 70, 72, 73, 75, 79, 80, 81, 82, 83, 86, 88, 89, 90, 91, 92, 93, 94, 95, 96, 97, 99, 100, 104, 105, 106, 108, 109, 112, 113, 114, 115, 116, 117, 118, 119, 120, 122, 123, 125, 126, 128, 129, 131, 132, 133, 134, 137, 138, 139, 143, 146, 149, 150, 151, 152, 154, 155, 163, 165, 171, 173, 182, 182–193, 183, 186, 189, 193, 194, 199, 200, 201; *see also* names of individual tribes
Inter Caetera (papal bull of 1493) 48, 127, 145
Iroquois Indians 12, 100, 106, 112, 195

Jay, John 174–175
Jefferson, Thomas 1, 2, 7, 95, 111, 136, 141, 151, 152, 153, 154, 176, 177, 178, 179, 180, 181, 198–199
John, Elizabeth 3, 64
Joliet, Louis 106–108

Kamchatka expeditions 158, 159
Kelsey, Henry 132–133
Kino, Eusebio Francisco 68–69

Lachine Rapids 104
La Salle (René Robert Cavelier, Sieur de La Salle) 20, 21, 69, 108–110, 111, 133
Law, John 114–115
Lewis, Meriwether 2, 7, 8, 36, 38, 39, 152, 159, 180
Lewis and Clark expedition 2, 10, 11, 24, 25, 34, 35–36, 37, 46, 92, 93, 102, 111, 152, 154, 159, 174, 180, 181, 183, 188, 190, 191–192, 198–199
Linguest, Pierre Laclède 124
Louisiana (French colony) 111, 112, 113, 114, 115, 116, 118, 122, 123, 124, 126, 134, 168, 176, 178, 179, 180, 198, 200, 201–202
Louisiana (Spanish colony) 125, 126, 168–169, 170, 175, 176, 176, 178, 180, 181
Louisiana Purchase 1, 2, 4, 46, 72, 177–181, 182, 184, 199, 202
Louisiana Territory 2, 6, 12, 109, 125, 135

Mackay, Donald 89–90, 93
Mackay, James 89–90, 91–93
Mackay, John 93
Mackenzie, Alexander 2, 44, 149–152, 172–173, 178
Malaspina, Alejandro 82–84
Mallet, Paul 120–122
Mallet, Pierre 120–122
Mandan Indians 10, 34–37, 88, 89, 90, 91, 93, 102, 118, 119, 155, 188–189, 201
Marcy, Randolph B. 26, 30, 32, 186
Maritime traders (Indians) of the Pacific Northwest Coast 10, 37–40, 189–190, 201
Marquette, Jacques 106–108

Index

Martínez, Esteban José 74, 80–81, 144–145
Meares, John 80–81, 144, 145
Métis 4, 102, 103
Mézières, Athanase de 27–28, 73
Mission Indians 10, 40–44, 190, 201
Mississippi (river and region) 1, 5, 6, 10, 20, 23, 50, 53, 54, 67, 71, 72, 81, 85, 86, 90, 93, 94, 95, 105, 106, 107, 108, 109, 110, 111, 112, 113, 114, 115, 117, 118, 121, 123, 124, 129, 133, 134, 135, 136, 137, 141, 152, 165, 166, 168, 169, 175, 178, 179, 180, 181, 195, 200
Mississippi Scheme (or Bubble) 114
Missouri (river and region) 7, 10, 24, 33, 35, 44, 46, 69, 72, 84, 87, 88, 89, 90, 91, 92, 93, 102, 107, 109, 111, 113, 115, 116, 117, 119, 136, 152, 153, 155, 167, 168, 170, 171, 176, 177, 178, 180, 186, 190, 199, 200

Napoleon Bonaparte 152, 178–179, 180, 201
Natchez Trace 166–167
New France 96, 97, 98, 99, 100, 102, 103, 104, 105, 106, 108, 111, 113, 118, 121, 126, 129, 131, 156, 195, 196, 196, 197, 201, 202
New North West Company (XY Company) 152
Nez Percé Indians 11, 46–47, 191–193
Niza, Marcos de 13, 54–55
Nolan, Philip 175–176
Nootka Sound conventions between Britain and Spain: First convention (1790) 145; Second convention (1793) 145; Third convention (1794) 145–146; Final convention (1795) 146
North West Company 4, 35, 89, 93, 100, 101, 102, 138, 141–144, 149, 150, 152, 154, 155, 172, 189

Oñate, Juan de 63, 64, 65

Passage (mythical waterway across North America) 5, 6, 7, 8, 81, 87, 89, 90, 95, 96, 106, 108, 116, 117, 118, 119, 125, 126, 128, 130, 131, 134, 138, 139–140, 144, 146–147, 150, 155, 158, 172, 177, 178, 193, 194, 196, 201, 202
Pérez, Juan 78–79
La Pérouse 80, 83
Pineda, Áverez de 50
Pond, Peter 171–173
Portolá, Gaspar de 75–76
Potlatch ceremony 39–40
Pretty, Francis 128–129
Prismatic approach 1, 3
Pueblo Indians 10, 11, 13–16, 17, 18, 28, 57, 60, 61, 63, 69, 70, 71, 182–183, 201

Pueblo Revolt see Pueblo Indians
Puget, Peter 139
Pyramidal height-of-land theory 5, 7, 8, 111, 135–136

Quimper, Manuel 81–82
Quivira 57, 58, 64, 67

Radisson, Pierre Esprit 131, 132
Requerimiento (document of Indian submission and Spanish overlordship) 49
Rezanov, Nikolai Petrovich 162, 197–198
Richter, Daniel K. 11–12
right of deposit (in New Orleans) 94–95, 176, 179
Rocky Mountain House 112, 154, 155
Rocky Mountains 6, 37, 38, 44, 47, 69, 86, 102, 109, 114, 119, 123, 132, 136, 138, 149, 150, 152, 153, 154, 155, 171, 172, 179, 180, 199
Rogers, Robert 136
Ronda, James P. 1
Rubí, Marqués de 72–73
Rupert's Land 6, 112, 131, 132, 135, 138
Russia 1, 2, 3, 6, 41, 49, 73, 74, 75, 76, 77, 78, 79, 80, 85, 87, 88, 95, 139, 140, 147, 151, 157–164, 173, 178, 182, 193, 194, 197–198, 201 202

St. Denis, Louis Juchereau de 22, 114
sea otter fur trade 3, 10, 37, 38, 41, 79, 81, 125, 139, 140–141, 144, 147, 157, 158, 160, 161, 162, 164, 173, 194, 197, 198, 202
Serra, Francisco Junípero 41–42, 75, 77
Shelikhov, G.I. 161–162
Sioux Indians 10, 23–26, 33, 136, 186–187, 201
Sitka 3, 5, 37, 80, 163, 164, 197, 198
Spain 1, 2, 3, 6, 11, 13–22, 25, 27–34, 41, 42, 43, 45, 48–95, 108, 109, 110, 114, 116, 117, 119–127, 129, 133, 135, 137, 140, 144–148, 157, 162, 163, 164, 166, 168, 169, 170, 174, 175, 176, 177, 179, 180, 181, 182, 183, 189, 193, 194, 196, 197, 198, 199, 201, 202
Sultzman, Lee 9–10

Talon, Jean 103, 106, 195
Thompson, David ix, 3, 154–155, 171
Tlingit Indians 158–159, 163–164
Tonti (or Tonty), Henri de 110, 114
Trans-Mississippi West 1, 2, 3, 4, 5, 6, 7, 8, 9, 17, 30, 31, 47, 49, 58, 69, 70, 95, 122, 123, 133, 135, 136, 141, 151, 154, 178, 180, 182, 182, 194, 197, 198, 199, 200, 202
Treaty of Fontainebleau 71, 123–124, 125, 168

Treaty of London (Jay's Treaty) 85, 174–175
Treaty of Paris (1763) 72, 124, 135, 168, 195
Treaty of Paris (1783) 141, 144, 174, 177, 197
Treaty of San Ildefonso 93, 94, 126, 176, 178
Treaty of San Lorenzo del Escorial (Pinckney's Treaty) 85, 86, 94, 170, 175
Treaty of Tordesillas 49, 127
Treaty of Utrecht 112, 119, 135
Truteau, Jean Baptiste 89
Twain, Mark 169–170

United States 1, 3, 4, 5, 6, 10, 11, 12, 25, 33, 37, 46, 59, 61, 73, 79, 84, 85, 93–96, 98, 99, 102, 112, 125, 126, 131, 133, 139, 140, 141, 151, 155, 165–187, 189–192, 194, 195, 197–202

Vancouver, George 43, 74, 83, 146–147, 148, 149

Vargas, Diego José de 16
Vérendrye, François (the Chevalier) 119–120
Vérendrye, Louis-Joseph 119–120
Vérendrye (Pierre Gaultier de Varennes, Sieur de La Vérendrye) 36, 89, 118–119, 120
Verrazano, Giovanni 96
Vial, Pedro 33
Villasur, Pedro de 70–71
Vizcaíno, Sebastián 65–66, 76
Voyageurs (canoemen) 101, 104–105, 107, 111, 137, 150, 155

Weber, David 3, 15–16
Welch, Thomas 165–166
Wilkinson, James 170, 175, 176, 180

York Boat 144
York Factory 5, 45, 102, 120, 132, 133

www.ingramcontent.com/pod-product-compliance
Lightning Source LLC
Chambersburg PA
CBHW051213300426
44116CB00006B/549